In the Fields of the Lord

A Seerveld Reader

edited by
Craig Bartholomew

with an introductory essay
by
Craig Bartholomew and Gideon Strauss

piquant

**TORONTO
TUPPENCE
PRESS**

Copyright © 2000 Craig Bartholomew
This edition copyright © 2000 Piquant
The moral rights of the author and illustrators have been asserted.

First edition 2000
05 04 03 02 01 00 7 6 5 4 3 2 1

Published by Piquant
PO Box 83, Carlisle, CA3 9GR, United Kingdom
E-mail: info@piquant.net
Website: www.piquant.net
ISBN 0–9535757–8–0

Co-published by Toronto Tuppence Press
332 Senlac Road, Toronto, Ontario M2R 1R3, Canada
E-mail: ttp@icscanada.edu
ISBN 0–919071–06–6

A catalogue record of this book is available in the UK from the
British Library and in the US from the Library of Congress.

Canadian Cataloguing in Publication Data
Seerveld, Calvin, 1930–
In the Fields of the Lord: a Seerveld reader

Includes bibliographical references.
ISBN 0–919071–06–6

I. Bartholomew, Craig G., 1961– . II. Title.
B995.S431B37 2000   191   C00–932254-X

Cover image: *The Sower* by Vincent van Gogh.
Van Gogh Museum, Amsterdam (Vincent van Gogh Foundation)
Cover design: Sam Hill, Aquablade

In the Fields
of the Lord

Seerveld is a medieval nondescript place-name like van den Berg (from the mountain). Some serfs scattered about on lands outside the feudal lord's castle were probably called *des heren veld* (of the lord's field). In time the d dropped off, the h was elided, and the rest smoothed out to *seerveld*, a field of the lord. God has thoughtfully provided me, it seems, with a kind of gentle reminder of my creaturely working status. All I am is a nondescript field of the Lord for God to plough and cultivate and bring forth fruit in; God asks me only to be responsive, hallelujahing ground, a place for the Holy Spirit to have free play in. Everyman – van den Berg, van der Vennen, van der Ploeg – should also be *des Heren veld*. That is our *logical* service, says the Scriptures.

Calvin Seerveld:
'Christian Workers Unite!'

By collecting these occasional offerings into one basket Craig Bartholomew has blessed my life with a redemptive surprise: I catch a vivid glimpse and a palpable sound of how the LORD watched mercifully over my journey. The gift to me of Craig's time-consuming labour is remarkable, and I am deeply grateful.

The volume is dedicated to

my wife Inès, woman of patience,

who has practised a life of giving that quietly buoys love with rich, gritty shalom; and is presented in trust to

Anya, Gioia, and Luke,

who were children growing up when many of these speeches were being born nights, and took me on the road, and whose love, with their spouses, in caring for us parents (Psalm 127) moves one to grateful tears of joy.

Calvin Seerveld
Toronto, 2000

Plate 1 Inès and Calvin Seerveld on an Australian lecture tour, June–July 1987

Contents

Preface

In the Fields of the Lord has been years in the making. It represents the deposit of a life-time of Calvin Seerveld's work, and the scanning onto disk – most of the articles were written in the pre-PC era – and the editing process have taken many hours of patient labour. The gender language has also been edited to bring it into line with Seerveld's present writing practice.[1]

I had the idea for this Reader a few years ago while studying with Seerveld. His creative talks and papers are carefully crafted and rarely recycled. I became increasingly aware that there was a wealth of material he had written which was no longer readily available. In line with his creation-wide perspective Seerveld has spoken and written on a huge range of subjects.[2] In this Reader I have sought to make available a representative selection of Seerveld's writings on the Bible, philosophy, education, labour and art. He is also an accomplished hymn-writer and we have included five previously unpublished hymns. Readers should be aware that we have deliberately not included in this volume material that is readily available in other published works of Seerveld: our aim has been to make available some of the wealth of material that is not readily available.[3]

Seerveld responded very positively to the idea of a Reader and Prof. Bennie van der Walt of the Institute for Reformational Studies at Potchefstroom University in South Africa set the process in motion, for which I am extremely grateful. Prof. Seerveld has been wonderfully co-operative in the process of editing this volume into shape, and I am also most grateful for the help in the closing stages that Paternoster Press and Nigel Halliday have provided. My good friend Gideon Strauss, previously senior researcher at the University of

---

[1] Some of Seerveld's present gender language may strike the reader as strange. For example, Seerveld prefers 'Godself' to 'himself' when used in reference to God. It will be clear from Gideon Strauss' and my introductory essay that I do not always agree with Seerveld on these issues. However, I respect his attempt to avoid misunderstandings of God as male and have edited the gender language of his articles in accordance with his present practice.

[2] The originally spoken nature of many of the pieces in this volume accounts for their occasional nature. The origins of texts are carefully footnoted with each article in this Reader.

[3] Because of the occasional nature of most of the pieces in the Reader, there is unavoidably some overlap in material and argument. We have sought to reduce this where it seemed excessive but where appropriate we have let it stand. As regards *footnotes*, where the original publication used footnotes we have retained these and they are referenced by number. We have also inserted some extra notes, where we felt some additional historical explanation was necessary for a new generation. These are marked by an asterisk or, where there are more than one on a page, by a similar symbol.

the Orange Free State in South Africa and at present a theology student at Regent College, Vancouver, has been a great collaborator in the challenge to write a reader-friendly introduction to Seerveld's thought – his friendship and collaboration in this project mean a great deal. I am also extremely grateful to Robin Livesey, manager of the Flexible Learning Design and Development Unit at Cheltenham and Gloucester College of Higher Education, for allowing me hours of use of a scanner, and to the college's School of Theology and Religious Studies for providing me with such a congenial context in which to produce this Reader.

A smorgasbord of nutritious delights – ranging from popular to academic – awaits the reader of this collection of Seerveld's material. The title alludes to the fact that we are God's handiwork *and* that the world in which we live is God's good creation. My hope is that this Reader will help introduce people to Seerveld's thought and provoke us into labouring, like Cal, to serve up bread and not stones in our service of God and neighbour in our Father's world. Thus, we will become fertile ground in God's service and we will discover the extraordinary riches in the fields of the Lord.

Craig Bartholomew
Cheltenham, UK

Abbreviations

AACS	Association for the Advancement of Christian Scholarship
AFL–CIO	American Federation of Labour – Congress of Industrial Organisations
ARSS	Association for Reformed Scientific Studies
CBC	Canadian Broadcasting Corporation
CJL	Committee for Justice and Liberty
CLAC	Christian Labour Association of Canada
CRC	Christian Reformed Church
ICS	Institute for Christian Studies

Introduction

Bread and not Stones:
An Introduction to the Thought of Calvin Seerveld

by Craig Bartholomew and Gideon Strauss

'Is there anyone among you who, if your child asks for bread,
will give a stone?' (Matthew 7:9)

Calvin Seerveld is a major proponent of what is called the neocalvinist, or
Reformational, tradition of Christian thought and practice.[1] However,
although he has lectured around the world, his thought and that of the tradition he represents is not as well-known as it should be. At the end of a collo-
quium of some 35 Reformational thinkers in Leeds in 1996, Lesslie
Newbigin, one of the leading thinkers about the relationship between Gospel
and culture at the end of the twentieth century, poignantly asked, 'Why is this
tradition so little known in the UK?'[2]

Being little known should not be equated with being *irrelevant*. The neocalvinist tradition and the work of Seerveld in particular has much to offer contemporary Christianity. Seerveld has specialised in aesthetics and most of his
advanced academic work has been in this area.[3] However, the breadth of the
neocalvinist vision and Seerveld's wide-ranging interests and teaching

---

[1] The term 'Reformational' was coined by Seerveld in 1959 to 'catch several related meanings' (see Seerveld,
1980b:46). It identifies, firstly, a life that seeks to be re-formed by the renewal of our consciousness so that
we can discern God's will for action on earth. Secondly, it identifies an approach that honours the genius
of the Reformation, further developed by Groen van Prinsterer and Abraham Kuyper in the nineteenth
century, as a distinct Christian tradition out of which one can richly serve the Lord. Thirdly, it identifies a
concern to communally keep reforming rather than getting stuck in the past. In this last sense Seerveld considers the philosophical work of Dooyeweerd and Vollenhoven as continued reformation of the neocalvin-
istic tradition. Because not all neocalvinists would follow Dooyeweerd and Vollenhoven's lead in the way
Seerveld does, we will use *Reformational* to refer to those neocalvinists like Seerveld who build on Dooyeweerd and Vollenhoven's work.

[2] There are a number of prominent Reformational thinkers in the UK but within Christian circles and
scholarship the tradition and, more specifically, the philosophical work of Vollenhoven and Dooyeweerd
have not generally received close attention. Hans Rookmaaker is probably the best known neocalvinist
Christian thinker in the UK and his *Modern Art and the Death of a Culture* has been republished by Apollos
(Leicester, England, 1996).

[3] A bibliography of Seerveld's writings and speeches is contained in Zuidervaart and Luttikhuizen, 1995:
328–49.

of philosophy have ensured that he has spoken and written at a popular and academic level on a wide range of issues, ranging from high art to labour unions, beauticians and toilet paper! This Reader is a deposit of his wide-ranging intellect and creation-wide interests. In this introductory essay our aim is to outline the contours of the Reformational paradigm within which Seerveld works and to give some perspective on how he develops that paradigm in different areas.

Biographical sketch

Seerveld was born in 1930 and grew up in a strongly Christian home as the son of a New York fishmonger. He looks back upon this humble upbringing as full of dignity, his father's labour being a good illustration of the glory of what it means to be human (see 'Christian Workers Unite', pp. 242–43).

Seerveld's first taste of Christian education was at Calvin College in Grand Rapids, Michigan, where he did his undergraduate work. Here he developed advanced ability in French and German and majored in philosophy and English.

A major influence upon Seerveld was the arrival at Calvin of H. Evan Runner as a philosophy lecturer in Seerveld's final year. A remarkable intellect, Runner had grown up amidst the Reformed orthodox-versus-liberal theological clash in America.[4] He did his undergraduate work at Wheaton, where he developed a fascination with philosophy and classics. At Westminister Seminary Runner was influenced by Cornelius Van Til[5] who alerted him to the possibility of a *Christian* philosophy and the work along this line of Dooyeweerd and Vollenhoven in Amsterdam. Runner ended up doing his doctorate on Aristotle under Vollenhoven and he said of his exposure to this brand of neocalvinism:

> I began to sense the importance of the religious dimension of the heart and the covenant of God and what that means – that we live with God in His covenant, and that all the various aspects of our lives are embraced in that, and how that openness or closedness of the heart to His revelation which impinges upon us and to which we must respond gives direction to all the various expressions of our life, whether they are scientific or pre-scientific. That began to take on some shape, but only gradually, and I don't think I got that all worked out until I had begun to teach at Calvin, really.[6]

---

[4]For a fascinating account of Runner's development see Van Dyke and Wolters, 1979.

[5]Van Til was part of the group of Reformed thinkers who sought to develop a Christian perspective in philosophy. There are similarities and differences between Van Til and the Reformational school of Dooyeweerd and Vollenhoven. See, for example, the essays by Stoker, Dooyeweerd, Knudsen, and Mekkes in Geehan, 1980.

[6]Van Dyke and Wolters, 1979:348.

This perspective revolutionised Runner's understanding of Christian scholarship and cultural activism and at Calvin he functioned as a catalyst for a new generation of scholars and especially philosophers with a similar vision, one of the first of whom was Seerveld. The contours of this neocalvinist vision are elaborated below. Suffice here to note that central to Runner's perspective was that 'all of life is religion' in the sense that no part of life and certainly not theoretical thought is neutral, so that Christians ought to do their scholarship rooted consciously in a Christian perspective. Vollenhoven and Dooyeweerd's major development of the neocalvinism of Abraham Kuyper was their insistence that Christian scholarship requires a Christian philosophy. In his *A New Critique of Theoretical Thought* Dooyeweerd sought to articulate such a philosophy.

It was Runner's charismatic influence that prevented Seerveld from becoming the Christian Humanist that he was on his way to becoming, according to Seerveld's autobiographical 'The Informal Fantastic Life of a Believing Fishmonger's Son'. Runner's classes alerted Seerveld to the dangers of synthesising Greek and Christian thought uncritically. Christian scholarship can and should appropriate truth wherever it finds it but it must ensure that its edifice is integrally Christian from the root up. The danger of synthesis is that unchristian elements are uncritically appropriated. Thus, after a year of Masters in English literature at Michigan University and with a Fulbright scholarship in hand, Seerveld set out for Amsterdam to study under Vollenhoven and Dooyeweerd and take a closer look at Reformational philosophy.

Vollenhoven was in the process of developing and working out an integrally Christian method of historiography,[7] which has left its mark deeply on Seerveld. Under Vollenhoven's supervision Seerveld, after spending time hearing Karl Jaspers and studying under Barth and Cullmann in Switzerland, did his doctorate on Croce's aesthetic, spending a year in Italy being tutored by Croce's protégé, Carlo Antoni.

The appropriation of a neocalvinist world-view and its deepening into a philosophy set the frame for Seerveld's academic career. The basic contours of his memory had been schooled for a life-time's theoretical labours which are still continuing (see 'Philosophy as Schooled Memory').[8] Seerveld returned from Europe to the USA in 1957 and taught for a year at Belhaven College in Jackson, Mississippi. Then in 1959 he became lecturer in philosophy at Trinity Christian College, Chicago. In 1972 he moved to the Institute for Christian Studies in Toronto as senior member in philosophical aesthetics, where he remained until his retirement in 1996.

---

[7] For Seerveld's understanding of Vollenhoven's historiographical methodology, see Seerveld, 1993.

[8] That Seerveld retained his commitment to the same, basic philosophical contours he learnt under Vollenhoven and Dooyeweerd was made clear in his unpublished 'Remarks for Trinity Christian College Homecoming' in 1993: 'I still believe what I used to teach at Trinity, that God-ordered temporality headed for the eschaton of Christ's return is the core of what it means to be a creature.'

What is Neocalvinism?

To understand the fruits of Seerveld's work one needs to know about the fertile soil of the neocalvinist tradition from which he draws sustenance. During the second half of the nineteenth century, the Reformed churches in the Netherlands experienced a revival. This took the form not only of large numbers of personal commitments to Christ, but also of a vigorous social movement intent on proclaiming and advancing the Lordship of Jesus Christ over all of life. Participants in this movement believed it to be a faithful revival of authentic Calvinism, and easily appropriated the label that was stuck on their movement by its enemies: Neocalvinism.

Neocalvinism initially received its distinctive shape under the leadership of Abraham Kuyper (1837–1920). Kuyper started his working life as a pastor, and it was in the pastorate that he experienced an evangelical conversion. He renewed his interest in theology but now along orthodox lines and he went on to write hundreds of books and articles in which he sought to articulate and apply a Christian world-view to all aspects of life. He entered parliament in 1874 and was prime minister from 1900 to 1905. In all sorts of ways Kuyper embodied the vision that he so memorably expressed in his statement that 'there is not a square inch of the universe of which Christ does not rightly say, "That is mine!"' Neocalvinism refuses to limit Christianity to individual piety, theology and the activities of the institutional church, although it affirms the importance of these aspects of the Christian faith and life: Kuyper himself was an exceptionally productive theologian, a very popular preacher, and the writer of many volumes of warmly evangelical, if intently Reformed, daily devotions. But these aspects are not considered sufficient. For Neocalvinists, Christianity provides a world-view, a way of understanding all of reality, with radical consequences for every part of their lives. The broad outlines of this world-view are already clear in Kuyper's 1898 Stone Lectures at Princeton University (see Kuyper, 1987) – a manifesto of early Neocalvinism.

Al Wolters (1985:4–10), an expert on the neocalvinist tradition, identifies four key characteristics of the neocalvinist world-view, as follows.

1. *An understanding of creation, fall and redemption as the basic thrust of Christianity.* Neocalvinists believe that Christianity is not alien to life in this world. Consequently Christians should attempt to renew life in this world from within so that it conforms to its created purpose. In creation God has laid down His law, making possible *inter alia* all human shaping of artefacts and interpersonal relationships. The whole world belongs to God. At the same time, all of reality is under the curse of sin – and all of reality lies within range of redemption in and through Jesus Christ. There is a good cre-

ational structure for everything, but after the fall the direction toward the original creation purposes is opposed by a direction away from it.

Neocalvinism does not recognise any conflict between gospel and creation: they are not parallel or supplementary to each other, and the gospel is no evolutionary extension of creation. Rather, Neocalvinists understand the gospel to be the healing power which restores creation, in line with God's original design, and toward its originally intended consummation. This emphasis on reality as creation, sin as the misdirection of creation, and redemption as the restoration of creation suggests that the neocalvinist understanding of the basic thrust of Christianity is rooted in the motive of creation, exalting God in the first place as the sovereign Creator. As Spykman (1992:257–8) writes, biblically covenant and kingdom, two major biblical themes, are seen as a 'bi-unitary index to the meaning of creation. ... Covenant suggests the idea of an abiding charter, while kingdom suggests the idea of an ongoing program. Covenant is more foundation oriented; kingdom is more goal oriented. Covenant may thus be conceived of as kingdom looking back to its origins, but with abiding significance. Kingdom may then be conceived of as covenant looking forward with gathering momentum to its final fulfillment. ... This bi-unity is so intimate that we may say, In the beginning God covenanted his kingdom into existence.'

2. *An emphasis on creation law and creaturely diversity.* If redemption is the restoration of creation, then there is a God-ordained standard or principle of what is possible for every kind of thing, to which it must be restored, and by which it can be distinguished from other kinds of things. God is sovereign (a central, perhaps *the* central belief of Calvinism in all of its expressions). His Word is law for all creatures. His Law-Word establishes the possible structure and distinctive identity of every created thing: linden trees, cigars, human beings, states – everything. The order of creation is unchanging, a constancy grounded in the covenantal faithfulness of God. Neocalvinism is able, out of this conviction, to forcefully counter the seductions of the relativism and historicism of the modern age.

There is a close connection for Neocalvinists between creation and the rich diversity of things in this world. God not only brought reality into existence, but brought it into existence as a richly diverse order of distinct kinds of things. Paying attention to Genesis 1, Neocalvinists noted in the process of creation several separations – light from darkness, waters under from waters above, day from night – and the creation of living things after their kinds. It is this biblical idea of separation and kinds which motivates the neocalvinist emphasis on creational diversity. Herman Bavinck (1854–1921) – next to

Kuyper and Groen van Prinsterer the most influential Neocalvinist of their time – wrote that

> the world is a unity, but that unity manifests itself in the most magnificent and beautiful diversity. Heaven and earth were distinct from the very beginning; sun and moon and stars each received their own task; plant and animal and man each have their own nature. Everything is created by God with a nature of its own, and exists and lives according to a law of its own (Bavinck, 1901: 41–2).

Kuyper argued that the various human relations in society each possess a unique integrity, independent of any other human relationship, derived from the possibilities which God enfolded into reality at creation with regard to that particular relationship. Thus, for instance, the family has a sovereignty in its own sphere in the face of both the state and the church, and should not be internally made subject to these other relationships. The authority of mother and father does not require the rubber stamp of a party commissar or the holy water of a parish priest – it is received out of the very hand of God. But all human authority, every human relationship, is subject to the sovereign rule of God, proclaims Kuyper (as translated by Seerveld in McIntire, 1985:49):

> Get it?! Not one bit of our thought-world is to be separated and hermetically sealed off from the other pieces of our conceptual universe. In fact, there is not to be a fingerprint speck of territory in our whole human life about which the Christ, who is sovereign over everything, is not calling out, 'That belongs to me!'

This view does not deny historical changes in society, but rather emphasises the possibilities given in creation which provide room and set limits for the emergence of a wide range of different relationships in society. This emphasis is normally referred to with Kuyper's term of 'sphere sovereignty' (*souvereiniteit in eigen kring*), although many contemporary Neocalvinists prefer the term 'structural pluralism'.

For Neocalvinists, sphere sovereignty implies that a key task of Christian cultural activism should be to respect and affirm the created boundaries of human relationships while working hard to realise their distinctive internal possibilities. In Dutch politics this conviction has often found expression in the struggle to defend the Christian family, church, and school against the encroaching excesses of the secularising liberal state.[9]

The emphasis on creaturely diversity, particularly with regard to relationships among people, must be balanced with an equal insistence on the created coherence of all of reality. This coherence can be seen in the relationships among all things and derives not from anything in created reality, but from

God's creation of all things. The need to balance creaturely diversity and creation-wide coherence is often referred to by Neocalvinists in terms of sphere sovereignty and sphere universality.

Hans Rookmaaker (1981:113–15) describes this balance between the integrity of individual created things or societal spheres on the one hand, and the coherence of all created reality on the other:

> God's creatures require no justification. God has given them their value by including them in the totality of his creation. ... Art needs no justification. It is meaningful in itself, not only as an evangelistic tool, or to serve a practical purpose, or to be didactic. ... But if art needs no justification, it also does not follow that art is to be for art's sake. ... Art is not just there to be art, but is bound by a thousand ties to reality. Nothing is simply autonomous. A tree, a human being, a work of art – all are part of that wonderful fabric which we call reality; no thread can be missing without impoverishing the whole.

> So even if art has meaning in itself, it can never be on its own. It would wither and die. It is tied in two ways to reality. On the one hand, art deals with reality; it is about fear, hope, joy, love, our surroundings, the things we love and hate. On the other hand, art is used in reality. Music, rhetoric, poetry make up a large part of our social functions and religious activities; and architecture, furniture and textile design, interior decoration, painting and illustration provide the setting for our movements and actions. No matter whether art receives a prominent place or serves in the background, the fascinating truth is that the more it becomes engaged in reality, and the more concrete its manifold ties with our daily life, the more we will recognise that it needs no justification.

3. *An affirmation of the historical development of creation.* Neocalvinism has a deep appreciation for the historical development of human cultures and societies. Undergirding all human historical activity are the structural givens enfolded into reality at creation. There is no inherent conflict between the constant order of created reality and historical development. The progressive unfolding of creational possibilities in history through human cultural action deserves at least two cheers in the neocalvinist view, while taking into account the impact of sin. The development of technology, the advances of the sciences, the building of cities, and the disentanglement of various distinct relationships in society (often referred to as 'differentiation') – are all fundamentally appropriate human responses to God's command to realise the possibilities of creation, the cultural mandate (see Genesis 1:28 and 2:15). It is the responsibility of Christians to affirm and

---

[9]It is possible to abuse the notion of sphere sovereignty, as South African Neocalvinists did when they supported racial and ethnic apartheid. For a nuanced discussion of apartheid and Neocalvinism see Strauss, 1996.

advocate such advances in the context of the coming of the kingdom of God – while opposing their misdirection away from the glory of God. In recent years Neocalvinists have become more aware of the temptation to see one's own culture as the culmination of all human history, a temptation to which an earlier generation of Dutch Neocalvinists occasionally succumbed. Critical caution needs to be exercised in identifying normative cultural unfolding.[10]

4. *The recognition of an ultimate religious conflict.* There is a war raging at the deepest level in every society and within every human person – a struggle between the inclination to submit to God and the inclination to rebel against God. This personal and public conflict between the kingdoms of light and darkness Neocalvinists call 'the antithesis'. This struggle is not relegated to some spiritual realm above or alongside everyday life: it is a spiritual struggle for everyday life itself. The antithesis issues forth a clarion call for Christian cultural activity in opposition to every manner of idolatry, including the pervasive secularisation of late modernity.

The fruit-bearing branches of neocalvinist scholarship

Neocalvinism, with its emphasis on the Lordship of Christ over all of life, has produced rich fruit-bearing branches of scholarship. The philosophical and historiographical work of the brothers-in-law Herman Dooyeweerd[11] and Dirk Vollenhoven, and their colleagues, is perhaps the best known of these branches – the Reformational branch out of which Seerveld's scholarship has grown.

It is the task of philosophy, according to Reformational thinkers, to systematically analyse and pose a framework for understanding the interrelated meaning of everything created. Philosophy must draw on the vigorous imprecision of world-view to avoid pedantic petrification, while world-view must heed the meticulous plumbing of philosophy if it does not want to sink back into fuzzy, unconscious cliché.

Dooyeweerd, Vollenhoven, and their colleagues drew on the convictions of Neocalvinism to shape a theory of reality which is renowned for its complexity. Reformational philosophy is rich in promise insofar as it threads out the implications of the neocalvinist world-view for scholarship. Following Dooyeweerd's programme (see for instance in the first volume of his *A New Critique of Theoretical Thought*, 1984:541–2), Reformational philosophy has:

---

[10]See Seerveld, 1996a for a carefully nuanced evaluation of Dooyeweerd's idea of historical development.

[11]Dooyeweerd's work is better known than Vollenhoven's, which has not been translated as has Dooyeweerd's. The best introductions to Dooyeweerd's systematic philosophy are Kalsbeek, 1975 and Clouser, 1991.

- critically investigated the ultimate commitments undergirding some of the many conflicting movements of cultural endeavour (particularly schools of scholarly thought) throughout history and in our time;
- shaped a theory of the *modal aspects* or distinct functional facets of reality (perhaps the best known and most contested part of Reformational philosophy);
- studied various areas of everyday human experience to uncover the structure of and relationships among the various kinds of things;
- begun to develop a theory of knowledge or epistemology; and begun the outlines of a philosophical anthropology, or theory of the human person.

The Reformational cosmological theory developed mainly by Dooyeweerd has attracted some attention among Christian scholars. Less known, but equally rich in promise, is the historiographical methodology meticulously developed in particular by Vollenhoven. Seerveld has drawn more on Vollenhoven and less on Dooyeweerd than most other Reformational scholars. Vollenhoven applied his methodology to the history of philosophy, Seerveld has applied this methodology to the history of art and of aesthetics. This methodology traces how people respond to enduring challenges emerging out of the structure of reality, and how people are submitted either to the Spirit of God or to some or other spirit of the age.

Seerveld and Scripture

Scripture is foundational to Seerveld's world-view and scholarship. As he says, 'The Bible operates in my scholarship the way the Bible operates in the rest of my life, like an iceberg.'[12] Hence the ease with which Seerveld moves from Scripture to discussion of all sorts of issues and his tendency to start talks with a freshly translated passage or two of Scripture. Seerveld's goal is always scripturally directed life and learning, so that he might genuinely live *coram Deo* (before the face of God) and provide bread and not stones for his neighbours in his academic vocation. While in Germany on a Fulbright scholarship he learnt Hebrew and throughout his career has worked at translations of the original texts.[13] In Germany while studying under Cullmann Seerveld had to prepare for an exam in which he would be asked to translate some of the Letter to the Romans into German from the Greek. He tells of virtually locking himself up with the Greek version of Romans for days in preparation

---

[12]Seerveld: 'A few theses for discussion purposes in *Biblical Foundations*' (22 February 1990 and 26 March 1992), unpublished.

[13]For a brief discussion of Seerveld's theory of translation see Seerveld, 1991: 28–34.

11

for the exam, and finding himself confronted with God through this text and knowing for sure that the Bible is Holy Scripture.[14]

Seerveld also studied under Gerhard von Rad in Germany and shares with him a sense of Scripture as kerygmatic. Scripture is above all else God's Word and Seerveld has sought not only to do scholarship in the grip of Scripture, but to read and preach it so that God's people genuinely hear God speaking. Seerveld preaches regularly and each sermon is a crafted attempt to respond to the question he poses at the outset of his book *Balaam's Apocalyptic Prophecies*: 'How can a man or woman, educated or not, go to the Scriptures with an imaginative, childlike trust, hear its storied Truth freshly so that it re-form his or her whole life-time of activity and bear fruit worthy of our Lord rather than inhibit our creatureliness?' (Seerveld, 1980b:xi,xii).

Seerveld is passionately concerned that God's people learn to hear God speak through his Word – simply believing Scripture to be infallible is not enough. In *Balaam's Apocalyptic Prophecies*, subtitled *A Study in Reading Scripture*, Seerveld distinguishes four ways of reading Scripture. A *fundamentalistic* reading focuses on the vacillating man Balaam in Numbers 22–4 and asks what practical lessons Christians can learn from him. This takes Scripture seriously as God's Word to us but misses the narrative sweep in Scripture of God's unfolding purposes in his world. A *higher-critical, neo-orthodox* reading helpfully notes the connection of Bible characters with the Ancient Near-Eastern world of the day. To an extent it also recognises the literary nature of the Bible and the historical processes by which biblical books reached their present form. However, the view of literature is often outdated and the rationalism and scepticism shaping this method are unhelpful. Scripture is continually made problematic so that it is hard for God's people to come to Scripture as God's Word. Thirdly, a *scholastic* reading always looks for doctrinal propositions in the text it focuses upon. Thus, for example, Numbers 23:19 – 'God is not a human being that he should lie' – is immediately related to the unchangeable Being of God. Such a reading rightly recognises the interconnectedness of the Bible as a whole but easily misses the existential encounter with the living Word of God because the stories and diverse genres of Scripture are read *through* a propositional grid and *into* one.

Seerveld proposes a *biblically Reformational* hermeneutic. There are four key elements to his creative approach: firstly, see how the passage fits in the story line of Scripture. Secondly, discern the literary configuration of the passage. Seerveld often speaks in this respect of a *firefly method* of reading, i.e. a reading which is alert to repetitions that indicate the literary structure of the text.

---

[14]Seerveld narrated this story in a delightful interview with Anna-Liza Kosma for *Tapestry* on CBC Radio, 31 March 1996. Senior producer: Richard Handler.

Thirdly, examine the historical context in which the passage was written. Fourthly, listen to the kerygma of the passage in the context of the whole of Scripture. Seerveld (1980b:47) says of this way of reading Scripture:

> It listens for the Good News, but in terms of direction rather than maxims; it honours research as an enriching factor, not as a precondition; it acknowledges that the message of the passage is given to be confessed, but then positively instead of apologetically, and fully rather than only in matters of dogma and morals. This other way of reading the Bible is born out of what we call a Reformationally Christian perspective, and seems to me to do most justice to the riches of the Bible, letting its integrating, compelling force work itself out on our whole life in society and God's world.

Seerveld is happy to utilise critical insights in his exegesis and anticipates the literary turn in biblical studies in his sensitivity to the literary shape of biblical texts.[15] However, and rightly in our opinion, all these resources are directed towards hearing the kerygmatic focus of Scripture, so that the whole of the life of the people of God might be caught up by it. Thus, with Numbers 22–4 Seerveld concludes that there are two main messages. Firstly, Christians are called to be a community specially set apart by God to facilitate the blessing of God's reign among the nations of the world. Secondly, we are to rid our communion of modern-day Balaams for they are destroying the people of God.

Seerveld's aesthetic sensitivity to biblical texts is perhaps seen most clearly in *The Greatest Song*, a dramatic version of the Song of Songs, which has been performed many times.[16] His discernment of three voices is controversial,[17] but the performance is a masterly embodiment of aesthetics in the service of kerygma.

Christian education

Seerveld is passionately committed to the potential of education, a commitment which is evident in the amount of this Reader devoted to this subject. Every teacher, he suggests, should be unforgettable to his or her pupils, sparking their imaginations with wonder at the challenge of growing in understanding of God's world and so being equipped to serve God in his world.[18]

---

[15] *Balaam's Apocalyptic Prophecies* were first given as lectures in 1968, long before the literary turn in Biblical Studies. See also Seerveld's work on wisdom literature, especially his series of articles on Proverbs in *Vanguard* (see Zuidervaart and Luttikhuizen, 1995 for bibliographical references).

[16] Seerveld, 1988.

[17] In addition to the woman and her lover, Seerveld discerns the voice of King Solomon.

[18] See Seerveld, 1980b:104–6.

Not surprisingly Seerveld's philosophy of education endeavours to be unashamedly Christian. The gospel embraces the whole of life and Christians ought not to live happily with Greek notions of excellence and other non-Christian understandings shaping their education (see 'In Quest of Excellence', pp. 132–38). Education ought to strive for excellence but it makes a difference whether this is defined in Greek or in biblical terms. Like all of life education is not neutral, and Christians ought purposefully to allow the gospel to shape their thoughts about and practice of education. The Greek Sophists, Socrates, and Montaigne shaped the philosophy of education powerfully and these influences are still felt today.[19] For years now Seerveld has identified *pragmatism* as a particularly dangerous influence upon North American education.[20] Christians ought to be alert to the way different perspectives understand education and ought to consciously seek to develop an integrally Christian philosophy of education.

While Seerveld does not deny that God calls some of His people to be educated in state schools and to teach in comprehensive institutions, he believes that the logic of the gospel is that we need Christian educational institutions. Education is not confined to schools; the nurture involved in education is fundamentally the responsibility of the family. However, part of the normative differentiation of culture is the development of schools which specialise in the nurturing process, and, particularly in the later years, focus on particular areas of that education. Seerveld himself has always taught in Christian institutions and devoted considerable energy to developing such institutions.

For education to be Christian a community of educationalists is required who share a vision of education as equipping for service in God's world and are committed to developing a curriculum emerging from 'the inner reformation of the sciences'[21] along Christian lines. The gospel needs to be allowed to bear institutional fruit in this way. This is what Seerveld graphically describes as 'a Septuagint approach' in 'Perspective for our Christian Colleges':[22]

> The Septuagint approach breaks with the attractive but futile individualism of one Christian here and another there going off bravely to infiltrate the educating world. … Christian education will flower only where the Spirit has hands and eyes and feet – all kinds of specialists – who are competent (piety does not cover incompetence, whether it be the botched exegesis of a poem or a messy appendectomy) and united not only by a common faith and biblical commitment but also by their breathing excitedly and wholeheartedly this unifying, re-forming spirit I have mentioned.

[19]See 'Cultural Objectives for Christian Teachers', pp. 146–67.

[20]See 'The Christian School in American Democracy', pp. 178–91.

[21]This is a phrase coined by Dooyeweerd to articulate the way in which a Christian perspective shapes a theoretical discipline. Teachers need not themselves be philosophers but the development of a Christian curriculum requires a Christian philosophy in Seerveld's opinion. See 'Cultural Objectives for the Christian Teacher', pp. 144–45.

[22]See p. 148 in Part 3.

Also central to Seerveld's philosophy of education is the insistence that an educational institution has its own validity distinct from other parts of society such as the institutional church, politics or the family. Ideally, a school should not be governed by the institutional church. It should be Christian and the curriculum should be shaped integrally by the gospel, but it is an *educational* institution and not a church. Thus its main task is education and not evangelism or Word proclamation. Because its task is done in the gentle grip of the gospel there will always be overtones of testimony and evangelism but it will give itself to the task of excellence in education.

It is often feared that this sort of vision of Christian education will become isolationist. Nothing could be further from Seerveld's mind or practice. Separate Christian institutions are required, in his view, so that the Christian tradition can manifest itself in all areas of thought, but this is always to be done with awareness of and dialogue with other positions. Thus, when Seerveld taught about Marxism, he would find the best-informed Marxist in his area and bring him or her into his class so that the class could assess whether what they had been taught really fitted with the reality of Marxism as understood by its adherents. While teaching at Trinity Christian College in Chicago, Seerveld placed an advertisement in the University of Chicago newspaper: 'Wanted: articulate atheist to talk with Christian students. Send CV and statement of unbelief with reasons. Travel money and honorarium for the best applicant.' From the applicants Seerveld chose an apostate priest, sent him a copy of 'Logic Impaired by Sin' from Abraham Kuyper's *Encyclopaedia of Sacred Theology*, which he was to criticise, and to explain to the students why he was an atheist, and then take questions! This is the sort of dialogue that Seerveld is deeply committed to, but it can only take place if the Christian tradition is given space to develop its own insights and, for this, Christian institutions are required. As Seerveld said in his (unpublished) 'Remarks for Trinity Christian College Homecoming' in 1993:

> Biblically Christian disciplined education is one piece of cloth, having the leisure to learn God's way in the universe – from germs and antibodies, to embracing colour combinations, to speaking the truth in love to an unfriendly audience – and the time to become sensitive to the cries of Christ's body in history, remembering them as our stigmata, with neighbours, under the sure hand of the LORD tightly holding and guiding our lives till Christ returns.'

'Christian Camel Drivers Unite?': labour

This is the title of a talk which Seerveld gave on Christians and labour unions. While convinced of the necessity of Christian scholarship Seerveld remained unsure about the value of Christian institutions in areas other than education.

Overhearing a conversation between members of the Christian Labour Association of Canada (CLAC) catalysed him into a realisation of the importance of such initiatives, and a number of the essays under 'Work and Daily Life' in this Reader are addresses to the CLAC. In these Seerveld reminds us that work is a constituent part of what it means to be human. The fall problematises work and historically thinkers have developed a variety of often unhelpful perspectives on work. From a Christian perspective work is a means of 'hallelujahing Yahweh' and part of being redeemed means being set free now to start doing that in our work.

Separate Christian organisations such as the CLAC have been controversial even in Reformed circles and Seerveld devotes much energy to defending the propriety of separate Christian organisations. He sees them as a Christian imperative and relates them *inter alia* to the New Testament exhortation for the body of Christ to be one. Real hallelujahing of Yahweh in work requires communal action; individualism undermines such attempts, especially in our modern, secular context in which anti-Christian spirits dominate the work place. Christian labour organisations are to be real labour organisations shaped integrally by a Christian perspective, and for the good of all in their attempt to recover a Christian practice of work. Thus a Christian labour union will be open to all who feel free to affirm its labour policies.

Arts and the aesthetic

According to Lambert Zuidervaart (head of the department of philosophy at Calvin College and one of Seerveld's doctoral students) four claims constitute Seerveld's contribution to aesthetics (in Zuidervaart and Luttikhuizen, 1995:9–10).

1. *The aesthetic is part of the fabric of created reality, and aesthetic norms can be violated or ignored only at great cost.* The human ability to imagine, and the aspect of reality which conclusively distinguishes art from scholarship, play from commerce, a gallery from a pet shop – these are gracious givens in God's good creation. Seerveld writes (1979:287) that

   the fact that 'allusiveness' is a real kind-of-being-there, and therefore holds the limited, ordinational blessing and cursing power of what God said was good and needed to be responded within by God's creatures – that fact takes 'modal aesthetic' problems out of the realm of personal preference, dillydally trivia or adiaphora. …
   If the *allusive* mode of creaturely reality is denied or neglected, or, if in reaction to the fastidious idolatry of aesthetics, one decides to live in aesthetic disobedience, the result is aesthetic closure to life. And a man or a woman's life deprived of *allusive* shalom … is a very sad, impoverished kind of closed-down creaturely existence.

2. *The arts, despite their variety and their continuing development, are a unified sphere distinct from other spheres of cultural endeavour, offering opportunities for vocational service to Christians today.* In his retirement address to the Institute for Christian Studies, once more with particular reference to the need for scholarship in neighbourly service to artists, Seerveld (1996b:14–15) confirmed this claim that

> bona fide artistic reality deserves ontological backup … to forestall colonialisation by semiotics, media studies, or to have artistry get lost in the shuffle of important non-artistic affairs like gender, nationality and technological innovation, which do indeed impinge upon art. Sorting out this foundational matter of defining artistry in a changing world is practically hopeless, I think, if an artistic event/artwork is conceived conventionally and only in terms of its functions. Precisely because there are now so many more professional Christian artists who have questions about their task, it behoves aestheticians at home with the LORD in God's world to come through with supportive rationale and wisdom for the artist's specific, multifaceted calling.

3. *The aesthetic is not limited only to the arts, just as the arts have many facets other than the aesthetic.* According to Seerveld, we catch a glimpse of the aesthetic in the troth-ward flirting of courting couples, in the playful exchange of wit during a meal of good food and drink, in the diplomatic niceties of political life. Aesthetic obedience is not only a responsibility of professional artists, but is one of the responses to God's good creation which needs to suffuse – though not overwhelm – all of our lives. Also, artists in their art need to consider as much as courting couples whether they are trothful to their subjects and audience, as much as table-companions whether their artwork is apt for the social setting, as much as diplomats whether they are doing justice to all parties.

4. *The core of meaning of the aesthetic – and the distinguishing characteristic of the arts – is 'allusiveness' or 'imaginativity'.* Seerveld's contested insistence on the defining centrality of *allusiveness* to the arts and the aesthetic seems aimed in the first place against what he considers to be the vicious curse of 'Beauty'. Seerveld considers the tradition of Beauty to be 'perhaps the major stumbling block to a fruitful theory of art, a down-to-earth sense of the aesthetic, and a hermeneutics that can trust imaginative knowledge' (1984:16–18). In his view this tradition has led among evangelical Christians to a misconception of the task of art as mystically reminding those homesick for heaven of the beauty once lost and the lustre a-coming. Marshalling an army of exclamation marks, Seerveld campaigns against proof-texting efforts to theologise about the arts in the tradition of Beauty (1979:289):

Psalm 29:2 is as much and as little a proof-text for kneeling in church as it is for 'the beauty of holiness' = ? God?! Psalm 29 is really a command more to the angels! (as in Psalm 148:2) or to heathen god worshippers! ... to everything in the whole wide world! to prostrate itself (*Werft euch IHM ... hin!* translates Buber) before the Lord God Yahweh in his terrible majestic Holiness, who is speaking creationally! And Psalm 29 reverberates seven times with qol YHWH! Qol YHWH! Till one remembers Revelation 10:1–4, and any budding Christian aesthetician in their right mind who had been looking for infallible backup information on 'Beauty' here would have long ago thrown away notebook, pencil, even clothes, and full of fear and trembling be pleading like Isaiah 6.

In elaborating the implications of these claims Seerveld works for a turnabout in aesthetics to understanding, as the title of his inaugural lecture at the Institute for Christian Studies promised.[23]

A Christian Critique of Art and Literature and *Rainbows for the Fallen World* are dog-eared on many study and studio shelves – yet these are not the most enduring documents of Seerveld's contribution to our understanding of aesthetics and the arts. Far more enduring is the legacy engraved in the hearts and shaping the memory of the many people who attended his classes and seminars, or heard his lectures, sermons and talks around the world. Imagination is not only Seerveld's object of study: it pervades his life and marks his teaching style. The memory of his students is schooled in the contours of the neocalvinist world-view and Reformational philosophy, and flared with occasional pieces and conversations on 'gallantry as a recreative moment of life', or 'glory to God in the kitchen'.

Seerveld endeavours to help the people of God, in a time of renewal in the arts among Christians, 'to find out what art is like, why the Lord put this talent in our creaturely laps and how is art to keep its holy rainbow character rather than become a mirage'. He digs the humus of challenge, comfort, freedom and shalom into the fields of the Lord as he reminds us that 'ordinary art can be special, full-time service for the Lord [and] that aesthetic obedience is required of everyone by the Lord – artist or not' (Seerveld, 1980a:8–9).

For those working in the lineage of Kuyper, Dooyeweerd and Vollenhoven – and for those excited and encouraged by the work of Francis Schaeffer and Hans Rookmaaker – Calvin Seerveld has indeed brought about a turnabout to understanding in aesthetics. His life of scholarship testifies to the truth of his claim (1996b:4) that 'the dynamic of scripturally-directed learning is selflessly single-minded service, has nothing to do with careers or fringe benefits, but comes with the high cost of communal struggle as sinful people to be obedient together in making a redemptive difference on the secular educational scene.'

---

[23]Seerveld, 1974.

Conclusion

The remarkable range of Seerveld's thought is related to the comprehensive vision of Neocalvinism and Seerveld's wide-ranging abilities, which extend well beyond the scholarly realm. This Reader, for example, contains some of Seerveld's previously unpublished songs. Indeed, Seerveld regards the years he spent helping in the production of the Christian Reformed Church's new hymnal[24] as some of the most important work he has done. A hymnal shapes the response of the people of God to his Word, and Seerveld's commitment to this project symbolises the passion of his life: to live life *coram Deo* and to help others live similarly. A new hymnal is a gift to emerging generations to help them to continue to respond to God from within the same tradition.

Throughout his career Seerveld has worked creatively within the Reformational paradigm, and has developed that tradition in a variety of ways, not least aesthetically. Neocalvinism and Seerveld's Reformational work are significant for a variety of reasons. This century Evangelicalism has slowly woken up to the creation-wide dimensions of its faith and Neocalvinism has made a vital contribution to this process. George Marsden (1987:14) even speaks of 'the triumph – or nearly so – of what may be loosely called Kuyperian presuppositionalism in the evangelical community'.

But it is not just Evangelicalism which has awoken in a new way to these dimensions. Lesslie Newbigin's (1983, 1986, 1991) challenge to the Western church to confront its culture with the gospel is being taken seriously by many, even as the stronghold of modernity has wavered. David Ford, Regius Professor of Divinity at Cambridge University, in his inaugural lecture, *A Long Rumour of Wisdom*, speaks of the urgent need for the Christian church to recover wisdom in our day.

> I see the most important item on their theological agenda at present being the education of their general membership for living in truth and wisdom. As traditional habits and supports for faith weaken in the society generally, as faith becomes less a part of the atmosphere, so the need for thorough learning of the faith increases. A religion is at least as many-layered and complex as a language and culture, and *if people are to be more than tourists in relation to their traditions then there needs to be ordered learning of them and of their contemporary significance.*[25]

Ford goes on to deplore the scandal of the lack of such wisdom in so many areas:

> If one looks at formative discourses in our society in recent decades there is relatively little high-quality theological contribution. On the whole it is hard to think

---

[24]*Psalter Hymnal*, 1989. The index for 'Authors, Composers, and Sources' has 39 page references under 'Seerveld'.

[25]pp. 14,15. Italics added.

of theological treatments of the legal system, the economy, education, science, technology, medicine and the formation of our culture that have entered the mainstream of debate … theology has often allowed itself to be marginalised or confined within restricted areas of philology, history, sociology or philosophy.[26]

These lacunae that Ford identifies are precisely the areas that Seerveld has devoted himself to address, attempting to relate biblical wisdom to all of life, and to scholarship and aesthetics in particular. There are encouraging signs of a renewed concern among Christians to relate the gospel to our cultures, and in this respect Seerveld's work on aesthetics may be of particular importance. The tornado of the communication revolution is gathering muster around us and it is transforming our culture and privileging the visual. Andrew Walker (1996:98) recognises this challenge in his suggestion that 'Surely now is the time for the gospel to recapture a true iconography in a world where the image is replacing the written word.' An adequate Christian response to these changes will require honed aesthetic insight, and Seerveld is one of few who have systematically worked at developing such expertise from a consciously Christian perspective.

As modernity has increasingly been questioned in the latter half of this century, a new awareness has developed among some theologians of the need for a Christian starting point and for the 'Word to absorb the world' rather than vice versa. This 'postliberalism', represented by Hans Frei and George Lindbeck in particular,[27] holds creative possibilities for dialogue with evangelicals. George Hunsinger (1996) has, however, perceptively pointed out, that within Evangelicalism it is the tradition of Kuyper and Bavinck that embodies the most fruitful ground for such dialogue. This is quite right, in our opinion, but the sophisticated development of the Kuyper–Bavinck tradition that Seerveld embodies should not be ignored if that dialogue is to have maximum effect. Hunsinger (1996:149) notes that Kuyper and Bavinck are less entangled in the encumbrances of modernity than many other prominent evangelical theologians. It is to examine precisely this question of modernity that Dooyeweerd, Vollenhoven and Seerveld, plus many others, have devoted their considerable resources and their contributions will increase the fruitfulness of such dialogue.

Our aim in publishing this Reader is to make available the fertile deposit of a Christian tradition that genuinely attempts to tackle the questions that are at the heart of what it means to follow Christ today. For the fruit of Reformational scholarship in the work of Seerveld and his generation invites a younger generation to be grafted themselves onto these branches. Our hope

---

[26]p. 17.

[27]For an introduction to post-liberal theology see Placher, 1997.

is not that all will agree with what they read, but that it will facilitate a dialogue with a still too-little known tradition and a major exponent of that tradition. The passion of Seerveld's life has been to serve up bread, and not stones, to his neighbour/s in his life and scholarship. Whether or not one always agrees with him, Seerveld's writings communicate that passion ineluctably.

References

Bavinck, H., 1901. *Schepping of Ontwikkeling*. Kampen: Kok.

Bril, K.A., H. Hart and J. Klapwijk (eds.), 1973. *The Idea of a Christian Philosophy: Essays in Honour of D.H.Th. Vollenhoven*. Toronto: Wedge.

Clouser, R.A., 1991. *The Myth of Religious Neutrality. An Essay on the Hidden Role of Religious Belief in Theories*. Notre Dame, Ind.: University of Notre Dame Press.

Dooyeweerd, H., 1984. *A New Critique of Theoretical Thought*. 4 vols. Ontario: Paideia Press. (First published 1935–6 as *De Wijsbegeerte der Wetsidee*. Amsterdam: H. J. Paris.)

Elwel, W.A. (ed.), 1984. *Evangelical Dictionary of Theology*. Grand Rapids: Baker.

Ford, D.F., 1992. *A Long Rumour of Wisdom: Redescribing Theology*. Cambridge University Press.

—— (ed.), 1997. *The Modern Theologians: An Introduction to Christian Theology in the Twentieth Century*. Oxford: Blackwell.

Geehan, E.R. (ed.), 1980. *Jerusalem and Athens: Critical Discussions on the Philosophy and Apologetics of Cornelius Van Til*. New Jersey: Presbyterian and Reformed.

Hunsinger, G., 1996. 'What Can Evangelicals and Postliberals Learn From Each Other? The Carl Henry – Hans Frei Exchange Reconsidered', in Phillips and Okholm, 1996: 134–50.

Kalsbeek, L., 1975. *Contours of a Christian Philosophy: An Introduction to Herman Dooyeweerd's Thought*. Toronto: Wedge. (First published 1970 as *De Wijsbegeerte der Wetsidee: Proeve van een Christelijke Filosofie*. Amsterdam: Buijten & Schipperheijn.)

Kraay, J. and A. Tol (eds.), 1979. *Hearing and Doing: Philosophical Essays Dedicated to H. Evan Runner*. Toronto: Wedge.

Kuyper, A., 1987. *Lectures on Calvinism*. Grand Rapids: Eerdmans/Washington, DC: Ethics and Public Policy Center. (First published 1898 as *Het Calvinisme. Zes Stonelezingen*. Amsterdam: Hoveker & Wormser.)

McIntire, C.T. (ed.), 1985. *The Legacy of Herman Dooyeweerd: Reflections on a Critical Philosophy in the Christian Tradition*. Lanham: University Press of America.

Marsden, G., 1987. 'The State of Evangelical Christian Scholarship', *The Reformed Journal*, 37:12–16.

Newbigin, L., 1983. *The Other Side of 1984*. London: World Council of Churches.

——, 1986. *Foolishness to the Greeks*. London: SPCK.

——, 1991. *Truth to Tell: The Gospel as Public Truth*. London: SPCK.

——, 1995. *Proper Confidence: Faith, Doubt and Certainty in Christian Discipleship*. London: SPCK.

Phillips, T.R. and D.L. Okholm (eds.), 1996. *The Nature of Confession: Evangelicals and Postliberals in Conversation*. Downers Grove, Ill.: Inter-Varsity Press.

Placher, W.C., 1997. 'Postliberal Theology', in Ford, 1997: 343–56.

Psalter Hymnal, 1989. Grand Rapids: CRC [Christian Reformed Church] Publications.

Rookmaaker, H.R., 1981. *The Creative Gift*. Leicester: Inter-Varsity Press.

Schrotenboer, P.G. *et al.*, 1994. *God's Order for Creation*. Potchefstroom: Institute for Reformational Studies.

Seerveld, C.G., 1973. 'Biblical Wisdom Underneath Vollenhoven's Categories for Philosophical Historiography', in Bril, Hart, and Klapwijk, 1973: 125–43.

—, 1974. *A Turnabout in Aesthetics to Understanding*. Toronto: Institute for Christian Studies.

—, 1975. 'The Pedagogical Strength of a Christian Methodology in Philosophical Historiography', *Koers* 40 (4–6): 269–313.

—, 1979. 'Modal Aesthetics: Preliminary Questions with an Opening Hypothesis', in Kraay and Tol, 1979: 263–94.

—, 1980a. *Rainbows for the Fallen World*. Toronto Tuppence Press.

—, 1980b. *Balaam's Apocalyptic Prophecies: A Study in Reading Scripture*. Toronto: Wedge.

—, 1984. 'Aesthetics, Christian View of', in Elwel, 1984:16–18.

—, 1985. 'Dooyeweerd's Legacy for Aesthetics: Modal Law Theory', in McIntire, 1985: 41–79.

—, 1988. *The Greatest Song: In Critique of Solomon*. Toronto: Tuppence Press.

—, 1991. 'Footprints in the Snow', *Philosophia Reformata* 56: 1–34.

—, 1993. 'Vollenhoven's Legacy for Art Historiography', *Philosophia Reformata* 58: 49–79.

—, 1995. 2nd ed. *A Christian Critique of Art and Literature*. Toronto: Tuppence Press. (First published 1968.)

—, 1996a. 'Dooyeweerd's Idea of "Historical Development": Christian Respect for Cultural Diversity', *Westminster Theological Journal* 58: 41–61.

—, 1996b. *Philosophical Aesthetics at Home with the Lord. An Untimely Valedictory*. Toronto: Institute for Christian Studies.

Spykman, G., 1992. *Reformational Dogmatics: A New Paradigm for Doing Dogmatics*. Grand Rapids: Eerdmans.

van Dyke, H. and A.M. Wolters, 1979. 'Interview with Dr H. Evan Runner', in Kraay and Tol, 1979: 333–61.

Strauss, G., 1996. 'Footprints in the Dust. Can Neocalvinist Theory Be Credible in Postcolonial Africa?', *Acta Academica* 28 (2): 1–35.

Walker, A., 1996. *Telling the Story. Gospel, Mission and Culture*. London: SPCK.

Wolters, A., 1985. 'The Intellectual Milieu of Herman Dooyeweerd', in McIntire, 1985: 4–10.

—, 1994. 'Creation Order: an Historical Look at Our Heritage', in Schrotenboer *et al.*, 1994: 42–61.

Zuidervaart, L. and H. Luttikhuizen (eds.), 1995. *Pledges of Jubilee: Essays on the Arts and Culture in Honor of Calvin G. Seerveld*. Grand Rapids: Eerdmans.

The Informal Fantastic Life of a Believing Fishmonger's Son: Autobiographical Vignettes*

The fact that this evening we could, as the church keeps time, celebrate the ascension of Jesus Christ to the glorious power of ruling world history from the right hand of God prompts me to state clearly that I do not consider this happy occasion as a step in the assumption of Ehlers and Seerveld, a kind of Protestant beatification ceremony. This good gift from those of you at Calvin College who prepared this evening to include Inès and me has given me the holiday opportunity to remember paths diverging in the woods, and how incredibly blessed I have often been in taking roads less travelled by.

I realise autobiographical comment is the most slyly fictional of literary forms, heroicising the teller; but fictional narration can also tell truth. Following Walter Benjamin's lead on redemptive history-keeping (*These über Geschichte*, III-VI,XV,A,B), I should like to recall and relate to you, for what it's worth, certain little events which I now see were deeply significant at the time, or have become emblematic of my Chaucerian pilgrimage in God's world. I learned from Augustine's Confessions (VIII,5,7–10) long ago that our most important decisions are often almost involuntary because we are led to take certain openings by following a heart-deep vision in the mysterious recesses of human willing hid under the layers of one's limiting, congealed societal matrix.

But one's hindsight history is full of surprises. You could call the vignettes I tell tonight, 'The informal fantastic life of a believing fishmonger's son who went to Calvin College'.

A home of Christian piety, with secular schooling: West Sayville, Long Island, New York (1930–48)

On Saturdays, school vacations and summers, from age ten to twenty-two I sold fish next to my father, Lester Benjamin Seerveld, and his three hired men

*Full text of an address spoken in part at Calvin College on 16 May 1996 in thanks for being designated Distinguished Alumnus by the Alumni Board of Calvin College, Grand Rapids, Michigan. Michigan Congressman, Vernon Ehlers, mentioned in the opening sentence, was similarly honoured at the same ceremony.

Plate 2 Lester Seerveld (left) with employees in the Great South Bay fish and fruit market, Patchogue, Long Island, New York, during the early 1930s

in the Great South Bay Fish Market, Patchogue, Long Island, New York. During the war years 1941–5 it was a busy fish store. There was meat rationing, and able-bodied young men were scarce and drafted; so I experienced as a young teenager the confirmation of coming through in doing full-fledged adult work that was sorely needed, performing beyond my years. That's an important reason, I think, why – to the incredulity of my student colleagues at Calvin later on – I never seemed to need to rebel against my parents. Also, the dozen years of training in dealing courteously with our predominantly Greek, Roman Catholic Italian, and Jewish customers who wanted 'Is it fresh? fish,' honed me with a people-knowledge that has been invaluable in academia.

My P.K.* mother, Letitia Elizabeth Van Tielen, played the violin, and stood over my practising piano lessons from age six onward. My first public debut was in third grade with a three-minute memorised piece by C.P.E. Bach. So by the time I graduated from secular high school I had written the school song for the primary grades K–8, played piano well enough to make Musicians' Guild as freshman at Calvin, had blown tuba for four years, was taking a turn as church organist at West Sayville Christian Reformed Church with a

---

*Preacher's Kid.

Plate 3 The Great South Bay fish store in the 1950s, Patchogue, Long Island, New York

repertoire, I blush to say, which probably caused the gnashing of teeth of the one good church organist we had in the village who stuffily played Bach which nobody liked. I won fifth prize nationally in a pop-song contest sponsored by the *Senior Scholastic* magazine, and played string bass well enough to continue it for four years in the Calvin orchestra directed then by string bass specialist Dr Henry Bruinsma.

In those days, of course, we didn't dance, drink, play cards, or go to the movies. But somehow my Bible-believing parents were wise enough not to make such activities prohibited 'worldly amusements'. We just didn't do such things, and kept busy as kids swimming like ducks for whole days in the Bay or Atlantic ocean, playing pick-up baseball in the pastures with cow-flops as bases, organising crazy, imaginative treasure hunts. You were a marked person at the secular school if you didn't dance or go to the movies, but so long as you played varsity basketball and track you were accepted. That is, I had a good, rich homespun childhood – TV did not yet exist! I experienced unobtrusively, I know now, the shalom of genuine biblical piety my parents lived, without talking about it. It is not mythical. Biblical piety can be a wholesome reality that breathes fresh gentleness, patient wisdom and healing. It's a seasoned quality of life I still meet in the five Christians without guile I know today.

A Christian college education: Calvin College in Grand Rapids, then University of Michigan (1948–53)

My friend Dewey Hoitenga and I lodged the first two years at Calvin off-campus with a room in the home of my great uncle Johannes Broene, appropriately professor of abnormal psychology at Calvin. Our collegiate pranks were country-boyish, we were not mechanised: like running from 35 Calkins S.E. to the Franklin campus through a snowstorm in our bathing suits for Messiah choir practice, or one spring afternoon crawling the mile distance home on our knees, just to see whether we could do it.

I majored in certain profs at Calvin: Henry Zylstra and John Timmerman, whose Chaucer course impacted fishmonger me profoundly; William Harry Jellema, Henry Stob, and the gruff, warm-hearted Cecil de Boer. I also took a steady diet of languages: second-year French with Albert Broene, a couple of accelerated years of German with Boersma, so I got to read Schiller's long *Wallenstein* and *Maria Stuart*, three years of Greek with Radius, serving as his assistant correcting Latin exams. I couldn't see taking three-and-a-half years of Dutch to qualify for Calvin Seminary at the time with Van Andel, seven courses of Dutch instead of Shakespeare, Aristotle, John Donne, Gilson and T.S. Eliot?! So I became a double philosophy–English lit. major, and just played on the Pre-Sem. intramural basketball team on the strength of my Greek courses. Henry Zylstra had counselled me, 'Stay with foreign languages long enough to get into the literature.' That was sound advice.

My four years at Calvin were priceless, deeply formative intellectually. My high-school teachers had thought I'd continue in math and physics and become an executive with IBM, but at Calvin I discovered the world of philosophical ideas, the scintillating treasures of English literature and poetry under several masterful teachers, and the excitement of entering other cultures carried by fascinating, strange languages. I was well on the way to becoming a Christian Humanist, in the sense of wanting to probe 'the best that has been said and thought in the world', pulled loosely into an Anglo-Catholic Christian net, where Dante and Aquinas' christianising amalgamation of Plato and Aristotle seemed the genial way to go to avoid the 'safe' mind of hole-in-the-corner parochiality and to avoid slipping into acceptance of truncated secular horizons. My ideal was to go study seventeenth-century literature with Douglas Nash Bush at Harvard.

But then in my senior year at Calvin two significant things happened. Other normal things took place too: a student chapel I had prepared to give on Ephesians 5:13–20 was disallowed by Henry Van Til, chair of the worship committee; an editorial I wrote for the *Chimes* was censored out, and editor Wolterstorff ran a full blank white column where it would have appeared; President Spoelhof called in Nick and me for a chat over a demolitional book-review I had done on a recent prize Zondervan novel – Zondervan had just donated a goodly sum of money to Calvin for prizes in oratory – where the *Chimes* editorial staff had picked up a phrase of the review as headline, 'Not Worth Buying!' That's just local colour on a day in the life of Christian college students in the early fifties.

But what of significance happened to me is this. Firstly, instead of taking the usual overload of seven courses plus audits in my last semester at Calvin, I took only four courses, and read Keats for Dr Zylstra, not for credit but just for the fun of it, to go thoroughly into something for once. I read Keats' whole oeuvre of poetry, all Keats' letters, biographies of Keats, the secondary critical literary analysis extant on Keats – I became Keatsian; and it has left me an incorrigible Romantic to this day. If you had an ironic bent, you could say Keats helped save me from becoming a Thomist at Calvin.

Secondly, H. Evan Runner began teaching philosophy at Calvin in my senior year. I took his Modern Philosophy course among others. We began with the Greek Pre-Socratics, and a week before the end of the semester Runner said, 'Read Kant's first Critique of Pure Reason for next week.' The course was a pedagogical disaster in a way, but it spiritually changed my life. Not just because of the eccentric charisma, where the professor often got as good as he gave: once while Runner was reciting the roll-call of Renaissance philosophers – Pico della Mirandola, Pomponazzi, Bruno Campanella – a slower but colourful student in our class raised his hand, 'Campanella – is he related to the guy that plays for the Dodgers?' leaving Runner absolutely non-plussed, speechless.

What changed my life, I later came to know, was Vollenhoven's take on the history of Western philosophy Runner taught us, where a radically biblical appreciation for the historic Reformation led by Luther and Calvin called into question the synthesis of Greek and Christian thought we all normally practice, and posited as our scholarly calling to forge an explicitly scripturally directed philosophical categorial framework to couch the leading questions we theorists ask about structure, direction, knowledge, and to set up the conceptual priorities we pursue for understanding literature, politics, labour relations, emotional life, environmental tragedies.

As Calvin's graduating senior with the University of Michigan scholarship I went to Ann Arbor for my Masters in English literature. Because my Calvin English major was so strong I was allowed to take more classics, Thucydides and Aristotle in Greek, medieval Latin authors, and medieval history as well as Renaissance literature and eighteenth-century English with old authority Louis Bredvold. Coming back to Calvin's campus after that year, with a Fulbright scholarship in my pocket to go check out the following year this Reformational Christian philosophy in Amsterdam's Free University, I happened to meet Runner, thanked him for the help his insights had been for me at the secular university, yet there was one thing that bothered me: 'This Vollenhoven/ Dooyeweerd philosophy is so positive!' 'Exactly!' said Runner. 'You need to be biblically thetical before you turn critical.' That Vollenhoven wisdom has saved me over the years much grief.

One other deep debt to Calvin I remember which could be mentioned is very personal; so I'll trust you to hear it right. During my totally absorbing, highly competitive intellectual year at the University of Michigan I finally faced the life crisis of feeling the need to break my engagement to be married imminently. The person who really helped me sort out the tangle of keeping and breaking promises was Cecil de Boer (whose own tragic love story I had heard about as a student), who took me for a ride in his big car to an empty park. We sat at a bare picnic table, and I told him my story. As was his wont de Boer was brutally frank. 'If you haven't slept with her, if you don't love her, you don't need to marry her. But don't look at another woman for a year.'

That was confession and absolution in John Ball Park on a chilly spring afternoon between a philosophy prof chomping on his cigar and an uncertain student with his life in the balance, which exemplifies, in my judgement, a dimension of the Christian college education you can't touch with even the best John Hopkins educational philosophy of a prof and a student seated on the ends of the same log discussing Plato's dialogues.

Footloose country boy in Europe with the Dutch Kuyperian philosophical tradition at the Free University of Amsterdam: Amsterdam, Florence, Basel, Rome, The Hague (1953–8)

So I went to Europe as a footloose country boy on a generous US Fulbright scholarship when each almighty American dollar was worth four guilders, and stayed for five formative years, which became a blur of absorbing wonder and have remained a treasury of imaginative educational experiences to this day. I was far from the madding crowd of polished seminars in precise logical argument. I lived in an unheated garret (to be true to Keats), walked past the house where Spinoza had lived, went to the opera to pick up additional Dutch, could bike to the Rijksmuseum to muse before a dozen original Rembrandt paintings; and slowly I entered the Dutch university system where Vollenhoven picked up in his first lecture where he had stopped the year before. When a student dared remonstrate, 'But Professor, I was not here last year,' Vollenhoven patiently replied, 'Please consult with someone who was.'

You were on your own as student, and competed only with yourself in one-on-one oral exams. I caught Vollenhoven's eye by working through Diels–Kranz volumes in Greek on *Die Fragmente der Vorsokratiker*, and proved to Vollenhoven on his own criteria that Theagenes of Rhegium had a dualist philosophy rather than the monist one Vollenhoven had ascribed to his thought: on such painstaking details a prospective researcher can cut one's teeth.

It took two heady years to finish the requisite exams and pass the doctoral comprehensives in the systematics and history of philosophy with a minor concentration in Dutch language and literature. Then I hitchhiked over the alps to Firenze in Italy to learn Italian, armed only, I thought, with a carton of Camels which as non-smoker I doled out to those who gave me rides, since American cigarettes were worth more than gold in postwar Europe. But God also had a protective shield of angels around me I found out, after taking a couple of bad rides. Dropped off in the middle of nowhere one night I found a local cemetery for sleeping under the stars, thinking correctly it would be safe there. Waked by a tolling church bell the next morning, as I walked into the nearest village I was met by someone who said, '*Bon giorno.*' So I walked through that strange village and said the password to everybody I met, '*Bon giorno,*' and was answered with smiles and new phrases. What a way to learn another language! and to satisfy a young educated Romantic's wanderlust.

Next came a *Wanderjahr* in Basel, Switzerland, where I went to hear Karl Jaspers elucidate Kierkegaard, to follow Karl Barth's seminars – his lectures that year happened to be on 'angels' – to do New Testament studies in Paul's letters with Oscar Cullmann, and to learn Old Testament Hebrew taught in the German language. Second semester I read Genesis with Walter Baumgartner, about the last of the early Wellhausen Higher Critics still alive, who JEDPed* the book to bits in front of your eyes, but left you brilliantly phrase-style-conscious forever after. I consider it a special advantage to have learned Hebrew in German, because it gives you the extra time (the dictionary is Hebrew–German) to put a nuanceful spin on the gritty, concrete biblical language of the psalms and the prophets you want your children to hear in colloquial English.

Just one educational anecdote: Karl Barth was considered liberal by the Christian Reformed communion at the time; in Basel I discovered Barth was considered very conservative. I spent three months inching through *Kirchliche Dogmatik* 2:1 on 'The Word of God is/is in the Bible', lined up my questions – I wanted to get this straight from the horse's mouth – and scheduled my personal half hour with Barth in his study. I presented my carefully phrased questions, offered my cogent critical objections, and Barth gave me his genial answers, all in a little over five minutes. We talked out the half hour, but I was finished. I still thought Barth was wrong on this crucial point, but I had nothing more to say. He was a genius, and I wasn't. That was an incredibly

---

*Reference to the Higher Critics' division of the Pentateuch into four sources: J (Yahwist), E (Elohim), P (Priestly code), D(Deuteronomist).

important experience for me, to be confounded but not have my bearings shaken. As a matter of fact Karl Barth made Jesus Christ as the historical Son of God on whom everything turns more historically real to me that year than anyone ever had; and it took me ten years to work less desirable facets of Barth's theology out of my system.

At this point I became the husband of the woman with whom I fell in love (after the requisite year of not looking). Inès Cecile Naudin ten Cate was multilingual, a geography–history buff, frequenter of art musea, and in training at the Christlijke School voor Maatschappelijke Werk in Amsterdam, specialising in dealing with delinquent children. We met by God's providence in a snowdrift during the first vacation I ever had, on a student ski trip I took with Harry Boer to Saalbach, Austria; and we courted weekends later on when she worked in a *pouponière* (orphanage) in Mulhouse, a French city across the border from Basel.

Without Inès' Griselda-like support for my workaholic life, needing rifts of monastic solitude in the (basement) study, the many-splendoured years of extraordinary fullness I have enjoyed would not have been possible. Our first year of marriage, for example, was ten months of honeymoon based in one private room plus use of kitchen inside a small, high-rise apartment inhabited by an extended, fairly dysfunctional Italian family in Rome: Inès learned the language and explored the city and its ancient culture with the Dante Alighieri Society, while I read 50 volumes of the late (1866–1952) Benedetto Croce's writings under the tutelage of Carlo Antoni, Croce's protégé, first non-Roman Catholic professor at the Università di Roma. On Saturday and Sunday Inès would show me the highlights of her discoveries in Rome that week. Her *grote vergissing** of marrying me has been an untold blessing.

Taking a Reformational Christian direction in college teaching: Jackson, Mississippi, and Trinity Christian College in Chicago (1959–72)

Prospecting for the job I needed in the US from Europe was not easy in 1958. Calvin College was not interested in me for philosophy. The University of Michigan offered me, without interview, a trial one-year position in aesthetics and history of philosophy (I knew DeWitt Parker's chair was vacant). Then Bob Vander Vennen wrote me visionary letters about coming to teach philosophy and English literature at a small Belhaven College in Jackson, Mississippi, which at the time was determined to become 'the Calvin of the South'. Comparing a good, pastoral letter from William Frankena on my options next

---

*Great mistake.

to Vander Vennen's compelling letters set the stage for my deciding, in some deep way, to go South, and into the Christian educational circuit. In that turbulent first year of teaching (ten new courses!) a number of faculty called certain irregularities of leadership to the attention of Belhaven's trustees. The trustees felt it uncomfortable but necessary to back the president who then decided this college was no longer going to become 'the Calvin of the South'.

When asked whether I wanted to stay at Belhaven the next year, I said, 'No' (this was in May 1959), and we decided to try to follow the Vander Vennens to Trinity Christian College which might open in September. Al Plantinga had been offered the position in philosophy at Trinity, but turned it down. Then Tunis Prins had accepted the position in philosophy at Trinity. I flew up to interview for teaching German – I needed a job – the only position still open. As I got off the plane in Chicago I was told Prof. Prins had had a non-fatal heart attack and had withdrawn his acceptance; would I be willing to be interviewed for philosophy?

So as third-choice candidate of Trinity God gave me a surprising opportunity to refine and develop my mixed inheritance from Calvin and the Free University of Amsterdam into a programme that was radically biblically Christian (naive as a dove) yet ground professionally fine on the inheritance of Western civilisation (wary as a snake in the grass).

Trinity from the start was Calvin-friendly. William Harry Jellema had inspired the Trinity core curriculum of Bible (6 hours), English (6 hours), philosophy (9 hours!) and history (9 hours), to be required of all students in the first two years. Two hours of Graeco–Roman philosophy dovetailed with three hours of Graeco–Roman history, and the same for the 'Medieval', and the 'Modern' periods, was the required (5 hours) three-semester sequence of 'Ancient', 'Medieval' and 'Modern' Mind courses (6 hours philosophy/9 hours history). There was also an initial three-hour philosophy course required for first-semester freshmen and women whose content was not specified by Jellema.

I vividly remember an early visit to Trinity, before we opened, by Dean Ryskamp and President Spoelhof who suggested that that first philosophy course ought to be a basic course in logic (following the Aristotelian paradigm), to teach young students how to think straight. 'But,' we firmly demurred, 'we wanted the beginning students to learn to think *christianly*.' So the introductory Philosophy 101 became a course in systematic Christian philosophy with Reformational grit which thetically (1) put a critical spin on the ensuing semester studies of Plato, Aquinas, Hume and Kant, and (2) provided an encyclopaedic interconnection of philosophy with all the other areas of specialised study – literature, biology, mathematics, psychology, political science, economics, theology.

Because this Kuyperian/Vollenhovian/Dooyeweerdian vision proleptically proceeded unpolemically for a goodly number of years, the sixties and seventies at Trinity Christian College were very special 'banquet years'. A gifted young faculty had no face to lose in admitting they still needed to flesh out what the biblical perspective meant specifically for conceiving music theory, the history of physical science, urban sociology, reading literature, and we were proactively helping one another in finding the Way philosophically integral to one's professional discipline.

At a certain point Trinity authorities wondered whether this robust, often unsettling challenge to the standard American way of thinking and doing things was really wanted, an academic approach which seemed to go paired with Social Action Seminars we held: we had African-American evangelist Tom Skinner talking tough to a packed-out Palos Heights church filled with displaced Roseland CRC white believers, and Christian Labour Association of Canada representative Gerald Vandezande locked in sharp debate with an AFL–CIO bigwig from Chicago on the violence to human work-rights exerted by the secular 'closed-shop' labour policy. When that philosophical tilt was mistrusted, some of us Trinity profs went to Toronto, and others found good places of blessing at Dordt and Calvin College. Inès and I gratefully salute those former colleagues present tonight – Trinity's backhanded gift to Calvin – and are simply glad at God's mysterious ways.

A call to teach graduates philosophical aesthetics at the Institute for Christian Studies: Toronto, Canada (1972–95)

Canada was fresh terrain, where I heard in the sixties first-generation Dutch immigrants singing Genevan psalms in unison with a good pipe organist syncopating the beat in tempo, so that you knew without a doubt the CLAC members being threatened on the assembly line and construction site and taken to court by the secular trade unions had the stock of persecuted Huguenots in their blood. The Institute for Christian Studies in Toronto was a community of scholars geared to Christian graduate studies, begun by a survivor of Dachau, a book-seller, a maverick preacher or two, and a couple of level-headed Dutchmen who remembered what Kuyper's vision had initiated in the Netherlands, mentored by the peripatetic, embattled Runner: I was gradually invited into this dove-and-snake organisation (cf. Matthew 10: 16), and finally in 1972 offered a position to specialise in researching and teaching philosophical aesthetics. How is that possible in our secularised North American world! – they will pay me for this too (maybe)?

So as family we moved to the superb cosmopolitan metropolis of Toronto, Canada, where you had the cultural distance to see more sharply the dark sides of American corporate business monopolies, and where our gradeschool children, Anya, Gioia and Luke, had to learn to ice-skate fast if they wanted to exist in school. Let me try to catch in one anecdote, an illustrated remark, and a potpourri of highlights, the kaleidoscope of blessings Inès and I have experienced in close to 25 years of ICS life in Toronto.

More than 15 curious people appeared for my first graduate seminar in History of Aesthetics. Assignment for the first session was Boileau's *L'art poétique* (1674), French text (this was bilingual Canada), because I wanted to sketch in slowly the historical background in art, literature and theory which set up Kant's third Critique, which I thought was pivotal for shaping the theoretical problematics of modern aesthetical reflection. The first session did not go swimmingly, as I recall; and in the following weeks student faces glazed over and gradually wholly disappeared. They had come to get 'the Christian answers' to their artistic problems, but I was concerned to wrestle in detail for a year and a half through Kant's *Kritik der Urteilskraft* (1790) contexted by European rococo art and the Winckelmann–Mengs 'neoclassical' culture that was hospitable to Schiller, Hegel and so on until Nietzsche, Heidegger, Gadamer, and Adorno came along.

Only three or four Junior members remained in philosophical aesthetics by the end of that first year. I survived the crisis of teaching self-confidence, shifting from American undergraduate to European-style graduate teaching, I think, largely because of the calibre of persons like Lambert Zuidervaart and Barbara Carvill who were there at the beginning: they wanted a mentor, not a guru, and trusted me enough to work like angels to help me realise that graduate students often know more than the prof about certain things, so you can become an exhilarating team, pursuing communally the right systematic questions and complicated historical answers that may bear conceptual shalom. I have been blessed with many gifted, younger generation investigators who like children that adopted me have enriched my life copiously.

The Institute for Christian Studies was not an 'ideal' organisation; ICS Senior members and staff did not live by Ideals. I came to know it as a genuine concrete community of sinful saints trying to put creatural ordinances into practice under the searchlight of Holy Scripture in obedience to the Rule of Jesus Christ on earth in history. It was not an Ideal but accepted policy, for example, that every prof received the same wage, newcomer as well as old-timer, to get rid of at least one source of competitive envy, when you joined this monastic order. Each person would give you all the shirts off his back if you needed them, and walk with you ten miles of sorrow, not just two. They also might try to knock your block off; but in the fierce old days we usually retreated to end with sessions of earnest prayer, tears and hugs that would have made even Promise Keepers jealous.

Because the Institute was becoming a formal academic institution out of a former kind of L'Abri centre for brilliant misfits fleeing the secular university system and anti-intellectual evangelical church backgrounds, philosophical

Plate 4 Colleagues from the Institute for Christian Studies on retreat at Georgian Bay, 1973: Bernard Zylstra, Henk Hart, Arnold de Graaff, Calvin Seerveld, James Olthuis, C.T. McIntire

seminars had all the priority. But the Senior members still criss-crossed continents, giving topical lectures at meetings and conferences on most things under the sun. When *The Banner* editor De Koster, who seemed to hate us in those years, once wondered out loud to me how like the devil could we be out reforming in so many places out of all proportion to our miniscule size, I didn't dare reveal the secret that just maybe, thanks to the praying *kleine luyden**in Canada, Christ might be multiplying our pitiful five loaves and two fishes to the thousands who were at a loss and hungry for bites of whole-grain bread and fresh fish instead of warmed-over crushed stone and fricasseed scorpions. (There is probably still a little unredeemed edge to this last remark.)

A few highlights: the Christian Labour Association of Canada, the Psalter Hymnal revision committee of the Christian Reformed Church in North America, Sabbaticals with the family

If I were to list a few highlights for me during my task at the Institute for Christian Studies, Toronto, it would include the following. (1) I made two

---

*The little, unimportant folk.

addresses to the Christian Reformed Church ministers' institute held before synod in 1970. The organisers would not officially sponsor my illustrated lecture entitled 'The Meaning of our Nakedness', but allowed me to do it on my own personal responsibility: it touched a responsive chord in those present – no trouble at all. The organisers had no problem with my prospective title for the other lecture, 'A Modest Proposal for Reforming the Christian Reformed Church', because they had not caught the allusion to Jonathan Swift's literary essay by that name, and were therefore taken aback by my first sentence recommending we close Calvin Seminary.

(2) Etched in my memory is the dark night in Smithers, northern British Columbia, where I was trucked in to speak for less than ten lumberjacks and mill-workers in a CLAC local. They may not have understood a whole lot of what I said – I forget the topic – but they knew this young professor was fighting on their side against the ruthless secular antagonists; so they were shod again for the battle to claim justice. Their rugged profiles and gnarled hands reminded me of every good thing I had learned intuitively from my Dad in the fish market, and you knew, in spite of our sin, God's pillar of fire was present and visible that evening, as if Smithers – which is a long way from anywhere else – was the centre of God's universe. You could sense the burned retreat of evil principalities and powers in the stubborn hope ignited in their believing eyes. Such contact gives an academic person life!

(3) When I arranged for the important atheist aesthetician from France, Mikel Dufrenne, to lecture at ICS for a few days – it interested quite a number of University of Toronto profs and students across the street too – I set up lodging for Dufrenne at Roman Catholic St Mike's guest room. No one had warned me about the expensive complications which arose when Dufrenne arrived, because of the mistress he always took along with him on his speaking engagements.

(4) Bert Polman and I became good friends during the many years we somehow spliced in extra sub-committee meetings together and wrangled time to fly down to Grand Rapids for Thursday-night-to-Saturday-night, non-stop work sessions in the Psalter Hymnal revision committee. A couple of times we were put up in the Harley House. After a particular twelve-hour day of sifting texts and melodies and hard decisions, trying to relax naked in the Harley sauna, another portly naked fellow asked us to explain what we were doing. It's about encouraging our communion to temper its sweet diet of 1800s songs; it's like helping our Reformed parishioners to become more Catholic in their hymn repertoire and harmonies – Taizé, Southern Harmony, British Psalm Praise; or it may even be making the Genevan psalms relevant to the rock-and-roll generation. I remember his uncomprehending, bemused smile as he left to take a cold shower. But that twelve-member Psalter Hymnal committee is the place where for almost ten years I most deeply experienced

and was buoyed by the living troubled–comforting reality which is communion of the saints.

(5) Sabbaticals were genuine respites from routine, and wonderful refreshment for my projects in aesthetics, but it was not easy on the children, even though family time in strange lands became subliminally very dear. We were not tourists, we always lived somewhere – Heidelberg (German schools), Montmartre, Paris (one bedroom for five people), London, England (frequent theatre and too many art musea), München (a small Olympic village apartment not that far from Dachau). You wonder about such disruptive yet unforgettable times with your children, because you have inoculated them against settling down to a North American standardised conformity, and that could mean irritating cultural displacement.

(6) It was great fun to be on the organising committee for the World Congress of Aesthetics held at Montreal in 1984, vetting papers from Russia, China, Europe, the Americas. A couple of us inaugurated at that time the Canadian Society for Aesthetics/Société canadienne d'esthétique. The infighting among the directors jousting for power between francophiles from Quebec and Anglophones from Ontario and the Canadian West was very stressful. I was considered to be Dutch (who spoke German and Italian) and therefore neutral; they trusted me to count the secret ballots. Maybe that's partly why I came to serve as first co-president. The most valuable fruit of that connection is the friends I gained who cannot (yet) believe the biblical message, but for whom I mean something more than a *scandalon*. Every follower of Christ deserves a couple of unbelieving friends.

Looking back at joining the Institute for Christian Studies I think I received Rachel immediately in Toronto, as it were, for the first 14 years or so of honeymoon service there, and then apparitions of Leah appeared on the scene, so to speak. I can freely testify, however, as Joseph once did (Genesis 50:20), that no matter my own sin or any evil directed my way, God has marvellously always turned it to good so that today the LORD has preserved in a new generation a generous number of dedicated, serious co-workers making their own *Pledges of Jubilee*[1] in philosophical aesthetics, methodology of art history, hermeneutic theory, and popular cultural philosophy.

The mysterious fact that Calvin College has granted me from the Institute for Christian Studies, Toronto, this unexpected honour as Distinguished Alumnus could have the angels smiling along in heaven tonight and on Saturday with various ones here, because the LORD's army of angels like it when God's mixed-up people come through tough times and temptations to go it alone, and then are surprised, as sinful saints, by the joy to be

---

[1] Lambert Zuidervaart and Henry Luttikhuizen (eds.), *Pledges of Jubilee: Essays on the Arts and Culture in Honor of Calvin G. Seerveld* (Grand Rapids: William B. Eerdmans, 1995).

found in celebrating one another's gifts in play for the Lord this side of the grave.

May God bless you, Calvin College, with the communal vision and stamina to be scrupulously, joyfully faithful in your thetical and critical educative task, resolute, open-handed, historically sensitive, and restoratively busy in our Lord's amazing, prodigal world.

Part 1

Hearing the Bible

1 Reading the Bible at Home as a Family*

In our Reformed tradition we read the Bible at meal-times. This is more important than most of us normally realise for our parental obedience to the Lord.

There are all kinds of external pressures today, in our hurried, secular world, that work against our keeping this good habit going. But there is also an internal bug that can ruin Bible reading at meal times: not having a Reformed idea of what the Bible really is, and not knowing so well how we are to read it so it doesn't become a formality. I'd like to explore this problem we all face every day.

Reformation focus

We grown-ups need to become like children again and remember that the Bible is God telling us a story. The Bible is the true story of the Great Deeds of God, as Herman Bavinck put it (in his *Magnalia Dei*), telling us what the Lord wants generations of men, women and children to do in response. S.G. de Graaf highlights the same point: the Bible is the story of Jehovah as the Covenant One revealed in Jesus Christ who calls us to be God's special people and to act like God's adopted kids.[1]

The Bible is about God's provident rule over the world and especially about God's leading God's people on to deliverance from sin and misery to a rich life of praise. The Bible is not about men and women, with God also in the picture.

The Bible is not about Joseph and his brothers, telling us we should act like Joseph did, and then God will reward us. The Bible is not about Saul and David's fighting one another, meaning that you and I must respect the government even when they visit witches. The Bible is not about the little Jewish girl in the house of Naaman or about Zacchaeus up a tree. But the Bible is

---

*First published in *Calvanist Contact* 34:1636 (17 March 1967), 8–9.

[1] *Verbondsgeschiedenis* (1936); first part translated by Elizabeth and Evan Runner as *Promise and Deliverance* (St Catharines, Ontario: Paideia Press, 1977).

telling us how God provided for God's people through Joseph's faithfulness, how God cursed God's people through the vanity and sin of Saul and David. The Bible is telling us about what God did for heathen Syrians through Naaman's servants and Elisha, and is pointing up to Christ's compassion for an apostate son of Abraham, Zacchaeus. This difference in focus is the difference between an understanding of the Bible by a church of the Reformation and an unreformed conception of the Bible.

We parents are called upon to give our children a sense of the fact that God, the Covenanting God, is talking to us in the Bible. God said, 'Let there be sunlight and moonlight and twinkling stars; let there be worms and bugs and creepy-crawly things. And I will take care of you better than I take care of the butterflies and flowers; so obey me, my child. ...' 'Wow! Is that what God is like!' exclaims the child. That would be a Reformed way of reading the Scriptures. But one should not read the Bible with the focus: 'Dare to be a Daniel, dare to stand alone, etc.' or 'Don't ever deny Jesus, as Peter did, three times in a row.' That is not a Reformed way of reading the Bible to your children.

If we treat the Bible like 'lessons on how to act' – even if we come up with good lessons – it never has the punch of hearing God speak to us in God's book, telling how God moved and moves among real people like us. And then one has lost the Reformed focus that rivets one's ears and eyes upon God's covenant-keeping, gracious judgements and deeds, with their focus in Jesus Christ.

One continuous, true story

We grown-ups also have to let it sink in that we need to learn to read the true story of the Bible to our children as a story, as a narrative, as a single book that starts with Genesis 1 and goes on to the last chapter of Revelation. The Bible is a whole. If you pick up a novel and read pages at random you cannot expect to get the point of the book. So, too, you cannot read the Bible properly without the whole story in the back of your mind when you read certain chapters.

Early Christian pioneers in Canada, especially on the plains (where there are so many Bible colleges), learned to read the Bible as a story-book. During the long, lonely nights they would read it for hours, leafing through it to look at pictures but also listening to the story of God's Way with his Old Testament people, of Jesus' ministry on earth, and the results of Pentecost in Asia Minor and on into Western Europe.

Early Canadian Christians did not read the Bible to find proof-texts for arguing whether supra- or infra-lapsarian doctrine was more orthodox. They did not read the Bible like a manual of texts to do personal evangelism. (I'm for documenting doctrines as well as catechism with scriptural study references, and I believe a mature Christian will know his or her Bible well enough to have passages on the tip of his or her tongue when conversing with unbelievers. But one should not use it like a machine-gun, the way many sects do.) Early Canadian Christians read the Bible like a continuing story, and all the pieces were fitted into the one narrative fabric.

I believe that the Bible is Holy Spirit-edited for us with the continuing story character as most fundamental. And we should begin to open up the Bible to our children that way. My parents read to me from the Bible story-book before I went to bed, and they read the Bible to us later at the table too, as one long, true story. That means that if we, as parents, want to lead our children into the Bible story – and don't have hours on end to keep reading it through to them – we need to know the key passages that hold all the details together.

For example, it helps to know that the point of Genesis 37–50 is made in 50: 20. You can read the 40 chapters of Exodus and the 27 of Leviticus as a story only if you know that Exodus 19–20 is the crux, and that Romans 3: 1–2 gives you the proper glasses to see that all these regulations are not like traffic laws and parking-tickets but are meant as God's hedges to keep God's children on the right path so they don't get hurt. When we read Numbers and Deuteronomy as a story it helps to know that those books are summed up in Deuteronomy 33: 26–9. Also, one simply must realise that the rest of the Bible leans on these first five books. If one does not know or love this section of the Bible story – how God selects a people to live out God's Will – it will be hard to understand the rest of the Bible fully and well, like pretending to grasp a novel if you leave off the first twenty chapters.

So far I've listed two points about reading the Bible. We must read the Bible (1) so that those listening say, 'That's our heavenly (Covenanting) Father talking !' and (2) so that listeners experience passages as sections of a literary whole, simply because God's Word is a unified book.

A home is not a school and it is not a church and it is not you, all by yourself. A home is a home. In a family-home setting the Bible should be read differently than in a schoolroom Bible-study, and differently than in the official church service. The Bible is always the Covenant God telling a true story – at home, in the school, in the pulpit, in your own room. But in each of these different settings the cast of its reading should be different.

Bible reading for children and to children at *home* should be predominantly an imaginative reading by parents as (true) story-tellers. It must seem to be natural and unstudied, as if you are recounting what once happened. Bible reading at *school* (depending upon the age-level) is rightly a studied reading, where the teacher deepens the students' reading with literary analysis and historical ordering (like synchronising the kings and prophets and outlining

Paul's missionary trips) and study of doctrines, because school is all about studying things.

Bible reading at *church* is the most important activity in the service. Scripture should be specially spoken and heard there to be convicting of sin and assuring of forgiveness. And each of us adults and our children need to be encouraged to face Scripture with God *all alone* and to learn there to wrestle with God's written Word so that we gain a thorough, heart-seared mastery of its true story passages.

It is worth asking whether we have been one-dimensional in our method of reading the Bible, always 'studying' it like the street-map of a foreign city, without ever being able to walk through it like a neighbourhood we know thoroughly. And it is worth remembering that the meal table at home is not a school desk nor a pulpit: it is a family meal table surrounded by children.

Things to remember

I think we parents need to be prepared ahead of time to read the Bible to our children in a story-telling way (again, depending on their ages). I have a few suggestions:

1. Parents have to know a lot more about the Bible passage they read in a simple way to their children, so they can fill in historical details, emphasise what is important, cut off irrelevant reactions, and focus on the main thrust of the passage – in the light of the whole Bible.[2]

2. Family Bible reading should be predominantly playful, imaginative, a story-telling in everyday language that arouses wonderment and interest (giving information too, yes, but in a narrative context so the children get the sense of a continuing true story of God's activity). Bible reading at home should come through like an epic or a ballad or a historical narrative. And we parents must learn to be freshly surprised about what God says to us in the Bible, to hear it like a child with our children. God used a she-ass to correct Balaam! God wanted David's Psalm 51 in the Bible! Christ called the religious leaders tombstones! We must get the Bible to live for our children – not fictionalising or dramatising it. We must let God's amazing doings with Jonah, and with Paul on the road to Damascus, and God's dictating Leviticus 19 to Moses, come through without

---

[2]Although S.G. de Graaf is a little too Christological in places (e.g. there is no biblical evidence, I think, for making Solomon a type of Christ) *Promise and Deliverance* is good help in preparing one to read the Bible in a Reformed story-telling way to children.

tying it up into neat, dogmatic packages at the supper table. We must let the whole panorama of the story work deeply into our children's consciousness, and tell it to them in a natural, contemporary idiom.

3. Family Bible reading needs to be a very settled habit so that it fits in as a normal part of the meal rather than seeming like an extra chore. Getting the right habit expectation among children is hard, but a good meal helps the Bible reading to go better, and good conversation at a meal gives a more lively sense that the Bible reading will be interesting. A good Bible-reading can save a mediocre family get-together. That is, reading the Bible to one's children is part of a larger life setting, and one can develop the home setting as well as learn to be a true story-teller.

4. The Bible passage read will never come through to our children as the Covenant God speaking directly to us, as something important for us as a family, as something to be newly discovered, if it is not that to us parents. There are no clever tricks. If one reads the Bible woodenly or like a distant document or like so many verses that we have no idea of how they all hang together, that is the way it comes through to our children. My own parents gave me Exodus, Judges, Proverbs 22, parts of Isaiah, Romans 8 and other passages. We need to have certain favourite passages too that will light up our children with excitement because they are so terribly rich and meaningful to us. Then we will be obeying the first paragraph of Psalm 78 and will be living with Psalms 127 and 128 as parental children of God.

2 The Gospel of Creation*

Ancient Egyptians worshipped the blazing sun. The pagan Greek saw Apollo riding his chariot through the sky, until philosophers like Anaxagoras studied the meteorite that fell at Aegospotami in 468 BC and said, 'They're not heavenly bodies, they're just hot stone.' The demythologised hot solar rock took on new importance with Copernicus and Bruno who made it the centre of the universe. Even a modern person may yet get down on his or her knees to put an adapter on one's gas and oil furnace to catch the heat from this source of energy.

But it takes the Bible to tell the truth that the sun is a servant of the Lord. The glorious, formidable sun is not a matter of fact so much as a minister of God, as faithful as the angels, whose testimony is more sure than human tradition. The sun waits, along with the trees too polluted to breathe well and with animals suffering wounds, for the redemption of our bodies so that its service be fulfilled and it may rest from its labours.

Again and again the Bible stresses that the name of Yahweh is praised from where the sun rises to where the sun sets. The name of Yahweh–Covenanting Lord of faithfulness–is held up high for all nations to see, and the people native to the earth are called to chime in with pure offerings of 'Hallelu Yahweh!' 'Don't tell me,' says Paul to the Jews and Gentiles at Rome, 'that you and your neighbours never heard the Good News. Didn't you ever see the sun run along its God-appointed race track?' Each day of sun and rain, of dappled things and finch's wings and pileated woodpeckers, is brimming over with news of God's great deeds.

Scripture cuts off such sentiments as Edna St Vincent Millay's 'O world, I cannot hold thee close enough!' The praise of nature is not in the Bible to elicit introverted, pantheistic feelings about the fall colours or to encourage God's people to have tremulous, Romantic experiences of the sublime 'out in the country' (an eighteenth-century, citified term) while the urban world goes to cultural hell. And you miss the meaning of Psalm 19, or 104, or 148, if you agree that you should just look at the sun and moon, fire and hail, fruitful trees and cedars, young men and virgins, so that your *I* meets the *Thou* of these innumerable individual presences filling the world, and we bask in the encounters of mutual love and praise.[1]

---

*First published in *Christianity Today* 23:4 (17 November 1978), 18–19.
[1] See Nathan Scott's 'Prolegomenon to a Christian Poetic' in his *Modern Literature and the Religious Frontier* (New York: Harper & Brothers, 1958), pp. 50–52.

As I understand God's Word, 'the contemplative poetic look' is a gnostic version of the human vocation: the artistic stare is not enough to save anybody or anything. What counts is whether the human response to creation levels pride, builds up Christ's body, and compounds the praise and thanksgiving of God's myriad creatures. God tells us that the creaturehood of non-human creatures is good, deserves respect, is worthy of cultivation, is to be emulated and sanctified by prayerful thanksgiving on our part.

Starkly put, creation is a revelation of the true God, as Psalm 19 tells us. God speaks through the glossolalia of God's creatures day and night; God witnesses through the path of the sun, through seed-time and harvest, of God's providing care. The covenanting will of the Lord is not secretive, oracular, or far away, but as close as the solution of salt in water, the breathing of a newborn child, the way of a man with a maid, the fine line of an older generation's pedagogy next to indoctrination. Children of God are asked to trade their talents in interpreting *creation*. That's what *Christian* philosophy is all about, what *Christian* aesthetic theory wants to plumb for its service, the very rationale of *Christian* scholarship and *Christian* education.

When you want to find out how God ordered plants to grow, you don't go study the synoptic Gospels. You go examine plants with a sharp knife and a keen microscope. If you need to discover what chinks in a person's emotional makeup are apt to crack wide open in later life and how you should put an arm around such a one, you don't go read Proverbs for details on neuroses and psychoses. You study the case histories of emotionally disturbed people and examine others who display psychic health, make notes, reflect, and bite your fingernails as psychotherapist lest you mess up the life of somebody Christ died for. If you must decide, so you can give leadership on whether Chagall's stained-glass window, honouring the late Mayor Daley in the Art Institute of Chicago, is more or less significant than the striking piece by Abraham Rattner that takes a whole wall of the downtown loop synagogue, you don't read Paul's letters, the Psalms, or even Isaiah 40. Instead, you study art and the artists and slowly begin to make an aesthetic judgement that will bring relative blessing or a curse to those whom it influences.

Although God's people necessarily *go first to the Bible* for the Lord's disciplining and setting our consciences straight and for a right understanding of doctrine, we *must needs go search creation* for drafting our fallible, Christian solutions to the problems facing us in our sin-cursed world and society.

That's nothing new. But I'm saying (with the authority of God's written Word, Psalm 19) that no Christian need be uneasy about whether a study of biology, psychology, or aesthetics serves the Lord. Creation is a revelation of God's will, and if you are humbly studying plant *creation* or emotional or artistic *creatureliness* and are busy trying to discern the will of God there, what more could one ask for as a kingdom mission and full-time Christian service.

Of course, if your biological theory is Lamarckian or Teilhard de Chardinian, and your psychology is soft-Skinnerian or Jungian, and your aesthetics is Crocean or a mixture of Hume and Dewey, you should be very uneasy as a Christian. Otherwise, you perjure the plants, the emotions, and the arts.

Yet, we must not succumb to the temptation to use the Bible as an answer sheet to check out our biological taxonomy, our chart of personality types, or to determine 'What now is art and music?' That would be a cheap misuse of the Bible and express an illegitimate, immature desire for a ready-made, instant Christian culture that shoves off on God what he entrusts *us* to do. What we need is a richer grasp of *creation* in our Christian philosophy and evangelical theology, and a new, urgent sense of doing scholarship as a community of *saints*.

Don't misunderstand; I am not talking about 'a natural theology'. I think that a *biblical* understanding of the *doctrine of creation* is the backbone of a Christian cultural philosophy and a theology worth its biblical salt. The glory of the Lord God is indeed being revealed everywhere – deafeningly – so nobody has an excuse; but some people are religiously deaf. Only when the Holy Spirit unstops the ears and opens up the heart can you make saving sense out of the creaturely glossolalia.

Evangelical believers are so busy thinking, talking, and acting out salvation, with nary a second thought about creation, that before you can say 'Afghanistan' we are caught up in quasi-world-flight heresies and are 'saving' disembodied, uncreaturely people. One cause of this abnormality, I'm afraid, is that many of us walk around with a lightweight Bible and act as though all the Good News for modern humankind is in the New Testament and the Old Testament is out of date. But *creation* is Good News, and it is found in the Bible, especially in the Old Testament. A believing knowledge of creation brings hope because creation, understood biblically, reveals the perversion and broken power of sin, as well as of salvation. Inflation and unemployment in tandem is not an inevitability. Racism is not ineradicable. Camp art and mental breakdowns among the saints are not necessary. We are not locked into evil. We can turn from sin to God, who will save us and God's creation. That is enough to leave you limp.

3 Psalm 30 and Ephesians 5:15–20[*]

My Bible reading and remarks mean to interpret what has just happened and to introduce what is coming. I read the psalm from David's works numbered 30, a song which came to be used when the believing Jews held the regular reconsecration service of God's house (cf. John 10: 22 regarding 1 Maccabees 4:36–59 and 2 Maccabees 10:1–9) and would be very appropriate for commemorating Christ's ascension into heaven after his death, burial, and resurrection. But Psalm 30 is good for all seasons.

This is the Word of God:

I am celebrating You, LORD God, because You pulled me back up; You did not
   let my enemies enjoy themselves at my expense.
LORD, my God, I cried out to You, and You have made me whole again –
let me breathe again! after being so close to those who have gone down into the
   opened earth.

O you faithful folk of God – all of you – sing out and play music to the
   covenantal LORD God!
Let there be thanksgiving in remembering God's holy presence:
if sudden ill wrinkles for a little while from God's grievous anger,
our having life and being alive issues from the LORD'S gracious favour.
If some evening you have to spend a night weeping,
there shall be – count on it! – broken cries of joy when it is morning.

I said to myself, I did, when I was disarmed, at ease,
'I shall never be shaken up' –
LORD God, by Your gracious good will You had set me up sturdy, a mountain of
   solidified strength,
but when You turned your face aside, I was shaken, completely bewildered.
I called out to You, LORD God! – I begged my Lord for mercy –
'What good is my blood to you? In my going down into the bottomless pit?
Can dust praise You? Can broken clods of earth announce your steadfast
   faithfulness?
Hear me, O LORD God, be gracious to me!
O LORD God, be my helpmate …'

---

[*]Meditations at a conference on church music and liturgy, Toronto, July 1982.

Tja! You have turned my weeping about death, You have turned it around for me
(Lord) into dancing!
You have undone my sackcloth of mourning, and girded me with gladness!
so that my deepest insides may sing and play music for You, and I not be
devastatedly stilled –
O LORD God, my God, I will give You thanks forever and ever and ever!

The Old Testament psalms primed for thanksgiving worship and the New Testament prayers to our Father in heaven have cosmic range. All creatures praise our God and King. All nations with their leaders and races of people are invited to join the throng of children who give priority to praise of the LORD. And the LORD God revealed in Jesus Christ hears the wide-ranging pleas we make for the bread we need daily, the forgiveness we need hourly, and the deliverance from all kinds of evil that trouble God's people off and on, it seems, life-long.

What is so captivating about the psalms is that they let us people be genuinely human before the face of God. Our shame is out in the open. Our joy spills over bodily. There's no cover-up. No guilty consciences making pious faces at God. In the psalms you confess sin, accept forgiveness and start toward healing, and recite before the congregation what the LORD has done for you, and say, 'Let's sing "Praise God from whom All Blessings Flow!" LORD, do not stop the work you started!' (cf. Psalm 138:7,8; 1 Corinthians 15: 54–8).

And many psalms, like number 30, compress the most variable moods you can imagine – from despair to exaltation – almost into one breath. That way the psalms catch the pulse of our life and death.

You can have a wedding and go to a funeral in the same week. You can watch your grandchildren frolic on the lawn and see bombing destroy Beirut people on TV, at the same time. A stranger at your right hand can be converted into a child of God, while a friend on your left has an emotional breakdown.

That's life, says Psalm 30, life lived historically before the face of the covenanting LORD who alone makes secure, and who always comes through for those who plead and argue with God in faith, love, and hope: 'Don't let me go under, LORD, even if I deserve it! If I'm gone, my praise of you will be missing' (30:9,10; cf. Psalm 6, Isaiah 38:10–20).

That's a heartbeat of the psalms which can give our church song and liturgy grit and laughter. Because such argued testimony *de profundis* is couched in the certainty that for those who belong to the LORD, who trust God as the LORD of our lamentable mourning as well as the giver of dancing, the final Word for the faithful will be not crutches and tears, but dancing, rejoicing always, hallelujah! (cf. Psalm 150; Revelation 5; 19:1–10; 21:1–22: 5).

Let's thank the LORD now with all our heart for the Lord's steadfast love which strengthens us who may have weak knees or false mouths, to exercise ourselves for more obedient service.

★ ★ ★

I read a short paragraph from the letter of Paul written to the young churches of Asia Minor, the letter we call 'to the people at Ephesus'.

This is the Word of God:

So watch out carefully how you walk around. Don't act like stupids but live as wise people do, really regaining the sense of timing, because our days are deceptive.

What I mean is this: don't become fools, but get to understand what the will of the LORD is. Don't get soused with wine – that's a pure waste – but be filled up, so to speak, by the Spirit. That is, sound out to one another psalms and hymns, spiritual songs, singing and making music wholeheartedly to the LORD. Keep on thanking God the Father for everything all the time, in the name of our LORD Jesus Christ (Ephesians 5: 15–20).

People who interpret the famous phrase in this passage – 'redeeming the time' (King James Version) – to mean 'keep busy doing something useful', often don't seem to read the rest of the paragraph. The point of 'redeeming the time' – the NIV almost says 'capitalise on the opportunity' – is the directive from the LORD not to get lost in the cut-throat opportunism of business practices in the city, the off-colour jokes colleagues indulge, the riotous sexual parties and the bacchanalian flow of strong drink to celebrate a hard day's night (5:3–14); but the point is to find yourself in singing psalms and hymns, playing recorders and drums and horns together for the LORD. That's 'redeeming the time' according to the Bible: 'making a joyful noise to the God of our salvation' (cf. Psalm 98)!

We do well to hear this Word of the LORD if we value our life, no matter how much it turns our way of thinking upside down, because our age is indeed deceptive on what counts. The normal frenzy of secularism – its hurry, leisure ethic, confusing mammon – worms its way into our routine too. Only when God's people get back again a sense of timing, of knowing in their heart what time it is, will we be wise women, men and children who sing, instead of secular go-getters.

The New Testament here is not recommending we raise singsongs and song services to the status of a sacrament. A personable song-leader and our usual entertainment mentality can turn singspiration into as manipulative a device as the warm-up band which softens up an audience before the star performer takes the podium to do their thing. Even tremendous choral or congregational singing on Sunday can be as little evidence of Spirit-filled lives as speaking in tongues, if there is no love shown in dealing with one's brother and sister, one's unfortunate or handicapped neighbours during the week (cf. 1 Corinthians 12–14). There is no salvation in the performance of music itself, liturgical or otherwise.

But there is both sanctification and good news possible in music, and the text of Ephesians 5 hints that people made wise by the Holy Spirit will put song at the core of the new life in Christ. Because Holy Spirit-disciplined song is the most winsome way to announce the coming victory of the LORD – that's what time it is!

The Bible says the LORD God is redeeming the world God loves (cf. John 3:14–21), not we creatures. Our ministry of reconciliation is pure thanksgiving (cf. 2 Corinthians 5:17–21). So, just as the sinful saints are called to pray without ceasing while we work out with fear and trembling the salvation God effects in us (1 Thessalonians 5:12–21, Philippians 2:12–16), just so we are told to sing without stopping as we prepare the way of the LORD on earth because God has already made God's glorious coming sure (cf. Psalms 30, 33, 40, 100, 1 Thessalonians 4:1 – 5:11; 2 Thessalonians 1:3–12). It's the right time in history to sing. We are in the last days, after Christ's resurrection and before the Night come, when it is the will of the LORD that God's people not just say but *sing* their certainties (cf. Ecclesiastes 11:1 – 12:7; 1 Peter 1:13 – 2:10).

Because it's time for God's people to sing even while we bury the poor, we can be glad for sad, believing melodies from African Ghana that weep comfortingly – 'Jesu, Jesu' – with those who are weeping. Because it's time to sing bravely in the face of the enemy whose walls are falling down (cf. Joshua 6), we can be grateful for toccata improvisations on the Geneva jigs that will baffle the devil with our incredible rejoicing. Because it's time to sing in suburban churches too when God's people unload their kaleidoscope of burdens and joys of the week to be picked up in festive, encouraging communion in response to the good news of God's Word, we can be thankful for strong Welsh tunes with words from Canada today invoking the Holy Spirit to

> fill us with Your holy fullness, God the Father, Spirit, Son;
> in us, through us, then forever, shall Your perfect will be done.

The Christian life of song is complex and rich because the LORD's Rule is cosmic.

And we need to become mature believers who will patiently learn to experience the world-wide, history-deep, up-to-date communion of the singing saints. That in Christ there is neither Jew-psalm nor Greek-hymn, neither long meter-tempo nor Latin-rhythms that are tabu *if spiritual*. That in Jesus Christ there are Bible choruses and Genevan tunes, rounds and black spirituals, old Isaac Watts iambic quatrains – we must never let cheap words drive good texts out of circulation – and dissonant chords, if biblically conceived, composed, consecrated, waiting to be sung by all of us who belong together practising for the final hallelujah song of Moses and the Lamb (cf. Revelation 15:3,4).

Paul and Silas were not singing baritone solos as special music in the jail worship service. I imagine they sang from their guts – that's the vernacular for 'wholeheartedly' – through tears. Their spiritual song woke up their captors and fellow prisoners to faith in Jesus Christ (cf. Acts 16:14–40). That is the mandate we are called to make good on in church, or anywhere, for singing our psalms and hymns, spiritual songs, making music and dancing for the LORD.

As our times become more grim, let us have no fear, little flock, says Luke 12, because it pleases God to give you the kingdom, the Rule of the earth, its principalities and powers. So, filled quietly and deeply by the Holy Spirit let us make music and keep on singing all kinds of good spiritual songs to one another, thanking God the Father for everything in the name of Jesu the Christ our Lord.

4 Reform Needed in the Church on Sensing God's Holiness and our Sin*

I have understood our speaker to say something like this: the biblical revelation of sin is out of service today, and the God in whom we trust on our dollar bill has become a Great Therapist in the sky who not only blesses America but will eventually solve all our individual problems for us. To make our theology attractive to the secular mind, the church has poured so much popular cultural water into its biblical wine, many worship services don't even have the alcohol content of weak beer.

Correcting our predicament could begin by recognising sin as being foolish, out of touch with reality – humans proudly overstepping limits God has set – so that you become destructive; sin is human vandalism, and necessarily self-abuse. The only way to recover the discipline of wisdom is to begin again standing in awe of the holy LORD, pleading for grace.

Since I agree with the thrust of Professor Plantinga's remarks, I should like to contribute to the reform invoked by selecting a couple of points to explore more deeply – first, sin, and then, how to meet the holy God and express it – and, for discussion purposes, I'll suggest a few concrete steps our repentance might take.

Sin is a tough nut to crack without breaking your theological teeth. It is a temptation for intellectuals to turn sinfulness into a generality. Gordon Spykman in his new book, *Reformational Theology, a new paradigm for doing dogmatics* (pp. 301-36) notes that the Apostles' Creed, and also John Calvin's *Institutes*, wisely follow Scripture's restraint in not giving separate, honoured placement to sin, but conceive sin in its alien surd character which finds its *modus turbandi* between God's good creation and Jesus Christ's salvation only in the repentant saints' confessing the forgiveness of sin. So we don't need a new doctrine highlighting sin, but a fresh, convicted consciousness of sin in its destructive filthiness.

'Folly' may not be the best term today to raise a biblical consciousness of sin. 'Folly' to me, has overtones of Aesop's moralising animal fables where the weaker and slower outwit the stronger and faster. 'Folly' recalls Erasmus' humorous *Encomium Moriae* (1509), and 'folly' rhymes with 'jolly'. But there is

*An invited response to Cornelius Plantinga Jr at the January Lecture Series held at Calvin College, Grand Rapids, Mich., January 1993.

absolutely nothing funny about sin. Maybe we could say sin is ontological masturbation, and the stymied, short-lived pleasure and inversion of masturbation makes graphic the tantalising repugnance of sin, to an observer.

A tricky, troublesome thing about sin, however, is that observing sin (in others) does not, I think, help one to confess sin oneself, and without leaders confessing sin I doubt we can give followers a vivid, biblical consciousness of sin. This past Sunday evening I was exhorting in church on John 3 and Ezekiel 36, trying to make plain the sorrowing intensity of the prophet's colourful vocabulary, in the plural, on the dirtinesses, crookednesses, filthinesses of God's people – the best Hebrew–English dictionary says a basic translation for *gilulim* is 'pellets of dung' (which has a very forceful, contemporary Canadian–English equivalent): to make the point I finally quoted Ezekiel on 'our abominable lukewarm crap', and as young heads looked up at the pulpit I explained that Ezekiel often went to extremes, and never use that four-letter word unless you are down on your knees praying, 'Lord, forgive me my dirty … sin.' But it still felt lame, as if I was one of Job's friends.

'Colouring outside the lines' is probably too genteel a desription of the despicable banality and perversity of our sin. The vivid biblical consciousness of sin Cornelius Plantinga is asking us to learn demands an awareness that at the core of our/my deed contrary to the LORD's holy, merciful will at the core is profanation, repulsive, no-effort betrayal. You bite the hand that feeds you; you stab your *friend* in the back; you give God a respectful Judas kiss of deceit in public. But again, at-arm's-length diagnosis of sin sets one up for the self-righteous consciousness we need to break through. So I don't see any way for us to recover having the humbling biblical revelation of human sin and God's holiness take us aback if we are not led to *confess* sin, that means, ask to be forgiven.

Especially we who are Protestant in tradition do not know well how to confess sin redemptively, or entice one's neighbour to the confessional which provides emotional relief and a chastened life under the joyful miracle of forgiveness, rather than searing guilt, fearful depression, and a programme of work-righteousness. Could we share thoughts on how our churchly communions might institute with authority a redemptive confessional? If we have effaced 'church' democratically into a town meeting with lecture, musical performances, collection of monies, and fellowship, then a ritual of *public* confession of sin would be a disaster, a spectacle and recipe for hypocrisy, like praying for show on TV. And I am not after more private pastoral counselling or intimate group therapy, but a bona fide confessional where sin could be admitted in person and the Lord's cleansing forgiveness – the good news of Psalm 130 – could be actually experienced.

In the meantime how could we deepen and deploy what I often find the best section of our Sunday morning liturgy, when we communally confess our sin, receive the Lord's assurance of forgiveness, and hear again direction for new life. Could you identify for a moment with the voice singing the 'I' of Psalm 141?

GENEVAN 141

I am crying, LORD, please come quickly!
Did you not hear my spoken prayer?
I deeply yearn to know You care.
My lifted hands still bring thanksgiving –

Guard my lips from mouthing words twisted.
Stop my enjoying sin as sweet.
LORD, strip my deeds of sly deceit.
Keep my poor heart from turning wicked.

When a trusted person corrects me,
I know the hurt brings healing grace.
How sad when judgement is not faced
until one's crooked life is wasted.

Your concern and power amaze me:
Lord, do not empty out my life!
Frustrate each wily tempter's vice –
let me walk past their traps in safety.

It gives me a tremendous sense of God's wonderful *holiness* at this place in the liturgy, after confessing Psalm 141, to have especially a woman's voice read from Psalm 103 declaring that the LORD does not deal with us according to our wickednesses, but in God's *chesed* wipes away the muck sticking to us, as far as East is from West. Would there be some way for us who claim the anointing of Jesus Christ (Heidelberg Catechism question and answer no. 32) to structure more firmly into our Reformed context – not a do-it-yourself project – the repentant exercise of such priestly service(with a Lutheran flavour) to one another, including our neighbours young and elderly?

The other point I bring to the fore is this: it would be a mistake, in my judgement, to blame the demotion of God in the church – from the majestic Holy One revealed in Exodus 34:67 to gofer – blame such dethronement on 'popular culture.'

Professor Plantinga's general critique is correct and trenchant: as a church communion we have become soft on sin, sweet on God, ignorant of the depth of biblical faith, and try to be entertaining in our worship services. In the name of outreach we have tended to secularise the horizontally extended arms of the church. Coming out of an authoritarian skid on rationalistic ice, we have oversteered into the emotional mush of manipulative media.

Instead of fingering scapegoats – the 'Grand Rapids Machine' by outsiders, 'popular culture' by the educated Establishment, 'traditionalistic old fogies' by the ultramodern generation – instead of bewailing loss and assigning blame (which is often mostly protecting one's own turf), could leadership not agree that the American way of death – whether you spell it 'greed for comfort', 'power of success', or 'self-praise' – has indeed infected the church we are and love? Hadleyburg has been corrupted. Then whoever opens one's mouth is called upon *not* to yank on the general emergency brake and *not* continue a secular skid with business as usual, but to destroy one's *own* household idols and offer concrete historical *reform* in one's area of communal responsibility, which faithful deeds will ripple out and foster that awe of the Covenanting LORD God which slowly builds up wisdom in Christ's body on earth.

Let me be specific on theology, liturgy, and language. (1) I have become ever more thankful that my birthright included the Reformed confessions. The Reformed theology I learned from my parents and in catechism gave biblical structure and focus to my life: the glory of the Covenantal LORD God who cared for me as footloose country boy, though a sinner, in Jesus Christ, and by the Holy Spirit keeps me joyfully busy in God's world during the advent of Christ's coming to consummate history. Calvinian theology remains the best theological pudding I know, not that I haven't stirred in strengths from Lutheran, Anglican, Roman Catholic and Pentecostal emphases too over the years.

A way to bring living knowledge of the Sovereign God Creator, provident Ruler of the nations, compassionate Redeemer of the whole world, who lies beyond our ken in heavenly splendour yet is the source of daily miracles, whose Word is tried and true: a way to make the awesome God we are to serve vivid and winsome to the micro-chip generation is to accent Old Testament preaching, to emphasise as believers of the New Covenant an Old Testament biblical theology. I don't mean we go back to the basics of God who is transcendent but immanent, who predestines salvation but permits 'free choice', where the trinity is made a logical puzzle or mandala, and then once you have orthodoxy you balance it with orthopraxy, and so on and on. One can smother God with distinctions, knocking in attributes plank by plank, just as one can sell out God as an ineffable 'high'.

By Older Testament preaching I mean proclamation which instructs people to read the earlier testament in all its literary and historical intricacies, promises galore, so one comes to see Deuteronomy as a cornerstone of the whole Bible, and to hear from the double-book of Samuel how the incredible God used pop-song writer general king David in his utterly messed up life for the good of God's people, so one meets the LORD God of the veteran killer angels in Isaiah 6, the cosmic Wisdom with servant Cyrus and others in chapters 40-45, 60-62, and witnesses directly the intimacy with which a lamenting Jeremiah struggles in hand-to-hand combat with the LORD.

That is, if preachers can get themselves out of the way and confront the current generation with the amazing inscrutable LORD of the Older Testament, who still is as close as a parent giving us life-breath, concerned with my pain, who works with eccentrics and the drop-outs recorded in Hebrews 11, and will save anybody in Jesus Christ, tangibly lead us today by God's booked Word and Holy Spirit, then we may, God willing, reverse the trend of superficialising ignorance that Cornelius Plantinga has documented.

(2) If part of our problem is 'theological' – that people walk around, as it were, with only a pocket New Testament or the red-lettered gospels, so that God becomes shrivelled up into a portable Jesus-as-buddy, a contributing irritant that hinders reform of our Sunday worship services – where we indeed need palpably to meet the awesome God, is, if I may use a philosophical term, a prevalent mentality of nominalistic individualism that ruins 'liturgical order'.

I do not fault God's people, the laity, for wanting something 'interesting' to happen in a worship service, so much as the leaders of worship who perhaps inadvertently hinder worshippers in a Sunday morning service from meeting God – which is astoundingly more gripping than pastoral pleasantries, announcements, and homegrown or obviously professional 'special music'. I leave particulars for discussion, but posit as a challenging principle for our Zwinglian-crossed Reformed communion to consider: to recover a sense of God's holiness in a worship service it would help greatly if ministers, liturgists, and musician participants all had a vivid sense of their following an integrating order of worship, to which they willingly and imaginatively *submit*.

I learned that from Gerardus van der Leeuw a long time ago: you float free in a sermon, in exhorting or expounding the booked Word of God for the people gathered then and there in life's changing circumstances; but the liturgy, the age-old – not sacrosanct – weathered order for public worship, hammered out through centuries of persecution and reformation – where the congregated faithful prepare to meet God, to come clean on their sin – and, fortified by the Holy Spirit, hear God speak, and then respond by celebrating the culminating sacramental presence of the Lord in Christ's body and blood, so that you break out uncontrollably in a doxological paean of thanksgiving – this liturgical order is bigger than a preaching elder. This churchly rubric for congregated worship bears up the preacher and everyone else, primes one and all to be on your knees or standing in reverence, forgetting your self, and focusing you before the Holy One surrounded by angels.

Liturgical order carves out the cathedral space and trembling pregnance conducive for us humans to experience God's terrible reassuring holy distant closeness. If liturgical order is understood to be simply quaint custom, a disposable routine, then one is opting for experiment. While experimentation in congregational worship can be exciting, a corrective to stodginess and rote, continual experimentation with liturgical order is hard on finding God at home, and Sunday worship becomes something different than an occasion to meet God face to face. If a pastor starts to act Sunday mornings as a Master of Ceremonies in charge of a variety of events, and if a 'liturgy committee' thinks its task is to put democracy to work in the congregation rather than be judicious ministers of Grace, church worship of God tends to be subverted to vaudeville. So we need educated liturgists, for whom 'epiphany' is not a foreign word and for whom 'ascension' is not an optional service – gift subscriptions to *Reformed Worship* are a must – and we need shepherding pastors who respect the catholic rubric for worship as their *regula cultus* before they graduate from seminary.

(3) A final comment on 'language' is my opening to ward off both élitism and vulgarity as we try to find ways to recapture for ourselves and our generation the unspeakable holy glory of the LORD God in a day when a documentary photo of atrocity and a slick plug to buy hard liquor can be found on facing pages of Time magazine, as if that's normal, and where both God and sin have been domesticated to pet projects and pet peeves.

Seventy years ago Klaas Schilder warned in *Kerktaal en Leven* (pp. 139-73) not to pull back and fashion a special holy language for church, or an overly artistic one, as if reverence entails stylised artificiality, a euphuistic dignity of well-turned phrases. The prime requirement for the language of worship is that it be disciplined and drenched with love, for God and neighbour, because then one will seek out and find what speaks truth to the other's hearing! The publican's stifled cry in the temple, *hilosthet moi ti hamartoli*, was convicting, but so was Miriam's requiem mass composed as a desert folk-dance with castanets and drums. God's awful holy deeds can be acclaimed in faith by deafening skilful noise (Psalms 33,150) as well as by anguished silence (Habakkuk 2:20). Proscriptive formulae are a mistake, attempting to bind the Holy Spirit.

I once heard a British heavy metal band play 'Jesus Loves Me' as an encore at the Greenbelt Festival, England, before 25,000 people standing outdoors on a Saturday midnight, and to my stupefied ears, under the soaring intensity of the lead guitar, the piece made biblical holy musical sense. I do not say we should play it to perk up the image of the national American broadcast of the 'Back to God Hour'; but popularity does not necessitate cheapness. Jesus' parables with bread and fish drew large crowds because he spoke with no-nonsense authority, but he did not compromise the depth of his hard message. The Genevan jig psalms were popular with the Huguenot martyrs in the European 1500s and 1600s, although the melodies seem esoteric to many ears today pacified by shopping with muzak. We mortgage our confessional birthright if we buy indiscriminately into – even on the cautious installment plan – the commercialised pandering of the electronic church. But our older generation needs to face the fact that we are being told that the Word of the church of our generation on God's holiness and sin has in great measure *not been credible*. And if the disoriented generation of today cannot stomach the meat of the gospel, and we cannot make it palatable, then people go for milkshakes.

Perhaps you have seen the recent mass-distributed 36-page covered brochure of the Christian Reformed Church agencies? Four-colour, oversize, multiple-photo narrative, lots of white space, expensive paper, tastefully done: the image of corporate American business, end-of-year report, upbeat, upscale, upmarket. The glossiness – it's too nice for where the world is – made me ashamed. I would have preferred a black and white handbill on newsprint for our 'suffering servant' of a church in Canada, or a graffiti scream of frustration at our parochial puncture in Christ's body this past year, and some word-image to catch and bring back into the picture the failures of faith in our communion in the last while.

Nothing teaches God's holiness and our sin so much as bringing them together. I could play you a 40-minute tape, an extraordinary one-woman song-piece composed by Ron Melrose, director of music at an Episcopalian church off Central Park in uptown Manhattan, New York, the story of Mary Magdalene. Her 'Seven Men' song snaps out 'Don't worry, Daddy' melding the shout from abandonment by her father and her father's brother's abuse with the 'Abba' of Romans 8 and the terror that Jesus, who had become her friend, is going to leave her in the lurch now too. The whole song sequence has an astonishing ring of biblical truth, operatic verve, Broadway beat, Brechtian punch, yet undiluted gospel on how God's holy mercy can encompass our rotten sin. So I know it can be done, also in a worship service.

We are indebted to Cornelius Plantinga for his sharp-sighted diagnosis of a troubling pain in our body. I can't go into it now, but maybe we pale-faces could learn from our believing black brothers and sisters how to humble and convert performed lament and praise in a worship setting into a *consecrated folk* – not mass, not pop – *folk liturgical service* that carries the exuberant sorrow for sin of a ninth chord with the grit and excitement of its forgiveness before God's holy face to those who are outside the joy of somebody's saying 'Amen'. We could also do worse, I think, than be moulded by the lingo of the Psalms (cf. Colossians 3:16), and translate their range of *colloquial reverence* for our neighbour to hear.

Psalm 131

LORD, my heart is humbled now:
I have stopped my haughty frown,
curbed my dreams to fit my gifts;
yes, at last I have calmed down.

Like a child near mother's breast
I have found contentment, rest.
All God's folk, hope in the LORD;
soon God's Rule will be restored.

Selected reading

Brecht, Bertolt. *Die sieben Todsänden der Kleinbärger* (1933). Frankfurt am Main: Suhrkamp, 1959.

Liturgical Committee. *Report 3, Agenda for Synod of the Christian Reformed Church*, 1968, pp. 8-72.

Myers, Kenneth A. *All God's Children and Blue Suede Shoes: Christians and Popular Culture*. Westchester, Ill.: Crossway 1989.

Plantinga, Cornelius, Jr. 'Fashions in Folly: Sin and Character in the Nineties', an address at Calvin College, 14 January 1993.

Ridderbos, J. *Het Oude Testament in Onze Prediking*. Kampen: Kok, 1922.

Ridderbos, Nicholas H. 'De Verhouding van het Oude Testament en het Nieuwe Testament', *Gereformeerd Theologisch Tijdschrift*, 68 (May 1968) 97-110.

Schilder, Klaas. *Kerktaal en Leven*. Amsterdam: U.M. Holland, 1923.

Spykman, Gordon J. *Reformational Theology: A New Paradigm for Doing Dogmatics*. Grand Rapids: Eerdmans, 1992.

van der Leeuw, Gerardus. *Liturgiek*. Nijkerk: G. F. Callenbach, n.d.

5 1989: In the Year of our Lord's Forgiveness*

To forgive another person for a wrong you suffered demands that you be generous and resolute. To forgive takes stamina. Forgiving is not like eating pie à la mode or chocolate pudding. To forgive is a difficult act a person takes. It is not just a congenial attitude where you 'let bygones be bygones' and muddle through. In fact, although forgiveness has to be a decision which starts deep down inside your gut, unless you carry through on being reconciled with the one who has hurt you, forgiveness does not happen.

The core of forgiveness, according to the Bible, is to make good for the wrongdoer. Forgiving is like setting the bankrupt person up in business again, with your own finances, or like letting the criminal go free, with your blessing. To forgive is to lift off the burden which hopelessly weighs down the other person, even when it serves him or her right. For somebody to forgive is for somebody to atone for the destruction one's neighbour did, to make it good, and give the offender a new start.

God forgives you and me sinners

The Bible says God had Jesus Christ become a baby, grow up in trouble, and be bloodied with death, in order to give us free the new start we need (Romans 3:21–6). I wonder whether we believers appreciate the fact that just because God's grace is free does not mean it came cheap. There was only one eternally begotten Son of God the LORD had to lose.

It hurt God to forgive us people. God got wrinkles in God's forehead and became depressed, so to speak, heartsick (Genesis 6:5–7), at human atrocities. God felt jilted when God's own people committed adultery again and again with sexy gods like Money and Power and Licentiousness (Numbers 25; Hosea 1–3; Ezekiel 16; Matthew 6). It broke God's heart to be tortured and shamed on the cross while *we* jeered (Isaiah 53).

But that is what God did in Jesus Christ to set us criminals free. God put up the capital to take us out of bankruptcy. God sacrificed Christ's only

---

* First published in *The Banner* 124:1 (2 January 1989), 8–9.

begotten life to save us from execution in the electric chair. It was painful for God to forgive us, especially while we were still stealing and fornicating and acting the hypocrite (Ephesians 2:1–7). But God does forgive those who cling to the Word of the Lord and confess that Jesus Christ was resurrected from the dead as our substitute (2 Corinthians 5:16–21; Philippians 2:1–11).

Why is it so hard to forgive?

Normally it is the injured party who is called upon to do the forgiving. It is usually the weaker person who has been taken advantage of by the stronger who do not even think they need to be forgiven – is it the victim who must forgive? It really seems odd that if you have been damaged by somebody who doesn't care, you not only have to bear it, but you have to grin and forgive it too?

People who have been hurt by somebody get angry. It makes you feel better about yourself to resent the injustice. If you've lost face in an argument or been slighted in public somehow, you take to the media, if you can, to caricature your opponent. If someone has stolen something precious away from you – someone you loved, a position you coveted, or one of your securities – it seems natural and legitimate to fume with indignation and try to get even. After all, the other fellow did something wrong.

It is hard for us men and women to forgive, because bitterness is sweet. An impatient husband, an annoyed wife, a provoked child, all want to be compensated for their just irritation. And it is so self-satisfying to hold a grudge, we sinful people can hardly ever give that up. But grudges and resentment in the body of Christ are like a hidden cancer that never goes into remission. Bitterness keeps on destroying love and communion of the saints, world without end.

The unforgiving stalwarts

Much of our secularised world is unforgiving in its very network of connections. How could a successful business forgive the poor, or anybody, since hard-nosed competition as a way of life neither asks or gives quarter. An educated professional has little room in North American society to forgive the ignorant. To 'excuse' sloppy secretarial work or to 'forget it' when an important lab test is botched, avoids going the extra mile of forgiveness, of making good yourself what was inexcusably mistaken. Who has time for that? And the ethic of 'permissiveness' makes forgiving impossible, because anyone's doing wrong is denied.

In the church it is the legalist hunter of sin who is unforgiving. The Pharisees and cross-examining lawyers of Jesus' day thought they had the adulterous woman dead to rights, and were concerned to test Jesus' orthodoxy (John 8:2–11). Let the witness of the illicit sex throw the first stone, said Jesus (updating Deuteronomy 17:6,7 with Matthew 7:1–5), and doodled in the sand. Church leaders who want to be both *witness* and *judge* of someone's sin have it wrong, and are filled with self-righteousness, as if they themselves are the law. Such would-be leaders of God's people cannot be forgiving.

God's calling us to forgive and to be forgiven is critical

Forgiving is no trivial matter. If you do not forgive the one who has done you wrong, that is evidence you have not received God's forgiveness: such is the straight biblical truth (Matthew 6:14–15). The Lord has made good for us humans in Jesus Christ unconditionally (Ephesians 2:8–10), but if we try to accept God's gift of forgiveness without sharing its blessing, we forfeit our own fundamental pardon (Matthew 18:21–35). The unforgiving person shows that he or she has not really repented before God of one's own brutality and pride.[1]

Many of us also need to be forgiven by those we have hurt. That's difficult to arrange. All of us who are comfortably well-off need to be forgiven by the starving children of the world who think we are unconcerned. All of us who have health and work and friends need to be forgiven by the sick and the unemployed and the lonely who may think we make-believe they are not there. If we think we have nothing to be forgiven for, we fool ourselves and pretend we do not sin (1 John 1: 5–11). If we remain unforgiven by our neighbour, our faith-life becomes sanctimonious and sterile.

Would it not be a good project to forgive somebody in January or February? Start with a person in the church who has ruined something you hold dear. Take away their (perhaps even unwitting) guilt – can you imagine? – and give them a new start in your experience. What a gift to give! And don't try to get credit for it, because that would spoil the very gift you are resolved to give away in Christ's name. Forgiving an enemy will be a shock to him or her (cf. Romans 12 quoting Proverbs 25:21).

And is it not time, 1989… in the year of our Lord's unspeakable forgiveness, to ask for forgiveness from the many neighbours, and especially brothers and

---

[1] Anyone who has been cruelly violated as a child, or sexually, often does not have the strength or presence of self to be able to respond forgivingly. God understands that, and calls upon the body of believers to bring healing slowly and surely into such a person's life, so that the grace of forgiveness may someday find a place to reside there.

sisters in Christ, whom we have judged and found wanting, whom we have disparaged and written off: *we* ask to be forgiven! It would change the way the church at large operates.

When a mother or father teaches their child to pray, they bring blessing to a coming generation. If the current older generation in the church were to show forgiveness to one another, it would blow fresh air – a holy spirit – through the stuffy corridors of argument, recriminations, and factional leadership we always seem to bequeath our children, and would instead give the younger generation a genuine blessing and head start.

6 Glory to God or Christmas?*

You remember how it all started, the first announcement of Christ's birth day: once upon a time when Quirinius was governor of Syria, there were some shepherds out in the fields around Bethlehem in Judea keeping the watches through the night for their flocks. Unexpectedly an angel of the Lord stood over them and glory of the Lord shone all around them, and they were deathly afraid. 'Don't be afraid,' said the angel to them. 'Good news! Great joy to the world! Today in the city of David is born to you a Saviour who is Christ the Lord!' And suddenly there was with the angel an enormous army of angels praising God, saying, 'Glory to God in the Highest! Peace on earth to people of good will!' Then the angels went away.

As soon as the devils heard this divine news broadcast, I imagine they became damnably infuriated. They were not enjoying themselves on earth at all, and here comes more bad news: Joy to the world. Peace!

So the devils got busy and spread the word around (and are still busy rumouring it today): That was no news broadcast. That was a divine commercial advertising God's latest product. It was heavenly all right, simply divine. How sweet the name of Jesus sounded in that angelic choir. Beautiful angels. Let's hope God makes it an annual affair – I just love good music.

An insidious attack! To turn attention away from the message to the music separated and sentimentalised; to praise God's angels down to choir boys. The fact of the matter is this: those angels were not the white-robed cherubs of our Christmas cards. Those angels were war veterans of the Egyptian, Assyrian, Babylonian and many more campaigns, mighty creatures who wielded fiery swords and had killed thousands and thousands of enemy soldiers in one night. They were not out for a lark in the dark to sing a delightful carol or two. Their song came in the dead of night, a tremendous Alleluia of good news. 'Praise God the King who tonight has changed history! as the Lord said God would.'

The jealous devils who did not get to sing in that choir of long ago did one other thing. Their archcomposer got together his best musicians to write a better song, and the result is that well-known chorus popular even today:

> Glory to Christmas in the highest!
> And on earth, peace and goodwill to humankind.

---

*Chapel meditation at Trinity Christian College, published in *Campus Scope* 3:7 (December 1963), 2.

Devilishly clever. Satan is a master of simulation. It takes a Bible-sensitive ear to hear the difference. 'Glory to God in the highest'; 'Glory to Christmas in the highest'. If anyone wants to know what secularisation means, here it is: the heart of the matter gets lost and the hollow shell is celebrated. But God knows about the satanic plagiary and God has plans. As St Paul ominously suggests: the next time God sends the mighty angels out on choir tour it will be with trumpet accompaniment, and that performance will be too terrible for sentimentalisation and shall put an end to all worldly parodies.

What is the point? No merry Christmas celebration? No, the point is this: there is more than one song in the air; know which song you are singing; and if it be *Gloria in excelsis Deo*, find out whether it be a confession of the heart or just something that melts into the background music of seasonal greetings.

God hates sham and God hates having other gods beside the Lord – which does not mean that God hates celebrations. That is precisely what we have been waiting for in the Advent, the big birthday party next week where God self gives out the presents to whoever comes, the very presents God's angels announced long ago: the Joy of safety, of restoration to a Loved One; the Peace from fear that passes all understanding because it is permanent in the Lord.

Let us interrupt our work briefly then, take a vacation as the shepherds did to go to Bethlehem for a rest – true parties are restful. Let us go then, you and I, with a grateful laugh, singing in Spirit and in Truth, to commemorate the birth of Christ our King whom God's angels proclaimed. Glory be to *God* in the Highest!

7 *Christmas* means Lord of the Angels and Kids Playing in the Street*

Have you boys ever met God? Did you ever shake hands with God? Did God say anything to you last week? Or your parents, maybe – did your parents ever tell you, 'Oh, yes, a long time ago, one night, God knocked on the door and we let God in for a while… .'

Once upon a time God took walks with Enoch. Another time, the Bible says in Genesis 18, God stopped off at Abraham's house near Sodom and Gomorrah and had some toast and veal chops for supper. God even spent more than a whole month with Moses on Mount Sinai once, getting to know one another first-hand, like friends (Exodus 33:11). But after that, it seems God showed up more in dreams and visions that special prophets saw during the night.

Zechariah was one of God's prophets. He worked among the left-over Jews in Jerusalem who came back from being war prisoners in faraway Babylon, where Daniel had to go. One night God gave Zechariah eight dreams in a row. Those left-over Jews live as if I'm still faraway somewhere, said God, as if they never see me! They've even stopped building the temple for me.

Two years after those eight dreams, Zechariah reports:

The Word of God, Lord God of the Angels, came to me again –

This is what God, LORD of the Angels, says:
I'm all excited about the special hill in Jerusalem – Zion –
(where they are building the temple);
I'm so worked up about it I feel warm, as if I've got a fever!
Do you hear what the LORD God is saying?
I'm coming back to that special hill called Zion, and
I'm going to live smack in the middle of Jerusalem!
And Jerusalem will be called 'the City-you-can-count-on', and
that special hill of God, LORD of the Angels, will be called
'a Mountain-where-things-are-clean'! (Zechariah 8:1–3)

*Meditation given at a Calvinist Cadet Father and Son banquet, Willowdale Christian Reformed Church, Ontario, 1980. Published in *Perspective* (Newsletter of the Association for the Advancement of Christian Scholarship) 14:6 (Nov–Dec. 1980).

Five hundred years later God did show up in Jerusalem. Jesus was born as a baby who wet his pants, skimmed stones on Lake Galilee, and played around as boys play today. When Jesus grew up he healed people better than a doctor and told kids and grown-ups stories about how to live, because he was God! But the people in Jerusalem said, 'If you're God, beat it!' And they killed him.

But Jesus Christ, who was God on earth, walked out of that grave alive! and went back to heaven where he came from.

So God is gone again? You never see God now, not even on the TV news? The prophet Zechariah had more to say.

> This is what God, LORD of the Angels, says:
> A time is coming when old men and old women too
>   will sit around in the open squares of 'the City-you-can-count-on',
>   each one with a cane in his and her hand because they're so old,
>   and the widest streets of the city (when I come back, says the Lord)
>   will be filled with boys and girls too playing around right in those
>   widest city-streets!
> This is what God, LORD of the Angels says!
>   If you left-over people think that's just too preposterous a sight
>   to believe can happen in the days still to come,
>   well, don't think it looks unbelievable to Me!
>   – this is exactly what God, Lord of the Angels, says!! (8:4–6)

Do you know what that means, 'God, LORD of the Angels'? What do angels look like? Are angels those little boys in diapers who shoot arrows at teenagers to make them fall in love around Valentine's Day?

No! Angels are tough, more like hockey players. Angels form an army of which Jesus is the five-star general, LORD. I'm not kidding – this is in the Bible. The devil is an angel on the other side, and the devil is tough. He knows judo. The good angels Michael and Gabriel are a lot stronger and faster than Bobby Orr and Phil Esposito put together. (The angel on the picture by artist Albrecht Dürer is more what an angel looks like.) One angel of the Lord killed 185,000 Assyrian soldiers in a single night, to protect God's people in Jerusalem once upon a time.

The angels, veterans of lots of fights, sang when Jesus was born, because they knew Zechariah's prophecy. God is going to show up now, and there will be peace on earth, and kids will be able to play right in the streets! Glory to God in the highest!

That's right. 'Jesus saves' means 'Jesus makes you safe, from all evil.'

> This is what God, LORD of the Angels, says:
>   That's right! I'm going to make my people safe!
>   Free them from countries where the sun rises

and from countries where the sun sets.
I'm going to bring them all back so they can live in downtown Jerusalem!
And they will become people-for-Me,
and I will be God-for-them – I will!
so you can count on it and live without ever getting hurt, safe! (8:6–8)

It wasn't much fun for Jesus to be born. But God did it to show up in person again, to convince people they should get clean. But the Jews in old Jerusalem said, 'You can't count on us', and 'We are clean enough, thank you.'

So when Jesus went back to heaven to prepare for coming to earth as God one last time, He sent the Holy Spirit and gave us the Bible to find out how to start building for His *new* Jerusalem and how to get clean so you can shake hands with God the Father.

God is coming to our city in person pretty soon. That's the only thing 'Christmas' is good for, to remind us of that. So we had better get things clean – our talking, thinking, feeling and hands. If you read the Bible and come to say, 'I believe in Jesus and am sorry for my sin, and I belong to Jesus and want to obey God', then you'll be able to enjoy the big Day coming when God shows up again.

Not only will old people be able to sit around safely in downtown Toronto and Chicago and New York, but you boys, and girls too, will be able to play road hockey at Finch and Yonge, right in the middle of the streets, safely! And the angels standing around here tonight, watching protectively, will serve as referees.

You see, God's excited about coming back to meet grown-ups *and boys and girls* he can count on, because God wants to live right in the middle of us all. So remember Bethlehem tonight, but remember our city too, because that's where Christ and all God's angels will show up next.

Father in heaven,
Don't let any boy or girl be afraid of anything, Lord.
Help us all to know you are not just a baby,
but the LORD of the whole world, with an army of angels!
And you're coming back soon
so we can work and play safely in the city streets.

Thank you for Jesus Christ. Amen.

8 Psalm 115*

leader: Not for us, LORD, not for us,
But do something glorious for Your name!
Make something solid and shining to show Your covenanting
Grace and utterly dependable faithfulness!
Why should the peoples all around say,
'And where now is their God'?

people: Our God is in heaven!
Every thing that pleases God, God completes!

leader: Their 'gods' are solid gold and silver, (but) made by a human hand.
Their fake gods have a mouth but cannot speak;
they have eyes but cannot see!
Ears they have but cannot hear;
A nose is there, but they cannot smell –
Their hands cannot touch things.
Their feet cannot go for a walk.
No sound passes through their throat …

people: Like them become those who made them!
Like them become all those who feel secure with them.

leader: Israel! get to feel secure with the LORD God:

people: a relief and a protection is the LORD for such people.

leader: (Priestly) house of Aaron! bind yourselves only to the LORD God:

people: a relief and a protection is the LORD for such people.

leader: You (newcomers) who fear Yahweh! trust – trust the LORD God:

people: a relief and a protection is God for such people.

leader: The LORD God has kept us in mind: God shall bless –

people: Bless the house of Israel!

---

*Translation by Calvin Seerveld for responsive reading (1969).

Bless the (priestly) house of Aaron!
Bless those who fear the LORD God!

leader:– the unimportant ones together with the very important ones

> May the LORD God prosper you, you and your children.
> May you all be blessed by the LORD God,
>   who made heaven and earth.
> Heaven (you know) belongs specially to the LORD:
> The earth is what God gave for the sons and daughters of
>   humankind (to tend).
> Dead men and women do not praise the LORD,
> not one of those who have gone down to where it is deathly still.
> But we people here, let us bless the LORD
> from now on and for ever more!

people: Thank God – hallelujah!

9   Meditation: Singing Psalm 137*

By Babel's running waters, there is where we sat it out,
and cried hard as we remembered Zion.
We hung up our harps, stuck there among the Euphrates poplar trees.
Yes, that's where those who made us displaced persons demanded,
'Could we have those song lyrics again?'
Our tormentors commanded, 'Jump for joy! Sing us one of those Zion-songs!'

How could we ever sing one of the LORD's songs on that home ground strange
  to God?
If I ever lose my respect for you, Jerusalem,
may my right hand lose its grip;
may my tongue be stuck to my gums, if I do not remember you,
if I do not honour you, Jerusalem, above my greatest joy.

O Lord, remember that (terrible) day for Jerusalem,
remember the Edomites who said,
'Strip her down! Strip her down! Raze her to the ground!'

You daughter of a Babel! You violating bitch!
Blessed is the one who takes vengeance on you
for the evil way you worked your retaliation on us!
Blessed is the one who grabs and smashes your evil children
against the rock (Psalm 137).

I have two wishes. I wish I could sing psalms in the streets with my fellow
believers in North America the way the Polish workers sang their songs in
defiance of a repressive government. And I wish – even though I'm afraid of
what it entails – I had the deeply seasoned faith to sing Psalm 137 so it would
not be sung in vain.

Just as a Dutchman saw the centre of Rotterdam the day after it was
bombed to bits by the Nazis in 1940, and just as a Japanese woman resident
of Hiroshima moaned, stupified at what had been her home city the day after
6 August 1945, so God's poet back from Babylonian exile grieves at the Holy
City gutted by marauding unbelievers.

---

*First published in *The Banner* 117:10 (15 March 1982), 12.

Babylon Streams Received Our Tears

Plate 5 Psalm 137, from the *Psalter Hymnal* on which Seerveld collaborated

The psalmist remembers when the enemy poked fun at Israel's consecrated psalms. Sing it for our entertainment! they ridiculed.

The psalmist remembers how Esau's descendants egged on the captors to crush Israel so completely there would never be a son or daughter of believing Jacob left to wander around. And then the psalmist pleads with God not to let the Lord of history be mocked but to finish off those who preyed on God's people, so that the ones dedicated to violence would themselves be wiped out!

74

I have never suffered under the occupation of enemy troops the way my wife once did. So my eyesight needs to be sharpened to see that God's people in our day are plagued by the evil angel and his cohorts.

Every time I sing 'O Canada' and the last stanza of 'My country! 'tis of thee' while approving the manic stockpiling of missiles in larger and larger barns, exporting hoards of weapons to countries who cannot even give their citizens food, I myself am defiling the praise of the Holy One, who alone makes secure (Psalm 33).

Suddenly Psalm 137:5,6 breaks through my guard: if I am not ready to curse myself for not putting the kingdom of God – the new Jerusalem – above my greatest joy, well-being, pleasure, love, or what have you, then I am not serious enough in my faith to take up the ceremonial curse against the enemies of God's people. And then I have lost the bounce to my faith in the Lord's salvation.

The beatitudes of Matthew have no teeth if you deny the curses in the psalms against hardened evildoers. And the curses of the psalms have no good news – they are not taken biblically – if they are not heard as intercessory prayers by saved, sinful people for Godless sinners and enemies – enemies needing to be covered by the blessed blood of Jesus Christ to end their atrocities.

So I have two wishes, no, three, I could relate. I pray that the Holy Spirit strengthen my heart of faith through the Word of the psalms to give me as an adopted child of God the grit needed when the hard times come. I wish I could practise singing Psalm 137 to a sturdy Welsh melody in church to get ready for singing it in chorus on the streets in front of those who persecute God's people around the world. And I pray that my children not have a father and mother who missed the comfort of the awful Lord, who went through hell in loving us and who protects us by putting the curses of the psalms against the whore of Babel (cf. Revelation 18:2–8) in our mouths.

Therefore, let your forbearance be known to your economic neighbour and to your political enemy, for vengeance – sing about it! – belongs only to the Lord (Psalm 137:8,9; Romans 12:14–21; Philippians 4:4–7), to whom be blessing and honour forever and ever more.

Part 2

Philosophy

1   A Note on a School of Thought and Disciples*

Benedetto Croce (1866–1952) may be the most penetrating thinker Italy has had since Galileo. Carlo Antoni, professor of philosophy in Rome, knew Croce's thought inside out and was Croce's best friend. But his life long Carlo Antoni refused Croce's attractive offer to manage his fabulous library in Napoli. 'The man was too big,' said Antoni. 'I could not breathe freely in his shadow.'

There is a pathetic seasoned wisdom in this confession. It epitomises a situation as old as philosophy itself: with every big thinker there comes sooner or later a paralysing school of thought. An original thinker with new ideas inevitably attracts a following, and a following inevitably seems to break down slowly on into a decadent school of thought. Where does the fault lie? And must I as thinker either enter into this pernicious circle or be condemned to a solitary normality and putter about by myself?

Every philosophy not directly and actually grounded in the confession of biblical revelation is just asking for the trouble of these two alternatives. Every philosophy uncritically begun in a sovereign Reason, with analysis that professes not to need any grounding, is bound to yield a school of thought or a fragmentary run of eclectics. Every time a big thinker has so begun and students have come from everywhere to learn his or her ordering of theoretic knowledge, the dead end is already begun. Philosophy is theoretic knowledge, and unless philosophy is grounded in a reality deeper than theoretic thought it remains exactly what it is: theoretic thought, theory, hypothesis. And once a student has accepted one person's hypothesis one can only work out its logical consequences, or try to combine it with another hypothesis and its logical consequences, and so on. The distinctions become finer, the relations more and more complex, but the end result is still only hypothesis. And your own reworked hypothesis is closer to this big thinker or to that big thinker; you belong to this school of thought or to that school of thought.

No wonder the person on the street feels closer to the scientist who gives one a television set and sulpha drugs, while the philosophers define and

*First published in *Reformed Journal* 7:6 (June 1957), 27–8.

redefine and talk like politicians. No wonder, too, that Paul spoke so feelingly against philosophy and the traditions of humans.

A philosophy grounded in the confession of biblical revelation is no longer hypothesis. It is theoretic thought dominated by a supernatural power that is Truth. Here is the opportunity to escape a school of thought: a person philosophising, personally continually quickened and chastened by the Holy Spirit self. Here is the opportunity to develop a *community* of thought where the big thinker as well as the student come from afar is subject to an over-powering Sovereign.

But pride brings about the fall. It is easy for the big thinker to become proud of his or her original thought, or more subtle, to become proud of his or her humility. And with age and the accumulation of devoted students comes a softness partial to acclaim. The dedicated young students catch the vision as well as the words, but they, too, can become proud. They have a handle on the universe and a ready answer for age-old problems. Their eye begins to wander from the Holy Spirit to the master philosopher, and instead of checking Scripture they begin spending more time exegeting him or her. Even more sad than a school of thought is this community of thought gone wrong in master and discipleship. The community is not a community when it is a patriarchal family. A body is not a body when it is a head and little heads.

It is a fact that after Plato came the Platonists, after Thomas came the Thomists, after Calvin the Calvinists, and after Barth the Barthianists. It is also true that a school of thought is a dead end, and that only Jesus Christ deserves disciples. There are two ways out of this theoreticism and pride. The one is for thinkers to sulk alone, to be jealous and lonely, to play socratic games and ply the sceptic's trade. But there is no room for individualists in the kingdom of God. The other way is for thinkers to build a community of thought by keeping close to the foundation of thought, Jesus Christ. Somehow only Jesus can keep a person humble enough. Somehow only God's Holy Spirit can lead a thinker through the shadows and give him or her a place to stand where one can breathe freely, together with another.

2 A Note on Philosophy at the Free University of Amsterdam*

There are frequent references in the Christian Reformed Church to two Dutch thinkers, Dooyeweerd and Vollenhoven. To help get at the point of what these two philosophers are saying, I should like to sketch two of their ideas.

The first idea is what Dooyeweerd calls the *Wetsidee*. The *Wetsidee*, says Dooyeweerd, is the trinity of questions every philosopher willy-nilly answers with his philosophy. A philosopher answers them whether he or she is aware of it or not.

What one answers to these three questions gives the cast to all of one's thinking: (1) What is the absolute Archè? (2) Where lies the epitome of meaning? (3) What is the fabric of the universe? A Christian philosopher has his or her answers too. My answers, the answers of a Logos–Revelation-directed philosophy, suggests Dooyeweerd, will be these: (1) Sovereign God revealed in Jesus Christ; (2) the dedicated redeemed human heart; (3) Time. That is, Dooyeweerd is proposing here that these are the necessary presuppositions of a philosophy which uses the Bible as touchstone.

In giving content to this first answer of the Christian *Wetsidee,* Vollenhoven has distinguished different kinds of laws which the Sovereign God has revealed as the guidelines of creation's activity. There is the command of love which God puts to every person's heart – Thou shalt love me; and a person takes his or her time saying Yes or No. There are the unchangeable structural laws God laid down in creation, e.g. the difference between the concrete human being and one's religious heart, or the number and order and meaning of the aspects of reality. There are the changeable structuring laws God laid down in creation for the realising of his blessed plan, e.g. reproduction, cultivation, a person's need for a man or woman. There are also the disciplinary educative relative imperatives people declare in trying – Yes or No – to apply God's demand of love to concrete situations in our fallen world, e.g. Paul's requirement that a church officer be the husband of one wife. Generation after generation, says Vollenhoven, comes and goes and lives out its life's span in this theatre of the Sovereign God.

The second answer of the Christian *Wetsidee* has to do with heart and meaning. Anyone who has studied St Paul has been struck by that riddle

---

*First published in *Reformed Journal* 8:2 (February 1958), 16–18.

Plate 6 Bernard Zylstra, Calvin Seerveld, Glenn Andreas, Th.D.H. Vollenhoven and H. Evan Runner, in Grand Rapids, Michigan, 1959

interior homo, the innermost self of a person, the non-existing yet existential core of a person that is never loose from one's body (Paul's *soma),* the whole person who acts. The *interior homo* is not a Greek psyche nor an immortal soul but the biblical centre of a person, the fulcrum moved by the transcendent wonder power or the transcendent sinful power to make a concrete individual human say Yes or No to the loving God, to head one for Resurrection or Death. This *interior homo* is what Dooyeweerd is getting at with his talk about heart. And this concrete human when overpowered by the Holy Spirit, this concrete person when set in Jesus Christ, working away at living under the law of the Spirit: this Dooyeweerd posits as the mysterious radical religious unified meaning of all creation.

To get at the third answer of the Christian *Wetsidee* Dooyeweerd needs to analyse Time. It is an historical fact that modern philosophy has busied itself with exterminating Substance. Berkeley was among the first to scrap it altogether. Since Kant, and after Bergson and Husserl, Time has winnowed Being mostly out of existence so that for the young existentialist Heidegger there was no ontology anymore, just a chrono–logy. Dooyeweerd is a chrono–logist too, in this sense: Time, cosmic time, is the stuff of the universe, the deep awful meaning of creation; all flesh is grass. Cosmic time is the structural order and the actual duration in which every thing God made lives; it is the transcendental apriori of reality. Time is the proof of all creation's self-insufficiency and total dependence upon its Creator. Time is the silent demanding coherence, the real solvent for all the fabricated antinomies we stumbling humans in pride or ignorance may make.

The second idea I should like to mention is Vollenhoven's method of historiography, his way of recording the answers philosophers have given to the *Wetsidee*. Every method has a little madness; it sees some things very well and inadvertently slights others. Vollenhoven's method arose out of his long preoccupation with the Pre-Socratics. Like Heidegger he believes that the fountainhead of all philosophy lies among the early Greeks before Plato. Unlike Heidegger he does not find it to be the Garden of Eden which we must recapture; it is rather the source of theoretical misery whose sins have worked themselves out to the third and the fourth and the hundredth generation. And that is Vollenhoven's method for writing the history of philosophy: tracing the sins of the Pre-Socratics out to the hundredth generation.

Since these pagans did not know the Lord God who created and ruled heaven and earth, they could not have a Christian *Wetsidee*. They took reality to be an ordered kosmos, and they absolutised something in it, idolised it and interpreted everything else in terms of it as consistently as they knew how. And they did this in different ways: with or without gods, monistically or dualistically, statically or dynamically, with an indefinite number of combinations and variations. From the records available Vollenhoven finds certain kinds of interpretations, types of conceptions, recurring again and again, generation after generation, new ones springing up and old ones petering out but many holding strong, naturally combined with the peculiar personality of a new thinker and with the changed spirit of a later era, but structurally at bottom the same old attempted interpretation of reality. So arises a kind of topography of the development of Western thought, with longitude and latitude: the structural inheritance of a thinker and the contemporary milieu of a thinker give you the two axes needed to plot his or her position.

When Christ became flesh and dwelt among humans, convicting them of Truth, says Vollenhoven, it unfortunately made too little impact upon theoretical thought. The Church Fathers accommodated their inherited pagan interpretations of reality as best they could to the Trinity, put Plato's ideas in a Divine Mind or exchanged a Prime Mover for a Creator. Not until the Reformation, especially along the lines of Calvin, proposes Vollenhoven, was there a radical break in Western thought – despite the necessarily accompanying continuity. Even after the Reformation the pagan types of conceptions persisted, but for the first time since the later Augustine there was a clear-headedness of purpose and a corporate will among a few to ground even theoretical thinking biblically rather than bring God's Word in afterwards.

This is part of what Dooyeweerd and Vollenhoven are saying, as I understand it. I think they deserve a reading by the Reformed community in America and a little honest discussion.

3   Philosophy as Schooled Memory*

Once upon a time, to separate Reformational thinkers from ideologues, Hart took to speaking of philosophy as a tool.[1] I heard Evan Runner use this terminology a couple of times, hesitatingly, back in the sixties too.[2] One still comes across this perspective occasionally, which is saying something like this:

> The *Philosophy of the Law-idea* is the best tool Christians doing philosophy have at present; so we should use it. When a better mousetrap is built, then we will use that. We are not wedded to Dooyeweerd and Vollenhoven's philosophical method as Charles Saunders Peirce professed he was to his bride of scientific Reason.[3] We follow Christ and are committed within his body; we do not believe in a man-made, systematic philosophy. Just as Barth thanked God he was not bound to Luther and Calvin the way Thomists were tied to Thomas,[4] we may be thankful we can use Dooyeweerd's philosophy only as a good tool of the trade.

This position feels comfortable also to those who suffer from the 'once bitten, twice shy' syndrome of Augustine after he was fooled by the Manichees.[5] Once one is cured from having been an ideologue, one is tempted to curry a kind of 'ecumenical tolerance' toward differing philosophies.

I honour the intent to keep our philosophical pattern of thinking humbled to continuing reform. Party-line scholastics are a burden to an original

---

*First published in *Anakainosis* 5:1 (September 1982), 1–6.

[1] See Hendrik Hart, unpublished inaugural address, 'The spiritual unity of Christian scholarship', at the Institute for Christian Studies, Toronto, October 1967.

[2] In 1982 Dr Runner makes his hesitation explicit in a rejection of the conception. See his 'The Christian Philosophical Enterprise in the Light of Biblical Prophecy', speech for the Second International Symposium of the Association for Calvinistic Philosophy, Zeist, photocopy typescript, p. 56.

[3] 'The genius of a man's logical method should be loved and reverenced as his bride, whom he has chosen from all the world.' Section 5 in 'The fixation of belief' (1877) in *Values in a universe of chance. Selected writings of Charles S. Peirce (1839–1914)*, ed. Philip P. Wiener (New York: Doubleday Anchor Book, 1958), p. 111.

[4] 'Es tat der Kirche nie gut, sich eigenwillig auf einem Mann – ob er nun Thomas (seien wir froh, dass wir keinen Thomas haben und brauchen!) oder Luther oder Calvin hiess – und in seiner Schule auf einer Gestalt ihrer Lehre festzulegen. Und es tat ihr uberhaupt nie gut, prinzipiell ruckwarts statt vorwarts zu blicken ... als ob sie eben doch nicht an den kommenden Herrn glaubte!' *Die Kirchliche Dogmatik* (Zollikon, Zürich: Evangelischer Verlag, 1951), III,l: ix.

[5] Confessions 6.4.6 '... sicut evenire assolet ut malum medicum expertus, etiam bono timeat se committere ... .'

thinker's legacy because they are essentially Philistine, one-party disciples of a human thinker. And it is true that when any real community of philosophers ('the Amsterdam school') – rather than an eclectic assortment of diverse thinkers doing their thing under an assumed, common name ('Society of Christian Philosophers') – try to establish their identity, the marks which distinguish their identity come at first to be hotly held. Given the factional infighting among professional philosophers, it doesn't take much to push deeply held convictions and years of training in a certain philosophical mould to the status of non-negotiables. And young students of such a philosophy can push it into surrogate gospel. 'Ideology' is a word for thought-idolatry. 'Tool' relativises such passion.[6]

But if philosophy is thought of as a tool, such thinking is liable to occasion error in conception and judgement that can greatly damage the edificatory power (= building durance) of Christian philosophical activity. Philosophy is not like a hammer or saw or forklift to pile things up in a corner. Philosophy has an instrumental side to it, but the 'tool' aspect of philosophic task is more like the FBI (undercover critique) or Peace Corps (exploratory, agricultural service in foreign territory) than like the work of a mechanic, a tool diemaker, or an expert who repairs people's thoughts, cleans up their talk, or gives them a programme to build the Great or a Marxist Society. Such use of philosophy, I think, denatures its gift to specialised interests, no matter how legitimate the interests. If philosophy as 'tool' were to connote 'architectural firm' that the special sciences like biology and psychology and political science and economic or literary theory call in when they want to think out a joint-plan to help them all think under one roof, fine. Or, if philosophy as 'tool' casts the philosopher into the role of janitor to the sciences (instead of 'king' to replace the 'queen'), a kind of *ancilla scientiarum*,[7] one may have a fairly accurate, partial picture of things. But philosophy is much more of a pace-setter among the many sciences than 'tool' suggests. Philosophy is more like the basement of a building or its architecture than being the 'tool' of a front door or fire escape to get in or out of a house.

Perhaps it would be better, however, to let the dead metaphor of 'tool' go, and try to formulate the matter exactly. *A philosophy is a categorial framework that is conceptually in place in someone's consciousness and acts as a schooled memory in which one's theoretical activity is embedded.* A given person's philosophy is always becoming and be-going, unless one settles into it like a rut. But the philosophy one 'works' with is not something you have. The philosophy has you as theorist and scientist. Much as your mother-tongue, which you learn even

---

[6]Cf. C. Seerveld, 'A note on a school of thought and disciples', see pp. 83–84 above.

[7]Cf. C. Seerveld, 'Skeleton for Philosophy 101 at Trinity Christian College', mimeograph (1960), pp. 11–12, 16–18.

before you can speak, determines your world of conversation, so one's philosophy, veritably functioning as a schooled memory, becomes the reservoir shaping your ideas and conceptual world.

Dozens of distinctions need to be made, and many supplementary points should be articulated, but right now I am after only one corrective, central point: philosophy is not a tool, it is not an instrument of thought, because philosophy is the fundamental thought-framework within which scientific thinking takes place. (My tentative position on this defining point harks back to the tradition of both Western and Eastern reflection of wisdom, before European positivism denied conceptual frameworks as committed-patterns and American pragmatism instrumentalised everything it touched.) Therefore a philosophy is much more deeply entrenched in one's subconscious makeup, if one is philosophically literate, than 'tool' would make one think. Augustine's insight on 'willing', that the more deeply the whole person is involved, the harder it is to will 'freely',[8] is pertinent too, I think. To change one's philosophy is almost as difficult, deep-going, and traumatic, as altering one's personality through years of psychotherapy. A philosophy is not disposable or fixable or replaceable like a diaper or getting a new lawn-mower. A philosophy is one's habit of schooled consciousness, the natural underwear or skin of every scientist and academic.

Let me make one terminological precision. In my book not everybody is philosophically active. Every human creature, I believe, lives out of some *faith* or other, existentially attached by *commitment* to the true God revealed in Jesus Christ and witnessed to by the Holy Spirit, or to a nogod. Every faith-committed human creature who is sane shows a way-of-life. Oftentimes one's way-of-life may remain unconsciously operative, determining the (relative) cohesion of choices, priorities, and routine of daily activities one lives out. (This is so for isolated tribes of yesteryear and also applicable for many citizens of today's secular society who have lost much conscious sense of the fact that their 'normal' life-pattern is quite parochial, really, in the light of millennia of history, rather than universally valid, as they dumbly assume.)

Sometimes people become aware of their way-of-life which can be held but not expressed. I am willing to call such consciousness of (one's) way-of-life a world-and-life view, a *Weltanschauung*, a 'vision' one is ready to 'confess' in words or stories (cf. myth), pictures and liturgy (cf. rites), that one self-consciously recognises is relative to others and believes to be true (or 'better' than others). You don't correct a crooked way-of-life by adopting a straight world-and-life view.

A philosophy, as I understand it, is similar to a way-of-life and to a world-and-life view (1) in its encyclopaedic, systematic compass, and (2) in its being

---

[8]Confessions 8.8.20.

an out-working of one's underlying faith-commitment. But philosophy has an analytically defined consistency. Philosophy marks an educated consciousness trained in making careful distinctions and in identifying precise relationships. A philosophy takes a very conscious, considered stand on the interrelated meaning of things.[9]

You don't need a philosophy to be a Christian. You don't even need a *Weltanschauung* to be a disciple of Christ. You need a walk with the LORD, the Way-of-life the Scriptures teach, for example, in Micah 6:6–8, Matthew 5–7, Romans 13:8–10. But if you have a confessional vision or *Weltanschauung* with your way-of-life, a Christian must make earnest in having them both biblically in line. (When one's way-of-life and *Weltanschauung* happen to be at odds, one lives a troubled existence, for good or bad, depending on whether their coming in line follows the shalom of Christ's Rule.)

Every academic and practising scientist – and that includes college and university students coming to think for themselves – are in the throes of being formed within, of firming up, or of altering a *philosophical stance* in their particular studies. The reason for this is that academic study is done within a categorial framework because one's professional concepts and ideas are loaded by their assumed interconnection. For Christian theory in any discipline a Christian philosophy is necessary. This is the rationale for the Institute for Christian Studies to exist at its task.

A given philosophy is a result of certain philosophical thinking. But a philosophy is not inert, a residue. It may hang around a thinker's neck like a dead albatross, but a philosophy serves more responsibly as a halo around one's thinking. Like a schooled memory, I proposed, philosophy is the hidden reservoir one taps before one knows it when you reflect with scientific precision: the fund of experienced, ordered knowledge which orients one's ongoing, controlled perception; the structured apriori foci one has adopted for tying definite thoughts together. That is, while a philosophy is 'a definite body of thought', its substance is categories rather than concepts; and categories order analysis but are not themselves conceptual 'answers'. Categories make answers possible. And a specific framework of categories limits the theoretical questions one asks to which one goes to find scientific answers.[10] While admitting to thinking out of a categorial framework seems restrictive to a thinker proud

---

[9]Seerveld, 'Skeleton', pp. 1–3, 7. Cf. S.U. Zuidema, 'Philosophy as Point of Departure' (1961), trans. E. van der Woude, in *Communication and Confrontation* (Toronto: Wedge, 1972), pp. 124–8.

[10]'A question is really an ambiguous proposition; the answer is its determination. ... Therefore a philosophy is characterised more by the *formulation* of its problems than by its solution of them. ... In our questions lie our *principles of analysis*, and our answers may express whatever those principles are able to yield.' Opening paragraphs of Susanne K. Langer, *Philosophy in a New Key* (1942) (New York: Mentor, 1953), pp. 1–2.

Plate 7 Seerveld and Lambert Zuidervaart at the Dooyeweerd Conference, Dordtrecht, Netherlands, 1994

of one's tolerance, unless one has philosophic cohesion as a professional thinker, I dare say, you are eclectic, uncritical, or muddled.

The fashionable term since the 1960s[11] has become 'paradigm' or 'model'. An insightful dissertation by J.H. Santema, which deserves more attention than it has received,[12] distinguishes 'knowledge models' (KM) and 'manufacturing models' (MM), and shows the pitfalls of confusing 'technical diagrams that serve as blue-print instruments for making something' (MM) and 'analytic constructs that teach one to identify key features of something' (KM). In my judgement a 'categorial framework' is more part of a scientist's human consciousness than either a 'knowledge model' or 'manufacturing model' and is even more fundamental a girder in advanced theory and scientific conception than what Kuhn argues for.

We all know how hard it is to talk across 'paradigms' in philosophical debates. That difficulty is evidence of how deeply ingrained a categorial framework is in one's consciousness. That's not bad, in my judgement. That is

---

[11]Cf. Thomas S. Kuhn, *The Structure of Scientific Revolutions* (1962) (University of Chicago Press, 1970), xii–210; and earlier, for example, Ludwig von Bertalanffy, 'Theoretical models in biology and psychology', *Journal of Personality* 20 (1951–2): 24–38.

[12]J.H. Santema, *Modellen in de wetenschap en de toepassing ervan: Historische en systematische beschouwing vanuit christelijk-wijsgerig perspectief* (Delft University Press, 1978), x–243. There is an eight-page summary of the study in the English language, pp. 186–93.

the nature of philosophy. But one should not avoid that trouble of communicating on theories of art or knowledge or dogma or historiography by playing down one's philosophy as merely an (important) 'tool'. No more than one should solve the problem by becoming a scholastic ideologue. Or be a candle-holder looking on by observing that philosophies are societally and historically conditioned and you particular individual have a particular societal history. Of course, but, once one has come of age philosophically, one stands with one's philosophical conception as a working categorial embodiment of the truth, so help you God, or Reason or Utility. That's why the clash between philosophers is bound to be as passionate as a vow — Peirce saw that correctly.

When one believes philosophy acts like a schooled memory, one will be less ready to try to turn it in for a new model to cut one's conceptual grass. Teachers and students of philosophy of different fields will be extremely wary of the traditional philosophies of people come down to us from unbiblical sources, as living options today. And Christians will be more thankful for the categorial framework formed in the generation of Vollenhoven and Dooyeweerd, Zuidema, Mekkes, K.J. Popma, van Riessen and sundry other saints. A reformation in cultural direction did happen historically once upon a time; Luther and Calvin were not just reformist. The same is true in philosophy, it seems to me: the neck of 'reason' was radically broken, at heart, in the philosophy of the cosmonomic idea. Its categorial framework is biblically directed, humbled enough to be rich in philosophical blessing, breathing a Reformed Christian tradition that is still too little known in scholarly circles.

We can keep this schooled memory a diaconal ministry best by continuing reform of its neo-idealist, phenomenological setting[13] and by giving away, in translation, its wisdom to our neighbour, recalling its key insights for giving conceptual direction that honours the Lord in issues of our day.

---

[13]Cf. Robert Knudsen, 'Dooyeweerd's philosophical method' (1962) in mimeographed collection entitled *Reflections on the Philosophy of Herman Dooyeweerd* (Philadelphia, n.d.), pp. 9–31; and Knudsen, 'Transcendental method in Dooyeweerd', *Anakainosis* 1:3 (April 1979): 2–8. Also cf. Albert M. Wolters, 'An Essay on the idea of Problemgeschichte' (Free University of Amsterdam doctoraalscriptie, 1970); Wolters, 'On Vollenhoven's Problem-historical Method', in *Hearing and Doing: Philosophical Essays Dedicated to H. Evan Runner* (Toronto: Wedge, 1979), pp. 231–62.

4 Philosophising Beauty*

That story about the early Greek philosopher who was out one night thinking, thinking deeply looking up at the stars ... and fell in a well ... ever since that story got around, people have persistently thought of philosophers and philosophy as being starry speculation out of touch with the facts of life. Unless one makes philosophy one's profession or unless you have studied it extensively in college, you very possibly share this widespread opinion: *philosophy is learned speculation more or less out of touch with down-to-earth reality*.

The trouble with this widespread opinion about philosophy is that it generally has been *correct*. Brilliant old Plato wrote an impractical political constitution because he was so fascinated by certain ideas which he himself said were out of this world. In the Middle Ages, while the butcher, baker and candlestick-maker lived in squalor and at behest of pope and prince went off to fight Holy Wars, the philosophers stayed home, and almost to a person argued among themselves fine points of language and logic and how many angels can dance on the head of a pin. To the shame of modern philosophy, German philosophy in the grand style, Adolf Hitler made the very same point: he did not execute philosophers and professors of philosophy because they might oppose him and work toward his overthrow; he put them all away in a comfortable old castle, and let them philosophise together merrily, harmlessly. By and large, unfortunately, philosophy has always been academic, closeted, eccentric; and although its ideas do seem to sift down gradually and help shape history, philosophers and philosophy have regularly been out of touch with their contemporary situation.

That is why my speaking before you cosmetologists of America today is odd, and at the same time most important. For my conviction is that philosophy is not harmless, that it should not be speculative, that it can have its feet on the ground and address itself with power to the daily workaday life about it. Given the opportunity to speak to you influential people, I became curious. Could I, as a classroom teacher of philosophy, say anything worth your while? What in the world has philosophy to do with cosmetology and cosmetics?

---

*Full text of an address given on 15 July 1960 at Morrison Hotel, Chicago, after the luncheon on Mississippi Day of the National-Interstate Convention of State Board Examiners of Beauty Culture and Hairdressing (Cosmetology). An edited version was published in the *American National-Interstate Council Bulletin of Cosmetology* 15:1 (September 1960), 3–5.

NEWLY ELECTED OFFICERS — (Seated, from left): Evelyn Wilburn, Jackson, Miss., *second vice president;* Elsie T. Tinsley, Bozeman, Mont., *president;* Aurie Gosnell, Aiken, S.C., *first vice president;* Vera Malchow Reed, Fargo, N.D., *treasurer.* (Standing, from left): Freda G. Bidwell, Hartford, Conn., *historian;* Ela Lovelace, Hot Springs, Ark., re- *vice president;* Lorrayne Piens, Minneapolis, Minn., *corresponding secretary;* Tressie Arnold, Sheveport, La., *fourth vice president;* Rose A. Couture, Nashua, N.H., *third vice president;* Florence McLaughlin, Atchison, Kan., *fifth vice president;* and Pearl Ware, Phoenix, Ariz., *editor-in-chief.* NOT PICTURED: Don Fitzgerald, Juneau, Alaska, *sergeant-*

Plate 8 Officers of the American National-Interstate Council of the Boards of Cosmetology at the national convention of cosmetologists, 1960

From the very beginning of Western history, the relation between philosophy and cosmetology has not been cordial. Philosophy began as something Greek, Western: hairdressing and cosmetics is something Eastern, Oriental in origin. Six centuries before Christ, here was the first troublesome confrontation of West *vs.* East, philosophy *vs.* the art of physical beautification. The phenomena of curled hair, mascara, chalk-whitened skin and perfumed robes entered Greece proper from Egypt, Babylonia and points East by way of Asia Minor where the Greeks had established colonies. And this fashion of hair-curling and cosmetics captivated Greece proper, Athens, just about the time that the first philosophers were starting to argue that the *mind* of man is what is important, *not the body*; in fact, to bother about skin and hair is to go soft, seductive, something a woman would do – and you know, of course, that for the classic pagan Greek philosophers women and other animals did not count for much. Do not rob the Greek nation of its vitality, said the philosophers to the beauticians, and do not distract us with your unguents and gold-dusted hairdos from our thinking.

But, countered some of these early Greek barbers and beauticians, the hair we cut and dress lies close to your head where the thinking gets done! We know we are on holy ground; as a matter of fact, our work is *sacred*. Every haircutting and embellishment is a ceremony of purification. We are priests and priestesses of Beauty to your head! And that is precisely what they were: the first barbers and beauticians were priests and priestesses.

UNIQUE, INTERESTING ADDRESS: *Here is Dr. Calvin G. Seerveld, PhD., Trinity College, Worth, Illinois, as he spoke at a luncheon of National Inter-State Council members on July 15, 1960, at Hotel Morrison in Chicago.*

Plate 9 Calvin Seerveld at the cosmetologists' national convention, 1960, with Vice-Preisdent Evelyn Wilburn and Inès Seerveld looking on

No, said the philosophers. You work with the body, *strike one*. It is effeminate, *strike two*. On top of that, your worship of hair and skin is superstitious, *strike three*. Out!

This original opposition of mind against body, philosophical thinking against the art of physical beautification, an opposition and antagonism which arose in a pre-Christian milieu, did not change much in the so-called Middle Ages after Christ. Many a Roman saint and philosopher of the early church fulminated against curling irons, rouge red paint, and that soap that had to come from Gaul to bleach the hair of fashionable ladies in Roman society. Many people still cut off and saved for the Judgement Day the locks of children (a pagan custom still practised somewhat sentimentally today); but the dominant cosmetic code of the times propagated and enforced by the medieval church – where philosophers had turned theologians! – was this: long straight hair for man and woman only occasionally attended. The Old Testament injunction to priests not to cut hair and beard really applies to every Christian, said the medieval authorities, and Peter and Paul outright condemned elaborate hairdressing. Emulate Samson if you must, but rather spend time in pure thought and celibate prayer, not in priming the body. In other words, the original pagan philosophical disqualification of hair-styling and cosmetics became a theological policy and stern reality in the Middle Ages.

Then happened what always happens when something naturally good has been wrongly disqualified and suppressed. At the breaking of the Renaissance, hair-styling and cosmetics came to the fore with a vengeance. The concern of emancipated courtly ladies, and lovers for the body and beauty, together with such earthy discoveries as the circulation of the blood – you don't massage the scalp to get healthy hair until you know about the circulation of the blood – together, the beauty-conscious ladies with new-found techniques went wild. You know how the story goes; long curls, waves, bobbed hair, egg shampoos, scalp washes in milk or – if you happen to be Queen Elizabeth I – in wine. Famous sculptors turned beauticians, adding precision and status to the profession; it became widely acknowledged that haircutting was not an ignoble business, but an *art*. And the men began shaving again!

Cosmetology finally snowballed into that infamous pompadour of the eighteenth century where the hair was kneaded with pomade and flour, drawn up over a cushion of wool, twisted into curls and knots, decorated with artificial flowers, and left unopened for several weeks – it took a skilled barber to put it up there – and when the head of hair was opened later you needed a sublimate powder to kill off the bugs that had multiplied inside! No philosophical argument could stem this tide, and ecclesiastical bodies could only frown and condone what they no longer could control.

At last there had to be a law to crack down on cosmetic extravagance. And there was. In 1770 the English Parliament passed the following, to wit:

> That all women of whatever age, rank, profession or degree, whether virgins, maids or widows, that shall, from and after such Act, impose upon, seduce, and betray into matrimony, any of His Majesty's subjects, by the scents, paints, cosmetic washes, artificial teeth, false hair, Spanish wool, iron stays, hoops, high heeled shoes, or bolstered hips, shall incur the penalty of the law in force against witchcraft and like misdemeanours, and that the marriage, upon conviction, shall stand null and void.

The point is this for our purposes, that in modern times, since the Renaissance, the art of physical beautification has won a prominence and such influence upon women (and illegally, at least in England, upon men) that philosophy ought to reopen its condemnation or investigation of the phenomenon.

That brings us about up-to-date for our systematic analysis of the contemporary situation. After the pompadour and French salons and the law of 1770, there was the tapering off nineteenth-century episode of wigs and the beauty parlour, and the early Victorian problem of hair being so long and freely oiled that you had to call in the furniture renovators after a banquet to re-do the backs of the drawing-room chairs. All this only made philosophers (if they thought about it at all) want to laugh at hair-styling and cosmetics.

Has then philosophy today nothing to say to cosmetology in the twentieth century, the age of machines and world wars and psychoanalysis, except laughter? To get at this, first I should like to interpret critically this history of the problem I have sketched. What does it all mean, this philosophy *vs.* the art of physical beautification?

It means that both theorising philosopher and practising cosmetologists have always assumed that a person is made up of a mind and a body. The philosophers have, without fail, contended that the body is so impermanent – and its adornment worth so much less than cultivation of the mind – that hair styling and cosmetics should be neglected, if not rejected, since it interferes with the truly important and essential activities of men and women. Beauticians, on the other hand, throughout history, have concerned themselves with man and woman as an object worthy of beautification, a body, something physical in which a person can find lasting enjoyment and happiness, thereby implicitly denying – or at least omitting from their purview of the person – any mental or spiritual factors there might be.

My point is this: that the age-old dichotomy of the human, the view that a person is split up into a mind or soul and body, a view developed in ancient times, intensified in the medieval period, and as powerfully latent in the modern era as ever – my point is that this split-up view of the human (no matter which side you take) is a misconception of a person that philosophers have traditionally fabricated and in which cosmeticians to this day have operated. Further, that this divisive, dichotomistic view of a person must undergo a critical re-formation if philosophy is to get its feet on the ground, and if cosmetology is to develop into the significant educative force of which it is capable.

I do not intend to try to give you a full-fledged course in a reformed anthropology in my last ten minutes. I should like to conclude by giving you two cents' worth of philosophical observation on the state and meaning of cosmetology and cosmetics in 1960. I propose to do this by spelling out briefly what seem to me to be the three basic perspectives in which cosmetology can be, and, as a matter of fact, is being practised today. My critical delineation of these three perspectives is guided, naturally, by a reformed philosophical anthropology which is deliberately trying to work out the implications of the thesis that a person is not cut into mind and body, but is an integral *whole*. To spell out such perspectives is what, from my position, philosophy has to say to cosmetologists and cosmetics. Nothing spectacular. Philosophy must simply try to bring to theoretical, systematic clarity the various possible perspectives which condition and colour such cosmetological training and work. From there it is your problem. And, as I understand it, your State Board Examiners are largely responsible for the standards and directions, the tendencies, emphases, perspective, which cosmetology takes in the various American states. I cannot expect you all to agree with the alternative I favour, but I do hope I shall be intelligible.

One perspective which can rule the training and operation of cosmetologists and their patrons is what I shall call the 'Cult of Beauty' perspective. In this perspective it is *Beauty* which determines, motivates and shapes all that is done. Beauty is never quite clearly defined. (I don't think I shall be divulging any trade secrets if I say in passing that philosophers themselves have been looking for Beauty with a capital B for two thousand years, and I am afraid, if you will pardon the scepticism, that they may be looking for that black cat in a dark room that isn't there.) Beauty is never quite clearly defined, but adherents to the 'Cult of Beauty' believe it is a certain pleasing if not perfect proportion. This Beauty is believed to be the key to a full life, happiness, even fame; it is both the driving force and jealous goal of action. Beauty is virtually worshipped. This is what 'cult' means.

For the 'Cult of Beauty', then, beautification becomes the magical operation. The steps of beautification become a ritual exercised religiously by its devotees. I was taken to be such a devotee the first time I went to a barber in Rome. As the barber finished cutting he mixed a creme in my hair. I protested inarticulately in my best Italian as he began with a second creme. My sounds were apparently generously interpreted, for he began pouring from several more flasks and bottles onto my shortened hair with such enthusiasm and finesse that I became still. Suddenly I sensed that I was being anointed as a kind of sacrificial offering to Beauty. As it was, I walked about Rome for two days, glistening and stinking like a sacred cow. Devotees of Beauty, however, honour cosmetologists as priestesses; their worship of Beauty is not comic opera, but tragically serious.

Just this must be said: worship of Beauty is pagan. By 'pagan' I do not mean 'primitive'. 'Pagan' by definition means simply 'not Christian'. Christians do not worship Beauty, neither physical nor the capital B variety. To say that the 'Cult of Beauty' perspective is pagan is not to cast aspersions upon obvious patron saints of the cult. It is not saying that the 'Cult of Beauty' is not a responsible way of thinking or a hard-working way of living; in fact, the 'Cult of Beauty' probably always lends a successful cast to the profession of cosmetology. To say that the 'Cult of Beauty' perspective is pagan is only to say that wherever this intensive, limited horizon sets the tone and pace of cosmetology and cosmetics, whether it be in Ancient Greece, Renaissance Italy, Pompadour France or Hollywood America, you have the pagan alternative dominating cosmetology.

A second perspective and live alternative which can rule the training and operation of cosmetologists and their patrons is what I shall call the 'automatic beauty salon' perspective. A 'beauty shop', understood exactly, is a strange animal. You have butcher shops, bakery shops, fender shops, and beauty shops – as if beauty were something like spare ribs, a loaf of bread and an undented fender. In the 'automatic beauty salon' perspective, beauty is a commodity anybody can buy, provided you have the money. Beauty is not worshipped, for it is something done by skill and machines, handled by trained experts who efficiently, painlessly, and as their technological know-how permits, supply the *demand* for beauty.

Beauty in the 'automatic beauty salon' perspective is considered a necessary of life, like bread and water, nothing unusual. This perspective makes the trip to the beauty salon no longer a pilgrimage but more like a medical check-up. Visit your dentist three times a year. Is your hair too long or going straight? Head for the barber and beauty shop. 'Five barbers – no waiting', and you whip in and whip out in less time than it takes to change oil.

This is the 'automatic beauty salon' perspective, and it is secular. 'Secular' does not mean immoral. 'Secular' means simply that 'the heart of the matter is gone'. Human cosmetologists become reduced to flawless technicians getting pay, and customers become patrons receiving automatic treatment.

The secular 'automatic beauty salon' perspective, a peculiarly twentieth-century perspective, is apparently not bad for business; but if it captures the American cosmetological industry and planning in its entirety, it will not be long – it has happened to restaurant services, shoeshine boys and others – it will not be long before IBM puts out an automatic machine with a cavity in it into which you insert your head, the brushes close in, you close your eyes and drop several coins in the slot, the vials burst and presto! you come out with a blonde permanent wave in your head. While this last example may be a caricature, the reality of automatic beauty shops is not, and has disheartening, unhuman possibilities.

A third possible perspective – you understand there may be more than three basic perspectives, and seldom does one of these perspectives appear stark and unmodified in policies on Main Street – the third perspective which can rule the training and operation of cosmetologists and their patrons is what, for want of a better designation, I shall call the 'style for a woman' perspective. In this perspective, Beauty is neither idolised nor considered a commodity, but is viewed wholly as a matter of style. Not every person can be 'beautiful' – whatever that means; but everyone has the capacity, even duty, to be *groomed*, and that includes aesthetic enhancement as well as hygienic care. The 'style for a woman' perspective believes that style is to be given by competent men and women to others as a service, a rather *intimate* service – shampooing and styling is not far away from the biblical foot-washing – and that this service is necessarily performed in a sphere of leisure. To become stylised is a luxury, not a bare necessity; therefore the performance deserves the restfulness, colour and celebration that goes with moments of luxury.

In practice the 'woman styling' perspective turns beauty salons into houses of beauty where you are met not by a clinical physiologist who addresses herself to bodies and heads of hair, but by cosmetologists who are aware that here comes a whole woman at leisure. And the competence of such cosmetologists is measured by their ability to give the woman style, coaxing out hidden beauty à la Frank Lloyd Wright, with a level of conversation and modest personal interest that relaxes and invigorates the whole woman. Cosmetologists dominated by the 'style for a woman' perspective are dedicated to the end of making every act of cosmetology an exciting and fruitful brainwashing – not leaving it limp and cleaned out, but sparkling clear, refreshed. No unspoken promises of Beauty are made. There is just that assurance of hair styled and sculptured about one's most comely features, during a pause that refreshes physically, emotionally, intellectually, spiritually, all ways.

This 'style for a woman' perspective seems to have a Christian warmth and sanity about it. By 'Christian' I do not mean moralistic nor humanistic. By 'Christian' I mean something done in Christ's name, whether it be the proverbial cup of cold water or the caress of a comb. When the 'style for a woman' perspective puts dedication and depth into the work because the worker realises its importance before God, working with a human being, a whole person created by the Lord God with glories waiting to be developed then you have action that is 'Christian'.

If there is anything our tottering social and political affairs need today, it is action permeated by the dedicated warmth and open joy of Christian sanity. Such action can be shown and taught by the cosmetologists. I am told that women dress more for other women than for men. When you have styled the hair of your clients, and they return home, would it not be fun once in a while to put a flower artistically in their hair? (Men, I think even philosophers, would like this touch of feminine style, 'style for a woman'.)

And that is my final point: you women can, and do, have great influence upon men, probably no matter what you do. You delegates to the National Convention have the opportunity, influence and responsibility to make one or another perspective for cosmetology felt throughout America. The 'Cult of Beauty', the 'automatic beauty salon', the 'style for a woman' perspective: what perspective you emphasise in the education of cosmetology, and what direction you bring to the public, will more or less determine what cosmetology and cosmetics means for us in America in the 1960s. That is why I challenge you, no matter what the philosophers do up in the clouds, you who are down on earth, choose wisely. It has happened before – I am not joking – and shall happen again: *which way cosmetology goes, so goes the nation!*

5 Philosophical Historiography*

The significant contribution of Professor D.H.Th. Vollenhoven of the Free University, Amsterdam, to the historiography of philosophy is practically unknown in America. This is especially unfortunate for the evangelical Christians here because Vollenhoven has much help to offer us in the studying and teaching of philosophy. To make him more than a name which rhymes with Dooyeweerd for those who read no Dutch, I should like to sketch briefly the basic idea of his method for writing the history of philosophy.

Working in terms of the Christian perspective developed by himself (*Calvinism and the Reformation of Philosophy*, 1932), Dooyeweerd (*Philosophy of the Law-Idea*, 1935), and subsequent Reformed scholars in the Netherlands, Vollenhoven let certain ideas guide his approach to the historiography of philosophy. (1) The philosophical analysis of every person is concerned with and bound by the same actual reality. Since (2) reality is actually the ordered work of the Creator-God, a world dominated in time by fallen humans, who along with their activity are able to be saved in Jesus Christ, therefore, (3) all philosophical theory in its analysis of reality cannot help assuming some kind of stand toward the crucial matters of the structure, Origin, troubled state, and meaning of everything together 'under the sun'. (4) In the stand that various philosophies take on these fundamental matters lies the key to a critical understanding and comparison of their various contributions to the analysis of reality.

As this working hypothesis was already beginning to order his judgements of the many philosophies under observation, Vollenhoven one day was struck by the similarities in certain conceptions of Eddington, Einstein, and Archimedes. Why were they so closely alike? Soon the idea occurred to him that maybe there were definite types of philosophical conceptions, certain systematic philosophical interpretations of reality, which kept recurring throughout the history of thought. Vollenhoven went to find out empirically. So as not to get caught in the Hegelian trap of reading modern concepts and subsequent developments of thought back into earlier history, Vollenhoven began his investigation at the simple beginnings of early Greek philosophy. What do these pre-Socratic philosophers analyse reality to be? Naturally he ordered

---

*First published in *Journal of the American Scientific Affiliation* 12:3 (September 1960), 87–9.

what he found an individual philosopher had to say around what that philosopher said concerning the structure, Origin, troubled state, and meaning of reality; for these matters – this is the thesis hidden in Vollenhoven's working hypothesis – constitute the crux of a philosophy.

Two things gradually developed from Vollenhoven's pre-Socratic studies: (1) the main categories he has used to expound and judge Greek and all subsequent philosophy of Western civilisation; and (2) unmistakable evidence that there are a number of basic philosophical positions which have won adherents generation after generation since the very beginnings of philosophical reflection.

One carefully defined category Vollenhoven works with is 'Monism' and 'Dualism'. He discovered that these pagan, pre-Christian philosophers always eventually decided that reality was basically One or basically Two: one world, one stuff, or one pair of contrasts – in which diversity had to be explained; or at bottom two worlds, two stuffs, or two initially separate and independent realms – whose connection had to be explained. And he found that this decided Monism or Dualism of a philosophy determined to a surprising extent what kind of cosmology, anthropology, and theory of knowledge developed. This sounds somewhat like William James who said that if you know whether a person is a Monist or a Pluralist, you probably know more about the rest of his or her opinions than if you classify a person any other way. But Vollenhoven's 'Monism' and 'Dualism' penetrate much deeper than James' loose pragmatic ideas of the one and the many, mere mathematical analogies in social intercourse. To hold to Monism or Dualism, explains Vollenhoven, is to hold a distorted view of reality. How so? Since these Greek philosophers did not know the faithful Creator-God, who rules the universe by the law of God's sovereign will, and since Jesus Christ in whom everything created must live and move and have its meaning was not known to them, these Greek philosophers (who by nature were also inescapably and restlessly religious creatures) sought the origin and meaning of things within the cosmic structure of reality – which cosmic structure their observation could not escape. But because they sought and found within created reality what is not actually there, these Greek pre-Christian philosophers distorted the very cosmic reality they were trying to observe. Invariably they absolutised some part or aspect of created reality and made it the permanent Origin which gave meaning to all life and thought; and just as invariably, that part or aspect of created reality which did not get absolutised became disqualified and was considered the troubling factor to life and thought, i.e. something evil. The Dualists, for example, idolised a divine spirit realm of transcendence and lamented any captivity to the non-transcendent material realm, while Monists, for example, found their fragile cosmos constantly threatened with chaos by antagonistic higher and lower forces within one world. And such a pagan schizo-fragmentised reality plagued Greek anthropology and theory of knowledge no less severely than Greek cosmology.

Vollenhoven's speciality is showing from the texts that a given monistic or dualistic philosophy occurs again and again throughout all history, sometimes due to the direct influence of one thinker upon another, sometimes arrived at independently a hundred years later, always modified by the peculiar personality of the new thinker and the changed spirit of a later era, but at bottom the same old attempted monistic or dualistic philosophical interpretation of reality. For example, the materialistic Monism of Thales is a philosophical position essentially held by Leucippus and Democritus, Aristippus, Epicurus, Lucretius, and others all the way down to Gassendi and Sartre.[1] Again, a certain severe dualistic habit of thought first simply developed by Xenophanes has been virtually shared by such varied thinkers as Parmenides, Marcion, Arnobius, William of Ockham, and Karl Marx. Before one protests such results – there are, of course, other carefully delineated monistic and dualistic lines of thought extant – let him examine the convincing evidence Vollenhoven has assembled.

Ueberweg (*History of Philosophy* , 1871) and other good historiographies of philosophy are mostly a series of responsible, incisive monographs. Windelband (*History of Philosophy*, 1893) indeed attempted to trace the relation, show the influence, and suggest the kinship of various philosophies; but, unfortunately he dealt principally with epistemological concepts, which are less basic to philosophies and are therefore less significant for their interrelation than the ontologies with which Vollenhoven works. In contrast, it seems to me that the terms Dooyeweerd uses in his historiography of philosophy – form–matter, nature–grace, nature–freedom – are more characteristic of a thinker's *Zeitgeist* than the peculiar systematic structure of his philosophical conception. The forte of Vollenhoven's method of writing the history of philosophy thus is this: the structural inheritance of a thinker is made embarrassingly clear upon laying bare his or her underlying position toward those few, crucial perennial problems of philosophy; and that same thinker's relation to contemporaries of different lines of thought can be shown precisely. Indeed, it can almost be graphically plotted.

As for the Christian shock in Vollenhoven's thorough method? His point is that without the forming light of God's Word-Revelation upon a person's philosophical conception, that person's philosophy always has and necessarily shall miss the glories of creation and distort reality into one of various reasonable ways. Also, Christian philosophers who seek to mediate and accommodate

---

[1] It is impossible to go into the complex qualifications which would do justice to the richness and circumspection of Vollenhoven's historiographical analysis. Also, the temporary misjudgement of a certain thinker's thought would not invalidate the worth of Vollenhoven's method.

themselves to one or another of these distorted interpretations of reality must settle for a Christianised distortion and forfeit the insights and praise that a philosophy shaped and re-formed by revealed Truth affords. For example, evangelicals who profess to hold to a 'contingent dualism' must face up to the possibility that they may be somewhere in the traditional, orthodox Roman Thomistic line of thought, where God gets pulled down into people's theoretical patterning of reality and where created reality itself is distorted into the ambiguously begrudged 'material matters' below 'the finer things in life'. Such is the exact and critical historical consciousness Vollenhoven's historiography fosters.

6 A Christian Tin-Can Theory of the Human Creature*

Now is a good time for scientists who profess that their life-consciousness is gripped by the Good News for modern people to exhibit a conception of the human creature that is really new instead of just a reshuffling of old ideas, replete with pagan dilemmas and dead ends. By 'new' I mean a conception of man and woman that rings an exciting bell of blessings for theoretical analysis and professional praxis rather than frustrations: a conception that straightens us out, the psalmists would say, and affords a prophetic integration of how we do things in the laboratory, at home, in our hobby, as student, citizen or whatever. We need to have the presence of the Lord biblically embedded in our understanding of humanity, or we have sold out on our Christian birthright, no matter how often we import God into the environs of human nature afterwards.

With these foolish, brave words I mean to say that committed evangelicals who have grit to their faith would do well to shuck the age-old belief in body and mind, or the formulation that says body, soul and spirit is the composition of a person. To think that a human is an embodied soul, or an animated corpse, or a rational animal with a heaven-bound spirit, or some other stock combination of a soul and a body, frustrates scientific analysis of humans; it is contrary to experienced fact, and is unsupported by the scriptural givens. Many secular scholars, dissatisfied with the honky-tonk, commercialistic exploitation of men and women in our society, predicated on a materialist design, are also looking for some new thing on the nature of the human today. Maybe we can help them if we truly do have a new, that is, a biblically fresh vision.

Psychosomatic effects and Christian theology

Everybody knows, of course, that so-called psychosomatic disorders have been a reality long before the invisible industrial management strain, or before the invisible university professorial and administrative tensions produced visible

---

*First published in *Journal of the American Scientific Affiliation* 33 (June 1981), 74–81, based on an address given at the 25th Annual Convention of the American Scientific Affiliation, Bethel College, Minnesota, in August 1970.

ulcers that can be cut and bleed. But trying to analyse psychosomatic troubles with the neat, theological categories of body, soul and mind, inherited from Plato, does not work well. Even a faculty psychology, pendent from the Aristotelian–Galenic view of the human as having a vegetative soul, sensitive soul, and superimposed rational soul giving distinctive form to the material body, is inadequate, like trying to engineer a space shot with Ptolemaic astronomy.

Recognition of the reality of subconscious processes in human makeup has also demonstrated how artificial and scientifically impotent the traditional, church-sanctioned, dichotomistic anthropologies are. And the pressing need for a reformation of mind or soul–body problematics can be clearly seen in the quandary of modern psychiatry. Psychiatry has done everything from boring a hole through your skull to giving you a soft soapy talk while reclining on a couch, in its effort to get an analytic, scientific, therapeutic finger on the desires and pains, ideas and values swelling through human behaviour. Psychiatric methods have been dangerously blowing in the wind, says zoologist von Bertalanffy, because the fundamental, apriori framework with which modern psychiatry approaches the human is uncertain or askew – something no amount of data research can make good (*The Mind–Body Problem*, p. 30).

It is right at this point, I believe, that Christian philosophy should minister to specialised scientists, but not with a learned rehearsal of philosophical conceptions of people from Anaximander to Jean-Paul Sartre, nor with a cavalier dismissal of those 25 centuries as a nightmare of pseudo-problems from which linguistic analysis shall save us. Needed instead is an encyclopaedic conception of the human which gently sacrifices that sacred cow of 'the (substantial) soul' inside a person's body without defacing the person into a molecular combination of physique and biosensitive operations with epiphenomenal values rotating around like electrons. To study a person as a physical phenomenon is a gross inhumanity; it is like observing a water drop form in a person's eye and say 'she leaks', instead of 'she cries' (de Boer, p. 10). But what has passed for non-naturalistic, 'Christian' reflection on human nature – whether in its Augustinian, meso-Platonic, freewill hassle of a person, or in the scholastic, intellectualistic version canonised by Thomas Aquinas – such reflections on human nature, have been, in my judgement, ersatz Christian and a stumbling-block for down-to-earth Christian scientific analysis. Our Christian conception of the human must feature the peculiar richness of a person's God-responsive creaturehood while accounting for what meets the daily eye, and not yoke exacting, first-hand examination of a person with other-worldly, dogmatic baggage.

I do not wish to take the time to berate medieval theology for the fix we Christians are in, but theology that has not minded its own theological business, deepening our confessional life with insights proper to that facet of our interwoven existence, has always tyrannised other responsible, Christian reflection. The Roman curialists learned their lesson with Galileo and never put Darwin's writings on the Index, but evangelical theology has by and large not had the benefit of that historic training. Even today, conservative theological pamphlets flood the market with judgements on the age of the earth that make Christian geologists squirm. However, all that concerns me now regarding man and woman is this: it does not make good sense to theorise backwards from a supposedly known *post mortem* condition of humans (about which Scripture tells us passing little), extrapolate logically back from existence-after-death to the now for determining how a person must be found constituted. Such theological dictation is particularly egregious when it is so uncritical of its conceptual debt to a tradition of Orphic cult, Pythagorean mystique and Plato's *Phaedo*, especially if it misuses the Bible as a text-book source precluding direct investigation. The Scriptures – Calvin said it right (*Institutes*: 1,vi,1) – are the glasses *through* which, for example, we can look anew at human nature.

A Christian philosophical conception of a human being

I sketch here what might be the basic elements in a Christian philosophical conception of a human being. I shall call it the tin-can theory of woman and man.

A leitmotif through my presentation is this, that each human creature is only one, a whole one. All special scientists – biologists, physicists, psychologists, sociologists, linguists, economists, ethicists, logicians, aestheticians, mathematicians, theologians, political scientists – each may take out their particular microscope to get a bead on a man or woman, but you may not, like the proverbial blind persons feeling the elephant, think you have the whole picture when you have a hold of the trunk or the tail, its leg or the hide. Scientists must beware of the temptation to parcel a person into pieces, even only as a working method, for such a working method really presumes that the human creature is a synthesis of separate, functional compartments. Because a man or a woman is one, single, whole creature, it is the philosophical task to establish an overview, interdependently with findings of the special sciences.

Christian philosophy is not theology in non-ecclesiastic dress. Christian philosophy is philosophy: a systematic, synoptic analysis of things which focuses on their interrelational meaning. Like every science, philosophy too has a theoretical character; it abstracts to get at the law-side of things, i.e. philosophy tries to approximate the structure of what holds for certain things and their functionings. Christian philosophy tries to grasp the structural contours which hold for a person, in such a way that the truth of Psalm 8 – 'you have made them almost like a god' – gets obediently and fruitfully, however fallibly, disclosed in quite earthy terms.

A basic philosophical assumption: individuality-structure

A fundamental, cosmological assumption I make is the thinghood of whatever is extant. Individuality, for me, is not a guilty philosophical problem until proved innocent; but the individuality-structured way we are constantly confronted I unquestioningly and happily acknowledge as a creational given. Our God-ordered universe is a population of various kinds of concrete, individuality-structured things – that is how God set it up. To be created means to be a cosmically ordered, irreducibly different, definite individual thing, one identifiable and re-identifiable thing among other comparable entities. Intrinsic to every creature or creational item is an enduring identity which bears a certain typifying and foundational closure to its singular configuration, which is established and maintained only by the fiat of God Almighty.

This confession on individuality-structure will sound to someone raised on Hume like a *deus ex machina* bow to convention, unworthy of philosophic tough-mindedness. But I would persist, because the idea of thinghood not only explicates an important dimension of what creaturely, created existence actually means but the philosophical idea of thinghood also corroborates our ordinary experience with an antinomy-free simplicity unknown to the old substance-philosophy accounts of individuation and individual permanence. Sophisticated attempts like that of Russell who, correctly avoiding substance, tries to explain away a-piece-of-matter as a string of physical events linked together – especially when that scientistic shredding of things is given general application (Russell, pp. 243–8) – always strikes me as some sort of *homo ex machina* solution, because sooner or later, unless you evasively beg the question, either *Bewusstsein überhaupt* (consciousness-in-general), 'a single unified spatio-temporal system' or some other demythologised god of Humanism rears its head to guarantee what is a daily occurrence and a normal assumption – the individuality-structured thinghood of whatever is here or there and everywhere around.

More than two decades ago, the noted Oxford scholar P.F. Strawson, in his painstaking study entitled *Individuals*, stated clearly that a general philosophical justification intending to solve the 'problem of other minds' is impossible to give; in fact, even the demand for a solution to the problem cannot be coherently stated (Strawson, p. 112). If he had remained consequent with that confession, his book would have had a shocking character similar to walking outside the walls of the university in emperor's clothes. But, while disclaiming any proof-making, Strawson still argues, and argues persuasively, that material bodies are the indubitable basic particulars and the concept of person has a primitiveness which simply must be admitted because our language, the conceptual scheme we as a matter of fact do have of physical things and other persons, calls for it and operates that way (Strawson, pp. 53–8, 110–13). Because Strawson wants to affirm the reality of individuals whose identity is

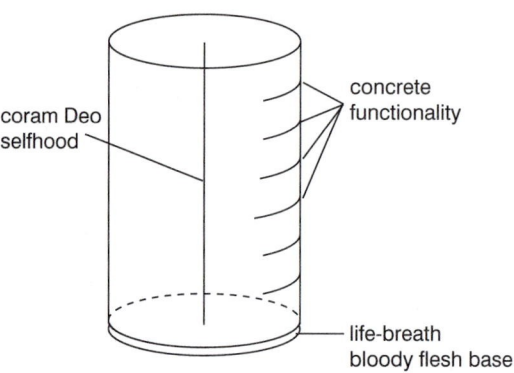

Figure 1 A tin-can model of woman or man

more than a numerical or qualitative or monadic type-individual identity, one that can withstand change of place and time (Strawson, pp. 32–4,125,131–4), and yet because he is unwilling to profess it as a pre-philosophical assumption, Strawson courageously (his reticent Kantian back to the wall, so to speak) goes ahead and 'makes a case for it', with as much pseudonymic distance as possible, in an essay of descriptive (only 'descriptive'! he says) metaphysics.

The predicament of this keen thinker, along with others, makes very convincing to me the fact that this lasting uninterchangeable identity of one thing or another remains unapproachable to theoretical analysis. Individuality-structure is a given initially accepted or initially denied by philosophical theory and subsequent investigation. Our everyday experience of the macro world attests to its existence, I think, as a basic ordinance of reality – this is what Strawson is trying to work off of and something the Gestalt psychologists latched onto – that we normally perceive things first-off as whole configurations and fairly certainly recognise in a naive way whether it is the same one, an identical one or a different thing. (The micro particles of physics need special attention because sub-molecular physical entities, as largely theoretical constructs, have an identifiability-dependence upon the entire abstractive, scientised condition and lack the concrete, independent character of macro things. It is very important right here not to give scientific *experiment*, if I may coin a word, primacy over ordinary experience as to which points to the primary order of created reality.) But the fact that we normally prehend macro objects as identifiable wholes does not *prove* an individuality-structured setup to a sceptic who simply disbelieves it, anymore than the fact that we see the sun disappear and that it is the evening and morning of a new day witnesses to the secularist that our Lord is the faithful Creator.

Many more observations and qualifications must be made, of course, about 'things'. A blade of grass or the wind, a crow or my neighbour is never known disconnectedly as a completely separate, singular entity. But every thing is always like a thread on the loom whose warp and woof of quantity, extension, gravitational forces, energy, growth, sensibility, formativity, style, significance, conceptualisation, use, and still more features as properties or latent qualities, totally enmesh the thing. Individual things also only exist as members of a kind; it is one of the plants or animals (despite the invisible crossover line), the inanimate physico-chemical kingdom, the human race, or angel creatures. Everybody knows that each thing within animalkind, for example, falls into a subgrouping dependent upon a common genetic or internal morphological structuration. Further, most macro things, despite their integral simplicity, have other individualities complexly interwoven within their wholeness, like the heart, lungs and stomach, for example, of a squirrel. But the original, whole thing is more than the sum of its internal organs, skin and nervous system, for their subordinated role is defined by the thing's singular configuration. Ordinary experience, it seems to me, bears that out again: a squirrel that has just been shot is not conceived of as a ruptured brain, collapsed lungs, stilled heart with four feet and punctured fur, but is taken to be a whole, dying squirrel. To notice, accept, and assume the enduring oneness of individuality-structuration does not mean you think every thing is blankly simple.

So the fundamental, cosmological assumption I make – which is the cornerstone for my tin-can theory of woman and man – is that individuality-structure is an ontic given holding for creation. The multiple functions of an individual thing are indeed present and can be differentiated, and the whole complex, integral, concrete thing is certainly open to development, deterioration and proliferation; but the identifiable, single prime which undergoes all such change and eludes theoretical determination is simply a structural creational given. Every attempt to locate that irrefragable oneness of a thing in some mysterious, hidden focus as a tension of functions (as Monism does) or to pinpoint it as the relation of parts (as Dualism does – as if a relation could be prime!) is going to lose the configured wholeness of a blade of grass, the planet or a squirrel. And then you have lost a lot. Because that leading idea of individuality-structure catches most perceptively the import of the biblically revealed truth of creation in that the very singularity of the thing, as well as its whole relative, temporal existence, is utterly and thoroughly dependent upon the creative-sustaining Logos of God who cares for it directly, whether it be sparrow, hair on your head, lily of the valley, or zygote.

The skeleton of a Christian philosophical anthropology

Few people on the street deny thing-character to subhuman existents, that a rock, tree or an animal is of one piece. But it is with woman and man that especially Christians on the street have balked. There seems to be more to woman and man than meets the eye, and the 'more' to humans is usually thought to be more than something like the back side of a box in one's visual field. There is something special, different, 'spiritual' in the human creature.

I should like to disarm the man on the street or the woman in the home with the fact that woman or man is a creature, and as creature woman or man is a temporal, identifiable, individuality-structured thing. A human creature is also of a piece, whose single existence manifests itself in all sorts of ways – a person is so big, with such a shape, moves, has weighted mass, breathes, feels, forms, can play imaginatively, talks, thinks, socialises, saves possessions and spends them, fights, loves, prays – all these ways of concrete existence, which constitute the person's corporeality, are all manifestations of the one same, individual subject. A woman or man is a single, full-bodied, tin-can functioning unit, a prime individual thing grounded with physico-organic functionings and qualified by selfhood. Every constitutive factor of this configuration, including its bloody-fleshly base, is human only as and because of the integrally constituted, inseparably bound-together nature of the whole self-dimensional structure.

The normal features, as well as the selfhooded peculiarity, deserve emphasis. The person has a this-one nature and an unbroken fabric of concrete corporeal existence simply by being a created individuality-structured creature.

Again, the unrepeatable singularity of a given person cannot be scientifically established. Characterological studies may pinpoint persistent act-features; handwriting experts (presumably) identify a definite and recurring temperament; autobiographies get written, and good old fingerprints seem to approach documenting that woman and man exist one for one, an unquestionably individual creation. But at rock bottom you have to believe that the fellow who has put on 20 pounds, divorced his wife, gotten false teeth and learned Swahili ten years later, is still the same person. Actually the impenetrable mystery of the gift of individuality is guaranteed surely and only by biblical revelation – even beyond the eschaton (cf. 1 Corinthians 15:38).

As to the seamless unity of a woman or man's many-sided activity, much could be said. One crucial matter is this, that a human's energy, metabolic processes, desires, ability to control things, attempts to imagine things, communicate verbally, think, and other distinct functions are not to be understood as 'faculties', some sort of autonomous powers which she or he has corralled and tries to keep in subjugated order. No, all the discernible ways humans can act are the very defining, cosmic, operating order of reality which each then as an individuality-structured entity enjoys. These ways of being-there in God's world which a woman or man bodies forth are facets of God's ordinances for all kinds of things, their existential reality. And the full-bodying tin-can human breathes, feels, opens a door, thinks, and does all the rest, not as if these were ontologically separate compartments one 'participates' in; but all the many mutually irreducible ways in which a woman or man functions are interpenetrating, intra-related moments of his or her concrete existence. For example, there is power not only in a fist action but also reverberating within a person's desires and speech and loyalties. While a woman's feelings are not her thinkings, there is always emotional content inside thought, and there is a creational pressure to have emotions thoughtful. There are analogies of vitality in activity beyond one's muscles, in a woman or man's conversation, occupational routines or church life. And there are elements of economy anticipated in one's physical acts, aesthetic response, and social relations. In fact, this tin-can solid, this cohering pattern of ordered, enduring activities is the proper meaning of corporeality.

That is an important point, because centuries of Western intellectualism have reduced the conception of corporeal and body to the cussed abstraction of 'matter', to what is hard, intractible, this physical hulk about us, and pointedly disparaged it as animal baggage, but much too real for comfort. And that web of misconceptions has played havoc with our reflection on the human creature's created glory and over-all cohering reality. Any concrete durable act of a person, I would maintain, is bodily expression – human speech, insinuation, penetrating reflection, are all corporeal acts. Words and thoughts kill as surely as rocks and bullets; a brick wall indeed stops a truck, but I have seen parental emotional upbringing stop a twenty-year-old more permanently in his tracks than any brick wall. Nicodemian scientists must learn that while poisons can end a person's breathing and brain waves, certain secular ideas can finish off a woman or man completely for good, as the New Testament puts it, when the Lord punishes him or her both 'body and soul' in hell (Matthew 10:28). That is, the whole gamut of a person's concrete action should be designated corporeal. The functioning tin-can person is a body. A woman or man is not incarnate, as if like Christ once was not yet human there is a human substance possibly not yet fleshed out concretely. If a person be incarnate, where does the 'carnage' begin? with his or her speech? craft ability? feelings? or only physique? Where does a woman or man's 'body' stop and start? Is the promise of a love-act or sentencing one to jail, so that the other winces or knows joy, less corporeal, less bodily an action than bleeding or falling down a flight of stairs?

Do not misunderstand me. Because angels are as real as cement I am not saying prayers are like digestion and toothaches are mental. Only this: the whole blanket of activities, all the ways a person is in concrete action is him or her bodily, corporeally there. And there are no second-class citizens in kinds of human activity. There is, to be sure, an order of conditioning: when push comes to shove, organic health gives psychic life stability; good psychic integration certainly strengthens analytic development, and if psychic life is disturbed, it quickly shows up in malfunctioning social intercourse and frequently blocks confessional activity; a measure of technical competence is prerequisite for all forms of art, language, science, and societal leadership. And discovering the interlocking order and dynamic of support and enrichment among the complicated ways a woman or man functions has important implications for education. Physico-organic functioning also has special foundational character; it is the life-breath base of a woman or man that God gives and God takes away. As underpinnings, then, such bio-physical, bloody-fleshly functioning grounds the other activities, not as some 'primary stuff' they shape and direct, nor as a set of neurophysical processes that maintain an isomorphic correspondence with the more cultural workings, but just as the founding, undergirding element needed, given by God, cohering in structuration with selfhood, to constitute a living, human individuality-structured creature. A person is not an animated corpse anymore than he or she is an embodied spirit: woman or man is a self-hooded thing with physico-organic base. (Once God pulls that physico-organic rug out from underneath you, so to speak, your natural given time is up and that human one goes to be with the Lord or to hell, says Scripture. The left-overs or remains in this aeon are not human, not part or piece of a woman or man; although the remains are often the *object* of human devotion and distinguishable for a time from a carcass, the remains of an animal, relatively soon the corpse shows it is but dust left.)

What makes *this whole* creaturely *thing* a *human* individuality-structured existent, what makes us people men and women rather than male and female animals, is this: we are built selfhoodedly open, and ready to be receivers of God's Word. Men and women are religious creatures: individuality-structured entities called to act out the self-conscious (communal-conscious) office of being *coram Deo*, serving lords of the universe. Peculiar to a woman or man's existence is that the whole richly concrete corporeality a human is has a thrusted bent to it. That person's existence is thrusted, innerly focused and intrinsically referential of all one does and means toward the true or some pretended Absolute Origin: that is woman or man's being in the image of God. All human's bear God's image. The worshipping-dependent, structural peculiarity of human creatures remains intact and is not annihilated by sin. Unbelievers betray the *imago Dei* by their restlessness, which leads to their distraction and eventual damnation. Manly and womanly believers, sinning saints, witness to their thrusted nature, glory in it, as they reflect and reveal God's ordinances.

The crux of my position is that the selfhood, the concentrated heart-specialness of a woman or man is not a separable from the body, the human's concrete functioning, nor is selfhood independent from being the lever-window-focal point of woman or man moved by *sarx* or the Holy Spirit. Selfhood or 'heart' or 'soul' is the unconscious structural opening-gateway thrust of a person's inescapable relation to God under the Word-command, 'Love me above all. Praise!' This is why I use the tin-can metaphor to describe woman or man. What defines a person is not an entity inside the person but is the structured thrust of the whole, as invisible yet as all-determining and as inseparable as the axis of a cylinder. A tin can (cylinder) also has the graphic, humbling connotations that may stop us women and men from thinking more highly of ourselves, as earthen vessels, than we ought to think.

It is the structural before-God position that provides a sense-of-self to human activity, i.e. a sense of a concentration point below consciousness which makes all one's operation personal. A person acts personally, intentionally toward things in reality and realises such intention by active deed. Such built-in, reflexive act-character adds the dimension of shame to a person's life – animals do not blush and are never naked – so that this monitoring tête-à-tête reservoir of silence in one's own preconsciousness (conscience = knowing with) is an important and delicate feature colouring all human doings. This inner room for embarrassment can be a hidden check to avoid what ruins one's self. This selfhooded preconscious depth is also able to be corrupted by false guilt-feelings or secularly defaced and levelled out so it is virtually inoperative, defacing the three-dimensional richness of human existence into a one-dimensional creature easily programmed for direct reactions to stimuli. But this creational sense-of-self in women and men is one important reason why human sexual relations can never be animalistic: they can be debased, wedlocked, full of joy or orgiastic, but they are always human.

Humankind in community

Integrally interwoven with the self-act-structure of a person is one's being a fellow-creature. *Mitsein*, a being bound together with other selves in society, neighbourhooded, is what characterises humankind alone. This non-genetic, interpersonal bond of communal consciousness is a given for every member of the human race because by its very creaturely specialness every human creature stands directly under the same central command of 'Love God above all and your neighbour as yourself.' Men and women who still exist in the first Adam experience this innate, neighbourhooded given as a societal burden or make of it a distorted ideal: those who live in the second Adam accept it gratefully as a task within which we are called to be patient and gracious good Samaritans.

Sin

No understanding of woman or man is biblically Christian and complete without also showing how the reality of sin fits into the picture. Animals are not sinners, but individuality-structured humans are. Sin is not an animal-bestial lower roughness in humans needing to be rationally overcome. Sin is also not simply devilish control of human nature. Since Adam's fall, I believe, sin is a fully congenital human condition. Sin is not due to our creaturely temporality. It is also not a passing functional state of affairs, although it shows up functionally. As a sinful religious creature, a person is foolishly in proud, idolatrous rebellion against God. Sin is the whole-hearted, turned-in-upon-itself direction of religious humans (pride) and the rooting of oneself in creation at large or in one's own self (idolatry), which is unlawful ground for ontic rootage, usurping God's prerogative of being the jealous Absolute Origin and Direction-giver for existential human meaning.

Despite ignorance or sincere intentions, if one does not keep God Almighty's Love-command, that person is breaking it and is therefore ignoring or violating God's central directive. While sinful, woman or man does not stop being woman or man, does not lose religious selfhood, does not lose touch with the world, but he or she does ironically deprive the self of its ground for being there. This apostate orientation also threatens the human creature with meaninglessness and the riddle of a disintegrating cosmos, since the focal point – the God-focused, viceregent calling to creaturely lordship in Jesus Christ – is lost. Sinful humans lose themselves by depending upon and giving total allegiance to creaturely things or creaturely activity, like science, for example.

One may be saved from this condition *in* time, through the work of the Holy Spirit, by being made a member of the body of Christ which is historically busy, in fear and trembling joy, to reconcile affairs of the whole world back to God, keeping the Lord's Word for all reality, since all creaturely reality was made by God and through God and for God. The heart of Christians is wholly turned, away from selfish-centredness, converted, transplanted and set in Christ; but the concrete reforming of their bodily acts takes time and often comes on inconsistently wagging its tail of sanctified feelings, skills, holy imagination, language, scientific analysis and societal relations behind.

The whole person

The fact that such a constellation of philosophical anthropological ideas together recognise the persistent unity and identity of the whole person defined *coram Deo* in history on earth is what marks them as biblically Christian. Traditional philosophical anthropologies have been unbiblical in so far as they misconceived the spirituality (the structural, to-God's-Word response-ability relatedness) and corporeality (multi-sorted ways of concrete action) of the human creature and theoretically abstracted and hypostatised spirituality into a spiritual part (a substantial soul) and corporeality into a somewhat begrudged, that-too, material part (a body one has for a while). Such God-neglecting analysis, begun by pagan thinkers who explained humans *per se*, has been largely accommodated rather than critically reformed by Christian theoretical thinkers; the synthetic Christian, conceptual result has usually defined a person *in se* and added a relation of one to God or Jesus Christ. Secular thinkers by and large define a person *pro se*, and then have the problem of what to do with our selves. But the to-God-relatedness is what defines people, and only this idea of *coram Deo* structural centring, I think, has the ontological wherewithal to stop the theory of woman and man from losing the unity and identity of the human creature as only one whole woman or man whose total corporeality must be directly obedient to the Lord, rather than letting him or her be fractured off into pieces where, for example, one talks about being a Christian *and* an athlete, or a Christian *and* a scientist.

Implied reorientation for theory of knowledge

Let me give one brief hint of the kind of reform a Christian tin-can philosophical anthropology entails, for example, in the theory of knowledge. Every special scientist, as well as artists and every thoughtful person busy in daily life, works with a stance on knowledge. Most unchristian theories of knowledge infecting the cultural air we breathe assume a dichotomistic anthropology or a reductive one, and have impoverished and warped our knowledge of knowledge.

I have presented an idea of woman and man as a self-hooded, flesh-and-bloodily based, individuality-structured creature operating within all kinds of God's creational ordinances, a creature who is a sinful, neighbourhooded, religious woman or man belonging to the body of Christ or who is a card-carrying member of the *civitates mundi* which is passing away. As historically developing human creatures, we whole humans are aware of other knowable, similarly cosmonomically ordered creatures, whether human, animal, plant, stone, artefact, or whatever. But most unchristian theories of knowledge assume a different setup than tin-can communions of humans in touch with other whole creatures.

The basic outline which unchristian theories of knowledge approximate, in several variants, assumes that there is a low-down sensing body either mysteriously linked or tenuously joined with a purely mental, thinking apparatus, and this localised combination is confronted by a bump-into-able world of stuff that can be weighed, measured, pin-pointed and double checked. In addition to such bump-into-able facts in the world there may also be abstract ideas called values, which at least some people consider important.

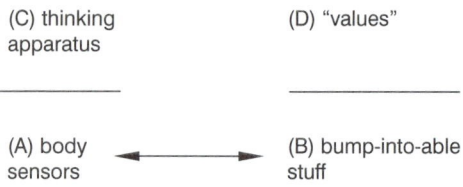

Figure 2 An unchristian theory of knowledge

There are many lengthy disputes as to exactly how these factors jibe to produce valid knowledge. Does (C) or (B) initiate the process? How do (A) and (C) interact? Can (D) be proved if (A) or (C) is the last court of appeal? But my point here is that the whole setup is humpty-dumpty awry. Because of the partitioned human nature and the split world assumed, knowledge conceived within this unchristian setup has no intrinsic responsibility to be God-obedient, or to be interrelated with other kinds of knowing acts, or to be aware of its historical datedness. The split mind/body, thinking-camera model of registering facts and maybe affirming values has to import history and personal human responsibility and God-relatedness *afterwards*; it also neglects kinds of knowing that don't fit these two sorts, 'sensing' and 'thinking'.

The tin-can vision of woman and man, however, begins by assuming that our human consciousness of other things is a self-reflective field of depth-awareness that is simultaneously subjective, multifaceted, variously normed, and called to bring about Christ's Rule in history. From the tin-can perspective human knowing is always full-fledged bodily human action. That holds for human thinking and human sensing too – they are intrinsically subjective, relative to moments of guessing, mistaking, pain and even hoping, called to be holy (cf. Philippians 1:9) and called to be true, that is, called to be full of compassionate wisdom (cf. John 16:13).[1]

Even scientific knowing, which is an important, controlled modification of everyday knowing, takes place in the same setting and is liable to the same basic conditions and norms, because scientific knowing is also human knowing. The peculiar x-ray problematising of creaturely things into fields of specific functions which special scientific scrutiny effects must be judged not only by the standard of accuracy but also by the norm of correct relatedness to other knowledge and to whether the scientific comprehension fills out the Truth

---

[1]One of the first projects needing attention in a theory of knowledge working out of the viewpoint of a Christian tin-can, philosophical anthropology would be making a case for the interdependent existence, validity and richness of other kinds of human knowing, such as the hunch, or an imaginative grasp of things, of the kind of deliberative weighing of political intangibles we call prudence – all of which are not reducible to either 'sensing' or (pure) 'thinking'. Cf. my essay on 'The Fundamental Importance of Imaginativity Within Schooling' in *Rainbows for the Fallen World*.

itself. A tin-can philosophical anthropology, which will develop its own kind of scientifically precise knowledge, can be of service to Christian special scientists and help them find ways to couch their accurate psychological, biological or physiological points within a limiting and directing network of knowledge such that the specialised results give body to Christ's lordship of the world. If one's special scientific knowledge is not itself philosophically integrated with an anthropological vision that is true to our whole, tin-can status directly before God, no amount of prayer or church attendance or theological piety afterwards can make it Christian scientific knowledge acceptable to the Lord.

Conclusion

Medieval Christians usually allegorised nature into an earthly fact with a correspondingly heavenly meaning. We evangelical Christians have often pushed the biblical faith we hold into our professional scientific acts in the same easy, bloodless way. But such an atrabilious approach to creation – especially if one is treating the human creature scientifically, trying to fashion a philosophical anthropology – underrates the creaturely object examined (for creation is revelation!) and overrates the scientific analyst into a type of God-discerner of meaning (who may postulate 'spiritual truths' on top of 'the facts'). If we could but begin to see woman or man as a tin can for whom Christ died – Christ did not die to save soul-pieces for a post-mortem existence – then we can begin to catch the full meaning of 'the resurrection of the body', when the Lord comes again, and begin to track down the implications of 'sanctification of us bodies' now, reconciling *all* we bodily are, including the most professional scientific knowing, quietly into Christ's service.

Bibliography

Baker, Herschel. *The Image of Man*. New York: Harper & Row Torchbook, 1947/1961.

Barrett, William. 'Negation, Finitude, and the Nature of Man', in *Irrational Man*. Garden City: Doubleday, 1958, pp. 251–61.

Berkouwer, G.C. *The Image of God*. Grand Rapids: Eerdmans, 1957/1962.

Boliek, Lynn. *The Resurrection of the Flesh: A study of a confessional phrase*. Grand Rapids: Eerdmans, 1962.

Calvin, John. *Institutes of the Christian Religion*, trans. Ford Lewis Battles. Philadelphia: Westminster Press, 1960.

Cullmann, Oscar. *Immortality of the Soul or Resurrection of the Dead? The Witness of the New Testament*. London: Epworth Press, 1958.

de Boer, Theo. *Wijsbegeerte en Wetenschap omtrent de Mens*. Free University of Amsterdam: Philosophical Institute, 1968, 16pp. mimeograph.

de Graaff, Arnold. 'Towards a New Anthropological Model', in J. Kraay and A. Tol (eds.), *Hearing and Doing: Philosophical Essays Dedicated to H. Evan Runner.* Toronto: Wedge, 1979, pp. 97–118.

Dooyeweerd, Herman. 'The Idea of Individuality-structure and the Thomist concept of Substance', in *Philosophia Reformata* 8 (1943), 65–99; 9 (1944), 141; 10 (1945), 25–48; 11 (1946), 22–52.

—. 'De leer van de mens in de wijsbegeerte der wetsidee [32 propositions on theory of man], in *Correspondentie bladen van de Vereniging voor Calvinistische Wijsbegeerte* 7 (1942), 134–43.

—. 'What is Man?' in *In the Twilight of Western Thought.* Nutley, New Jersey: Craig Press, 1960/1965, pp. 173–95.

Eichrodt, Walther. *Man in the Old Testament*, trans. K. and R. Gregor Smith. London: SCM, 1951.

Hook, Sidney (ed). *Dimensions of Mind: a symposium.* London: Collier, 1960.

Huber, Max. *Mensch und Tier: Biblische Betrachtungen.* Zürich: Schulthess, 1951.

Jeeves, Malcolm A. *The Scientific Enterprise and Christian Faith.* Downers Grove: Inter-Varsity Press, 1969.

Jeremias, Joachim. 'I Corinthians 15:50', *New Testament Studies* 2 (1956), 151–9.

Kummel, Werner Georg. *Das Bild des Menschen im Neuen Testament.* Zürich: Zwingli-Verlag, 1948.

MacKay, Donald M. 'Man as a Mechanism', in idem (ed.), *Christianity in a Mechanistic Universe and Other Essays.* London: Inter-Varsity Fellowship, 1965, pp. 51–69.

Morris, Desmond. *The Naked Ape: a Zoologist's Study of the Human Animal.* New York: McGraw-Hill, 1967.

Nicholls, William (ed.) *Conflicting Images of Man.* New York: Seabury Press, 1966.

Platt, Jorn R. (ed.) *New Views of the Nature of Man.* University of Chicago Press, 1965.

Russell, Bertrand. *The Analysis of Matter.* London: George Allen & Unwin, 1927/1959.

Seerveld, Calvin. *Cultural Objectives for the Christian Teacher.* Seattle: Pacific Northwest Christian Teachers Association, 1966.

—. 'Gone with the Resurrection', *Christianity Today* 2 (31 March 1958), 11–13.

—. 'The Meaning of Silence', *International Reformed Bulletin* 10: 3 (July 1967), 6–19.

—. *Rainbows for the Fallen World.* Toronto: Tuppence Press, 1980.

—. Review of L. Verduin, *Somewhat Less than God: the Biblical View of Man*, in *Christian Scholar's Review* 1: (Fall 1970), 78–80.

Strawson, P.F. *Individuals: an Essay in Descriptive Metaphysics.* London: Methuen, 1959.

Van Peursen, C.A. *Lichaam–ziel–geest.* Utrecht: Erven J. Bijleveld, 1961.

Vollenhoven, D.H.Th. 'Het geloof, zijn aard, zijn structuur en zijn waarde voor de wetenschap', in *Levensbeschouwing en levenshouding van de academicus.* Utrecht–Nijmegen: n.v. Dekker & Van de Vegt, 1950, pp. 71–7.

von Bertalanffy, Ludwig. 'The Mind–Body Problem: a New View', *Psychosomatic Medicine* 26: (1964), 21–45.

—. 'Mind and Body Re-examined', *Journal of Humanistic Psychology* 6 (Fall 1966), 113–38.

Part 3

Education

1 What Makes a College Christian?*

Maybe you know Kafka's story in which a man picks his solitary way past rubble and scorched earth until he encounters a huge deserted apartment building. He enters a door, hesitates, then climbs a cement staircase high up into the building. And up there somewhere he stumbles upon a long corridor down which he begins to poke his way wonderingly. A chance premonition makes him turn off into a room, a little bathroom. And there, lo and behold! a fellow sitting on the sink, hunched over a pole, fishing in the bathtub filled with water. The visitor looks the situation over carefully and finally dares to say, 'You're not going to catch any fish in there.' And the other fellow says back, 'I know it' – and continues his fishing.

Kafka's story of the defiant bathtub fisherman is a keen analysis, it seems to me, of contemporary education without Jesus Christ. A difference between Kafka's post-war European university and the secular twentieth-century American college may well be that the Americans are still expecting to catch fish, but the story holds.

Facing the real issues

And now a question. What is a Christian to do about it? Shake one's head, smile, and wander off out to where there is some fundamentally fresh air and flowers? Or, like a liberal hail–fellow–well–met, pull out one's fishing tackle and sit down beside the man, letting one's own line dangle dialectically in his tub, too? What is a Christian college? A separate, specially built bathtub stocked beforehand with approved edible fishes, so that Christian education becomes one big sanctified fish fry?

We Christians, I think, would be much less timid about what we are doing educationally if we had a clearly developed understanding of what a Christian college is, what spirit must drive it on, and exactly what is going on in academic America today.

---

*First published in *Christianity Today* 7:23 (30 August 1963), 1103–05.

On church-relatedness

A church-related college is not necessarily a Christian college. Many private American colleges today are church-related simply because some devoted clergymen started them in the nineteenth century, and the historical relation has been maintained because the church, like a distant rich uncle, puts up the desperately needed money in the spring of the year – provided that the Bible department hasn't gotten too far out of line and any student immorality has been kept out of the headlines. Moreover, if a church has betrayed its centuries-old Christian confessions, the fact that the college is 'church-related' means little.

If 'church-related' means that the college is church-dominated, and the church be orthodoxly sound, then you may have the machinery for a Christian college. But is it the church's business to run a college? The church may give birth to centres of advanced scientific study and prop those young institutions up like saplings during their infancy; it has done so, thank God. Because a college is not a church, however, some of us contend that it is a mistake to subject one to the other, that is, to let one kind of social structure dominate the internal workings of another kind of institution. Whenever that happens, both become denatured. That is why some Christian 'colleges' actively dominated by a church are not so much colleges as lay seminaries, restricting themselves predominantly to the church-like business of mission, ministry, youth-work training, with nary a major in sociology, French, or mathematics; and denominations running a full-fledged college today soon, if they lack the worldly-wise Romanist restraint of watchdog control, find themselves with a million-dollar building programme on their hands for dormitories, science buildings, and gymnasia – a rather devilish distraction from the church's first love, the pastoral care of its many members and preaching the Gospel.

Sincere subscription by the faculty to certain theological dicta, and a measure of honest piety and prescribed morality among the student body – if you will not misunderstand me – even these pearls of great price do not yet make a college biblically Christian in its workings. I have no patience with existentialistic quibblers unwilling to pin themselves down to confessional standards; and the anomaly of 'required chapel' and proscribed liquor is no laughing matter, because those regulations are at least hard-headed attempts to meet terribly basic problems. But we evangelicals must resist the temptation to rest our case for Christian college education on the Christian environment we maintain, for it is full of holes. My church has long had an unwritten rule against attending the movie theatre, and then television came in the back door – *fait accompli*. Prohibition of the modern social dance on campus – rightly so – has not stopped students from petting indiscriminately in the dark.

Yet it is especially for our Bible-believing creeds and signal virtues that unbelievers know us and defer. We are law-abiding citizens, a credit to any community, minding our own religious business; thank you for letting us shine 'this little light of mine' on our 25–50–200 acres. Why, we wouldn't hurt a fly. But maybe biblical Christians should be hurting flies, should be training to stand up even to dragons without apology but with the flaming sword of the spirit – demythologised dragons like the Russian bear – and if need be, to a new kind of American centaur with elephantine hide and donkey's head. The most impeccable 'Christian' college will always be something of a tatterdemalion. What shall it profit us if the secular world comes to esteem us for our inoffensive, genteel behaviour? For the sake of our suffering Lord, we should perhaps cultivate less pacific qualities, those with more biblical grit and Wesleyan vigour.

The learning process

So, you say, if church-relatedness and moral perfection do not make a college distinctively Christian, what does? The living presence of the Holy Spirit in the very matter that makes a college a college – *what goes on between a teacher and student.*

Strip away all the fringe benefits of a contemporary American liberal arts college – not co-eds necessarily, but choirs, clubs, and college publications, if they are not made academic disciplines: the core of a college is still its *wissenschaftlich* educating action. That is its reason for being. A college is not a Robert Shaw Chorale, Rotary Club, newspaper business, or convalescent home. A college is that intimate association of a professionally competent, practising investigator in a certain field with a young inquiring follower, who together, really communally together, leading and questioning, searching and finding, take some aspect of God's world, however small – atom, irregular verb, or the nuance of

> idle as a painted ship
> Upon a painted ocean

– and examine it until its meaning is discovered. Education, I dare say, is basically learning to make distinctions, uncovering and interrelating the meanings of different things. If education takes place it will involve a communal examination of created reality in which some new understanding of its nature and workings is born.

God or an idol

And this is the Christian insight on education: that such examination and its results take place inescapably within the framework of a dynamic religious perspective. By 'religion' I do not mean the Christian faith, Sabbath consecration, or moral acts in general. By religion I mean that inescapable, structural God-relatedness of humans, that deep-down unconscious bent of being dependent upon some Absolute that every person has, that *sensus deitatis* (sense of deity), the directedness of one's self toward the true God or toward whatever one takes to be divine, final. By 'perspective' I mean focus, the simply lived-out, expressed, or carefully articulated hanging-togetherness of a sane person's thought, word, and deed. So I assert as a biblical position that whether a person eat or drink or abstain or study, whatever he or she does issues either from a heart committed to the true and jealous God Almighty revealed in Jesus Christ through the Scriptures or from a heart attached to some temporal idol, whether bacchanalian or as sophisticated as Reason. As Deuteronomy 30 puts it: human action is on the road of life and blessing or on the road to death and a curse: choose whom you will serve!

To realise that the delicate, triggering process of education is the working out of one's religion, that learning is full-fledged worship of God or denial of God, that the fine sifting and fallibly deciding that 'this theory is so, and that problem is false, and the other clue is worth pursuing' is all couched in and simultaneously giving body to one's stand toward God or against God – to realise all this is altogether sobering, and exhilarating! Because where two, teacher and student, are gathered together in Christ's name, there God's Spirit is. So the teacher's fear and trembling at what rests so trustingly in his or her hands need not be a Kierkegaardian agony: it can be an overflowing rush of hope that, despite the blind mistakes and shortcomings, out of this work something glorious may come – their growing in the fear of the Lord, because the Spirit is nearby, blessing. Only that – a teacher and student in the very activity of learning growing in the fear of the Lord – only that makes a college Christian. All else is vanity.

It takes more than devout Christians to make a Christian college. The free gift of God's grace and the play of the Holy Spirit inside *wissenschaftlich* investigation are needed to establish it.

2 A Reformed Christian College*

Students and Friends of Trinity College,

We are gathered together to consider what lies before us and to ask help from God who is Almighty. Our meeting here is not just a formality, but in the overwhelming presence of angels and demons and the Lord of these hosts, we are pressed now at the beginning to declare ourselves and make our communal vow, as it were, promptly and sincerely. For if we would expect Almighty God to keep blessing us few people in what we are trying to do, there must be no mistake about where we stand and what Spirit drives us on. It is within this context that I am glad to take up the faculty's mandate to greet you all at this second convocation of Trinity Christian College.

This is the second convocation. This means that the opening of a Reformed Christian college in the Chicago area is starting to become a regular occurrence, an annual ordinary affair. For many of you it is still a first, something extraordinary, new, alive with the exciting unknown; but after the shine of the day has worn off, things hereabouts will strike up a rhythm that turns the strangeness to you too into the ordinary. This very ordinariness of our second and continued assemblage, the very ordinariness soon of our daily operation again is what those hard-headed and tough-hearted parents of yours who had the vision to initiate the Trinity movement hoped and prayed and worked for. We who are now to enjoy such marvellously ordinary activity must get the eyes to see the glory of the Lord in the commonplaces around us and must also call up the stamina and imagination to develop the trust given us if we would keep the faith of our parents and keep it alive. What that trust is – and it involves student as well as professor – I should like to try to delineate again at this second convocation. That is, I propose to sketch very simply the contours of Trinity Christian College and then say briefly and quite bluntly for what the faculty has called you together.

College

Trinity is a Christian college. That means, for example, it is not a high school. At a high school, where everybody has to go, I am told that the teachers lead

---

*Second convocation address at Trinity Christian College, Palos Heights, Illinois, 12 September 1960.

Plate 10 Seerveld teaching philosophy in the basement at Trinity Christian
College, Palos Heights, Illinois, 1959

the students to water and try to make them drink. I am also told that there
always are a lot of horses that simply will not drink water. And this recalci-
trancy obstructs the other horses' drinking and tyrannises the horse master
who is hired to make all the horses drink. At Trinity College, where not everybody has to go, the horses are led to water but not forced to drink. The professors are so busy drinking themselves, protecting and encouraging those

trying to drink, they have no time to bother with the others who stay high and dry on the river-bank wanting merely, as the expression goes, to horse around. At a college, these animals are put out to pasture, without water.

As a college then, Trinity is not an advanced high school; the whole sphere, structure and attack is different. The college is a centre for scientific studies. By 'scientific' I mean investigation, searching investigation which aims at depth and precision, the concentrated attempts to grapple with a problem, whether it be chemical, literary or whatever, grapple with it until you have analysed it, related it to other knowledge and come up with a simple, hard-won contribution of your own. College is only the beginning of such study, but it is the beginnings of such serious, exacting investigation which assumes both dedicated determination and this, that the elementary matters of the subject at hand have been learned. Old and New Testament studies at college do not repeat Bible stories and rehearse catechism but assume that knowledge and build enriching theological research upon it. Historiographical studies at college do not drum on dates, data and anecdotes, but assume some grasp of chronology and retention of events so that the probing interpretation and critical relation of key persons and historical movements can be begun. College study depends upon the completion of high-school work and does not, cannot prolong it and stay college.

It may be that there always will be a couple of skeletons in the college closets, certain elementary work that creeps in for college credit, like review of English grammar, beginning German and Dutch. But – I think this may be on public record – Trinity College intends to start college English with American Literature, German studies with the classical authors, and intends to do this on the shoulders of nearby Christian secondary education which with its new curricular studies is fighting for the wherewithal to upgrade and solidify the quality of basic work done there. For Trinity College to do less, to let the temporary skeletons in its closets become permanent fixtures, would be for Trinity College to forfeit its right to be.

Christian college

Further, Trinity Christian College is not a professional or semi-technical vocational school sometimes graced with the name of Junior college. Trinity Christian College does not specialise in turning out engineers, businesspeople and schoolteachers; it is not geared to the student's learning a trade, making money or becoming stop-gap aid to primary education; Trinity does not aim at being 'practical'. If this is hard to understand, it is because it is hard to understand that people do not live by bread alone. While technically trained engineers, business administrators and schoolteachers will incidentally be coming out of Trinity, that is not what we are after, that is not for what Trinity was established. And do not be fooled. No institution of learning can itself in two or four years make you into a schoolteacher any more than it can make you into a businessperson or an engineer. It can give you the meat to grind and the know-how of the machinery, but the making of teachers, business-people and engineers is done on location in the press of life – something which academic college training by definition is not and cannot be without annihilating its collegiate character.

To say that collegiate activity, the programme of Trinity, is not 'practical' does not mean it is impractical anymore than not to live by bread alone means you must live without bread. The point is simply this: at Trinity Christian College you do not learn to bake bread, however useful and expedient and proper learning to bake and make your daily bread may be. Trinity is not a centre of practising for paying professions. It is a centre of scientific, that is, theoretical studies, a centre of Christian theoretical studies which serve not to supplant or extenuate the daily workaday life of a person but to deepen, inten-sify and brighten it, whatever it be, with the glory of the Lord.

Now it is precisely this last, the central thrust of Trinity Christian College which sets it off from the usual run of the Middle-West liberal arts colleges. We too are so-called liberal arts minded in that, of the several basic kinds of studies required here, no one of them is permitted a preponderance over the others; *belles–lettres*, biology, Greek, history are all considered equally impor-tant, integral factors of a liberally rounded college education. Despite the runaway success of Russian technology, for example, Trinity will not join the wide-spread attempts to out-Russian the Russians by overbalancing the cur-riculum with mathematics, physics and technological studies; such a pragmatic manoeuvre might get a person on the moon but it is still narrow-minded, il-liberal education. In so far as Trinity does not overbalance the curriculum with 'hard science', Trinity is a liberal arts college. But we are not liberal arts minded into thinking that study of language, chemistry, literature, philosophy – the liberal arts – will liberate one from ignorance, prejudices and a humdrum mentality, as the credo goes; we do not believe that application to the famous trinity of the Good, the True and the Beautiful will set one free, create a higher type of individual able to change society and relieve the world of its ills.

The stand of Trinity Christian College is rather this: we study everything because people do live by every word that proceeds from the mouth of God, and since God has spoken and speaks here, there, everywhere in the world and its development, God's sustained creation. It is a person's privilege, it is God's command to those who are qualified, to search through all the areas of cre-ation and all the varied aspects of human activity – nothing of God's play-ground is off limit – it is our task to seek out everywhere the wonders of God

Almighty's work and enjoy the discoveries with childlike surprise day in and day out forever. This burden is light. Further, the stand of Trinity Christian College is this: all the arts and sciences and theoretical studies of creation disclose the handiwork of our Triune God when the languages of these varied and complex fields are heard and seen by biblically honed ears and eyes. Thus, in the time-consuming job of learning these special languages of God's creation and of training the eyes and ears, unless the professor and student get to see the handiwork of God, unless professor and student grow in the fear and adoration of the Triune God, realising more intimately that Jehovah covenant God does hold all things in God's hand, that all things were created by Jesus Christ, that it is indeed the Holy Spirit who leads into all Truth, unless professor and student grow in this scintillating awareness, grow in grace, the diligent pursuit of knowledge and wisdom is in vain no matter what gets done, whether we learn to speak with the brilliant tongues of orators and angels and throw a satellite halfway to heaven, it is still a meaningless, Towering Babel and clanging cymbals, it is empty, vanity.

This stand is very sober, severe, Calvinistic. It is also the rationale and strength of Trinity Christian College. It is our trust and birthright. If Trinity Christian College should ever fall for or accommodate itself to the truncated humanistic trinity which with its liberal arts simulates the Christian programme and gradually breeds a secular, worldly-wise sophistication and the unlovely mentality of more–educated–than–thou intellectualism, if this befalls the Christian college, then those hard-headed and tough-hearted parents who support this centre of theoretical studies by the sweat of their praxis will have the right to be disenchanted, for Trinity Christian College will have failed in its distinctive calling and we might as well go elsewhere.

Reformed Christian college

Please understand me well: this unrelenting Christian religious focus of every theoretical study here does not make Trinity education a pious powder-box affair of moralism and ill-timed devotionals. Dr Vander Vennen will not say everytime sodium chloride dissolves in water, 'You see, it was providential.' Prof. Musch will not say, '2 and 2 at this Christian college equals 4 plus.' Miss Bossenga will not say, 'All right, today we are going to cut up Christian frogs.' At the same time, never forget that simple classroom biology is always subtly couched in a God-fearing perspective or dominated by some god-less religious view such as the positivistic macro-evolutionary dogma; and if you think that graduate chemistry and higher mathematical theory has not long had its nature and tack set by a dehumanising and deterministic naturalism commitment which has finally exploded into a crisis, you have never heard of

127

Hiroshima. The problem is complex, yes, but the direction is clear: out of every college classroom study in this building – biology, chemistry, mathematics, philosophy, history, psychology, theology, literature, German, Latin, and if we taught Chinese you would hear it in Chinese – comes the quietly moving, almost unobtrusive, subconscious but strong, pulsating song, 'This is our Father's world ... we are here for Jesus' sake ... come, Holy Spirit, with all your quickening powers.'

Because every faculty member here present today is of one mind on this, wholeheartedly dedicated to the Reformed Christian philosophy of education, Trinity packs a drive and power few American institutions can know. Here there is a scrupulous tenacity to get every particular matter right and master it thoroughly, for if you misread the psychology or physiology of humankind you miss glories of God, and if you leave grammar shoddy, in a sense, it is indeed the King's English you are mutilating. Here at Trinity also is a singular intramural communication and rapport among the different branches of study, because each faculty member is jealous for his or her own discipline yet fascinated by the other fields, thankful for their enriching complementation and correction, happy that he or she does not bear the brunt of having to say it all, secure in the realisation that all of his or her colleagues, in their own ways, are trying to project the same total picture at which he or she is working. This invigorating, concerted study of the faculty which works its way down to the students too is not just an *esprit de corps* on the campus, not even just plain communion of the saints, but is the full-fledged, peculiarly Reformational reality of the Christian community in collegiate action. Trinity Christian College is only as big as a mustard seed but it is a live fragment of the *civitas Dei,* and that will be the secret of whatever impact Trinity makes as a Reformed Christian centre of scientific studies upon its surroundings.

The wise people who first conceived Trinity's curriculum decided to make explicit what lay implicit in its peculiarly Reformational nature. They made philosophy and history requirements of freshman and sophomore studies along with biblical theology, composition and American literature. Maybe you wonder why?

Theological study makes immediate sense, for it drives one persistently back to the biblical source of our inspiration and what more effective plan could be devised for supra-denominational ecumenical consolidation than careful examination of the historic creeds of the Protestant Reformation. As for literature in one's native tongue: there is probably no better, less technical way to point out to apprentices the glories of God in creation than to have them read quality poetry and prose, for poets and prose writers sensitively re-present the world around them and cannot help but uncover glories, Christian or no, even though those without Christian humility look so closely and stare so intently they are blinded.

But philosophy? Philosophy has always been a joke or had a bad name outside the little circle of its devotees with pipes and severe brows: philosophers look up at the stars and fall in wells, busily try to find black cats in dark rooms that are not there. Study philosophy, has long gone the feeling among evangelical Christians, and you will lose your faith. These reactions, unfortunately, have generally been correct. By and large philosophy has been speculative, eccentric, out of touch with down-to-earth reality; and whenever a lonely Christian did go off to the state university, the predominating pagan, scholastic or secular philosophy in which one steeped oneself often caught one and regularly distorted whatever biblical view of reality one may have had. That is why sturdy Roman Catholic institutions of learning to this day have theology on top ready to clamp down on philosophy whenever it reaches a certain point. That is also why evangelical Christians in the nineteenth century withdrew from intellectual pursuits or desperately tried to fight fire with fire, picked out the least offensive, most idealistic branch of philosophy and taught it as apologetics. The founders of Trinity Christian College, however, did not follow the Romanist way of theological domination and had no intention of being apologetic about philosophy, since the genius of the Reformation makes clear that even philosophy can be brought in subjection to Jesus Christ, and no one science, not even theology, may dictate to all the others, because it itself can be in error. The curators of the college asked for philosophy radically captive to Jesus Christ; they asked for critically Christian philosophical studies at the very core of the curriculum to put Reformed grit into the education and to fortify the tensile strength of the whole undertaking with its unifying, interrelating, reforming perspective. That is the kind of philosophy Trinity offers: not a strait-jacket of final answers but a probing introduction into the few crucial, fundamental questions of reality and an attempt to focus and translate into theory the Light which illuminates these basic problems; and that philosophical theory gets worked at not in a world-and-life-viewy way but systematically, scientifically, professionally trying to form a live body of thought that can be scrutinised, pruned and developed.

And history? Historiography then joins philosophy in a measured, critical examination of the roots and growth, troubles and glories of our civilisation. Together, history keeping philosophy's feet on the ground, they look at the major contributions of Athens and Rome before the shadow of a Cross brought consternation to the brilliant glare of intellect there. Historiography and philosophy together next go tangle with the monolithic medieval period, piecing out the little beginnings and sprawling dark ages which followed the Light of the resurrection. Finally, with sharpened analysis, philosophy and historiography lay bare the possible structural and existential living alternatives which face a person today, some variety of the fabulous humanistic Renaissance which swept from the streets of Florence up to the individualistic, relativistic, bloody alleys of the French Revolution and only now in the twentieth century seems to be losing its poise, or, on the other hand, part in a Reformation which takes sin, salvation and gratitude to Creator God so seriously and unambiguously that it maintains that not to humans but only to the jealous Triune God be glory and dominion, now and forever.

In other words, all this painstaking historical and philosophical study of centuries of world events, ideas, men and movements, is done here not for its own cultural sake but to make unmistakably, documentedly clear the basic religious struggle in the world to find meaning and the terrible meaninglessness of all directions outside Christ-centred endeavours. A sense of tradition, a sense of the biblical Christian tradition is what we are after, so that as a people we do not get lost like squatters in secular America, do not flirt with the perpetually accommodating Romanist line or succumb to the touchy pietistic Christian approach, but on the solid ground of Reformational Christianity, with a host of witnesses – Augustine, Luther, Holbein, Calvin, Bourgeois, Bach, Kuyper – we go out to attack and reform as a united body and build as a testimony to the Lord on earth a peculiarly powerful, contemporary, apocalyptic culture. All this searching and struggling investigation at Trinity Christian College within a scandalously open dedication to Jesus Christ is meant to leave those so trained impassioned for the concrete glory of God and unafraid, because they have been instilled with the fear of the Lord and given respect for a heritage of great price.

Paideia

The gist of the matter has been said. Trinity is a Reformed Christian College with philosophy and history serving as academic backbone to the Christ-committed training. This is the kind of institution to which the faculty now calls you as a student body. There remains just this: for what has the faculty called you together?

In Greek it is called *paideia*: disciplining, breeding, formation, unfolding, chastisement, nurture, *paideia*. Each professor wants to see the student find *paideia* in his or her classroom, but he or she cannot give it to the student. A habit of disciplined thought, a hammered-out decorum of Christian warmth, a chastised character, a competence to lead and follow intelligently, a perspective, *paideia* – for a student to get that takes time, and one has got to catch it oneself, unobtrusively like a case of poison ivy. If we teachers fail to communicate, if we fail to fire you with zeal for the calling – the Holy Spirit who broods around the corners and classrooms of Trinity College knows all of our shortcomings. After several weeks of faithful work, after a hard beaten semester or even a year on our part, maybe the Spirit will blow gently and a new look at things will come upon one here and one there, unawares, a vision of what we actually are doing, and there will be a rush of joy and determination in the hard work, a sudden thankful gladness that you are busy about your Father's business. That is *paideia kuriou,* the fear of the Lord, and it is that for which the faculty has called you together. If you fail to get *paideia,* if you fail to get educated, if you fail to become a genuine Christian student, we teachers fail too. A teacher is nothing without a student. You have got us there. We are in this affair together.

Conclusion

I conclude very simply. Trinity is a free college. It does not have the insurance, stability and rigidity of a state-controlled or church-controlled institution. We are free to develop or degenerate academically as the curators and faculty see fit; we are free to enlarge our vision or stiffen spiritually at the election of every trustee; we are free to flourish or flounder financially as God moves the hearts of the few people who know what is going on here. We are so freely, helplessly dependent upon the mercy, protection and guidance of God alone that it drives a person instinctively to one's knees – something truly Reformational. And now that the second year of Trinity Christian College has begun in all its desperately important ordinariness, we cannot turn back. Trinity is no American crash programme but a long-term investment of the Reformed faith, and we students and professors who stand here with the gifts, the promises, the trust, must trade the talents of the Master and bring increase: or it would have been better for us if Trinity had never been born.

Let us go then together to work it out with fear and trembling, vigour, sacrifice and joy, with one holy passion, secure in the knowledge that if we remain faithful to our calling, the Almighty One will supply our needs and send blessing till the LORD come.

3 In Quest of Excellence*

Part 1

> I pray this: may your love flow over into (your) knowledge, every perception, more and more, so that you may discern what is truly excellent (so that you may) be single-minded and beyond reproach until the Day of Christ, filled with just action by Jesus Christ for the glory and praise of God (Philippians 1:9–11).

Whenever on a Sunday morning you go sit down in a congregation of the saints and look around at the motley, quiet, and even night-clubbing-clad members of humanity of which you yourself may be one – obtuse, well-meaning, overfed, spiritually so homely – nevertheless, nevertheless! you can believe (help my unbelief) that what pulls each one there is more than his or her unlovely humanness; it is really God's Spirit; and that is why it is good to be there on a Sunday morning all together, with your weaknesses showing.

I wonder if somewhat the same holds for our convocation here – Christian schoolteachers are saints too – where one could probably look around and see elegance and ruin, advancement and heartaches showing through on people one once knew or even doesn't know (our desires are so transparent and the history of our sins works itself out with such alarming clarity into our idiosyncrasies): but what pulls us all here together? Is it Quest of Excellence?

As the flush of a new school-year wears off into the grim business of correcting papers and meeting PTA crises, to find out, to enjoy, to glory in what really binds us individuals together, one could do worse as saints than listen to Paul's prayer for the saints gathered at Philippi.

Implicit in Paul's words is critique of the Excellence of his day as not being truly excellent. Paul was captive in the Rome of Nero and Seneca, epitomes of the Roman brand of Epicureanism and Stoicism dominating the age. Roman millionaires were buying up the best Greek statuary with the wave of a hand. Grandiose, glittering, gross is what was approved and prized in Paul's day. Except, of course, by the philosophers, armchair prigs that they were. Excellence they sought, not in the solid material state, but in the contemplative life, safely raised high above the acute responsibility of effec-

---

*Address to the Midwestern Christian Teachers' Association, Chicago, published in *The Banner* 98:6–7 (8/15 February 1963).

tively shaping society from the dirty inside; so an effete, cynical moralism is all they could offer, ending in a kind of sour-grape consolation, even a half-oriental quietism.

All this the roving tent-maker and missionary Paul had in mind when he prayed for the Philippian saints. He knew that the Hellenistic Excellence was attractive, while decadent, and had stopped his listeners on the Acropolis short of the Christian dynamic; the Hellenists were too confident in their own struggles for glory and were simply so cosmopolitanly curious about new things that they could do no more than laugh when they were preached the central message of the Christian faith, Jesus Christ's resurrection from the dead, which demands a single-minded, earthy response from a person.

Did you know, historically soon after, notwithstanding Paul's caution, it was largely Christian schoolteachers who chose Greek Excellence as guideline and smuggled it into the church? The original Socratic–Platonic struggle to achieve what is superior, the fascination with a first-rate performance that bowls over the *hoi polloi*, the conviction that true knowledge, true virtue – knowing the difference between good and bad – upon which everything rests, is something within one's ability if one only undergoes professional training: these Greek themes were taken up by the Near-Eastern Christian Teachers' Association of Alexandria in the second and third centuries after Christ. The moral and mental Excellence every Christian needs depends on academic proficiency, said Clement and Origen in their Christian catechetical school, turning university; and we can promise you that Excellence, growth in grace, by virtue of study here.

What that Excellence and grace amounted to, because it was primarily pagan-conceived and man-made, can be seen in its more relaxed, modern counterpart, the Excellence and grace of the Gentleman produced by Cardinal Newman's university: pious insight and superb manners, a paragon of tolerant virtue, imaginative, modest, informed refinement *par excellence*. Only a tiny secular step away is Matthew Arnold's civilised Hellenist, the well-read disinterested commentator on reality who approaches everything with 'the tone of tentative inquiry'. And ever since Clement's *Stromateis,* this respectable, humanistic, ivy-league Excellence has plagued and undermined Christian education.

It would be a shame if this convention of Christian teachers were in quest of some such kind of Excellence, because our calling lies along different lines. Search out what is truly Excellent, says Paul, who disclaimed the use of any rhetoric, yet could quote Greek poets back into the face of his opponents. Find out in a given situation what's up, what really counts, and grab ahold of it boldly. Learn to recognise the crucial differences, the fine line between a lie and the truth, leisure and loafing, the wink of love and a lewd look. This is no prim call to academic perfection or a gentlemanlike morality: this is the religious matter of where you shall be found on the Last Day. Scrutinise everything, test even yourself whether you be in the faith, says Paul; get into the habit of recognising what pleases God so that you will not have to stumblebum along but can live singly, passionately, almost unconsciously pure in the grip of the Lord Jesus Christ.

Until you are actually gripped by the Holy Spirit, you cannot know what is truly Excellent. That is why the key word to Paul's prayer is Love: let this Love given you, driven into you by the Spirit, work itself out into your everyday knowing experience, every facet of sensitivity you have, so that you may confirm constantly, wisely, what is truly excellent from what is pseudo-excellent. That Love is no gentle, contented-cow type of sentiment which pacifically enables you to peruse alternatives unattachedly and then pick out one that strikes your sanctified fancy. That Love *(agape)* has a turbulent, spontaneous rush to it that makes a person give and withhold his or her whole self because it is a living attachment to the holy God and therefore involves an intense, jealous, excluding power of discrimination, such as Christ had, who lovingly prayed all night before He picked his twelve disciples, who lovingly cleansed the temple, took spit in the face, and went through hell for dirty, stupid people – that's Love. And that kind of Love, worked in our hearts, is the only source of understanding what is truly excellent.

This all has critical implications for us who are in quest of Excellence with our students. If the key to true knowledge is this exclusive Love, and our students get away from us chock-full of information, techniques, and maybe polish, without the key thing, have we not failed them as Christian teachers and broken covenant with their parents who trust, hope beyond hope, we shall be able to do for their children what they themselves find so difficult to do? I do not mean to support pietism's view that the mission of education is to make persons Christian. The Reformational position has it right: vigorously develop already given *Christian* joy and command of the world; and anything less than that is less than Christian education.

Successful education is not necessarily Christian. In fact, Success is the peculiar Excellence pushed hard nowadays by almost every secular educational salesman: my programmed learning kit and apparatuses work! My rapid-reading machine works! Our novel approach backed by two years statistical study with a Ford Foundation Grant works! So? The Russian educational system works too. *What* does it work in a child? Unqualified Success is no virtue; it could cover a multitude of sins … for a while. Given the broken nature of humans, I suspect that in every stunning success something of real value got lost in the process. And the intimate nature of Christian education – or is this in dispute? – must not get lost, must not be sacrificed to some hard-boiled success programme.

That is no invitation to go back to the Middle Ages, although there is not too much danger of that. Our danger is rather to buy a product without realising we may have also bought an Excellence foreign to the workings of our Lord. And if you get something askew and it works, you are really devastated. Unless we want simply all-American boys and girls coming out of the Christian school – we who seem to be a pivotal generation in that arm of the body of Christ dear to us, no longer hid from the world – we have got to test by the Love of Christ the spirit of the new directions overwhelming us, whether they be truly Excellent, and not be afraid to fashion our own new transforming methods.

Part 2

The most serious problem in Christian education comes perhaps from the inside. One of my college freshmen, graduated from the Christian-school system, blurted out last week in a moment of despair, 'God help you if you're just left with the faith you've got after you get out of high school!' That is a testimony to what Kierkegaard saw, that it is sometimes easier to become a Christian if you are not one than to become a Christian if you are one. It is also a testimony to the dearth among us of that consuming Love that drove Paul over the face of the earth and which is the only way to prime our students in understanding creation for the indispensable, enlightening breath of the Spirit.

It takes a kind of charismatic competence in one's field – it cannot be done by mere rote, example, or ability – to lead a student on in learning to discern for oneself what is truly Excellent. You know that is true from the great Christian teachers you have had, who gave you more than the discipline studied, whose vision got through to your heart, shaped it, and stayed long beyond the blue books. That holds even more subtly all the way down to kindergarten. And it is our reasonable service! Charismatic competence.

Not much can be said about competence. It is not something you search for like a Holy Grail: mastery of the ABCs of one's trade is something you painstakingly work out over the years. Pray God more administrators will grow the imagination to take promising raw material and make it competent. (Be practical: like giving bonus-paid, round-trip fares to Europe for summer study to get competent, enthusiastic language study down into the grades and cut out this time-wasting foreign-language grammar in later years. What a tremendous boost it would give to genuine scholarship!) And pray God the boards who have to make the hard decisions behind the scenes will develop more Christian backbone to draw a firm and freshening line on the simple matter of trading talents and the diverse gifts people have, because no sin hurts Christian education so much as the persistent incompetence of shoddy work or ability proudly misfitted to a task. It undermines, kills the whole glorious spirit of the undertaking, makes it a laughing-stock; and Christ's name must not be made a laughing-stock before unbelievers. Not much can be said about competence, as about hypocrisy, because we are all involved: yet the Lord will ask those who oversee others for an accounting of their superintendency too: shame to God's kingdom and not individual embarrassment will be the balance.

A little more can be said about the contagious zeal (zealot! why not?) built into genuine Christian teaching. This is the way to answer, I think, the usual sophisms on what's Christian about your German, maths, and physical education programme? Don't you learn *derdiedasdie*? You got a different multiplication table? Do your boys pray before their foul shots?

A Christian German teacher, by his or her very unspoken respect for his or her menial job as a holy calling to conquer that terrain thoroughly for the Lord, teaches *derdiedasdie* not as a language requirement, not as a step toward diplomatic rank, but as the beginning, the way to get inside Hitler, Marx, Goethe, Luther, which a person must do to give meaningful Christian leadership in a world with a *Deutschland über alles.* This *Gestalt,* showing through unobtrusively and therefore terribly effectively in one's teaching, makes it Christian. And it is not moralising theologisms about the harmony of numbers reflecting the beauty of God in late Pythagorean fashion which makes arithmetic Christian: in a crackerjack course in geometry – when it is made plain between the lines that mathematics is *not* the answer to the world's problems but is indeed one vital theoretical service among others available to open up creation's secrets quite concretely – then it makes important sense in a Christian curriculum. If this cannot be got across in the silence of a classroom, with chalk measuredly marking the board, we should honestly admit that this is one part of day and night free from sacredness and outside the domain of Christian education. (Maybe we could save parents some money!) You also do not need to visit a post-game locker room, win or lose, more than once to sense whether the coach has couched his boys' basketball training in a Christian perspective or not (as a rough bout in skill and endurance for the sheer fun of the struggle to win, or as this hard professionalism abusing the refs, keen to the heroic adulation).

Students catching discernment of what is truly Excellent from their teachers are the rationale of the Christian school. And if a teacher does not get it across, practise it in his or her field, the whole business is a farce as Christian education, something far worse than not professing it at all; because, if there is one thing that revolts students more than incompetence, it is hypocrisy, preaching without a fulfilling practice – even if they live that way themselves. And so they stumble.

That leads me to say something else. It is time, maybe imperative, for us teachers concertedly, wisely, slowly, lovingly, with our students, to re-examine, re-form some of our sacred cows, such as evolution, dirty literature, certain theological thought-clichés (more than language), because sacred cows, if left alone too long become white elephants — if you can take the mixed species. Nothing is beyond re-formation except the living Word of God. This is what makes Christian education so exciting: we are not a monastic retreat; we fight live issues, grapple with the all-important problems, put questions again to old answers, not to get lost in a permanent Socratic dialogue but to honestly, faithfully carry along to Christian commitment those students who are 'Christians'. If this requires adult education too, okay then, adult education too. We have become so scholastic, to be reforming almost seems heretical.

This does not mean we go get the cows for shock therapy! That is the temptation, with a compensating anti-provincial chip on your shoulder. Shock only belongs in the pulpit, kerygmatic shock. Would that our ministers used it more often! But teaching goes by trust, by patient, communal unfolding of the problems and ripening of the decisions, all done within the bounds of our fathers' *faith*. Such reforming Christian teaching is dangerous in an age of unbelief, of course; and the practical St James gives a heart-stopping warning in his third chapter: don't many of you become teachers, my brothers and sisters, because the teachers' final judgement is much more severe.

Protect us, Holy Spirit! But this is our prophetic calling. I think that is why it is a joy to be here together this morning; what pulls us close is the bond of our common prophetic office. Kings have power; they rule by law and the sword; they speak, and it is done. The priests have the protective mystery of the sacraments and receive their tithe. The prophets of the Old Testament walked barefoot in the dust, were lonely and jeered at by God's people as they tried to make God's Word known, to bring the very vision without which God's people perish (Proverbs 29:18).

This last prophetic office is peculiarly our office as Christian teachers, so that, after one has struggled alone for a while, got lost in the drudgeries and problems of his own little locale, become discouraged maybe at how regularly your mistakes hit you back in the face every exam period, there is comfort in coming together — not self-righteously to congratulate ourselves that there are at least 1200 who have not yet bowed the knee to Mammon (if you want to make five dollars an hour to fix somebody's plumbing, you should get into plumbing; we need good plumbing in God's kingdom too), but — prophet! receiving grace to mould the lives of other human beings! And for this, paid? The comfort in coming here together, despite all our weaknesses and pretensions, rests in hearing God's Word again, realising that there is more to this teaching business than us: the Lord has need of us, and we may expect great blessings if we are faithful.

I conclude with a story, as it were, about Excellence. You remember that singular scriptural account of trepidatious Balaam on his way to Moab, who beat his balky ass until God let it speak?

And the ass said, 'What did I ever do to you?'
And Balaam said, 'You have mocked me by blocking my direction.'
And the ass said, 'You have ridden me every day, have you not? Did I ever injure you?'
And Balaam said, 'No'; and then God opened Balaam's eyes so he saw the angel standing there with sword drawn.

You see, Christian teaching is not moral indoctrination; it is also not intellectual clarification: it is religiously protecting those who ride us daily from the Way of Death, prodding them with the kind of dumb, passionate, forgiving Love Paul prayed would well up out of the Philippian saints, protecting and prompting those who ride us, lovingly, until God lets them discover how to find the Way themselves.

Excellence that pleases God is not the best our hands can bring, sophisticated refinement, or practical success: God wants the stubborn, unconditional obedience of our hearts. The Excellence we Christian teachers seek is to serve in Love – like an ass, the least in God's kingdom – letting the Lord God who is near, and God alone, bring the increase.

4 Perspective for our Christian Colleges*

It would be wise for would-be Christian colleges everywhere to examine themselves whether they be in the Spirit of God or driven on by some unholy spirit. There is one unholy spirit which has captivated higher Christian education again and again, beginning with the Christian university of Alexandria in the second century AD: the appealing, respectable, vitiating spirit of Christian accommodation to the traditions of humans. I am not talking abstractions. This spiritual force caught me at college, and maybe it will catch you. It is the driving concern to combine Christianity with the best that has been said and thought in the world, the moving attempt to fuse into one grand product the Christian faith and centuries of general human culture. And this Catholic, synthesising spirit has a devastating influence upon a Christian education.

How so? This tempting, synthesising perspective tacitly assumes that broad areas of human achievement are a religious no-man's-land and thus can be safely tucked under an inviolate compartment of Christian truths which have the last word on supernatural questions. Synthesis presupposes a compartmentalisation of reality, and therefore in education works with the idea of certain naturalised, neutralised fields of learning, having kicked Christian faith in God upstairs to an honourable presidency; and it is precisely this built-in split, the kind of separation behind the combination, that deranges an education committed to having all knowledge integrated in Christ. No matter whether you patronisingly 'make room for faith', as Kant said, or give God, theology, and ethics a solidly papal, authoritarian position above subordinated 'natural' arts and sciences, the profaning damage is done to education: certain studies are conceived of secularly, as being extrinsic to religious commitment, while revealed truths and their human interpretations are elevated, isolated, and made over-rationally airtight.

Historically a willing Christian synthesis with 'good' ideas and products foreign to Jesus Christ has always led to a synthetic Christianity, the biblical Gospel adulterated. When Clement and Origen, sincerely seeking to raise their Christian catechetical school of the second and third centuries above the level of *sancta simplicitas* and to make it apologetically attractive for unbelieving

---

*First published in *Christianity Today* 7:24 (13 September 1963), 1169–71.

intellectuals, invoked the best of Greek philosophy as handmaiden, it was not long before the handmaiden took charge of the marriage; and the resulting gnostic philosophical theology plagued the church for ages with Platonism, Aristotelianism, and general humanistic intellectualism.

So today, when the spirit of accommodation to the traditions of humans infects a college (maybe when it grows big and successful?), you may expect (1) that the purity and power of God's Word will be compromised by the reflection done upon it, and (2) born out of the fascinating robbery of gold from the Egyptians – especially if no 'infallible' Roman church is present to draw the limits and curb the pride – will grow a vaunting intellectualism, an unlovely frontier of sophisticated élite, orthodox on demand, but proud of what a person by himself apart from Revelation can do.

Freedom with no compass

Another unholy spirit that creeps like Carl Sandburg's Chicago fog on cat feet over a Christian campus is the spirit of scientistic Modern Freedom. Conceived in Renaissance magic and anti-Scholastic science, this evil spiritual dynamic is frankly unbiblical and at heart revolutionary. It is our *Zeitgeist,* the contemporary *dunamis,* dynamite raging in the wind on all continents. Freedom to revolt! Freedom to be an existentialistic question mark. Freedom to sell your neighbour for scrap if it further the *Uebermensch.* Freedom to have a planned economy, planned marriage, planned birth, and planned euthanasia by 1984.

What is hard to understand is why those who live and move and have their being in the grip of such a spirit still wish sometimes to parade under the old opprobrium 'Christian'. If a church, if a college, if a person would really be free from nineteenth-century values, eighteenth-century hymns, seventeenth-century creeds, and the sixteenth-century rediscovery of a 2000-year-old book of maxims, myths, and local histories, for a twentieth-century unitarian pottage, why not let a first-century name go, too? Would it not be more honest, parasites? Or is it more dignified to let the Latin biblical mottoes engraved on the cornerstones, like old soldiers, just fade away?

Students, understandably impatient to be caught up in our vigorous world and its mad problems, check your angels before you drop the parental traces. With all your getting at college, get Wisdom – let Wisdom get you, because the seductive whirlwind of Modern Freedom is a strong, beating wind, and it is suicide. That is what Santayana – no Church Father but a reprobate sceptic – said before the First World War: Modernism is suicide for Christianity. 'It is the last of those concessions to the spirit of the world which half-believers and double-minded prophets have always been found making; but it is a mortal

Plate 11 Colleagues at a Wheaton Philosophy Conference, Illinois, 1968: (back row) John Vander Stelt, H. Evan Runner, Peter van Nuis, Bernard Zylstra; (centre row) John Van Dyk, Peter Steen; (front row) Richard Russell, Nicholas Van Til, Calvin Seerveld

concession. It concedes everything; for it concedes that everything in Christianity, as Christians hold it, is an illusion.'[1]

The re-forming spirit

What perspective now envelops a college filled with the Holy Spirit? Can one say, 'Here it is' or 'There it is' (Luke 17:20,21)? Shall not every designation fall prey to the factionalism of 'This is of Christ, and the other is of Apollo, of Cephas or Paul' (1 Corinthians 1:10–13)? We are under God's command to 'test all things and grab ahold of what is good' (1 Thessalónians 5:21), not so much an identification of the elusive way God works as a call to reconsecrate all hearts in the revealed, foolish Wisdom of our undivided Lord. Are the fruits of the Spirit unknowable in education? Would you know what spirit drives a teacher and student held in the biblical vision that all life is lived before

---

[1] *Winds of Doctrine* (New York: Harper Torchbook, 1957), p. 57.

Almighty God, all life is religion in operation, all life including study itself is to be *agape* for Christ in action?

To be holy is to be set apart for God. To make holy is to call out, to reform, joyously to present something specially for God. Those in whom the Holy Spirit dwells, saints, holy ones despite sin, will charismatically be busy sanctifying, like Midas transforming whatever they touch into (unlike Midas) living sacrifices to Creator God. At least this will be the calling they recognise, the grounding, pushing motive power to their work. And everything lies there to be set apart for God: sex, race, chemical reactions. In fact, every creation of God is good, says Paul to Timothy, not worthless if able to be received with thanksgiving, for it is made holy by the creative Word of God and prayer (1 Timothy 4:4). To saints the whole world is a sacred burning bush where God speaks marvellous things, to be enjoyed. But human acts and products, institutions and traditions which have trampled God's burning bush with their shoes on, twisted and profaned it, cannot be enjoyed by saints, not even tolerated as something 'secular' next to what is hallowed, for what cannot be received with outright glad thanksgiving must be either rejected or re-formed out of the grip of sin, made holy again for God. And I pray, says Paul, that your love for Christ may flow over into your knowledge, every perception, more and more, so that you may discern the differences between what is holy and unholy (Philippians 1:9,10).

This sharp double-edge of love for the Holy One, the passionate thrust of this re-forming spirit involves more than evangelical witness to the unsaved soul and renewal of a sagging church. Reformation is global in touch, that is, has intense concern for all creation groaning and labouring under sin, as Romans 8 has it, and understands as its reasonable service bringing *all* human activity subjected to the feet of Christ. Savonarola was not a reformer but a revivalist used mightily by God in fifteenth-century Florence to convict men of sin, to challenge the immoralities of Pope Alessandro VI, to get men to burn their paintings and quit godlessness. Like Savonarola Luther preached sin and salvation, stirred the self-indulgent to come alive in Christ; and he re-formed song – what a salvage *ad gloriam Dei!* John Calvin too brought God's open Word to bear upon more than the church in Geneva, disciplining, re-forming social, economic, aesthetic, and political life by the Word's directing norms. The most sacred profession a man can choose, says Calvin, is politics, to become a civil magistrate, an 'ordained minister of divine justice', directly under God's law protecting the poor, weak, and oppressed irrespective of their belief – this is truly holy work, governing the world as God's viceregent (*Institutes* IV.xx.4,6).

The only ungrudging rationale as well as the necessary, qualifying characteristic for a genuinely Christian, full-orbed college education, I think, is this re-forming spirit with its cosmic outreach for the love of Christ as Sovereign

Lord of the whole creation. Jesus himself asked no less of us. No one pours new wine into old wineskins, he said, for the new wine will burst the skins and seep away, and the skins will be worthless too; you ought to put new wine into new wineskins (Luke 5:37,38). We Christians have the new wine. What needs fashioning are the new wineskins for sex in psychology, for race in sociology; re-formed wineskins in chemistry, too – or did you think the hydrogen bomb is not evilly ingenious chemistry? Difficult, certainly, partly because, as Jesus said, no one who is drinking old wine wants new wine right away; he says, 'The old wine is good enough for me' (Luke 5:39). Yet teachers and students with whose spirits the Holy Spirit of God testifies (Romans 8:16), how can they not be driven to make all things holy, acceptable to God?

Something earth-shaking

I once heard Karl Barth say, 'The best apologetics is a strong dogmatics.' Or as Abraham Kuyper puts it: you forsake the richness of the Christian faith if all you do is saunter around in other people's gardens with scissors cutting off a piece here and a piece there to make your bouquet. For God's sake! grow your own flowers![2]

We Christians must not let contemporary unbelievers condition our culture; it is mistaken sympathy or policy or whatever to force our Christian insights, adjusted, down inside their confining vision. To trust too easily the glittering results of a disbelieving culture is to play the biblical fool. And being our neighbour's keeper, that is, being called to genuinely understand him or her, to live sensitive to his or her predicament, must not make us forget that we Christians have something earth-shaking and important to say ourselves, which needs painstaking development and careful application.

Besides, since the work we do is our Father's business, in covenant with God who blesses us to the third and fourth and hundredth generation, all the theories and products we develop must conform to biblical specifications, no matter the measure of the day. The vocation of God's people in education is to build a highway for our God straight out into the desert, through the wasteland and rubble, so that the glory of our Lord may be revealed. Christian college education is not missionary activity to the unsaved but a workshop where Christians trade on their talents to become worthy servants, administrators of the world to which their Lord will soon be returning. And this is what the heritage of us protesting Catholic, Reformational Christians has always witnessed to in art, science, and institutions; it is this God-oriented,

---

[2] Abraham Kuyper, *De Gemeene Gratie* (Kampen: J.H. Kok, n.d. [1902–05]), 4th edn, III, p. 527.

Holy Spirit-driven, Christ-focused study of the world and society at which we believers today, constantly re-forming, touchstoning to the biblical vision, are to be abuilding.

A Septuagint approach

Needed for the Septuagint approach of Christian education are at least, say, 72 scholars who with unbending rabbinic concentration upon the cast and purity and purpose of their message steadily work together at embodying it plastically for the faithful and the faithless to see and read as they run. The Septuagint approach breaks with the attractive but futile individualism of one Christian here and another there going off bravely to infiltrate the educating world. Education by its nature demands concentration. Christian education will flower only where the Spirit has hands and eyes and ears and feet – all kinds of specialists – who are competent (piety does not cover incompetence, whether it be the botched exegesis of a poem or a messy appendectomy) and united not only by a common faith and biblical commitment but also by their breathing excitedly and wholeheartedly this unifying, re-forming spirit I have mentioned. The weakness in Christian *educational* impact at a Christian educational institution comes from the wedges between albeit confessing Christians, the fact that every scholar does what seems right in his or her own evangelical eyes, because they lack this common sense of religious direction and academic attack aimed at holy scholarship. If the Christian college has as its task to praise God not only with hallelujahs but in the difficult, time-consuming construction of Christian social theories, a Christian aesthetic, mathematics that bears out its unique and limited theoretical service in the kingdom of God, it must have more than a single educator to accomplish this; a Christian college demands a single-minded (uni–versity), re-forming community of, say, 72 scholars.

Basic to such a programme, I think, is the orienting architectonic of an outspoken if soft-spoken Christian philosophy – not philosophy in the sense of lingual analysis nor the traditional Satan-spired philo–sophia (trying to know all things, like God) but a Christian philosophy that is born out of Solomon's God-fearing request, 'Give me, Lord, an understanding, discerning heart so that I may lead your people' (1 Kings 3:9) in politics, art, physics, and the rest. An articulated Christian philosophical systematics – not just a viewy Christian outlook but a *wissenschaftlich,* worked-out ordering and systematic analysis of the interrelated meanings of things – is a beginning for a working Septuagint concentration because it helps all the various sciences on their communal way. Maybe, if evangelical and Reformed scholars dug more into this kind of scandalous study instead of seeking a rapprochement with liberal

Christianity or taking dialectical fishing trips with secular scholarship for its kudos, maybe then the Lord would bless us in ways our little eyes of faith cannot even imagine seeing.

Let no one mistake Septuagint concentration for isolation. The offensive Christian *Gemeingut* (what we hold in common) which it is our burden to develop must be translated into terms understandable by the rest of the world. That involves our knowing their language and having carefully scrutinised what especially they are mistakenly getting at in God's world at the moment so that we can catch the locus of their problems and without self-righteousness bring our answers to their needs. The difficult business is to learn the language without accepting their *Problemstellung* in order to bring our strange news to each in his or her own technical tongue. Septuagint translation is not monologue any more than it is dialogue; translation is prologue really, prolegomena, what gets said before the other learns to read the text directly with open eyes. I mean that the Septuagint echo to the blues is not more blues turned sweet nor a Bach chorale today but Mahalia Jackson's 'I'm goin' to muv-up a littl' higher'; the Septuagint response to Tennessee Williams' *Baby Doll* is not a Hollywood-censored Samson and Delilah plus moralisms nor a silent censorship but maybe T. S. Eliot's *A Cocktail Party* or an updated *Scarlet Letter;* the Septuagint answer to lingualised analytic philosophy is not more analytic philosophy Christianisedly twisted onto problems of 'Grace' nor a nineteenth-century Hegelian idealism but a systematic investigation of created structures under God radically re-formed from the age-old traditions of humans, which fastens upon the positive analytics' little tempest with simple insight and then moves on to wrestle with more significant problems. I realise a twentieth-century Septuagint in most fields will sound to our contemporaries a little bit as Chaucer did to Francis Bacon, somewhat old-fashioned; but so far we can go, and then pray hard that the Holy Spirit will interpret those mumbled utterances to them.

5 Cultural Objectives for the Christian Teacher*

To begin, let me read you Psalm 148. This is the Word of God:

Hallelujah Yahweh!
Hallelujah Yahweh all the way down from heaven and all the way back.
All angels – all God's veteran angels, hallelujah the LORD!
Sun and Moon, hallelujah the LORD!
Every star alight, hallelujah the LORD!
Endless end of the sky and hidden reach of the oceans, hallelujah the LORD!

They shall hallelujah the name of the Lord, for
God commanded and they were created.
God set them up for ever.
God made them an ordinance which they do not overstep.

Hallelujah Yahweh every crack in the earth!
All you dragons, whirlpools and burning fires,
Hail, snow, and smoke,
Wind wedded to the storm blowing where God speaks,
You mountains and little hills everywhere,
All wild animals, all animals near the house,
You snakes and birds on the wing:

(Hallelujah the name of the LORD!)

Rulers and judges on the earth, every nation,
You young fellows, you young women,
The older ones with grey in the hair, and any children:

Let them hallelujah the name of Jehovah, because
Only God's name is to be praised.
God's glory soars beyond earth and heaven itself.

The Lord God will shoulder the weakness of God's people.
And God shall shore up praise for all God's lowly faithful ones,

---

*Extracts from a lecture given at the annual convention of the Christian Teachers' Association of the Pacific Northwest, Washington (October 1964). Published Seattle: Pacific Northwest Christian Teachers Association, 1966.

for the sons and daughters of Israel,
the folk that stay close to God.

Hallelujah! Yahweh!

That psalm puts in a nutshell the thrust of what I have to say to you: that a
man and woman, especially the folk that would stay close to the Lord, stand
under the imperative of God's Word to join the chorus of angels and dragons!
and gigantic cracks in the earth, to join all creation in praising God! that all
human life – young, old or child – in its cultivation of the world hallelujah
Jehovah, maker of heaven and earth.

To make that biblical perspective concrete we need to square ourselves
away, not too pedantically, on what is being talked about: what is creation?
human life? what is God like? i.e. what constitutes the teachers' theatre of
operation? What do you mean by 'cultural' objectives? And can you give some
biblical precision to talk about 'Christian' teachers?

The state of creation

'This is our Father's World' is no pious shibboleth to lull us comfortably to
sleep: it is a revelation (Psalm 24:1) that sets the stage and dynamic of all
history and human life. And the response Credo in *Deum Patrem omnipotentem
creatorem coeli et terrae* affirms as biblically believed, not arguable or proved, that
the world is the creation of Jesus Christ's *pantokrator* Father.

That matter of fact – creation – can really open up our eyes to the human
situation. The awful meaning of creation is that the created is limited, held by
the eternal God to being timed. Time defines the nature of creatureliness; time
is what things are really subject to and bound by, it is the basic 'stuff' of the
universe. 'All flesh is grass', timed: there lies bare creation's essential self-insufficiency and total dependence upon the Creator.

The heavens as well as the earth, whirlpools, wind and animals as well as
people and angels, everything is bounded, ordered, structured by the all-
encompassing ordinances of God and subjected to the Past–Present–Future
temper of this cosmic ordination set by God. This World-time is the God-
instituted and thus binding way in which things keep on functioning. To be
created means to last so long in such and such a way under God's direct care.
And the Past–Present–Future makeup of this timed ordination is not simply a
before and after measured by sun and stars but is rather the *eschaton*-oriented
and thus 'once-only' duration of all things where Past–Present–Future are ever
trinitarily extant: that rock gets old, that birds grow up, that a man and woman
mature – one is physically young only once, socially single only once (and for
so short a time in America), morally naive only once (here lodges the pain of

repented sin) – that creatures live and move and have their ordered meaning in an inescapably one-time development, this many-sided historical process is their temporality.

It is also important to notice what you may consider obvious but what has tremendous philosophical implications, also for our topic, that what God created is various kinds of concrete things. Taking our cue from Scripture one can say that God did not create matter, spirit, reason, substance, qualities and the like; God created different sorts of individual things – earth, grass, birds, fish, man and woman. To be created means to be an irreducibly different, definite individual thing, one identifiable creation among other comparable creations. Intrinsic to every created thing is an enduring identity of some kind or other whose singularity is established and maintained only by the fiat of God Almighty. Individuality too is utterly dependent upon the creative-sustaining Logos of God. So intimately concerned with the hairs of one's head, cups of cold water and birds on the wing is the Almighty Creator.

Further, every created thing is some how; no individual thing just is. Every thing operates in various mutually irreducible ways; e.g. a man is fat, sad, aloof, poor, forty and Christian Reformed (to be one is not to be another). In fact the many different ways in which individual creatures can operate are the moments of God's ordering, ordinated duration, time, which constantly and completely conditions, binds, defines all creations.

Unlike creation the Creator God is not timed; the LORD God is A and Ω, the Eternal One Divine; any talk about God in time categories is overreaching intellectualistic speculation. Does that mean then God is time-less? God is neither in time (with a history) nor time-less (foreign to time): God is Lord of time; God holds timed creation in the palm of God's hand. That is, God's relation to the ordered-enduring theatre of creations is that of *kairos*, of fixing, determining, fulfilling time. God does not fill time up ontically like water in a sponge (pantheistic immanence; cf. Augustine's *Confessions*) nor penetrate time just potentially (deistic transcendence with occasionalism). God began time, has hallowed time, and shall perfect time. Only in the mystery of Jesus Christ does God enter time as are we creations. Christ was both subject to creational ordering and its undisputed Lord, e.g. he was rocked restlessly asleep in the boat on the Sea of Galilee yet able to stand up and say, 'Stop! Be quiet!' Neither God the Father, Son nor Holy Spirit is in time somehow other than that the Triune God disposes time, takes time for the believer-elect, continually realises time, i.e., activates human redemption of time.

In other words God, who in unique eternality personally rules time, provides comprehensively, in a way incomprehensible to human thought, the setup and course of creation, all creatures and creations. God's awesome and gracious providence, called Providence by Reformed theologians, must not be speculatively analysed *sub specie aeternitatis* into some kind of Univac up there but kept in the comforting (cf. Belgic Confession XIII), demanding biblical focus of the Creator revealed in Jesus Christ who slowly is working out God's Will through creation.

We men and women, as temporal, cosmos-bound, individual creatures, have a special nature before the Eternal Almighty One. A person, says the Bible, is peculiarly fashioned in the image-likeness of God (Genesis 1:26–8). A person is not God's (graven) image; only Christ is God's spitting image: a person is *in* God's image. That means that a person is created structurally unlike all other creatures, that a person peculiarly bears the stamp 'Made in Heaven'. A person inescapably carries about with him or her the sense of divine Origin: one is dependent upon some Absolute, one is religious, a worshipping, fearful (under Law) self (un)conscious creature, one's being is ex-sistent, inner focused and intrinsically referential of all one does and means toward the true or some pre-tended Absolute Origin. That is a person's being in the image of God. All people bear God's image; this structural peculiarity of human creatures is not annihilated by sin: unbelievers betray the *imago Dei* in *simulacrum Dei*, a rest-less fake, to their distraction and eventual damnation; believers, sinning saints, witness to their religious nature, glory in it, reflecting and revealing the glory of God.

Now matters get more offensive: religious humankind timed in the hands of jealous Creator God. This perspective makes our teaching existence live, empty or significant, and the state of creation itself pregnant – honour and praise should get born. There is a delightful rush if not urgency to it all because the actual existential time of humankind is God-given. Everyone is living on borrowed time; there is only so much time to a person before he or she must pay up or shut up. In this deep sense the world, creation, creatures, men and women are made up of time: not that an individual thing dissolves into time, but that every created individual is defined by it. When you give another time wholeheartedly, it is your self you give. One's time is very pre-cious; love is spending your time with someone.

The time of all people and everything right now is *Anno Domini*; we are in the last days (*post mortem et resurrectionem Christi*), i.e. our aeon, as the Bible calls it, is the Age of Sunday. Whoever holds that our time is that of Saturday Sabbaths (Jews) or a plain pagan seven days (Red Chinese and secular Amer-icans) are simply guiltily outdated. This New Testament era, our presently given time which the Old Testament age prefigured and prepared, is such that it admits Eternity – the coming Aeon (of Glory). Eternity is already begun, is in time! Eternity is not a timeless extra-temporal state (Plato) nor simply prolonged time (Aristotle and Oriental astrology) nor a supra-natural condi-tion (Aquinas); but eternity is time specially touched by the Eternal God, the Lord of Time; i.e. eternity is God-ordered duration glorified, perfected from sin.

All people are commanded to be redeeming their time, to be on time with their using that lent them and to be waiting for the last Day when the Eternal Lord with one masterstroke shall complete this redemption of time and make eternity fully come. Only persons gripped by the Holy Spirit are saving and trading their time for Christ's permanent sake; unbelievers waste this aeon (losing it lazily in a buried napkin) or laboriously make it empty! (squandering time on themselves in vanity). On that *eschaton*-day the final redemption of time shall end time plagued by sin (being wasted by fallen creatures) although time itself does not end, disintegrate: in that Day, time which was made good and hallowed by Jesus Christ's entering it assumes the completed, perfect tense – about which world Scripture tell us little more than that it is an unimaginable glory.

To be created then means to be timed, totally dependent upon the Word of God's mouth; and to be a human creature is to be moving with all of the groaning, pregnant creation toward the Last Day (Romans 8:19–23) under the Lord's command to be co-operating in the coming of God's Kingdom, the redeeming, reconciling of all things to the Lord through Jesus Christ (Colossians 1:20), not sinfully dragging your feet. That brings us to the juggernaut of a term 'culture'.

Culture as human cultivation of God's world

When God said to man and woman before they ever sinned, 'Bear fruit, mature, inhabit the earth; subdue and control the waters' fish, the sky's birds, and every living thing that crawls over the face of the earth', God was not just suggesting Adam and Eve sleep together, raise a Dutch-sized family, and have their children become fishermen, farmers and birdwatchers. 'Be fruitful and multiply' may include the satisfying glory of child-bearing, yet the thrust of this formula of Genesis 1:28, combined with the revelation of Genesis 2:15 where it states that Jehovah deliberately took humankind and put them in the garden to fashion it and care for it, is to dignify humans as the Lord's trusted viceregent over the whole cosmos. The injunction has a global sweep to it deserving the name of 'cultural mandate'. 'Cultivate further the garden of Eden' means that even before sin God expected this workable creation to be taken care of, to be dressed, moulded, cultured by humankind. From the very beginning creation was made to be unfolded, dis-covered and formed, watchfully built up by people toward some future Day. So Adam got busy right away and started naming the animals.

When God said 'Bear fruit, blossom out, civilise my heavens, sea and earth', God's Word was not a kind of exhortational invitation, RSVP, nor was it a forbidding order, stern and onerous: God's Word, as always, was a command graciously bringing blessing, rich abundant life to whomever obeys. We must hold on to that biblical truth that the original command given to representative Adam, and re-issued to Noah in an abbreviated way after the flood had punished humankind's sin (Genesis 9:1), that 'cultural mandate' was not and is not an imposition upon human life but a divine call for humankind to activate the built-in dimension of our nature to cultivate God's world in praise of God's holy name; and this enterprise is a pure joy! The 'cultural mandate' reveals humankind's peculiar privilege, one's own cosmic birthright, as it were, granted by the Creator. Cultural action, opening up creation's possibilities intentionally, self-consciously, with a view to succeeding generations' taking up the work with new initiative and bringing it to greater flower, this is the singular character of human hallelujahing the LORD God. Culture is not therefore something a person has to strain to do: it is rather a channel of worship proper to human nature and an activity in which one is inescapably engaged – presiding by God's delegation over the rest of creation's formation, development, from lowly weeding of onions in Indiana to Leonard Bernstein's composition of sounds.

The monkey-wrench to this exhilarating, responsible opportunity of bearing fruit in a way becoming to God, reflexively enlarging one's service of love to God, is that three-letter matter of fact called sin. Sin is peculiar to humankind; animals, plants and stones do not sin because their kind of existence lacks this structural God-relatedness called religion which defines humankind. So sin is not some animalic, bestial roughness in people needing to be rationally overcome; nor is it simply an evil, devilish control of human nature. Since Adam's fall sin is a fully congenitally human condition of a person's being existentially attached to trusting in something other than the true God. Sin is not due to our temporality, our creatureliness; to be created is not to be *per se* bad. Sin is also not a passing state of affairs, a deliberate act now and then against the will of God to do or not do certain things: sin is not a matter of immorality, ignorance, insanity, or even confessional 'disbelief'. Sin is the whole-hearted turned-in-upon-itself direction of religious humankind (pride) and the rooting of oneself in creation at large or one's own self (idolatry), which is unlawful ground, usurping God's prerogative of being rightful Absolute Origin. Despite ignorance or sincere intentions ('The road to Hell is paved with good intentions'), if one does not keep God Almighty's Law – Love Me – one is breaking it: sin is basically an anti-God direction, faithless infidelity, broken covenant with God and thus perversion of all that a person does.

The effects of sin are severe. It is a powerful impotency, a dynamic corruption bringing about the radical ruination of human nature; it cuts a person off at his or her root, turns existence (as utterly dependent thing) into proud existence (I am what I am here myself!). While sinful humankind does not stop being humankind, does not lose its religious self-hood, it does ironically deprive the self of its grounds for being, and the resulting apostate orientation threatens a person with meaninglessness and the riddle of a disintegrating cosmos, since the focal point – God-focused viceregent lordship – is lost. Sin, that is, one's embracing this usurping disintegrating power called 'flesh' in Scripture, is punishment itself, foolish separation from God – that which turns our temporality ending in the Great Sunday morning into the awful mortality of humankind, death, eventual permanent abandonment by God. Meanwhile, to the sin-full person the world becomes heavy, much too heavy for his or her would-be Atlas shoulders, and the joy of cultivation becomes a burden or an enervating escape.

This is our present, historically given situation: the possibilities of God's culture-able world are being opened by the human race, born cultivators, largely in a perverted, God-ignoring way because people are wrong at the roots, constructing self-glorifying Babels instead of shaping God-honouring gardens.

However, thank God! there is Good News: the Son of God, Jesus Christ, was sent to die and He rose from the dead to save the world, to set humankind straight, i.e. work powerfully by his Spirit in the hearts of apostate humankind to turn the elect of every race back to God and with them turn senseless, struggling creation into meaning. Some sinful religious human creatures are saved (only God knows who are not – appearances can be deceiving), saved from themselves by being uprooted out of the unlawful ground where they are growing wild on borrowed time (in money, fame, sex, even books as the teacher of Ecclesiastes showed), and transplanted into new ground, into the root of the new humanity, Jesus Christ, Himself, His body, where they can bear fruit pleasing to God become their own Father. Other sinful religious creatures remain lost somewhere in the wasteland pretending they are growing in virgin ground.

To these new men and women regenerated in Jesus Christ culture becomes a happy, voluntary response of beginning to reassemble all things in the world for Christ, what God has purposed to bring to a concluding climax for God when the time is ripe (Ephesians 1:10). The cultural objective of Christ-followers is to re-form out of the grip of sin, to be used by the Holy Spirit to transform what generations of faithless people have made tradition, transform such thought and practice or whatever it be until it is con-formed to Jesus Christ's lordship. The cultural objective of Christ-followers is to plant and water gardens nourished by Christ's root, to build buildings on the rock of Christ's foundation, to bring everything from onion weeding to symphonic music in subjection to God's Word, since all that creation offers rightfully belongs to God. Only such collection of the world's riches that is a veritable living sacrifice of a captivated heart is acceptable to the holy Creator God of heaven and sea and earth.

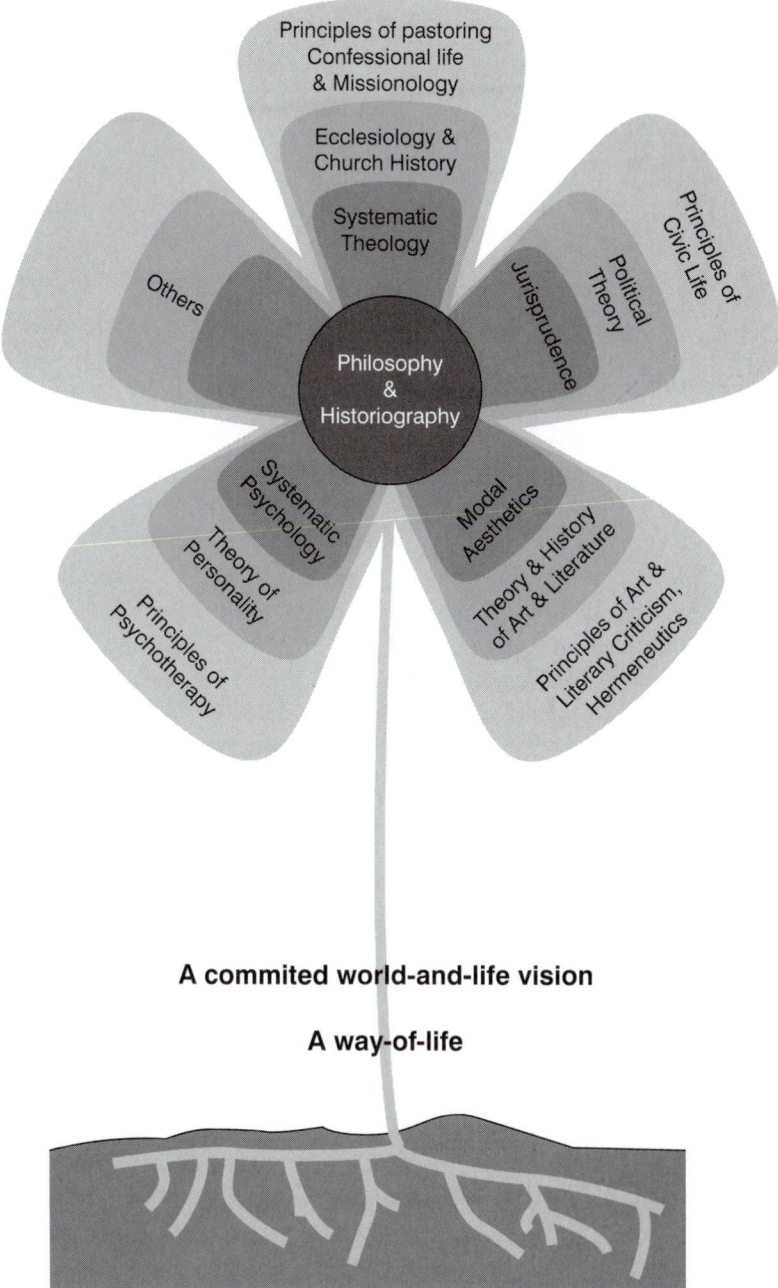

Figure 3 An academic (university) flower in God's world

If managing the storehouse of creation is humankind's God–given task and one is to fulfil it out of and through and to Jesus Christ while all time passes swiftly away and distorting sin would ruin one's best willed deeds, then the questions and problems about cultural objectives for the Christian teacher tumble out on the table. But first we must examine two basic and widespread 'Christian' approaches to the whole matter of culture, approaches that differ from the biblical perspective I shall be developing for you. We must do that fairly if we would get precise what 'Christian' teaching involves.

Withdrawal and compartmentalised Christian approaches to culture

For ages there has been a persistent anti-cultural stream within the church which has rightly been afraid of proud cultural sophistication and having its little ones stumble, seduced by the whore of sinfully framed art, sciences and social usages. A frequent 'Christian' reaction to this temptation of culture that flatters people and betrays God is to withdraw from such worldliness and reject cultural activity as far as possible. You may witness, preach, do mission work *to* the world but not get involved *in* such worldly business.

The ancient Church Father, Tertullian, is the most famous champion of such Withdrawal Christianity. 'What has Athens to do with Jerusalem? the [Platonic] Academy with the Church? What have heretics to do with Christians? … We have no need for curiosity since Jesus Christ, nor for inquiry since the Gospel has come' (*On Heretical Writings*, 7). You cannot serve God and Mammon; therefore, if you love God, forsake Mammon, the world and all its pleasures (St Augustine would quote 1 John 2:15–17); let the culture of our sinful world go to the devil where it belongs. If your heart is right with Jesus and your theological doctrine is biblically sound, that is what counts eternally; live by the Bible – that's all you really need to know, and stay away from rotten apples. And Montanist Tertullian righteously inveighed against cosmetics, dyed hair, bracelets (cf. Isaiah 3:16–24); even marriage was begrudged by him as something that would distract an individual's attention from service of the Lord, and marriage's pleasures are described as not much more than legalised fornication.

This rather grim reduction of human life *for the sake of Christ!* is actually a Christianised brand of Spiritualism known to the pagan Hellenic world. The cynic Antisthenes, in one of his writings, commended Hercules' choice for the arduous mountain road of virtue rather than the soft valley of sensuous vice; a reward not heroically struggled for in discomfort and self-denial is not truly a reward, or what's a heaven for? The puritanic Bunyan, exhorting one to a pilgrim's progress along the narrow road to the Celestial City despising the

Tents of Wickedness and Vanity Fair leading to destruction and the Lake of Fire, has also a touch of this other-worldly, anti-cultural asceticism.

It is true that Withdrawal Christianity sees better than most the crux of the matter, that Jesus Christ alone is the way to life eternal, and takes utterly seriously that God brooks no other gods beside God. But the mistake made is the abdication of humankind's lordship of creation and the attempt to withdraw locally, as it were, from sin. Withdrawal Christianity confuses the issues of Christian sanctification: purification before God and transformation of creation. Withdrawal would purify self of creation as if creation itself were sinful. Gospel talk about the narrow gate and broad way should not be misinterpreted to mean a fork in the road between a high road and a low road, for it entails a false separation from the world defined locally and puts part of God's creation permanently off-limits. The result is retribution by the back door, since one cannot stamp out sin by drawing boundaries. The Bible does not call Christians to walk a straight line of Do-this-Don't-do-that and you will be secure (and not thereby encourage indiscriminate fraternisation with wicked sheep and wolves). God's Word commands a Christian to be a marked person, gratefully functioning close to Scripture, a sojourner who hates sin and is busy subduing all of creation as one's king's business.

The Scriptures say clearly in Colossians 2:8: 'Look out! that no one beguile you by the philosophy and puffing-up seduction forged by human tradition, that no one capture you by worldly principles supplanting the fundamental directives of Christ.' That warning is reinforced by Paul in the famous 1 Corinthians 7: Because our temporal opportunity is so compressed (pregnant) … those working the world should not work at it as if everything depended on it, because the formed shaping of this world disappears (vv. 29–31). And it is possible that some need to make themselves cultural eunuchs for the sake of the kingdom of heaven (Matthew 19:12); it is indeed better for a person to cut out a part of one's projected cultural activity than for one as a fully active person to be thrown into hell (cf. Matthew 5:29). Nevertheless, the New Testament mandate to Christ's body here on earth working for the coming of the kingdom of heaven, praying that God's will be done on earth as it is in heaven, reinforcing the Old Testament call to hallelujah the LORD God, the New Testament mandate is for us to trade our talents – five, two or one – whatever it be, as God's own possession given us on lend-lease till Christ return to bless or curse the work of our hands (cf. Matthew 25:14–30).

There has also always been a respectable segment of the church which has professed that indeed Christ must have pre-eminence, but we are in the world too. Such a 'Christian' approach has rightly refused outright adoption of non-Christian culture but has wrongly been willing to honour it next to Christian cultural attempts, honour it as legitimate in its own right, incomplete of course, needing special finishing; but Christians should use, adapt cautiously for themselves what is good in unbelievers' work. Fusion of the Christian faith with good ideas and products not native to the gospel of Jesus Christ is all right, said the great Augustine in his later life, allegorically exegeting Scripture: just as the Israelites at God's command took gold and silver away from the Egyptians when they left, so we should steal from unbelievers whatever gems of truth and beauty and goodness they possess and revamp them to the glory of God.

The historical background to this accommodating compartmentalisation approach is the work of late Aristotle who posited a sensational realm of physics under a supra-sensational realm of metaphysics; Thomas Aquinas modified late Aristotle by having a territory of purely natural *recta ratio* common to all people as a self-contained prerequisite and preparation for the upper additional realm of church-faith-bound human activity and thought. There is the realm of natural, secular, civil good above which is the specifically Christian, churchy area of sacred matters where God's special Grace abounds; the world of culture can be relatively good and may be indulged in so long as no one is led astray but always ends up at the church door.

This plausible arrangement and approach to life and culture is not acceptable to the kind of evangelical Reformation Christian commitment I would present to you, one which holds that everything a person does issues out of one's faith-commitment to God or to an idol, and that all that a Christian does is or should be subjected to one's Christian commitment, to one's saying Yes to God, because the jealous God revealed in Jesus Christ demands a complete surrender, unconditional and total capitulation of all that a person is who would be one of God's, a Christian. Compartmentalised Christianity distorts the Scriptural opposition of Grace and Sin into the Grace–Nature combination which obscures the radical nature of sin and thus the triumphant sufficiency of God's Grace in the whole of creation. Revelation does not have all humankind naturally working toward Grace but says many are helplessly and/or wilfully lost in sin (*civitates mundi*), and some, overwhelmed by Grace, surprised by joy, are living wholly if weakly before God in gratitude (*civitas Dei*). The Bible does not ask Christians to give to God and the world on a comparative percentage basis, 10 per cent for God and 90 per cent for the rest, a kind of Christian schizophrenia. This compartmentalised approach hurries a loss in the sense of calling within the Christian community, secularises it!, as if there are a few professional saints and the rest, most of us cultural-minded people who are fairly good, keep wagging our sinful tails behind us. Rather, the Bible commands one to give all to God for God's blessing in order that a person be enabled to consecrate all that is done in the world.

It is true that unbelievers have shown much command of the world. This fact is frequently lazily described and commended with the term 'common grace', with the compartmentalising result that the need for Christian cultural objectives is blunted. Can't we have our unchristian culture and eat it too?

Let me just say this now: 'common grace' rightly describes, it seems to me, the state of affairs that, after the fall, creational structures did not become anti-godly but remained integrally valid. For example, after the fall, difference between man and woman remained in effect, and it was good; laws for motion, growth, feeling, thought, work and the like persisted, and this was good; God's command to humankind to love God also remained holy after the fall. What sin changed was human response to God, concrete marital relations, acts of motion, growth, feeling, thought, work, and the like. There must not be an antithesis between saved people and their created world because God has graciously conserved it, though it is plagued by sin; rather, because sinful people can turn God's gracious conservation into a common dis-grace, saved people must bring the saving grace at work in their lives directly to bear upon all God has held conserved, to develop it positively in a way pleasing to God. Just because unbelievers, who are not all suppressing the truth in unrighteousness, can live and move – indeed they have to – and develop culturally within the preserved ordinances of creation and in so far seem Christian because they act orderly and do get ignorantly at secrets of creation, stumbling by God's Grace on to significant control of our world: this does not permit the newborn Christian to be satisfied with a common culture Christianised. For then the Christian would be denying that he or she has the good news to set radically right what sin has misdirected and unbelievers are prostituting, however honourably. The Christian would then be selling one's peculiar believing birthright, one's right to be the proper lord of creation's development, if one did not show what light the Scriptures have for time-bound recreation as well as for eternal salvation. That 'The earth is the Lord's and everything filling it is God's' (Psalm 24:1) is a recognition missing in unchristian culture, an insight twisted in post-Christian secular culture, and a commitment that cannot be satisfactorily appended, circumscribed or applied like varnish to an object conceived without it, because the Lord is a jealous God.[1]

Our biblical calling is this: 'whether you eat or drink or whatever you do, do it all to the glory of God' (1 Corinthians 10:31), showing God's presence. As a person you cannot help but be busy culturally: since this is our Father's world, our cultivation of it must show we love God and recognise that all here belongs to God.

---

[1]See my *A Christian Critique of Art* (St. Catherines, Ontario: ARSS, 1963, pp. 25–6.

A believer's office: posting God's Word concretely in history

The famous Heidelberg Catechism has the question: 'But why are you called a Christian?' And the answer (no. 32) goes: 'Because I am a member of Christ by faith, and thus a partaker of His anointing (as prophet, priest and king), that I may confess His name, present myself a living sacrifice of thankfulness to Him, and with a free and good conscience fight against sin and the devil in this life, and hereafter reign with Him eternally over all creatures.' For a person to be a Christian is to receive over one's shoulders the wedding garment of prophecy, ministry and royal authority, i.e. to be appointed and qualified by the Holy Spirit to act, think, speak, teach in the name of Jesus Christ, the great Teacher, High Priest and Lord before whose footstool all things shall be brought. The Christian believer has the human office of being the responsible developer of the universe charged with the power and direction of the living Word of God. It is exactly that Word which it is the believer's task and joy to confess pentecostally in all its forming richness according to the measure of one's talents.

This Word of God, the Truth, which unifies all human life and sets humankind properly in the world is the summary of God's Law embodied fully in Jesus Christ: Love me above all, with your whole heart, soul, mind, strength, and your neighbour as your own self (Mark 12:30–31). God does not fall under that law; God speaks it. *Deus legibus solutus est, sed non exlex* means God stands behind and maintains the Command of Love justly, not respecting persons, and is angry at sin incurred; and God stands behind the Command of Love, faithfully sending God's son, our mediator, graciously to forgive sin. This God of wrath and grace is trustworthy, a covenanting God who uses this holy sovereign Command, as Luther put it, to teach people their misery, to lead one discipled to Christ (Galatians 3:24), and as Calvin added, to stimulate thankfulness in our hearts that it has been fulfilled for us by Christ so that we may freely respond under its guideline here in directing the traffic of creation.

Proceeding out of God's same mouth are the Words, the ordinances, the structural and structuring laws God has laid down in creation for the realising of God's blessed plan. These laws which the psalmist enjoyed studying – the marvellous works almost too wonderful to understand like the movements of heavenly bodies, the religious bent of humankind, the sexual difference in creatures, the maturation process of all growing, creeping things, the many prime ways creatures operate – all these laws of God which cannot be broken, escaped or made void, do not bind creation in polar opposition to God's Command of Love but find their hallelujah summation there. The manifold laws embedded in creation and which shall not fail till the Last Day, within which all things function, find their coherence in the Word of God which established them to be filled concretely in praise of God's Name. That is the dynamic to our temporal existence: the integrally structured, one created reality of God can be opened up obediently to its focus Jesus Christ or transgressed to the breaking down of humankind, society and creatures at large: homosexuality, 'brainwashing', cock-fights, drug use that stunts or ruins healthy processes, are perversions not of 'Nature', with no connection to Jesus Christ, but of God's holy Word–Law for creational development. This is where the peculiar cultural office of humankind comes in.

By 'office' I mean the position of authority a person exercises in a certain special relationship, authority granted one by God. Ecclesiastical office-bearers like elders, deacons and bishops, while selected somehow by people, receive their pastoral authority from God. People who win political office by election, hook or crook, assume its respective power not, as many voters think, by the will of the people or their own cleverness but under the delegation of the Supreme Justice of God. Fathers deserve the honour of children not because they begat them but because God bestows on them parental office. A person can have all kinds of office. One can also forfeit an office, be defrocked for heresy, impeached for injustice, declared unfit, null and void as guardian because of desertion. And it is no light matter in the eyes of God to have loosed on earth what was bound office-ially in heaven.

The broad cultural office of humankind with which God has graciously empowered humankind to act is not like the angels who willingly carry out God's direct bidding almost automatically down to the details. Humankind's cultural office carries with it the glory of one being an ambassador, a representative, and in covenant as child to Father, to apply God's Command of Love in concrete situations of our temporal, law-bound world. And this cultural office cannot be avoided as one's office as elder, statesman and father can be avoided. Therefore, a person is trying – or denying, to his damnation – to posit what the revealed Love of God makes imperative here and now in our sin-disturbed structured world: that is one's cultural office. The missionary must decide what in the sight of God is ethical for a converted Moslem with four wives to do – is he continually living in sin if he keeps them? Or is it an unusual opportunity to build up the Sunday School? And do you tell his sons to take only three wives, and their sons only two, and their sons only one, weaning them gradually in time to what the Scriptures direct? The political executive must declare whether it is just, in the light of God's Law, for the state to assume in a given civic disaster duties which are not normally those of government. The believing father must prayerfully posit for his children that the Word of God 'Love me above all and your neighbour as your own self' means this or that with respect to current social crazes and taboos.

All these kinds of imperatives which people posit in their varied offices – and every vocation (calling by God! cf. 1 Corinthians 12) practised by a believer presents him or her with the task to lead office-ially in that area – are disciplining, educative, relative positings by people striving to give flesh and blood to the skeleton of God's Law ordinances by the light of God's commanding Word. If the imperatives posited for language, art, thinking, health practices, emotional activity or whatever, are badly posited by believers, then God's people and all those who come within the influence of such norms will suffer. When the imperatives disclose a biblical insight, competence and wisdom, the many who follow them – converts, citizens or teenage children – will be blessed. This is the terribly responsible, full-bodied thrust of the cultural mandate to the believing Christian on earth: since humankind's chief end is to glorify God and enjoy God forever, let every believer preach and teach, posit concretely the full Gospel, God's Law fulfilled in Jesus Christ, the Good News, walking humbly before God in a way that enriches all areas of life with God's Grace.

One must beware of oversimplification. You may not hurriedly read 'there is no Jew or Gentile, slave or free, male or female' (Galatians 3:28), combine it with the Good Samaritan story, and say, OK, proceed with integration of the races as conceived by secular civil rights leaders. Jesus' conversation with the rich young ruler is also not a prototype for mission work among rich young businesspeople; and can one turn the 'other cheek' spirit of Christ's Sermon on the Mountain into a brief for political pacifism without man-handling God's Word? No biblicistic parsing and dead simple, forced application of the Scriptures is ever permitted us, although this does not mean the Bible gives no clear-cut direction for us in the twentieth century. The believer's cultural office involves much more wrestling with imponderables, agonising in the Spirit, searching the Scriptures with other believers busy at the same problems not to get textbook answers from the Bible but seeking to listen together to Revelation's humbling message which convicts leaders of their own sin, need of repentance and reforming till they slowly build up a plastic, sanctified, communal consciousness out of which they act, in fear and trembling, faith, love and hope that the leadership of their various specific roles be conformed to the revealed Will of God.

Disciples of Christ are not perfect right away because they belong to God. Yet despite a given believer's dangerous little learning, laziness, scandalous hypocrisy, he or she is still – the awful wonder of conversion! – graciously set in Jesus Christ. Salvation is God's turnabout of a person to God's service, a turnabout which is carried out but not yet concluded; transplanted sinful religious creatures must work it out in stumbling consecration until time be terminated and creation receive its hoped-for consummation in Jesus Christ's return. The heart of Christians is wholly turned, converted, transplanted, but the concrete reforming of their acts takes time and inconsistently comes on behind. As these beginnings of eternal life grow, obedience to the central Command of Love becomes more habitual since the Holy Spirit gets more of a person's 'members' under control: one grows in singleminded Gracious perception.

The complexity of creation's problems and the incompleteness of believers' consecration must not divert us from our calling: to try to translate our Christian captivity and allegiance into specific, comprehensive and meaningful historical service to God Almighty, in the realisation that only people acting out of wholehearted gratitude to God for their being taken up into the body of Christ are good stewards of the office and gifts entrusted them. And it is this evangelical Reformational spirit – prompted, for example, by Paul's words to Timothy that nothing of creation is secular but all is good, holy! sacred! if able to be received with thanksgiving and kept in the context of effective witness to God's glory (1 Timothy 4:1–11) – that offers us teachers sound biblical direction. Then we shall neither overestimate the effect of sin upon the world and reject all non-ecclesiastical realms as not significant to God, nor shall we underestimate sin's perversion of the world with its culture and try only to add Christian touches here and there; but we shall see that whatever one dedicatedly executes proportionate to one's full qualifications (whether as mother, senator or janitor) is full-time service in the Kingdom of God, and that especially Spirit-filled transformation of scholarship and teaching is vital for the Christian community's leadership in the world at large.

Christian teaching as patterning of biblical vision

What, then, is the nature of the teaching office and what makes teaching Christian teaching?

One teaches another, I suppose, whenever one gives guidance to the other along certain lines, whether it be folding diapers, changing a wheel, understanding a poem or tracing the path of a meteor. Teaching is the process of opening up someone to wonders, differences, actions not hitherto apprehended or performed. Teaching is basically, perhaps, helping one learn to make distinctions, uncover and interrelate the meanings of various things, bringing the new matters within one's power to do, like reading, writing and arithmetic. No one is a teacher without a student, without someone who trusts one's direction, who takes and follows the guidance on say-so authority, at least in some measure. Teaching is generally done by older creatures to younger creatures, although there is a vigorous reciprocal education at work from younger to older generation, hopefully in the classroom too.

Classroom teaching is what we are here primarily concerned with, i.e. professional teaching, teaching done by persons differentiated by the fact that their job is teaching – they don't work at something, they just teach! At least, that is the strange impression the first professional teachers in Western civilisation made, those itinerant cosmopolitan professors called sophists, who lived by their wits and tongue, who had to be popular teachers to receive an income to keep body and soul together, who most importantly instituted private education. Their teaching was avowed practical training: 'We shall give you mastery of skills that will get you ahead in the Greek *polis*, the technique of politics.' Their basic offering was speech, debate techniques, the art not of determining truth necessarily but of convincing hearers of a certain thing at a given time in a particular situation. 'We form your nature to meet the occasion; guaranteed political success or double your money back!' It was an unheard-of, high-powered, very successful type of teaching arrangement that bowled over the less specialised amateurs trying to run the government on the strength of their noble blue blood. But the slick Dale Carnegie slap to such sophistic 'guidance' – 'We'll get the job done and put you where you want to be, for a fee' – hollowed out Athenian leaders to sophisticated opportunitists for whom anarchy was semi-respectable.

The great teacher Socrates opposed the sophists because he judged teaching not to consist in transferring skills but in stimulating discussion, argumentative examination of life and a search for some objective Truth which, when known, would lead to the perfection of one's hidden excellence. Teaching is not putting predigested answers, methods and tricks in the hands of young people to corrupt them with quick success, suggests Socrates; teaching is being a mental midwife who never really 'teaches' anything but succeeds in arousing curiosity in other individuals to think for themselves and to come to know themselves. Such reflective inquiry may not appear very practical but it will be better for society in the long contemplative run. And it is this challenging the status quo, bite of Socratic dialectic, that has appealed to intellectuals through the ages, appealed perhaps fundamentally to their pride.

When Renaissance figures like Montaigne rose up against the humdrum pedagogy of the so-called Middle Ages, the catechetical indoctrination dinned by a Magister Artis into the brains of his docile disciples who compiled notebooks, cross-indexed concordances of approved maxims, split distinctions academically myriad times when there was a dispute, and passed for scholars – Montaigne spoke classical Latin as his natural tongue – these Renaissance figures pleaded for travel, 'experience', practical involvement as the proper teaching–learning situation. Their aim was to get a cultured, worldliwise gentleman as the result of the process, an updated facsimile of Socrates' never-ending inquirer and conversationalist. More modern Socratic enthusiasts have left the street corners and retreated to ivy towers where at least in current philosophical quarters 'the right method of teaching philosophy is to confine oneself to propositions of the sciences, stated with all possible clearness and exactness, leaving philosophical assertions to the learner, and proving to him whenever he made them, that they are

---

[2]Bertrand Russell, introduction to Ludwig Wittgenstein, *Tractatus Logico-Philosophicus* (London: Routledge & Kegan, 1961), p. xxi.

meaningless'.[2] Such teaching, in my experience, is the guidance of annihilation that frazzles into a brilliant cat–and–mouse game on split hairs or acts like a roulette wheel for urbane nondirective psychoanalysis.

Christian teaching, I shall be so bold to say, is not set up like sophistic practice or like leisurely Socratic contemplation. And possibly that breakdown covers most teaching without Christian fibre: academic guidance tending constantly toward functionalistic training to produce skilled practitioners, or mostly stimulus toward encouraging one to become a speculative armchair 'thinker', *honnête homme*, urbane critic. Neither objective fits the office of Christian teaching. That does not mean Christian teaching slights technical competence in a relevant field or disparages a honed intelligence and argued positions, but means it leads students in such *relative!* matters – skill and critical thinking are not the be-all and end-all of education – *relates* them to serve equipping students for every good work (2 Timothy 3:17) as servants of God. That does not make Christian teaching a round of moralising platitudes, catechetical pedantry or counselling on one's faith. It does mean that Christian teaching sees the crux of the 'guidance' to be setting the vision in which all discovery takes place, in casting the direction in which all new specialised craftsmanship and work is pursued; and this vision is given and caught subtly in the daily training.

Socratic teaching mistook a keen insight, took amiss by absolutising it, that education is a nice, intimate communal examination of some matter by questioner and answerer, leader and follower, teacher and student. For it is correct that academic teaching should be disciplined training by professionally competent people for the best a student is capable of, and it is so that there must be a little play, a dramatic push and pull in the process of teaching and learning because the knowledge gained must be self-earned. However, education conceived Socratically has a built-in sceptical block in that it is fundamentally unwilling to lead a student vigorously in a definite direction and is utterly unable to build up a body of knowledge which grows into a tradition enriching later generations. Socratic education chooses to be provocative and unfinished, expert questionings especially of the more intellectual while leaving the 'unthinking masses' to the sophists. It is indeed easier for teachers in the liberal arts to ask questions than to answer them; and I am afraid that the Socratic gambit of humility, resting in questionings is frequently a clever cover-up for lazy intelligence, a laziness which is irresponsible in the Christian community because it misses what makes Christian teaching such a glorious office: being used by the Holy Spirit to open up a talented life in definite hallelujah response to the Lord. Indefinite teaching, no matter how stimulating the Master teacher may be, does not build up a lasting Christian habit and body of thought, and such edification of a vision, a biblical vision, is needed to make teaching Christian teaching.

Patterning a student's vision is done schoolishly; Christian teaching is a scholastic enterprise, it is not preaching. Schooling has a 'distance' not found in earning a living or going places; there is a schematic suspension, a scientific pull-back from 'practical' involvement to schoolwork. Precisely there in that abnormal academic disengagement lies the tremendously engaged interpretative forming of Christian teaching: how maths is taught, as the Gospel Truth or as one aspect of human theoretical knowledge, how ideas are thrown out, in faith for the truth or in a cynical way that flips a child's commitment up on razor edge and lets it spin – right there, in combat with evil spirits and thrones and principalities, is where the office of Christian teaching is exercised or forfeited, where the Truth is professed concretely or one is set adrift, where the moulding and slow formation of Christian scientists, doctors and leaders is done or undone, where child hearts and minds are set in the Lord or unsettled. And only when teacher and student, in the very process of teaching, grow in the fear of the Lord, in the vision that they are both servants of God, that the teacher is a guardian of the student's unfolding as they develop together an honest stewardship in some area of the world for God, only then do you have Christian teaching. And only then does teaching lose the tendency to fragment into either a shard of job training or a piece of 'smart thinking', because then both professional training and philosophical orientation are not idolised human preferences but are complementing, down-to-earth expressions of the underlying, integrating, prophetic religious vision furnished to saints by the Holy Spirit. God's presence is needed for the patterning of youth's vision and must be passionately prayed for; for without the true vision God's people shall perish (Proverbs 29:18).

To keep exercise of such Christian teaching fresh, exciting for the teacher and stretching for the student, it is wise for both teacher and student to confront primary reality as much as possible – the bugs in biology, the documents in history, the primary sources in literature and philosophy. The artificiality necessary to scholastic work must not be textbookishly increased unless for very good reasons (of which there are more in primary grade). Parsing of secondary and sometimes tertiary material is not so healthy for learning or teaching as direct contact with the original material met first-hand. Secondary sources are valuable chastening tools, but if used uncritically, their problematics accepted, a Christian teacher is stopped from taking a fresh, reforming approach to that area of creation studied. This suggestion may make education a slower process, more 'inductive', but I think the teaching will go deeper, opening up and enlarging the student's perspective and command of the material till the student become conversational about the study rather than repeating barely remembered notes of hot-house compression. Such ripening in its time has a biblical unhurried, long-range determination about it, more easily fitted, perhaps, to the talents of varied individuals.

In passing I mention another natural ingredient to Christian teaching: that the teacher present the *Gestalt* of a field or unit of study, that the student see the whole in significant, selective, representative detail, neither be lost in atomic facts nor captured by full-blown, grand talk that lacks the discipline of detail. So important about seeing the whole configuration to a topic, the horizons of the study, is that there in the motifs of the *Gestalt* the religious motives at work can be better seen and critically exhumed: penetration into the religious forces at work in study is integral to Christian teaching.

Christian teaching is not the instrument God uses to save the world; it is not a weekday church either, dispensing Grace by Word and Sacrament. But the office of Christian teaching is a calling in which men and women prophesy, interpret the world with others for another generation as the Holy Spirit leads into the Truth that sets people free from themselves and lets them live out of God's hand.

The nature and necessity of a Christian philosophy

In conclusion, I should like to show why an articulated Christian philosophy is indispensable in fulfilling the authoritative cultural forming we Christian teachers practise. One's definition of philosophy already hides a philosophical position. By philosophy I understand the systematic, synoptic, scientific knowing, and results of that activity, which analyses all things and every aspect of reality that can be humanly so known, in their interrelated meaning. By Christian philosophy I understand precisely philosophy (not just an attitude or an ill-defined world-and-life view) whose basic philosophical ideas and hence systematics itself are prompted, directed, enlightened by the biblical Word-Revelation. Christian philosophy is not just philosophy done by nominal or even generally historical Christians who are sincere and spiritually kindly: the obtained result itself (which is more than good intentions or activity) must be checked out as Christian. It is not pagan philosophy Christianised by homogenising various Christian points into a system already set up without biblical orientation, nor is it secular philosophy pragmatically baptised by sprinkling into Kingdom service; it is also not philosophy mythologised, overcast by a nondescript quasi-religious appeal.

Christian philosophy is also not a finally achieved theistic system which presents the most complete, logically coherent network of knowledge on earth; Christian philosophy is not divine, not sanctioned by the Holy Spirit because Scripture – or even the creeds – are respected. Christian philosophic thought is just as fallibly provisional as non-Christian synoptic theory – although Christian philosophy may beware of antinomies more so than non-Christian philosophies and hence avoid many impasses. Christian philosophy is not found wholly in the Bible as if Scripture were fragmented philosophy and when you logically derived propositions from certain Bible texts and then carefully, systematically associated the logical derivatives you got a Christian philosophy. The object Christian philosophy takes for its peculiar analysis is not Scripture but all reality at large, analysis primed by Scripture.

The scandalous bite of Christian philosophy so defined is its profession that though it be mere theory, hypothesis, historically limited human knowledge, the crucial, leading philosophical Ideas which inform its whole systematic theoretical analysis are openly sought, admittedly taken on cue from, founded upon, grounded in the true *pou sto,** divinely revealed humanly understood Truth. That is why a mature Christian who is not just out to play games stands behind his or her correctible philosophy with oath sincerity, whole-hearted conviction, because one's fallible work is prompted by what, in the face of all tolerant, eclectic, positivistic, and sceptic nonsense to the contrary, one softspokenly and outspokenly knows to be the Truth, so help me God.

The Ideas of an ordered, timed world under God's Command in which Christ's body is what counts, these Ideas woven all through my remarks go back to the revealed Truth that the world is God's creation and that Jesus Christ came to reconcile sinful people in it to God, moving them to grateful life. Until the philosophical perspective suggested by these Ideas translated from the Bible story is shown awry I am intent to explore the implication for all science further.

That is my point at the moment: the challenge that a radically Christian philosophical perspective is necessary, because no teacher in any field at any level is free from assuming certain philosophically relevant matters, and it is highly important that these decisions have a Christian philosophical bent. Besides, a philosophy, if we do have one, must be wholly subjected too to our Christian faith-commitment.

All special sciences like maths, physics, biology, psychology, sociology, economics, historiography, literary criticism, are couched in a philosophical perspective. How so? Every operating science, besides consulting professionally with other distinguishable sciences, has this peculiarity: when a science defines a specific field of investigation for itself, and when the science as advanced theory brings its analyses to bear upon other disciplines and tries to say what its own conclusions imply elsewhere, then that special discipline is busy philosophically, encyclopaedically posing and establishing its interrelated meaning to other areas of knowledge.

When special studies are couched in a Christian philosophy it is recognised that such study has its limited integral task within the whole corpus of scien-

---

*A position taken on the fundamental meaning of things. Literally 'the place where I stand', from Archimedes' reputed remark that, given a *pou sto* and a long enough level, he could move the earth.

tific investigation, critically examines its judgements by the law of antinomy, and willingly admits that its Subject-ive specialised analysis comprehending Object-ive creation is openly achieved within religious horizons. Specialised studies that are Christian cannot help but lapse into witness every now and then because religious commitment does underlie it, but what makes maths and physics and aesthetics Christian in teaching is not the obvious personal devotion attending it but that the built-in pride of human scientific thought is broken and the technical results are presented to give body to the communal cultural structuring of reality going on in obedience to God's Command.

When no Christian philosophy gives coherence to the varied fields of study, disciplines may be favoured (for pragmatic reasons of convenience or for tradition's sake). With no Christian rationale the movement in a school or university is inexorably toward absolutised *ex cathedra* status for one's own study – curricular aggrandisement and a specialist's tyranny or the cold chaos of indifferent, isolated cells of research. Only when chemists get an explosive situation on their hands will they head for the theologians or sociologists; otherwise there is not much concern for what is going on at the other end of the building or campus. Such unchristian scientific study and teaching, at lower grade levels, often reduces its business to a routine check-out of sterilised data, manipulations, or summation of trial-and-error observation, mechanics done well with little long-range, Scripture-ranging reason. Such teaching has lost the dimension of biblical office and the Christian vision of one's being an equally necessary part of Christ's culturally active body.

A Christian philosophy is simply an academic translation and articulation of the biblical vision Christian teachers are called to hold out before their students like a God-sent fiery cloud to lead them through the wilderness. Christian philosophy need not be expressly taught by a teacher but is needed to help one withstand the seduction of over-specialisation and especially to help stir up the professing, prophetic element so often lost to professional activity. Unless the whole is seen and seen as meaningful service to God because this knowledge we work with is a prophetic response to God's Grace which touches all things, Christian teaching will mutate into disenchanted labour or an apologetic retreat.

6   Test the Spirits*

Graduates of Dordt College, 1965 *Anno Domine*, the first fourth-year graduating class in these first ten years of your college's existence, I congratulate you on being historically first, on persevering to the end of the course, and especially on the weakness of the achievement.

Dutchmen are stubborn, but they also have a head for business. To stick with something for ten years that does not turn a profit means something strange to the world at work. And for you students to have staked your career on an education still largely unaccredited by the world, as at my own college, makes a sophisticated eye looking this way wonder in unbelief, 'Why in the world …?'

To you all congregated here joyfully tonight because you have been foolishly faithful for so many years, joyful because you understand the biblical significance of the weakness of this historical first, to you I wish our Lord's continued, repristinating blessing. Ten years from now, forty, or should God ever bless you with a centennial, it will be much harder to bring honest Christian congratulations: when an institution becomes old, strongly established, respectably seasoned and learned like a Nicodemus, it is much harder to be properly weak, freshly ten years old, childlike as are those in the kingdom of heaven.

Since every end point in our life is also a beginning, since the Amen! at the conclusion of this evening's festivities starts you graduates off on the road more travelled by than the collegiate one, I read you the Word of Almighty God for the occasion:

> Beloved, don't you trust every spirit! Rather, because there are many false prophets roaming around in the world, *test the spirits* to find out whether they be of God or not.
>
> You can know whether it be God's spirit this way: every spirit which openly declares 'Jesus Christ came in the flesh' – that is God's spirit: and every spirit which does not publicly celebrate Jesus is not God's spirit – in fact, it is the spirit of the antichrist. You heard he was coming, right? Well, he is in the world now already.

*Commencement address at Dordt College, published in *The Banner* 105 (20 August 1965), 20–23. (A few paragraphs in this address are repeated in other pieces in this Reader. However, to remove them would have disrupted the flow of the argument, and they have been allowed to stand.)

But you belong wholly to God, children, and you *have* overcome those (anti Christ) because the Spirit in you is greater than the spirit in the world(ly ones).

Those (who) exist worldly speak the language of the world and the world listens to them. We are rooted in God: whoever knows God listens to us; whoever is not rooted in God does not hear us. This is how we (apostles) know experientially which is the Spirit of Truth and which the spirit of probing deceit (1 John 4:1–6).

It would be pure bunk for anyone to say that after being academically cloistered for four years now you are headed out in the wide and wicked world. It is probably so that there is more honky-tonk around Chicago where I come from than in North-western Iowa, and that Greenwich Village, New York, is a centre for experimental morals and profligate thought (I do not know what Sioux Centre is a centre for), but it is probably also true that there is as much sin and misery per square human inch here as elsewhere in God's world.

Just because the sorrow, pain, dirty tensions have been introverted à la Kierkegaard, Hawthorne, and Alan Paton fashion in our tradition does not mean we have escaped being worlded. And it would also be mistaken, I dare say, for anyone leaving Dordt to think that by setting up housekeeping on the Albertan prairies, getting immersed in the Christian school system, by taking a Christian Reformed charge eventually at points East or West, one could stay away from the big bad world. The devil is more subtle than any creeping beast of the fields. Worldiness is *in* the church. And the church is to be fighting *in* the world. This is the complicated state of affairs God's Word reveals. And central to this very revelation is what I read you from 1 John, the Bible-simple focus to all this complicatedness, that there are two spirits afoot in the world: the Holy Spirit of Truth and the unholy spirit of deceit, Christ and antichrist. As you children of faith shift now from academic studies into the concrete life situations of earning a living, it is critical – practical mistakes cannot be erased like theoretical ones – it is critical that you know the difference in spirits and decide as never before what to do about it.

Language of the world: deceit and success

What is so devilish about the spirit of deceit is its easy, respectable, far-reaching devastation. The lie is the perfect crime: no fingerprints, no mess, no getaway car needed; just close your mouth and the evidence evaporates into the air, while the evil dart spins on to its mark like a radioactive isotope. And there are so many interesting ways you can twist things: withhold just a speck of information; tell what is indeed so at the wrong time; merely wink suggestively. Deceit is so smart to do, elusive to track down, so spiritual in nature.

What has that got to do with graduating from a Christian college? This: the spirit of deceit seems to lodge peculiarly well among educated Christians. We are a good, decent people. We would never rape anybody on the street or burn a person's home down; but we might kill his or her reputation with a well-freighted word or poison the air with gossip not quite said. We will not be unorthodox, just neo-orthodox, not promulgate error, just be tricky in the wording, not outright evil, just deceptively fast with the context of things.

I am not talking moral peccadilloes – everybody here knows a falsehood when he or she tells one – but am trying to put a finger on what stymies the body of Christ, what constantly plagues the close communion of saints, what is antichrist among us, no less worldly because confessing Christians do it: bearing false witness of a highly refined, rationalised sort in society, the church, one's work. This is the special temptation of newly graduated professionals, jockeying for elbow room, who have knowledge to burn, flush with ideas, able to run dizzying circles around those pressed down in the workaday life of bread and butter. In the dizzy, exhilarating movement to get ahead and probe new ground, solve old problems, set different directions, the Christian child turned adult is apt to speak, think, and act too hurriedly to square it with his or her heart deep down or to listen in the necessary time-consuming way to the Word for guidance, with the result that a life without God-context develops. So the rush of well-meant impatience can become a pattern of detached living that forms a habit of gentle deceits, with all its attendant evils.

Whoever practises or responds to such self-deception and social chicanery is guilty of false prophecy, hypocrisy of the intelligence, fronting for one thing while being another. This is the language of the world, says Scripture, and do not fall for it because it is so common.

The same with success. Knowing the kind of solid training you got here, I suspect the devil will not try to come roaring in through your graduated front door, but he will amble in through the back. Maybe he has not been around here in the form he uses near Chicago, IBM recruitment officer joking with the undergraduate maths students promising to pay them money to go to computer training school, guaranteeing them $10,000 annually within two years – he slips the glint into their young eyes while the boys' Christian parents stand by approvingly; but the devil knows there is more than one way to skin a graduate. He can teach you to covet on a primary school teacher's salary too, morosely figuring out your rung on the salary scale, buy you with ministerial prestige in a community, plump you into a fat sleek parent relaxing on a plush living-room sofa wondering out loud why the children are not interested in 'kingdom service'.

I know, tonight is a heady night for you graduates: the handclasp of your Christian professors is worth much; the terrible intensity of the past classroom studies is sensed now as a sweet leisure you will never know again, the fact that next fall there are new fields to explore – it is all rightfully intoxicating! But do not trust the spirit of success, no matter how legitimate be its come-on. Success covers a multitude of sins in North America; but if success drives the life-breath out of you, no matter how much it be subsequently consecrated, it will turn your marriage into a wormwood of pay-cheques, your anointed teaching office into a bitter sinecure of musical chairs, the pastoral ministry into a showbox for a pompous ass.

That is what the spirit of antichrist does: turns the Christ follower into a fake. And the youth for whom you graduates now will be the older ones, especially the high-school age – even if they do not want to be openly Christian themselves – can smell a fake Christian farther away than a coon dog picks up his scent. God knows what havoc that brings into the Christian community. So diabolical is the success-babbling language of the world, splintering Christ's body into bits and pieces.

Antichrist pietism: public silence

Every spirit that does not publicly celebrate Jesus Christ come fleshly to earth is also the spirit of antichrist. That cuts quite close to home for all of us raised in country piety, because piety is a peculiar animal. *Pietas* means sincerity, a godly walk of life, simplicity, prayerful devotion, Bible study, and learning your catechism.

My boyhood was spent on the East coast near the ocean where nights you could hear the whippoorwill, Thoreau-like sounds in the woods, and the splash of phosphorescent waves on the beach and on Sundays families walked the couple of miles to church in their Sunday best while the church bells rang them in and it was a quiet enough, Puritan-minded town to pray in and learn honest piety. Perhaps there are comparable silences here far from the maddening crowd of city noises?

I am not saying biblical piety is a rural reflex, but I am saying that Dordt is known for its conservative piety and that maybe the blessing of your country quiet environs in the twentieth century is a contemporary God-send rather than an embarrassment. In the history of the church it has most frequently been the pious souls of the countryside who have brought renewal to a decadent church, breathed new evangelical life into its scholastic bloodstream. Could that be your task as college perhaps in the years ahead – to be the conscience of the Reformed community? I pray you do not become a bad conscience.

There is one thing, however, against piety gone to seed in pietism: it does not work out the implications of the Son of God's incarnation; it does not celebrate Immanuel (*God with us!*) but emphasises *our pilgrimage to* God. Therefore it has a broadly docetic, ascetic, spiritualistic bent. Pietism interiorises the

Christian life. The pietist believer fights the power of darkness in the inner chamber inside her or his house, not out on the historical street – which does not mean such battles are not as real as a hurled ink pot. The true pietist has terrible, introspective struggles because he or she is excruciatingly sensitive to every iota of his or her sinful consciousness and fiercely hates to offend, break the Law, in love for God. One is a backboned individualist who can say No again and again to temptation, who thinks to settle disturbing questions with prohibitionary silence, who pulls back from cultural involvement to devotional silence. Pietism bids one trust in God, keep your powder dry, and take time to be holy.

But not so! *All* our time should be holy, and if not, no amount of prescribed quiet hours can make it right with God. And we do not need to strive in cramped fashion to reach higher forms of moral purity: our spiritual exercises must have the free sunshine of thankfulness or they are abominations to the Father. The quirk in pietism, the antichrist in this dutiful, earnest silence, heroic omphaloskepsis, lies in its distorting locus of salvation and half-rejection of creation. Believers are God's children by adoption and may live out of grace, out of faith! We do not need to win anything or serve God as slaves (Romans 8:15). Also, our war with the evil spirits must not be reduced and hyper-focused to a mental or emotional one: Christ's coming fleshly to earth has not only redeemed created bodily activity but tells us God wants history as well as the final heaven to recognise God's Name; therefore, we must face the devil and his hosts like a human child, flesh and bloodily, on the historical street too and not pretend we are angels. The spirit of pietism would hem in Christ's lordship, and for that there is no biblical excuse.

What spirit then should drive you on, if neither the lie, nor success, nor over-pious silence? What is the spirit of Truth?

The spirit of passionate, discriminating love

The Holy Spirit of love: love God above all, neighbour as self, and world as the Lord's garden it is your joy to tend. That is not just a formula thrown out on Sunday, but the ever-present command of Love meant to work the reality of our being spirited, driven by the Spirit of Love – to be in love with God ! because God is in love with you.

I want to wear my people like a loin-cloth, God told Jeremiah the prophet. (Now a loincloth is a pretty intimate piece of underwear.) I do not want them left stuck in the mud, said Jehovah, but so close to me I can feel them when I stretch (Jeremiah 13). To that kind of jealous intensity – the LORD God, Lord of creation is our Lover! – God's people can only respond with one holy passion.

There has been some mix-up on 'love' in Christian circles. Some have rightly understood that the crooked Platonic idea of eros (love) has a person *get* for oneself, *passionately* desire selfishly to possess some good–beautiful object for self, and then wrongly opposed to it as biblical love the act of self-less *giving*, *passionless* gentleness, an irenic, unifying, good-will-toward-all type of benevolence.

The biblical *agape* (love) is certainly giving but it is also passionate, a spontaneous, self-surrendered giving of body and soul in life and death, the whole person acting as one living sacrifice of obedience to one's loving Lord. And that passion for God tempers biblical love on earth with the edge of discrimination. A believer, spirit-filled with the love of God, holds on to God for dear life, willingly binds oneself *only* to one's Almighty lover and covets *only* God's pleasure. Love means just that: the joy of spending your time together with that *special* one, doing things devotedly for your selected one's joy. Otherwise 'love' becomes a bland form of tolerance or an unctuous reduction of charity. Paul talked New Testament sense when he prayed that your *love* lead you to *discriminate* what truly counts in life so that you remain *single-minded* till the day of Christ's coming (Philippians 1:9–11).

You are aware, I take it, that the spirit of professing Jesus Christ in love seems excessive to the world. Too often, even in the church, moderation is preached: 'Don't get excited, go to extremes, be a zealot ...' But the Christian life of thanksgiving has no room for the grey mentality of reasonable moderation, a reflectively calculated state of prudence. The cautions of moderation are generally an Aristotelian reasonableness synthetically packaged as Christian and palmed off on the uneducated as the sane thing to do. Nowhere does Scripture ask a person to be temperate except in the sense of 'tempered' to coiled-spring vitality. It is the immoderate Mary and her broken flask of oil contrasted to the moderate Judas Iscariot, the irrationally good Samaritan next to the moderate Pharisee, Christ who went all-the-way versus the rich young ruler who kept the commandments moderately well – these are they who catch the apostolic and pentecostal spirit of the Scriptures. The Christian life is a love life of holy excess (Christ redeemed us to be a 'zealot of good works', Titus 2:14).

'But that excess business is dangerous; you will end up a fanatic ...' The Christian life is dangerous. It is a mark of our watered-down times that 'to be on fire for the Lord' is a martyred reality demythologised to a metaphor for modern pseudo-edification. Our logical service as lovers of God, says Romans (12:1,2), is to be going up in smoke for our Lord, a living discriminating sacrifice. We need to be turning the world upside down as Paul and Silas did, said their enemies (Acts 17:6), rather than be satisfied with armchair philosophising, contemplative 'love', sounding alarms from ivory-towered studies. This is what to love God and be loved jealously by God means in the Bible.

'Blessed are the meek.' Yes, those not proud in their own strength. It is so that they are not blessed who say 'Lord, Lord' all the time while they cut-throat the opposition. But 'meek' does not mean a docile Milquetoast, doormat mentality: that is a pacifist reading of the temple-cleansing, Christ's sermons and a denial of the power given him by the Father (Matthew 28:18) and available to Christ's body on earth. With such 'meekness' you have the sanctimonious pedantry that paralyses action; and if love is anything, it is action, deed by the hand, not talk.

The spirit of impassioned, discriminating love is the offence, offensive answer of the Bible to the spirits of silence and success. Such single-minded love is itself also the source of a person's ability to put spirits to the test and know whether they be of God or not. Not intelligence but this intimate love for God leads a person to sniff out what is the spirit of truth and what of antichrist.

If the spirit of passionate, discriminating love fills your post-graduation life as you lead God's people in the world, they will listen to you leaders, say the Scriptures, for you shall win their trust. Trust of the uneducated followers in Christ's body deserves to be won. It cannot be bought, propagandised, or argued for – thank God! – because genuine warmth and discernment of what is the Lord's work comes only out of a below-the-conscious-surface love response. Those rooted in loving God understand one another.

The fun of reforming cultural deed

'The Son of Man came eating and drinking' (Matthew 11:19); *Gaudeamus igitur!* Once one is caught by the reality of God on earth, shown off in Jesus Christ as human, and once one is filled by the holy spirit of passionate love for him, one cannot help but enjoy publicly celebrating the fact that Jesus Christ is Lord of creation and that to us believers come the unheard-of cosmic privileges of showing just that: the beginnings of Christ's blessed government everywhere.

This reality should bring the covenanted people of God a sense of joy in life rather than grim-faced duty. *We* are the ones specially shielded by an umbrella of grace in the world (1 Timothy 4:10)! The world and all its treasures is our inheritance (Colossians 1:12)! There should be more atmosphere of the Cana wedding and graduation festivities to the Christian life while we wrestle with powers of darkness. Once one is kept and caressed in God's love there can be more holy music through all one's activity, from auto-mechanics to learning Sanskrit. We must stay awake, watch, suffer, yes, but we do have the beginnings of eternal life *now*. And there is fun and excitement because God's world is full of surprises and God floods sin too with forgiveness upon repentance.

Can you graduates catch that vision? So you fellows are old enough to die in Vietnam. Still then, the tone of the third part of the catechism is our guide:

thanksgiving! That is what sanctification is all about: not that we get better, but that the Lord gets more of us under Holy Spirited love control so that we become not our own but possessed by God, God's Spirit – and that is not a stuffy business but a passionate love affair.

We must not make the secular mistake of imagining God to be up there somewhere while we ask God questions, 'Why is there hate among people? Why murderous killings? Why incurable cancer?' and we wait for the answers. No. Rather, actually God is there openly commanding us: 'Love Me above all, loincloth, and show it!' And some keep their backs turned … and some, with our feeble response of praise buoyed up by His Grace, are kept busy, laughing and weeping in faith till Christ come.

Why are you called a Christian? 'Because,' says the rich Heidelberg Catechism, 'I am a member of Christ by faith, and thus a partaker of His anointing (as prophet, priest, and king), that I may confess His Name, present myself a living sacrifice of thankfulness to Him, and with a free and good conscience fight against sin and the devil in this life, and hereafter reign with Him eternally over all creatures.'

For a person to be a Christian is to receive over one's shoulders the wedding garment of prophecy, ministry, and royal authority, that is, be appointed, graduated, and Holy Spirit qualified to act and think, speak, teach in the name of Jesus Christ, the great Teacher, High Priest, and Lord, before whose footstool all things shall be brought. The Christian believer has this human office of being the responsible developer of the universe, charged with the power and direction of the living Word of God. It is exactly that Word which it is the believer's task and joy to profess pentecostally in all its forming richness according to the measure of one's talents.

Does that need underlining? that which God said to man and woman before they sinned, 'Bear fruit, mature, inhabit the earth; subdue and control the waters' fish, the sky's birds, and every living thing that crawls over the face of the earth,' God was not just suggesting Adam and Eve sleep together, raise a Dutch-sized family and have their children become fishermen, farmers, and bird-watchers. The thrust of God's whole directive to humankind was to dignify them as the Lord's trusted viceregent over the whole cosmos. That is Dordt College's reason for being in operation, and no other.

And you should never forget that this 'cultural mandate', God's Word, as always was, is a command graciously bringing blessing, rich abundant life to whoever obeys in faith. Cultural action, opening up creation's possibilities intentionally, self-consciously, with a view to succeeding generations taking up the work with new initiative and bringing it to greater flower, this is the singular character of human hallelujahing the LORD God, and deserves our very life. Culture is not therefore something separate, optional, a dessert to the Christian life: it is rather a very channel of worship proper to human nature and an activity in which humankind is inescapably engaged – presiding by God's delegation over the rest of creation's formation, development – from lowly tillers of the soil to composers of six-part harmony chorales.

The monkey-wrench of sin distorts it all. But there is your task as Christian college graduates, in the special fields where you have been trained, to show the body of Christ and the world God's presence and leading spirit at work in art and science, ideas and reforms of society. You graduates have not finished with the cultural mandate but have only been primed to begin its business of reforming the traditions of humankind till everything be brought subject in obedience to Christ.

For you prospective primary- and secondary-school teachers, reforming cultural deed means the awful business of writing letters not written with ink but with the spirit – put the spirits to the test! – writing letters not with ink but with the spirit of the living God, not in tablets of stone (or paper) but in the fleshy tablets of (children's) hearts. So say the Scriptures (2 Corinthians 3:3)! Is it any wonder James says: Don't many of you become teachers, because we receive a more severe judgment (3:1).

The spirit of crafty professorial deceit may kill thousands of students, and success kill its ten thousands; but it is only the spirit of biblical love and joyful God-service that you before God must instill by educational osmosis in your charges – all the rest you do pales next to it! only that reforming biblical spirit does God use to save one and bring lasting fun to the world.

All of you graduates, top of the class to the bottom – it is not a matter of intellect and performance but a matter of love, knowing whom you believe and undissembling willing to test the spirits roaming around, to mark what is approved of God: all of you are called to join in public celebration of Jesus Christ come fleshly to earth, to build up a Septuagint articulation of that act of God historically and its cosmic significance for *1965 Anno Domini*. Even if the worldly ones do not hear us, do not listen, God does! and God's Holy Spirit shall communicate through our weak service or use it as judgement upon the world. Such is the offence, offensive answer of the Bible to the spirit of probing deceit: public, reforming Christian cultural action.

The body of Christ, hereabouts and elsewhere too, does not expect silence from you graduates. And if it be so that Iowa is noted more for its conservatism than its reformation of American life today, is it too much to hope that you graduates, from a solid base of piety, be among the first wave of Dordt-disciplined Christians with the eyes to see and the heart to respond to the Holy Spirit of discriminating love put to open reforming deed? so that two times ten years from now your students and children, come to this place, shall be able to glory in the same childlike weakness before the world you have tonight, strong in the Lord, and know that the faith of their parents, yourselves, was surely the living growing spirit of truth that inherits the world.

If you become discouraged soon at the scholarly success and manoeuvring innuendo of worldly ones inside and outside the church, remember, beloved, the Spirit in you is greater than the spirit in them. It pleases the Lord God to use the weak things of creation and history to confound the strong: you *have* overcome those anti Christ; therefore, be of good cheer. Work and laugh, give birth and sing, for the LORD God, your Almighty Lover, is coming soon to finish the work you here at Dordt have begun.

7 The Christian School in American Democracy*

The Pharisees once put their heads together to think up how they might trap Jesus in an argument. They sent him their disciples with those who were pro Herod the ruler.

'Teacher,' they said, 'we know you speak the truth, you truly teach the way of God; you don't care who it is, for you don't look people over first – tell us, what do you think? Is it proper to give tax to Caesar, yes or no?'

Jesus, who knew their conniving first-hand, said, 'You hypocrites, why do you try to test me? Show me the money of your taxes.'

The tempters brought him a small Roman coin. He asked them, 'Whose face and inscription is this?' They said, 'Caesar's ...' Jesus said to them, '(You can) give Caesar Caesar's things, (if you) give God what belongs to God' (Matthew 22:15–21).

Unless we follow Christ's wisdom here, the topic 'Christian education in a democracy' could trap us neat: go all out for the Christian school and you seem a little less than American to your voting neighbour and fellow citizen; champion the public institutions of our great American democracies and you seem to hedge on your devotion to the Christian school. 'Christian education in our democracy' – must the Christian citizen be divided? play off both allegiances in some kind of balance? dialectical tension, perhaps, dear to the hair-splitting heart of every Pharisee?

Christ's simple, elusive wisdom cuts short all such tempting, theoretical exercise: you can only give American democracy what it is got coming to it, if you know what you must give God. And God, in education and all of life, gets *everything* from the believer, doesn't God?

American democracy

To say just what 'democracy' means today is no joke. East Germany, the Soviet Union, and most of the Americas all claim to be 'democratic'. If we restrict

---

*Address to the 44th Annual Christian School Convention, Kalamazoo, Michigan, 11 August 1964, published in *Christian School Directory 1964–5* (Grand Rapids: National Union of Christian Schools, 1965), pp. 223–40.

the matter to the political setup constitutionally structured in the eighteenth century for the United States of America, then maybe we can start to identify certain features for a working definition. Then 'democratic' will be a government vested by frequent and secret vote of the people for representatives who, in tandem with executive rulers and an independent judiciary to safeguard the rights of individual citizens, seek to maintain a just order for all segments of society to operate freely at their respective tasks. Our country's 'democratic' conception limited federal and state governmental powers by written law; it guaranteed, again by written law, what it called inalienable human rights to every person, of life, private property, freedom of speech and exercise of one's faith. For its final authority the United States of America appealed 'democratically' to the sovereign, majority will of the People within its borders. It is this kind of polity, an incarnation of John Locke's ideas coloured by an Old England independentism and a rugged New England concern for the individual, framed in the honest theism and sincere deism of enlightened Southern planters. Why is it this 'Democracy', born in the American Revolution long ago, that has been envied, copied and parodied by insurgents throughout the world trying to turn feudal and tribal societies into modern nations? Why? Is American democratic government so inherently attractive to twentieth-century people?

To get closer to the stuffings of 'democracy', our democracy, we need to notice that American democracy has become more than a political order: it stands for a whole way of life that spells equality, freedom, and material prosperity for all people. This is what people everywhere covet and what we Americans in fact enjoy; it is more than fiction – equality, freedom, and material prosperity. That is very important for us American Christians busy with education to examine.

The Bible says people are equal before God and God's judgement upon sin. God is no respecter of persons; that people are unequal in talents, station and responsibility on earth, however, the Bible does not mind saying too. Our Declaration of Independence shifted 'equality' a notch: all people are created equal before Nature, and no government nor law may be a respecter of persons. That key political concept of impartial justice from the state has the blessing of truth with it, but because the biblical insight of a person's inequality among people got lost a bit in the shift, 'equality' has gradually enlarged its meaning somewhat indiscriminately. Today in America, if a person is not given equal opportunity in business, if a person is not equal socially to his or her neighbour, if he or she has not equal cultural duties, something is thought wrong – it is not 'democratic'! And such democratic equalising of people, the levelling de Tocqueville acutely saw at work in America already a hundred years ago, appeals to the many who would like to cut down to size people who have more privileges, substance, and ability than they have. This move toward a general 'equality', sameness among people is now part of American democracy.

Freedom too. The Bible says that a person is free who obeys God's law, filled with the Holy Spirit. Rousseau and the modern temper shifted things again: that person is free who to his or her own natural self can be true, unhampered by all sorts of civil and legal restrictions. This last kind of freedom is the spirit of the French Revolution, loose today in the cry and anarchy of Uhuru! To be sure, the liberty and looseness in the American republic, unlike the first French republic, was defined much more rationalistically by our founding fathers; yet there has been an undercurrent of this laissez-faire, better, let-me-be! don't-fence-me-in! wild Western taking the law into your own hands type of freedom in US history too. The dominant note of American freedom fighters, of course, has usually been the highly noble moral one, intent that people be free from war, free from fear, free from disaster, free from poverty. You could say, though, that if the accent is always on freedoms *from* without freedom *to* service of the living God, there may be the devil to pay with so much 'freedom' on our hands, even in American democracy.

I suppose the chief freedom, the most noted come-on of American democracy to the contemporary world, is our freedom to make money. And I can imagine the chagrin of a people which has tried to adopt our democratic machinery, swallowed our liberal advice, and then waited for the millennium, in vain; no wonder they cast about for other 'democratic' models. They do not realise that the incredible wealth of United States citizens has many reasons, the remarkably open, internally mobile 'democratic' society which still frees talent to produce its best, yes, but also rich and varied natural resources, an ingrained tradition of hard Puritanic work, a wide-spread fascination and apparent knack for technology, and – who knows why? – God Almighty's special blessing. This fact of prosperity, overwhelming affluence in American democracy, is both relevant and touchy when you begin talking about giving to Caesar and Christian education.

Do you see what I'm after? To make concrete the necessary relation of the Christian school in American democracy we have to feel into the state structure, the most crucial characteristics, and now the peculiar spirit of American democracy.

It should be said quite bluntly: the secular spirit of disbelief in the Christian God has hold of American democracy at its vitals. It is no secret to anybody that times have changed, that our colonial and Puritan fathers are past, that *Moby Dick* and the houses of seven gables via *Life on the Mississippi* have given way to *Catcher in the Rye* and *Blues for Mr. Charlie*; that the urban renewal 1960s impetus is sharply different from the spirit of '76 and the brain-trusted New Frontier is most unlike the good Old Frontier – that is no secret. It should also be no secret that in and out of the change to America, sparking it, has come a benevolent, tough-minded spirit called Pragmatism, and if that pragmatic spirit driving American thought and society today has become truly the genius of American democracy, as so many have said it is, then pray hard for your children, because this pragmatic dynamic is a hell-bent force with no use for Jesus Christ as Lord. I am not saying that all change is bad nor that secularism is an American trademark. I am being brash enough to say that the major winds of doctrine and life blowing through Western and world civilisation since the Renaissance, in spite of the Reformation, on our technologically compacted little planet, are a whirlwind, a Blue Devil's whirlwind causing people increasingly to forget the God of the Scriptures as ruler of human affairs. And this secular, intrinsically revolutionary whirlwind has blown into the American democratic way of life as the pragmatic directive.

Pragmatism trusts the scientific method to lead people on to greater wealth, equality and freedom. The pragmatic mentality gladly admits its results are never final and unblushingly continually expects good luck as it experiments further. It wants action and promises progress. If only we can bring our scientific know-how to bear upon all life's problems we will not only get a man on the moon but solve our economic problems, correct our military and political policies, agricultural surplus, racial tensions – if we will only try hard enough and all get together – all get together behind the infallible scientific method – it works! – and we'll plan us all into one great big happy, successful community where indeed no one will be more equal than another and freedom shall mean total security and there will be a Guaranteed Annual Wage. *All get together!* This Community-ism is the glove to the pragmatic hand, and it is ominous. It is not Communism, which has an élite to tell you exactly what you can do for your country, and it is not socialism, where everybody is brought legally into line with an international welfare working society. Community-ism is peculiarly American, and it has you adjust all right to the whole but uses much more subtle, decentralised social pressure appealing to your reason and community spirit, a little bit like the old Athenian 'democracy' (which had an unmistakable totalitarian grip on an individual person's life). Pragmatism would not mind a 'guided democracy' so long as it was *scientifically* guided.

Do not misunderstand me to be talking black and white. History never breaks clean like a prize-fight. I am calling your attention to this, that the leading spirit, the moving force at work in our beloved America is this religiously secular spirit of Pragmatism with its accompanying pressuring Community-ism, and that this spirit is at the vitals of American democracy because it is capturing the hearts of us people, damningly successful. It is a tempting, wicked spirit because it omits God; not that it drives Americans to repudiate God theoretically, just that it trains them to ignore God practically, as irrelevant. But you cannot ignore God the Lord with impunity. Success does not cover that kind of sin. And we people gathered here do not need to point fingers at a pragmatic Supreme Court or at liberal well-to-do Protestant churches and their community chested attitude, making believe the body of Christ is a volunteer outfit. We ourselves cannot retreat to Grand Rapids, Iowa or New Jersey and stick our head in some conservative sand till the wind blows over because this pragmatic spirit is so strong it is changing the chemical composition of ostrich-headed sand. The evil pragmatic spirit gets inside a home and school and church like radio-active material; you don't know it has hit you till you're burned. 'Will it be effective? If not, we shall not do it.' Hidden persuasion flattering our faithless intelligence. Diabolical! American democracy, all of it, is in our blood.

The Christian school

Comes then the Christian school. Is that ostrich-headed work? I shall not count the many Christians teaching at public schools and secular colleges or universities. I do not question their valid and missionary reasons for choosing such jobs, but they do not properly constitute Christian education in American democracy. For 'Christian' education means at least education done openly and formally in the name of Jesus Christ and for Jesus' sake, and not in the name of the Canadian or United States Government, in the name of Humanity, Freedom, or any other such name given under heaven. 'Christian' education is education where the Holy Spirit is publicly invited to come in and influence the very educational processes. It is education, further, where there is a conscious, willed, obviously concerted effort to proclaim in all its scandalous intolerance that the mind of Jesus Christ is the only true way for life and knowledge, in biology, history, literature, geography … Christian education is not a matter of getting together a group of teachers somewhere till you have a simple majority of confessing Christians, each able to let his little evangelical light shine, and let it go at that, because Christian education takes in more than individual human endeavour. It takes place when the presence of the Lord is felt, known, seen, evident in the studying, wrestled and prayed for *communally* by the faculty, administrators, the board as one person on its knees, the parents behind it, the students too if you are blessed. That is, Christian education, for me, means a Christian school. A place where you can write indelibly across the entrance for every passer-by to see, minister, business person, government official, every angel and devil in the neighbourhood:

In Jesus Christ are hid all the treasures of wisdom and knowledge (Colossians 2:3).

A Christian school is a society of parents organised to support an arm of the body of Christ, a *Christian* community (!) of teachers with the office to open up children to the wonders of God's world by the light of the Scriptures. I am aware of sham, that what is Christian education in name may in fact informally not be so – each one look to oneself – but where saints in communion, invoking the free play of the Holy Spirit, solemnly declare they shall articulate, however imperfectly, Christ's lordship for every area of creation and then proceed slowly *all together in faith*: there is where you must look for Christian education.

But how about that ostrich-headedness? Are Christian schools not built as safe places for the kids to grow up in, away from the big bad wolves? Are not Christian school societies actually Societies for the Prevention of Cruelty and Obscene Literature and Gross Wickedness to Children? like putting your heads communally in the sand?

There is a Christian school in my home town of West Sayville, Long Island, New York, because a series of ministers faithfully preached the gospel and the Word fell on good ground. I dare say that is why many other localities have Christian schools too. The Bible says so! 'Fathers, don't drive your children mad: bring them up in the discipline and formation of the Lord!' (Ephesians 6:4). You have really got to twist pragmatically to squirm from underneath that biblical imperative as a Bible believer. Back home the Christian school society was not protectionist – what from? The local grade schools and high school I was attending were manned by God-fearing Methodist and Congregationalist ladies and gentlemen (Oh, there may have been an evolutionist or two thrown in, but we kids could handle them with a little extra coaching from our parents), crackerjack New York schools, no Blackboard Jungle then. The Christian school society was not even a protest, but a genuine, positive response to the preached Word. It took years, certainly! Shaping the consciousness of Dutch people is not done in a day, and the best believers can be slow of heart, and you have to find the means. The beginning of classes finally in the church chapel was so pitifully small it had to be a determined act of faith. But I remember, as a teenager, when the Christian school got its own building, built by the men and women themselves under a Christian contractor; I remember the nights after supper, young and old men up on the roof nailing shingles in the summer twilight in great sweat and joy while townsfolk gathered on the sidewalk across the street to watch, somewhat incredulous at these crazy fishermen and clam-diggers; it had the excitement of building Noah's ark on dry ground and we knew it would rain. I know, it is harder to be simple and faithlike nowadays; the construction trade is much more specialised, and 4.5–5 per cent mortgages take longer to get and to pay; but again, I dare say there are many Christian schools throughout our nations, thank God, especially in Canada now, simply because believing parents responded to the Word of the Lord: 'Fathers, don't drive your children mad: bring them up in the discipline and formation of the Lord!'

I cannot believe the second-guessing insinuation that the major force behind our Christian school movement has been withdrawal, an attempt to close eyes and ears to 'the world'. Wherever that motivation has been mixed in – godlessness may be a context but not the ground – unless it is scotched soon there will be trouble because it is false! You cannot withdraw from sin! The Devil merely concocts a new brand inside the walls which, while it doesn't make the headlines, is just as dirty and mean and stupid. And there will be the trouble of young blood called to be saints in education tiring and leaving because you cannot build a glorious vessel for the Lord, you cannot build on a defensive reaction.

There may still be confusion and weakness in some minds on the Christian school's task (here I cut in closer to what we are after). Many evangelicals, in obedience to God's command, hold Sunday Schools correctly as mission projects, and then develop Daily Vacation Bible Schools, correctly, as mission projects, and then think why not increase our coverage from two weeks to nine months which we can do if we add the required state subjects in other fields – what a boost it will be to the home and the church – and so develop Christian Day Schools, incorrectly, as carry-over mission projects, a kind of church and state agency under one roof for Christian common-sensical (= pragmatic?) reasons. This is why you can find sometimes a strange secularism and revivalism existing side by side at so-called fundamentalistic Christian institutions, some areas admittedly untouched by Christian focus yet everywhere surrounding a genial, genuine Christian-hearted readiness to talk about Jesus Christ as personal Saviour, lacking in more dour Christians. But the Christian school is not a hybrid church and state. It is a separate institution in which Christian parents delegate their authority to others for the formal training and maturing of their Christian children. The Christian school is not aimed at regeneration but is busy with sanctification – any salvaging, 'saving', is wonderfully incidental; its job is to *teach*, not preach, to show the cosmic kingship of their Saviour Jesus Christ in God's world and what this means for daily life. This is what bringing children up in the discipline and formation, awe of the LORD is all about.

The formation is done schoolishly; it is a scholastic enterprise, academic. There is a 'distance' to schooling not found in earning a living or going places. In school you don't go to Antarctica; you find it on the map and look at photographs. In school you don't make an atomic bomb; you read about its physics in a book and demonstrate chemical experiments. There is a schematic suspension, a pull-back from 'practical' involvement to schoolwork, often mistaken by critics for impracticality because unfortunately this 'school' character helps a school system become a sanctuary for impractical pedants, a sinecure for the contemplative lazy candleholders who like to look on rather than act, who live as if the school world had no other world outside it to live in and conquer. It is also true that unimaginative misuse of this scholastic structuring helped all-

American Dewey and his angels to get rid of the baby with the bathwater, to make convincing that good education must be a real *life*-experience, *do* things with your hands! experiment! act! don't study German grammar; converse! don't study phonics; read! the norm for education is a *real* life-situation! The Christian school does well to catch in perspective what Dewey blindly absolutised, the importance of liveliness and fun and relevance in studying; but if you lose the schoolbookishness to schooling you have lost what distinguishes a school from playground, travel and on-the-job training. Precisely in this abnormal academic schoolishness lies the spring to the tremendous impact formal education can have upon a person's life. It is so that in a school you can add up a column of figures wrong without being put in jail; in a Christian *school* you can throw out some strange ideas without being immediately put under church censure; in medical school a student can disembowel a corpse wrong and thank God it was not for 'real': but in all this 'unreal' tentativeness, in this protected (!) trial-and-error pushmipullmi leisure that goes with learning, right there, unawares, how simple arithmetical errors are corrected, how a stinking hulk of flesh is respected, how the new ideas are thrown out, in *faith* for the *truth*! or in that Socratic, cynical way that flips a covenant child's commitment up on razor edge and lets it spin – right there, in combat with evil spirits and thrones and principalities, is where the moulding and slowly leading, formation of Christian scientists, doctors and leaders is done or undone, where hearts and minds are *set* in the Lord or unsettled. A child's underlying consciousness can be shaped at any age, hideously. This is the job Christian parents delegate to you teachers and me: bring them up in the formation of the Lord! Anybody who thinks that school formation is a rather harmless transfer of punchcard data, skilled manipulation, and maybe some 'values' the humanists talk about is quite shallow in his analysis. Schoolbookish formation gets down where you play for keeps.

This should be said too: because the Christian school is there for schoolish discipline, *paideia*, tempering, exercising, the plastic moulding of students in Latin, chemistry and literary criticism, any behaviour that interferes, blurs, or would chill the Holy Spirit's presence in the schoolbookish developing is simply out of place. And it is the high calling of administrators to minister to the teachers, to make Christian teaching possible, probable! by coaxing out almost unconsciously that so difficult, delicate, wholesome attitude among the student body for school work. A staggering ministry at the teenage level, it seems to me. Keen-eyed entrepreneurs are probably not building motels across the street from your Christian high schools as they have done near some suburban Chicago public school areas, just to be handy, but a beat, gang-like, careless spirit does not leave us untouched either. A Christian principal can expect, I suppose, when *Look, Life,* and TV run unchecked, radio-active, through the Christian living room, that a few of his girls will want to dress like bunnies and a few of the fellows will follow up a swiggled hip or rowdily depant the meek; but it seems to me it would be exhiliaratingly healthy for the Christian school as Christian school if parents were faced with the fact that the Christian school is not a moral reformatory and that attendance is a privilege as well as an obligation before God. And no administrator may cover up a weak spine with the formula *70 × 7* or hold back school expulsion as if it were church excommunication. So crucial is the atmosphere at a Christian school that a class with high SAT scores is a mockery unless the spirit of simple thankfulness and deep dependence upon God, of course in all its boyish and girlish unevenness, unless that holy spirit somehow prevail.

When an irate Christian parent filled with community spirit thinks to trap you in a self-righteous argument about the Christian school, yes or no? Christ's answer is: let that Christian parent take his little child and look at its face carefully; if he sees Caesar Augustus inscribed there across the eyes, then send him to the state school. No cajoling. Let the church preach the gospel! The Christian school does not have its head in the sand but is being weakly built upon the strong rock, the cornerstone of the kingdom coming and at hand. It is schools where the typical American democratically pragmatic spirit rules that have heads in sinking sand.

A just state: the free school

The Christian school is, as a matter of fact, in contemporary American democracy. That historical given, with all its complex blessings, still does not say how they should be related. That there has been so little friction between Christian school and American state is a testimony to the original intent of the early New England and Virginia provinces that schools form Christian people and that despite the continued watering down of that first ideal the United States government has officially maintained a 'friendly' disposition toward a figurehead Deity for its citizens. The amicability of Christian school and American state is also a testimony to the law-abiding respect for government and concern for civic good held by those Christian parents who were constrained by the love of God to set up schools radically subjected to the sovereignty of Jesus Christ, a testimony too, perhaps, of their uncertainty as to where they stood – conscientious objectors?

Right now, however, there is a suspense in the air, thanks to the Becker amendment and such stuff.* More people sense a shift in the wind; and while

---

*Around 1962 a New York principal stopped the ritual of oral prayer in a state school, and PRAY (Prayer Rights for American Youth) sued to continue the practice. The U.S. Court of Appeals, second district, then ruled that the First Amendment means that a state-owned facility is not compelled to let citizens pray there. In 1963 the Supreme Court refused to hear an appeal to that ruling. Different groups then organized to amend the constitution (the Becker amendment) to permit prayers in public schools.

they may not want to worship God, many Americans still do think it fair play to be honest to God, on a kind of person-to-person basis, especially if it is more apt to keep the standard of living up. But the shift in spirit informing the American democratic way of life from an enlightened rationalistic deism to the practising atheism of pragmatism does not let one so easily be honest to God. Let no one underestimate the drastic socio-political, economic–ethical changes taking place today on top of the change in spirit – people change homes like cars every few years; children are a population problem for contraceptives rather than an inheritance of the Lord; you can't step on somebody's toes in Cyprus or Vietnam without threatening to mangle somebody else's whole leg. The pitch and tempo of major changes in patterns of living and killing is so rapid, faster than a generation, that parentally posited norms cannot be applied in a pat way even by their grown children.

The Christian school in American democracy is a nice focus to the suspense. It could become, shall we hope, a crucial test of the Christian community's wisdom, witness and nerve. Evangelicalism with its built-in anti-cultural bias does not have the goods to show leadership here, I think; it will hang on gamely, preach the gospel of salvation, and seek to avoid clashes. A Roman Catholic ('common grace') Christian humanism does not have the passion to reform secular American life either, but is content to arrest and contain the malignancy while getting separate but equal due for itself. It is the Reformational Christian perspective which has the biblical insight to offer guidelines and directives that fully honour God.

I mean this: most people can tell the difference between a human and an ape, especially if it is a question of marriage. Astute biologists, however, who do not believe the creation story of Genesis have a terrible time trying to define the difference and sometimes end by wiping it out – they cannot see the things of God's spirit because they do not discern holy spiritually, say the Scriptures (1 Corinthians 2:14). Most people could tell the difference between a school and a church and a business and the state; but it is a mark of the blinding secular spirit loose in American society today that the government and business and school are often only semi-distinguishable. It is this 'principle', however, if you will, that Kuyper meant by sphere sovereignty, the simple, homespun, observable truth that a school is not a business and a business is not government and government is not an educational institution, and that all such radically different-structured institutions, school, church, business, and state as another one, are mutually bound to one another but mutually bound as equally sovereign whole institutions of an inviolably different sort, each with its own prerogatives, i.e. God-delegated rights peculiar to its office – the church as confessional fellowship to preach and administer sacraments; the business as an association for commerce and fair profit on services and goods distributed; the school as a parentally delegated institution to educate children;

the state as God's instrument to administer justice. It is this Reformational Christian insight which honours God's ordering in society for its godly walk that can direct us and preserve us in all the fierce change from chaos or totalitarianism. For when one institution, generally the powerful state, assumes as its own, functions not peculiar to its own structuration, the result sooner or later is societal stress, decomposition and great human misery.

This truth is quite 'practical' and has a very unpalatable, demanding Christian wisdom to it. It means that church and industry as well as state should assume before God their own kind of responsibility for the school without subtly seeking its control. The church may not say to the Christian school: 'Give us ministers, missionaries and theologians, else what have we to do with thee? We will support Calvin College only if you tack on a Seminary.' Industry may not say to the Christian school: 'Give us stenographers, nurses, engineers, technicians, and turn a profit now and then, else why should we invest in what yields no returns on our money?' Church and industry, if they would be Christian, must not try to make the school a seminary or a business and support it only if they directly get something out of it, but before God must help the school be a good school. They should ask for educated believers and educated clients (or will that hurt the persistent clericalism in the church and Madison Avenue's beamed appeal to the twelve year old mentality?) In turn the school, the Christian school, must fulfil its obligation to church and industry; produce students with a matured confession, a living appreciation of the Church's heritage; and give industry students who are not speculative but hard-working, efficient, time-conscious labourers with a vision of subduing the daily workaday world honestly for Jesus Christ.

In the same light the relation of Christian school to the American state should be seen. When the state would dictate to Christian parents and teachers' association, to the school institution, for example, that you teach the 'Christian religion' factually as no more than a factor, as economics or politics or race is a factor in American life and culture, or would dictate (should it ever come to that openly) that you teach that American Democracy is as important almost as the kingdom of God, then the Christian PTA says firmly No! to the American state and requests it to stop pressuring the school to become some kind of state agency but to return to its God-given limited task of not educating but tending to justice. The American state may demand of any school, including the Christian school, educated citizens; but it may not come inside and fix the educating. I know, there are moot points: to maintain civic stability the state sets, from the outside, minimum school standards; and in a crisis like the nineteenth-century inundation of unskilled immigrants the state felt itself forced to crash-programme more 'public' education in the interests of the commonwealth. The Christian community must just make certain that if the American states' idea of school standards and civil emergencies becomes increasingly secular, the squeeze play in education be met not with equal pragmatism and 'natural reason' but with a fearless, turning-the-other-cheek, witnessing Christian judgement. The Christian school is glad to produce American citizens who will defend with their lives our one nation, indivisible, under the living God, with freedom to obey God's laws, and asks only to be free in its own schoolish way to produce such patriots, who will also guard jealously the state's calling to prescribe equal justice for everyone.

Note well: the biblical sanity of sphere sovereignty must not be twisted into special pleading for a general functionalistic decentralisation, as if the state should look the other way while Big Business and Big Labour fight it out – such would be an unchristian abdication by the state of its political task. There is more social Darwinian, survival-of-the-fittest philosophy in laissez-faire doctrine than 'conservatives' are willing to see. The American state must signal and enforce just relations between its citizens, bodies of citizens and all institutions, legal and civil justice, neither more nor less! wherever it is necessary; otherwise there will be no 'free' industry, church or school. You need a just state to have the free school, the Christian school free to be a Christian school.

It is for this relation – a just state and the free school – we Reformational Christians, as one body, should work. To suggest just the dynamic of our work with the Christian school in American democracy I will say two more things.

1. The Christian school must stick to its radically biblical, Reformational Christian foundations. It is so tempting to cosy up pragmatically and become acclimatised to the American scene, be one of the boys, or, for example, become a parochial school. But in our consolidation as Christ's body, schoolishly structured, lies our strength: we know what a school is to be and what we are about educationally, and this Christian difference should not be apologised for at major educational councils and symposia but we should challenge that schools not free from church and state or business are not schools as they should be. And if the free Christian school needs money we might do well to check our running to philanthropic foundations, and first, last, and again, go to the Christian rich – who is poor? – who love God, and show them that our Christian school is God's school, that's why we are so New Testamently crazy about it and why you should be too. Let the Christian school be driven to appeal to the hearts of those rich in Christ rather than to the criteria of secular money. That spirit, in its naiveté I admit, strikes me somewhat more biblically than going to the state and arguing with Shylock, 'Give me my pound!'

2. We Christians in love with the Christian school as a response to God's grace upon us and our children must be spilling that love over toward American democracy. That means we are called to a communal Reformational Christian witness to the state. That does not mean we organise a pressure group to get a manger scene on the next Christmas postage stamp or go all

out to elect some Calvinist to the Michigan legislature or even necessarily lobby for a 'Christian Bus Bill': Reformational Christian witness to American democracy does not mean we seek a little place in the sun too. It must be made unmistakably clear to them that our zeal is Jesus Christ's cause, not the needs of his believers, us. As Citizens United for Christian Schools and therefore for Educational freedom – that's the priority and stress Kuyper put on it and what we need to hear from the C.E.F.* – as a National Union of Christian Schools we need to be making a national witness in Washington, DC, and Ottawa: that all life is religion in operation before God and that only in Jesus Christ is their hope for American education and American democracy. Do you see the scandalous bite that would have? And we believe that, don't we?! Only in Jesus Christ is there hope for American education and American democracy!?

Were you ever caught by what happened between Paul and Caesar's representatives, Festus and King Agrippa? Paul in audience was answering the charges of the Jews, and he swung into proclaiming Christ's rising from the dead as light for Jews and Gentiles. Festus interrupted with a loud voice:

'You're crazy Paul! Much learning has made you mad!'
'I am not crazy, noble Festus,' said Paul. 'I am speaking tempered true words. King (Agrippa) knows whereof I talk … You believe the prophets, don't you, King Agrippa? I know you believe them!'
And King Agrippa jested: 'In a minute you'll persuade me to be a Christian!'
And Paul said, 'Would to God not only you but all those hearing me here …'
Then King Agrippa got up and House Rules Committee Hearing on Bill 1521 was adjourned.

We need the National Union of Christian Schools testifying to the American democracy!

Senator Humphrey, do you believe the Christian Scriptures?

Can you imagine! Are we embarrassed? Don't we have the worldliwise humour and affront to beard the state in its den with the Christian Scriptures? That is needed to bear a Christian witness in American politics! That is giving Caesar what he has got coming to him and giving God everything at the same time. Not in a slapdash 'Brother, are you saved' fashion, but in the dead scandalous earnest of this outspoken confrontation that the biblical revelation of Jesus Christ is where government, press and school must go to take hopeful shape. That is giving Caesar even more than he thinks is coming to him!

---

*Citizens for Educational Freedom.

It is raining rather hard outside, in American democracy, secularly pragmatic radioactive rain. The Christian school is not a safe place to keep dry; our work on the roof is full of holes. So here we are: the Christian school in American democracy.

We must not divide our allegiance between Caesar and the kingdom of God. To Caesar, as the body of Christ united in faith and with a live sense of the reality of the power of the Holy Spirit to move people's hearts, to Caesar we must pay our communal biblical witness on power, justice, equality, freedom, sin ... the world, so that American democracy also, please the Holy Spirit, be conformed to the ways of our God. To the Christian school, as teachers, administrators, board members, parents, we give our very life-time, in stumbling consecration. Some of us may not see the end of the rain while we live, but we all may believe that the Christian school is an ark! ... ark of the Covenant.

'Didn't it rain, chillen? O my Lord, didn't it rain?!' sings Mahalia Jackson, with incredulity and surprise and gladness all bursting through the confusion of Noah's ark!? Judgement Day? Victory! all mixed together in the pouring rain – 'Didn't it rain, chillen! O my Lord! didn't it rain!'

As you head back to your big and little Christian schools at the end of the week, to the wilds of Northern Canada, sunny California, Celeryville, Ohio, North Carolina and West Sayville, be steadfast in the rain, beloved, unmovable, abounding always in the work of the Lord, knowing that your labour is not in vain in the Lord.

8 The Umbrella over Trinity Christian College*

Parable of the Vineyard

the prophet (in song):
>   Let me sing a song of one who loves me,
>   a song my lover wrote about his vineyard.
>   My lover had a vineyard on a sunny, fertile mountain slope.
>   He spaded it over and over with care.
>   He took out all the stones,
>   and planted it with vines to grow grapes fit for wine.
>   My lover built a sturdy watchtower in the middle of the garden.
>   He even hewed out of the rock a press to thresh the grapes there.
>   And he waited with hope [on that mountain slope]
>   for the choice vines to bear a grape fit for wine.
>   But all he got
>   was bitter, little pits in rot (Isaiah 5:1,2).

… Why should God not destroy us, in North America? Has the Lord Yahweh not already abandoned us, God's nominal, believing people and the land we possess? The signs of the prophetic Isaiah's time are present. The country is chock-full of idolatry; not just the primitive adulation for beetle-browed specialists at incantations, but an older, more tired, easy-going idolatry connected with prosperity. When people hanker to go first-class, when you feel a need for the latest conveniences or get into the habit of being just a mite spoiled, that is, greedy, you are an idolater, say the Scriptures (Ephesians 5:5). Idolising is to desire, revere, pay undue attention to, covet some little thing to help or flatter yourself. And this covetous idolatry is so unobtrusive, petty, and as common as TV sets.

When a person owns an expensive sports car and polishes its fenders to a sheen, it may express a decent pride of ownership – God shall judge – but it is true that the dumb thing can't talk back like the living God through God's Word: reflect your own image is the most a polished car-fender can do. Not to mention the mirroring done by the comfortable sofas in our middle-class

---

*Part of an address given at an all-college retreat, published in *Torch and Trumpet* 18 (January 1968), 2–5.

living rooms, the electric carving-knives and wall-to-wall carpeting: the costly churches many of us frequent may be Ebenezers – God *is* judging the congregations – but it could just be that the heavily mortgaged, plush consistory room stinks to high heaven like an idol, reflecting our superficial sense of values.

To hold and seek inert possessions, stuff not actually moving in the world for God's sake, is to be retainer for an idol. And when idolatry is present, says Isaiah, that is evidence of the Lord's departure: God brooks no other gods beside God.

It is no wonder then that a glamour-ridden society is empty of depth. Civil leaders of stature, righteous judges with authority, intuitive wise people are so rare in the Christian community and Western citizenry at large because the developing secular, social fabric of life, like the one Isaiah exposed, induces people to frazzle themselves in the busyness of polishing idols. There are so few preachers who make you glad to be in church, so few teachers able to give Christian direction in their field, so few parents not fumbling to manage their children because everyone of us today likes to have his or her fringe benefits and keep on eating them too. A godless, softening way of life has crept up on us and robbed us of the singleness needed to grow in faith, the focusing consecration Yahweh uses in people to work God's pleasure. Nobody knows anymore what it means to be 'holy ones', saints, marked 'for Life'!

So why should God not destroy us Americans with all our money in the bank! Why should the Lord not leave us to hell, us 'Christians' who give God so much lip, lip service, who are all dressed up on Sunday with no place to go for God on Monday?

There is no reason on earth why not. And Isaiah's prophecy has got to make clear to us gathered so primly here that *we* are contributing to the coming of that awful, final Day of the Lord as well as unbelievers. You and I are actively caught up in the shameless lawlessness that elicits and characterises the Lord's process of judgement anticipating the End.

You girls may not flounce those fascinating mini-skirts around the way they do in Europe, but there is more than one way to show off in public what has native charm only in private. And you men may not be rabble-rousers, but there are all kinds of collegiate hanky-panky for thumbing your nose at the creational norm of authority. And is there a faculty member born who has no foibles, no ability to grow a pet grievance, a blind spot or coldness that lames a community of love?

These are not questions of morality. It is a matter of disguised pride and not thoroughly knowing the totalness of our anointed nature as Christ-believers. You may not hate the American Negro as some of your elders do, and you may detest the hypocrisy of the established generation; but if we ourselves do not have the humbled guts to show an open kindliness to stranger and fellow at close quarters, and if we are not concertedly reforming the social order and world of thought in some small way because it is dominated by the anarchy of multiple idolatry, if we lethargically make the best of the most decent fashion still left in clothes, decorum and ideas, then we tacitly – with a kiss – further the disintegration of God's universe. And God gets that bitter taste in God's mouth.

You students all came to Trinity – why? Because it is Christian? James (*The Fire Next Time*) Baldwin lives in Istanbul because, he says with evil penetration, the Turks, for all their faults, at least are not pretending they are Christian.

To come to Trinity Christian College is to confess one's sin – then it is right. Then there is the relief from pretence, making-believe we are so good, and teacher and student together can cry out to God for mercy and time, direction; together we can ask God to come through with wonders like in the old days when angels destroyed the enemy and mouths of lions were stopped and God's people knew what to say before unbelief. In spite of the rotten taste, because Jesus Christ is our common Lord, come through now, Almighty One, and treat us … like leftovers, sophomores, freshmen, teachers needing repair and a touch of beauty, glory. …

Do you have any idea of how solidly your faculty are leftovers? Left over from the high-pressured rat-race American industry, cast-offs from other institutions too good for them, misfits here and there because of a biblically Reformational faith. What a motley group of teachers God has mysteriously brought together, counter to any human plan, with you students, hardly imaginable, from Japan to Africa, British Columbia to Mississippi, transfers from Swarthmore to Santa Barbara, Roman Catholic and Baptist, graduates from Christian highs and secular schools. Leftovers!? Willingly or unwillingly, uncannily, leftovers for Christ's sake? found now near Chicago.

Trinity is a college for leftovers. Not in the proud sense of being reserved for those few who have not yet bowed the knee to Baal, but as an academic workshop for those who have decided 'for Life'! and then been baptised by fire, by ridicule, misunderstanding, and yes, by the burden of carrying along the indelible marks of past sin, forgiven, but in the open. Trinity is there for those who have had enough of the lukewarm stink of nominal Christianity that deserves and gets Yahweh's judgement, and who, however weakly, have decided to be busy the hard way of praising God by faithful, daily exposition of God's revelation. Nobody gets transfigured, but there is a rough joy in helping one another learn to be 'holy ones' all the time. We have got to recapture the Old Testament sense of picking out a skirt and putting on your earrings festively for God's sake! to realise the Triune God's name spread on our faded cross-country sweat-shirts is only a feeble exercise in preparing for the day coming when Zechariah says even the horses' bridles will be emblazoned with the name 'Holy be YAHWEH' (Zechariah 14:20) because *everything* belongs to God!

The faculty is together as one person on that: we mean to master creation, reform the traditions of humankind and show Life-direction for culture that reveals the holiness of Yahweh, disclosed by the eye and hand and heart of a biblical faith. This unreserved commitment is what sets Trinity apart. No philosophy or theology, teachers or chance perfection distinguishes us: solely the communal faith decision to choose Life with the jealous God rather than stay halting between service and idolatry in study.

That is not a hard decision to make, says Moses; it is not difficult to grasp (Deuteronomy 30: 11–20): it is as simple as knowing who your father is. But to sacrifice your 'reason', your 'feelings' on twentieth-century matters in order to bow exclusively before the Way, the Life the Lord commands – single-mindedly finding out *His* ordinances – this approach on earth, plagued by all our stumbling, comes hard to a person until she or he is truly broken by the powerful Word of God into a 'leftover'.

So now we go, teacher and student, into a year that shall never be repeated. Teachers always plant students, and students – if you know the expression – pot teachers. You freshmen are the first at Trinity who we hope shall be four-year graduates, but for however much time God gives us so intimately together, because we are fighting not flesh and blood so much as wily powers, we shall need to pray hard for one another, through tiredness and tedium, mistakes as well as laughter; and God shall have to do a lot of weeding.

There is the fearful possibility that the Lord has left our nations and us as a people, a so-called 'Christian' civilisation. And there is always the shadow that someday Trinity will become secularised – the temptation to idolise sport and glory in winning over a rival, forgetting our first love; the temptation to scholasticise a human thought-pattern, to produce successful graduates, to cut religious corners because of the constant lack of money, and polish it all to a sheen with pious public relations people: these temptations are real. But this possibility and shadow only underscore the urgency of our being faithful now before the Lord with everything God has given us.

And this year, if the Lord has truly spoken tonight through God's Word, which we still have had the time and Grace to hear, then we may demand in faith, not doubting, that Yahweh hang God's cloud of love and fire of reforming power over all our convocated meetings. Because the Scriptures say so, we may believe that someday the whole earth shall be refreshingly filled with God's glory, but that now at least, the Grace, Word, Holy Spirit, Presence of the Lord God Almighty is held like an umbrella over Trinity Christian College, over all us leftovers ... an umbrella, like a grape arbour giving shade against the weltering heat, like a retreat, a place to run and hide from the thunder and pouring rain.

Lord God,

Wait with hope a little bit longer for us grapes to ripen.

Take every proud and lonely and scared and uncertain person here under your umbrella of awful Majesty, and knit us together in a way that astounds and makes onlookers curious of the Truth that moves us.

Do not dislocate our lives with war and faction and the curse of idolatry, so that we may sing of your Goodness rather than lament our sin.

Because your Son is our Lord, Father in heaven, we pray, establish the work of our dedicated, sinful hands, and do not take away the umbrella over Trinity.

(in song):

Yes, the striking glory [of the Lord] shall hover over all [the 'leftovers'] like an umbrella.

[The presence of the Lord Godself] shall be like a cosy grape arbour giving shade by day against the weltering heat, like a retreat, a place to run and hide from the thunder and pouring rain.

9 The Cross of Scholary Cultural Power*

To look at us tonight it would be hard to believe that each of us once came naked out of our mother's womb. And it is good to have festive clothes, abundant food and drink, splendour of shelter, with fatness and oil dripping down our beards and goldilocks. But the reality of your being honoured for intelligence and the fact that some of you imminently face a change of life from being an honoured student at this respected Christian college to becoming a cultural initiator outside Knollcrest society is serious enough to give us pause. What is at stake in an honours convocation at Calvin College?

By reason of your rich training in the arts and sciences, you now have a deepening sensitivity and skill to mould affairs on campus, and later on in consistory rooms, school houses, hospital rooms, ghetto streets, board rooms, and the ivory-inlaid halls of secular universities where your scholarships can take you. You have in your hand cultural power – no matter what the job market – many would covet. So I speak to you as a class of rich young rulers called by the Word of God to take up your cross of scholarly cultural power and follow only Jesus Christ. Otherwise the honours of this day will come to glitter like a Babylon built by gifted students and profs, backed by believing parents; and that would be as sad as idolatry rather than the joyous occasion of blessing we have gathered to celebrate.

Cultural power defined by Humanism

Cultural power only becomes a cross when it is marked by the joy of fasting before the Lord God. 'Culture' as Matthew Arnold understood it is never a cross. It is more like a secular Holy Grail or a perfect silver spoon one pursues by religiously studying the best that has been thought and said in the world in order to free yourself from stock notions and daily life trivia.[1] Enlightenment dogma that defined humanity by a refined taste, humanist learning, daring to think for oneself in an encyclopaedic, civilised way becomes with

---

*Speech given at the annual Honours Convention held by Calvin College at its Knollcrest campus at Grand Rapids, Mich. Later published in *Vanguard* 8:2 (Aug.–Sept. 1978), 19–22.

[1]See Arnold's 'Preface' to *Culture and Anarchy*, 1869.

Arnold establishmentarian. Cultured people are by definition a cosmopolitan élite, bred by the liberal arts university; and their authority resides simply in their educated intelligence which is broader and deeper than that of uneducated mortals, who often act like trained barbarians.

Much could be said, of course, about this influential idea of cultural power. It lives off the insight that men and women who ask transcendental questions with *weltanschaulich* focus exercise and open up folds of our consciousness left undeveloped by those who remain busy hewers of wood and givers of cups of cold water to the neighbour. Arnold's vision of Culture as the bulwark against societal anarchy threatened by nineteenth-century industrialisation suffers, however, from an intellectualistic vanity that adheres to earlier versions of the venerable ideal of 'the contemplative life'. Most telling is the fact that Arnold's conception of cultural power, epitomised in the breeding of Victorian ladies and gentlemen, is dated.[2]

Arnold's belief that classic literature is the truest bearer of humanising liberation has occasioned decades of polite civil war in academia between 'the humanities' and the (natural) science departments, the engineers versus the *philosophes:* but it is clear today that that fight has been a Screwtapian diversionary tactic to keep us from the truth. Contemporary painting, music and poetry allow themselves no less specialist and abstruse than the mathematical formulae needed for space shots: and the plastics from the laboratory of science have no more a corner on humanity or inhumanity than pop-art literature and entertainment. The truth is that all scholarly culture – science or art and literature – which is conceived, desired, enjoyed or even administered as *privilege* bears questionable fruit. Such culture cannot be picked up and carried as a cross.

Cultural power defined by Marxism

Correct, says the revolutionary Marxist theorist. The cultural power convocated here is in the tradition of the monolithic medieval church, the prestigious European university, and the capitalist state which rewards its sons and daughters who buy the system and score high with sweetness and light and managerial jobs, but spells oppression for the poor of the earth, dependent upon handouts, and the less fortunate who do not survive the competition in excellence. Enlightenment science and Matthew Arnold's literary culture promised us a brave new world but have instead maximised the misery of masses of people who do still count, even though they don't make it to

---

[2]Cf. Cardinal Newman's kindred contribution in chapter 8:10 of *The Idea of a University*, (1852).

college, and who are in misery, even while they guzzle beer and junk food, watching sports events on TV – the old bread-and-circuses combination pacifier. And Christians who for years have tried to still their spiritual heartburn by exporting pietist hymns and cast-off clothes along with medical supplies and the debris of western 'culture' in the name of Christ are really antichrist, a false witness, because they have not truly emptied themselves for their neighbours in need – you probably know this Marxist line of argument aimed at the soft underbelly of us who have middle-class status.

Marxist critique certainly touches a nerve centre in our honourable hypocrisy. But there is a curious ambivalence in Marx when he comes to formulate his own positive judgement on cultural power. Art, philosophy, 'religion' and political–cultural sciences are all secondary for Marx, superstructural to the basic 'material history' of humankind, the socio-economic means and productive forces which make things tick in society, he believes. Marx also was so anguished by the dehumanising humiliation workers suffered in factories, where humans are made accessories of machines, that he envisioned a future, communist society without division-of-labour divisiveness and professionalistic specialisation. So there is a curious pull-back at times in Marxist theory of culture and its embodiment: 'higher' forms of cultural consciousness must be ready to revert transparently to their basic class reality, and the complicating differentiation that goes with genuine historical development is looked at askance, as out of line with the almost tribal simplicity desired for society. I mention this because sometimes Christians who feel unable to live out their cultural calling wholeheartedly salve their guilty consciences by adopting a similar dialectical model wherein one oversimplifies the tie between one's work and the grounding faith-commitment, or mistakenly forgoes the necessary complexity of culture in our day in order to tow a party-line.

When all is said and done, however, the genius of the Marxist alternative to mainline, Enlightenment–Victorian, humanistic privilege is to take on cultural power as a weapon, as an instrument to attack the wealthy in power, in the name of liberating the poor underdog. As British Marxist literary critic Terry Eagleton put it:[3] 'Ideology is class struggle at the level of signification. Literary criticism is like demonstrating at the barricades, every bit as real!' I admit, I like that attitude of committed scholarship very much, but we must be wary. Marxist culture is intrinsically combative, debative, essentially unsettling; it cannot afford the kind of love which issues in shalom. Maybe that is part of the reason why so many neo-Marxists believe that the ultimate answer is to remain questioning, to deconstruct historical givens into self-conscious problems, to end by anti-systematically mounting a permanent cultural critique.

---

[3] At York University, Toronto, 13 March 1978.

Such a posture leaves one perpetually undermining the cultural status quo, often with great brilliance; but it is not the Way of carrying a cross.

Christian students cannot escape the question

By now you may be thinking: look, don't send us the bill for Humanism, Marxism, and the general secularising decline of Western culture just because we're having an honours convocation! This was supposed to be an evening of light entertainment, an impressive ceremony to occasion a little oratory, and then we have coffee, visit, and go home. Academicians are not the legislators of the world!

And I would agree, with a smile in my voice. It's just that academic work is our life-time. And at a convocation to honour academic scholarship, with all that stands for, if one takes it seriously, you put your finger on the crux of our life: is it faithful, relevant God-service or has it become at bottom a rather thoughtless, self-preening congratulation? I've not been posing a hypothetical question about whether you'd prefer to have a Trotskyite or Oxford don living next door. Quite concretely I'm trying to ask, myself too: does it make Christian sense for a student to pursue a major in *belles-lettres* in our day, while the stench of holocausts still hangs in the air we breathe? *Belles*-lettres? Can it be? What would make it responsible for a bright Christian student to spend years studying ancient Greek philosophy when multimillions of the world do not need to read Platonic dialogues, not even in 'Classic Comics' book form, but need clothes? Am I really worth a salary in God's eyes, paid for by Christian farmers, factory workers and plumbers, to do research in rococo art, literature, and aesthetics theory of the early eighteenth century when they at least can grow food, make tools, and fix toilets for their neighbour, while the most visible thing I can do is talk?

We all know the Christ-transforming-culture answers. It's the backbone of Reformed, quality Christian education. But I'm wondering out loud, and not just rhetorically, whether we do not sometimes interiorise that rationale to a motivation rather than make it the test of the pudding. Would it not be unconscionable for someone to conduct countless, expensive experiments or play marathon games of mental chess and then, when the results consistently turned out negligible or negative, say, as you tip over the king to signify checkmate, 'For the glory of God,' and apply for another grant?

Am I speaking for *une logique engagée,* that profs should spend more time outside the classroom than in it, justifying their scholarship by being consultants at large, gadflies on the hustings, speaking out on 'issues', 'doing things', rather than patiently shaping the consciousness of the next generation? No. Just like gambling occasions economic disturbances by getting money too quickly, unthriftily, out of or back into circulation, so the pragmatist pressure to convert academic reflection into quick-cash knowledge warps theory into expertise and denatures the living fabric of praxis into something like toothaches needing technical treatment. It would be a trap for a college to treat scholarly culture or practical wisdom as its 'business'.

My point is that the grand old tradition of 'Christian Humanism' has been put out of date by the enormity of our Enlightenment evil loosed in society and by the advent of operationalistic theorising as surely as gunpowder upstaged sword-play. You can still kill somebody with a knife and you can still be of limited help to somebody in Matthew Arnold's shoes; but our times are too grim for old-fashioned, time-honoured, cultural solutions infected by privilege. Political terrorists who have dirty hands instead of privilege spurn following Aristotelian logic and will not heed even the pope on his knees. Hidden persuaders who never read Dante or Shakespeare and commercialise our most human acts, from laughter and love to prayer, and therefore treat us mercilessly like small change, will never stop their rape because of an appeal to literary taste or 'reason'. Perhaps, because of our background, you and I might be able to isolate ourselves and our loved ones from the worst assaults on the streets and the air waves, and inch our way toward professional priggery – that's why other honours students at Christian colleges sometimes instead become cultural Molotov cocktails in society. But neither protected American prig nor revolutionary cocktail comes at all close to following Jesus Christ. In fact, the disciples of both Arnold and Marx miss entirely the security and excitement of converting one's cultural power and position of leadership into a cross, which opens up the way for one to join in exorcising Mammon from the land and begin to bring healing and hope to the damaged people all around.

The implications of cross bearing

I should like to leave that upsidedown joy with you this evening, even though I don't know exactly what that shall mean for you and me – the cross of cultural power. But I believe a metaphor carries as much truth as a direct statement of fact if it can shake some biblical sense into our heads, set our consciousness straight on the cast that our cultural power must have if it would be blessed by the Lord of history.

To deny self, take up one's cross and follow along with the Christ (cf. Mark 8:3–9:1), is not a stern demand for you to demolish your self-respect, accept a share of earth's troubles with gritted, Stoic teeth, and imitate Jesus' life-style by taking vows of poverty, celibacy, and total obedience to a superior. Christ, who revealed this good news about throwing away your life-time in God's care and letting the professional core of you be esteemed a reproach among snooty men and women, was not a Pharisee giving killjoy advice. Christ was talking to the people he loved and was saying: if you take the dearest possession you own, your life, your whole life – eating and drinking, awake or asleep, at work or in play, under stress or thankful – and offer it totally to me, renouncing all claims to its honour in your name, if you in living act dead to the world of privilege and stop warring to get ahead: blessed are you, my children! You have nothing to lose anymore! Laugh and be glad! you can live according to the 'as if not' of 1 Corinthians 7:29–31, intensely exploring the wonders of the world in the whole gamut of human experience but not using the world to pieces, not as if that's all that there be! Indeed, the age-old forms of worldly diplomacy, integrity, stewardship, gallantry, rhetoric, and analysis with a human face *are* disintegrating. …

Is there any way for us rich, young academic rulers to realise whether or not our professional work is being carried as a cross? And the answer is, yes. When the sons and daughters of Matthew Arnold and Karl Marx examine the products of our cultural hands and exclaim, 'Excellent! but what a crime – this scholarship itself covertly shows that it belongs to Jesus Christ – what a shame!' then we may know in the full integrality of our ordinary life experience the inexplicable gladness that comes from having confessed rather than denied our Lord in academic deed. But are there specific marks of the cross imprinted on scholarly cultural studies that show they belong to Jesus Christ? And the answer again is, yes, but not like medals or war campaign ribbons that one could order from a college or seminary catalogue: and I do not pretend the Institute for Christian Studies in Toronto holds a patent on them. The marks of the cross, the fingerprints of the Holy Spirit upon human activities and artefacts are discernible more like fruits.

It can be shown, given time, that the iconographic changes in rococo art are almost as important for understanding our modern art sensibility as the pre-Socratic philosophers are for grappling with the contours and pitfalls of the Western philosophic tradition. It can be demonstrated, further, how that insight saves people from an atomistic, monographic historiography of cultures and proffers to our twentieth-century consciousness the vision that there is nothing new under the sun (except the surprises of wisdom given by the Holy Spirit) yet simultaneously God carries out God's compassionate judgements upon generation after generation of believing and unbelieving cultural responses to God's call for praise and obedience. When such scholarly study frees people from the curse of coveting and chasing the wind of sweetness and light, one may thank God – and pay salaries – for the diaconate of Christian scholarly service. That the winsome slant of Christian scholarly insight is hard-won, by painstaking reform, and is not trumpeted as such, is worth remembering. Culture that is handled as a cross rather than as a privilege or an offensive weapon knows that it itself does not need to atone for things, ensure redemption, or proclaim a final judgement. Scholarly culture bearing the imprint of the cross is content to give direction and structural insights that demystify evil mirages while honouring the inescapable glory of creatureliness: and it attests with quiet sureness to a special *koinonia* of God's people that will last forever yet opens its heart wide to all, even enemies, who have lost their way in history.

You honours students who will continue your scholarly life in high places that are secular will be tempted, possibly, to a pact like Faust. Some of you will immediately declaim, *Carthago delenda est*! Others will enter the great secular universities of America more like T. S. Eliot's Augustine: 'To Carthage then I came, burning burning burning. ...' But every one of you, and every potential Christian leader, must make his or her peace sometime with the fascinating cultural power of secular learning. It is a matter of life or death that you pick up your cultural critique and carry your own thetical contribution as a cross. If that leads to the persecution Scripture promises – constriction of your analytic air, taboos on certain imaginative horizons, even cutting disparagement that hurts – rejoice and be merry! Shalom is not a matter of tranquillity. But never baptise the old, heroic defeatist Sisyphus myth into a martyr complex as if *you* had to play the role of 'Suffering Servant'. The joyful fasting which Scripture recommends (Matthew 6: 16–18) and which the Holy Spirit provides for all those who have got rid of every encumbrance of privilege and competition surpasses all humanist understanding!

What is at stake in this convocation honouring scholastic achievement at Calvin College? This, that everyone of you who dared to accept the honour of having your name printed in the programme is making a public vow (*cor meum tibi offero, Domine ...*) that you will use your scholarly cultural power not in the tradition of Matthew Arnold, not in the zeal of Karl Marx, but singularly in the name and hope of Jesus Christ, powered – God help you – by the Holy Spirit.

A challenge for real honour

Willynilly you have great cultural power for the well-being of God's people and for many far beyond its community. I plead with you, never let the crucible of your Christian college settle for a no-name brand of scholarship, an anonymous Christianity adopted for supposedly tactical reasons, nor ever get bogged down in the coalitions of faith *and* learning, faith *and* science, faith *and* literature, as though what is distinct were separate. Let the scholarly cultural power you have in trust be exercised surely and openly in the name of Jesus Christ. Then God will bless you and many others through you in the tough years coming.

Honoured students: take up your cross of cultural power joyfully, and follow only the Lord. As you learn to cavort naked before our God in your born-again scholarship – historiography, special sciences, arts, and philosophy – God will clothe you with patient insights and wholesome righteousness that will make the festive robes we wear this evening seem rags by comparison. And let us pray that even the disbelievers who spy on God's people will become jealous of the honours you bear in the cross.

10 The Pertinence of the Gospel of Creation for Christian Education*

Perhaps the most redemptive message we people of God can bring to our world in crisis is an articulate confession of creation. Given the mindless, technocratic bent of our hypertropic civilisation, I believe it is especially the Good News of creation which may get through to the leadership of our secular culture and open up their hearts to the healing of God's Grace. I should like to recommend, for us who hold a peculiarly academic ministry of reconciliation in trust from the Lord (2 Corinthians 5:17–19), that we give concerted priority in our generation to a biblically Christian philosophy of creational ordinances, so we can be truly mature, faithful stewards in our calling.

Let me explain what I mean in this brief comment of response to Dr Houston's address which has dealt largely with old line Creationism and new deal Existentialism and the Process Theology weed, all of which I too find basically unsatisfying as a context for Christian witness and scholarship today. When you trace the major shifts in world-view behind the current dominant options of world-view in Western thought, it points up the need for Christian thinkers to do something different today than has been done in the past.

Patristic leaders adopted an ordered world with God in charge. The earth was the centre of things, there was room for mystery, and spiritual activities were considered more important than mundane affairs. Various biblical notions shaped by the Ptolemaic cosmology, influence of Plato's *Timaeus*, and later on a Monarchian Aristotelian position, gradually fused to form a world-view of structured settledness that became the grammar of scholastic Christian theology, Dante's *Divina Commedia*, Gothic architecture, and the serf-on-the-street's outlook on the setting sun and location of hell.

Copernicus and Galileo upset the Ptolemaic apple-cart, dethroned Aristotle, and led to the Newtonian modern science view of the world, where autonomous man posits an interrelated world structure *à la* Kant: phenomena are causally determined, human morality fits into an optimistic teleology, and cultured man trusts human reason to give humankind its ideals and the truth. Christian theology by and large adopted this rationalistic world-view, often on

*Response to the address of Dr James Houston, President of Regent College, Vancouver, at a conference held by the Institute for Christian Studies and Regent College, at York University, Ontario, May 1975.

the strength of the private faith of its proponents. Of course, when the secularising acid in the Newtonian–Kantian world-view wore its theism down to deism, orthodoxy began to balk.

Finally, Newtonian Rationalism was relativised by Einsteinian science. And when World War I Existentialism, Bergson and Whitehead got thrown into the same hopper, shaken well together with American pragmatism, a much more dynamistic world-view gained currency. A recognition of the inescapable subjective human factor in observation of natural processes spoiled the old-fashioned belief in neutral objectivity and fixed rational verities. Recognition of the pluriformity of things examined by science and therefore the necessity of using methods other than mechanical physics to analyse organisms and society has introduced, further, a basic indeterminism.

What strikes me as significant in this overview is the tag-along character of the Christian contribution and therefore its continual embarrassment. Because the biblical world-view was identified by the Church Fathers with the Ptolemaic, when Ptolemaic astronomy was discredited in the sixteenth century, so was the biblical perspective. Because Newtonian Rationalism supported a theistic Christian orthodoxy, orthodox Christianity adopted Newtonian Rationalism. Now that Newtonian Rationalism is becoming *passé*, what does that mean for orthodoxy? And I hear Dr Houston facing us with the twentieth-century quandary: how do we recast a biblically Christian world-view out of its traditional, synthetically christianised Aristotelian, rationalistic frying pan without falling into the fire of neo-orthodox Existentialism and Process (natural) theology?

What we need first of all is an articulate confession of creation, a biblically rich doctrine of creation that manifests its eye-opening *Gospel* character.

Although I am not a church historian, I would hazard the guess that 'creation' has never absorbed church council time like the great heresies respecting the Trinity, Christ *homoöusios*, and any number of denominational armageddons. First- and second-century Gnosticism really denied the biblical credo on creation, but even there the battle was joined, I think, around *sophia* soteriology. The dogma of creation has always been there, affirmed, in the church's background of benign neglect, while we concentrated on 'salvation' and 'sanctification'. But could it be that Christians have fallen prey to being yoked with compromising world-views because we have lacked developed reflection true to Scripture on creation and made do with a more nondescript and therefore protean idea of 'Nature' we hold to be almost self-evident?

I do not mean we should put the best minds of the church to work conjugating the possible meanings of *ex nihilo fit* so as to pin down God's aseity or *modus operandi* during the six days revealed in the prologue of Genesis. And I certainly do not wish to promote the tireless debate on evolution and dating earth with carbon-14, which often seems to have the earmarks of the proverbial angels-on-a-pinhead controversial seriousness. An argued apologetic for creation may be as unredemptive a use of time as hammering away at a speculative theology which pretends the biblical notice of creation makes us privy to inside knowledge on exactly how God does things.

I have in mind, instead, our developing a large sense of creation from Scripture so that a sense of its Good News serviceability comes through. For example, the revealed fact that *creaturehood is good* (Genesis 1:1–2:4; 1 Timothy 4:1–10), meaning reliable, deserving respect, worthy of cultivation, to be received with thanksgiving, is a gospel that removes the No Exit sign from the world of the social scientists, who feel compelled to treat non-human reality as a brute *en soi* (Sartre's 'in-itself opaque substance') which limits our creative free-egos inherited from Fichte. The gospel truth that creaturehood is good lifts away the burden of *Weltschmerz* turned *Sorge* (Heidegger's 'Care') and foisted upon nations as a trap leading to extinction (*zum-Tode-sein*), and stops thinkers from believing that human existence must mediate meaning in history.

If we began to take seriously, for another example, the revealed fact that *creation discloses the will of God* (Hebrews 11:3; Revelation 4:11), that God speaks through God's creatures, that creatures are made and provided for daily by the Lord and testify of God's wisdom (Psalm 104; Romans 1:18ff) so that God's covenanting will is not secretive, oracular and far away, but as close as heaven and earth and the breathing of a child (Deuteronomy 30; Jeremiah 33:19–26): if we began to plumb the biblical Good News of creation that way, what horizons might it not open up for bio-physical science, commercial use of the environment and how you raise children in a city?

I am positing for your discussion that we opt for exploring and developing biblically first of all the doctrine of creation. I can only hint here that as I envision it, it will entail a reformation of theology away from God-scrutiny (*via negativa, analogia entis*, and the rest), away from God-talk analysis (humankind should only talk about God on one's knees or with a psalmist's Hallel, never like an Oxford don putting creaturely 'how' questions to the Almighty One revealed in Jesus Christ), and away from doing mission work with merely the Gospel of John, as if Deuteronomy be an outdated book of the Bible.

I'm only saying that Old Testament biblical theology will be crucial in our moving toward a world-view that proffers shalom in the twentieth century. And my concern is that any theological contribution to this philosophical problem Dr Houston has raised be permeated by the Calvinian insight that *omnis recta Dei cognitio ab obedientia nascitur* (all right knowledge of God is born out of obedience; *Institutes of the Christian Religion*, 1,6,2). Calvin's insight chiming in with 1 Corinthians 2:14 cuts off any move toward a natural law theology. And to escape the reproof of Hebrews 6 about staying immature, dogmatic theology, also about creation, must not just be a sanctified intellectual puzzle. Dogmatic theology about creation must touch life with insight and enable followers of Christ to show leadership that makes disbelievers in Christ jealous of the wisdom we have in earthen vessels.

What we need next, along with an articulate confession of creation – so that such a redemptive doctrine gets the context to influence contemporary cultural life rather than just stick out like a sore thumb – we need a biblically Christian philosophy of creational ordinances. That is required, I believe, for a mature witness in our day.

Let me close with just the rationale for this suggestion. (1) While God's people necessarily go first to the Bible for *nouthesia*, for getting their consciousness set right, for receiving redeemed vision, biblical eyesight, and while fear of the Lord is the head-start of Wisdom, we who become adopted children of God and are then indwelt with the Holy Spirit must needs go search creation for drafting our fallible solutions to the problems facing us in our sin-cursed world – which belongs to the Lord.

(2) If God's creational ordinances are good, disclosing God's will to those able to discern *pneumatikos* (John 14:15–27; 1 Corinthians 2:15,16), then the normal task of Christian philosophy as a systematic, encyclopaedic discipline, working in concert with Christian theology, physics, psychology, aesthetics and other disciplines, will be to emphasise the real structure and relationships of creation as the perduring *magnalia Dei*. Philosophising will be Christian, trading its talents of theory faithfully, if it aids other disciplines in discovering ordinances of the Lord in their fullness, so that God's people will be helped in ordering their lives obediently to God's Word in our complex civilisation.

My motivation for this proposal is evangelical: to make known the gospel of Jesus Christ that our redeeming Creator God has won the victory over sin and death and meaninglessness, and that those who repent and respond in the power of the Holy Spirit to God's gracious judgement and merciful love shall find blessing and creaturely fulfilment.

Missions have traditionally been oriented toward those who did not know the Gospel of salvation but who lived in a non-technocratic setting more dependent upon creational happening than upon people's control-devices. Missions within mainstream twentieth-century culture today, I am suggesting, should be oriented toward those who do not know the Gospel of creation but who live in a Westernised civilisation where world-flight salvation, promulgated by the church for centuries, has been letting the world-culture go to hell.

We as the people of God need to repent of that sinful mistake and bring healing to distracted, secular humankind where they are especially hurting, faced with the wrong dilemma of 'escape to heaven' or 'create it yourself'. We have the most trenchant biblical message to bring healing to this contemporary dilemma practically unused on our hands. I believe we should act quickly and prayerfully, as harmless as doves and as prudent as snakes, proffering the Good News of creational order which is fulfilled in the reign of our Lord Jesus Christ.

11 A Cloud of Witnesses and a New Generation*

I should like to tell you from the Bible why the Association for the Advancement of Christian Scholarship was begun. Then I should like to describe the nature and task of the Christian scholarship supported at the Institute for Christian Studies in Toronto and its necessity in the context of the pregnant present and the pull of the future. Finally, I want to present certain problems Christian leaders of our generation face so that everybody here will feel small enough to be thankful to God for giving us what brings us together on a Sunday summer afternoon in 1978 AD.

Biblical setting of the Association for the Advancement of Christian Scholarship

I need to read two Scripture passages to give us a sense of the difference and continuity between the first student study conference of the Association back in 1959 and the family conference this weekend which is the twentieth. Also, I think it is good to remember that the cloud of witnesses which surrounds us here stretches back for millennia, not just a generation or two. I will read the beginnings of Psalm 78 first, which is a folk-song by Asaph, a poet writing around the time of 1 Kings 6, let's say, a few years before Solomon dedicated the grand new temple being built for Yahweh.

> Prick up the ears, my people, to catch my wise direction!
> Stretch out your ears for the words coming out of my mouth!
> I am going to tell something in proverb form;
> I am going to let loose with prophetic riddles from long, long ago
> which we have heard before, and even understood –
> ones that our forefathers used to tell us …

*A manifesto for redemptive education given at the 20th annual AACS conference, Niagara, Ontario, August 1978, published as a *Vanguard Supplement* (November–December 1978). The AACS (Association for the Advancement of Christian Scholarship) is a body of Christians in North America and elsewhere who support the graduate Institute for Christian Studies in Toronto. From 1958 the AACS held summer student and family conferences on topics of cultural interest to people from all walks of life.

They did not hide it from their kids:
storytellers they were, to the coming generation,
recounting the bigtime things the Lord God did,
about the Lord's unshakeable strength you could count on,
and the extraordinary, truly astonishing acts of God –
you know, how God set up an ordering reminder in Jacob,
I mean, planted the live-spoken-covenanting Law right in the middle of Israel!
what God charged our parents to make known to their kids
so that the coming generation would really experience it,
so that those children still to be born would grow up
and tell it to their kids,
and set their foolish, unshakeable hope in God,
not ever forget the deeds of God
but instead, take good care of the tasks God sets
so that they would not become like their parents –
a stubborn, know-it-all generation whose heart never got settled,
whose spirit never held steady, solidly faithful to God ... (Psalm 78:1–8).

And then Asaph continues Psalm 78 reciting the amazing things God did to bring God's people up out of Egyptland, how the Lord practically carried them through the wilderness in spite of their pigheaded selves, and situated a later generation of the same folk in the lush, green land of Canaan and tried to get order among the tribes with judges and priests like Eli. God mercifully kept on forgiving their thankless worship of local gods and goddesses, and finally – the way this biblical folk-song puts it – God woke up and knocked the Philistine enemies of God's adopted children to smithereens, and picked out David to head up God's people and give them a sense of belonging to the Lord forever as God's specially chosen community of believers.

A time of expectation

Psalm 78 shows a festive expectancy in reciting the *magnalia Dei* (the great deeds of God) from the memorable past, as if God's people were ready to settle down now, pull together in Jerusalem, and the Lord would even surprise them with new kinds of great things.

There was that kind of trembling wonderment around twenty years ago when François Guillaume, Chairman of the Association, survivor of Dachau, spoke of the Association's unanimous opinion, 'for the time being, to bring together scholars and students in a yearly conference and to deepen and strengthen our awareness of the absolute necessity of Reformed Scientific Studies'. Of course, 'our deepest desire is for something more than a conference is able to offer: we sorely need an institution where the courses are taught in a Christian manner from day to day.' He also recalled a remark by Martin Woudstra (Old Testament Professor at Calvin Seminary) about 'the missing link in the fields of Reformed universities in the world. Discerning three wide fields, one in Europe, one in Africa–Asia and one in America, he mentioned the Reformed universities of Amsterdam and Potchefstroom, but observed that the third one was missing. In the whole American continent such an institution can not be found. Does not this fact seriously accuse us all? Let us say in faith with Nehemiah: "We, God's servants, will arise and build!"' (*Christian Perspectives 1960*, 1960, ii–iii) Well, as you know, Solomon's temple got built and dedicated; and the missing link was instituted in Toronto. I don't imply any connection, but I do sense historically there were comparable expectations. And now we hear Malachi 3.

A time of perseverance

A lot of spilled milk has gone over the Israelite dam between Asaph's folk-song and Malachi's monologue dialogue: the united kingdom of David split; the people's sins accumulated until the Lord had the Lord's house on earth razed by enemy soldiers, and men, women and children were deported, exiled, scattered like sheep on a thousand distant hills, until a couple of generations later still, the Lord brought a remnant back to the promised land. Malachi brought the Word of the Lord to those who were returned from the mighty city of Babylon. Malachi spoke to God's people after the new cheapie temple had been built under Zerubbabel, after the Israelites had squeaked through the plot of Haman, a descendant of Esau, to wipe them out in the Persian empire, and before Nehemiah arrived to lead them in rebuilding the run-down walls around Jerusalem. God's people had settled down to business again in the promised land; they intermarried a little (2:11), lived in more relaxed fashion with respect to the traditions of Sabbath observance, divorce, kosher food and tithes, all the orthodox customs kept by earlier generations (3:7–9). And some of God's people got restless: here they were finally safe, back in God's holy city – where was the millennium?!

This now is the Word of God:

> Your talk directed at me has been harsh, says the Lord God,
> and then you ask, 'Why, what have we been saying against You?'
> You have said, 'Working hard for God is a farce!
> What does it profit a man or a woman if we keep standing on guard for what God
>   wants done?
> What does it get you if we walk along with a long face before God, Lord of the
>   (mighty) angels!
> From now on let's face the facts:

"Blessed are those who have cheek to push for what they want,
because those who run roughshod over limits not only get ahead
but even dare God, so to speak, and get away with it.'"

Then the God-fearing people began to talk to one another, each one to his or her
neighbour:
'But Yahweh is listening with pricked ears, Yahweh hears (such crooked talk)!
And the Lord has a (big) sort of commemorative Book written in, so that it's there
to remind the Lord,
(the names and deeds of) those who wait attentively for the Lord God Yahweh,
who anticipate action respecting God's Name.'

– These (God-fearing people), says Yahweh, Lord God of the angels, are the ones
who will belong to me, my special possession, on the Day when I act,
for I have compassion on them as a father is compassionate with his own son or
daughter who works hard for him.

The time is coming when you shall once again see what makes a right-doing man
or woman different from a wrong-doing person, and
you shall be able to recognise the difference between someone working hard for
God and one who is slaving all right, but not for the Lord.

Yes, look out! The Day is coming, burning like a smelting blast furnace
– all those with cheek who pushed to get ahead and kept on running roughshod
over limits as if God were absent, shall now be bits of straw –
and that Day coming will burn them to a crisp, says Yahweh Sabbaoth,
so that there will not be even a twig or piece of root of them left over.
But the sun of redeeming justice shall climb the sky like a meteor and shine down
on you who really know me by name and patiently wait expectant,
shine down with (such) restorative, health-giving power in its rays
that you shall go out, stampede like young bulls (released) from the stockades,
and trample those who did underhanded things – they'll be just like ashes – under
the soles of your feet!
That's what happens on the day when I (finally) act! says Yahweh, Lord God of the
angels.
Keep on remembering, all of you, the law of Moses who worked hard for me,
the careful ordinances and ordering judgements I commanded him at Horeb to set
down for all Israel.
On top of that I shall send you the Elijah-prophet(s) before the Day of Yahweh
breaks, that great, awesome Day,
so that the prophet shall make the hearts of fathers and mothers reverberate again
with the hearts of their sons and daughters,
foster the hearts of children to beat again with the hearts of fathers and mothers,
so that I don't have to come and smash up the earth with a curse! (Malachi 3:13–4:6)

Plate 12 First seminar with Seerveld at the Institute for Christian Studies, Toronto, 1971–2: Barbara Carvill, Don James, Seerveld, Marion Johnson, Harry Westerhof, Charles Huischen

Plate 13 Junior members Adrienne Dengerink, Judy Jordet, Donald Knudsen, Allison-Ann McSwain, Carol Guen, with Seerveld, during a seminar tour of New York City musea, 1981

Plate 14 Junior members outside the Institute for Christian Studies, Toronto, 1989: (back row) Shari Luttikhuizen, Govert Buijs, Marcille Frederick, Henry Luttikhuizen (front row) Fran Wong, Barbara and Nigel Douglas, Priscilla Reimer and Seerveld

Plate 15 Junior members at a philosophical aesthetics seminar, Institute for Christian Studies, Toronto, 1992–3: (back row) James Leach, Scott Macklin, Greg Nations, Brent Adkins, Hamish Robertson, Craig Bartholomew; (front row) Greg Linnell, Andrea Bush

Telling stories to the next generation

What I am saying from Scripture is this: Psalm 78 gives the biblical directive and rationale for the Association for the Advancement of Christian Scholarship. Certain Dutch-Canadian immigrants with Reformed stuffings heard God command in Psalm 78 that fathers and mothers should tell their sons and daughters the great deeds of the Lord in history and should repeat daily what the law of the Lord means for knowing the world and serving one's neighbour in God-praising ways. That means Christian schooling, Christian high schooling, a christian university in Canada where the consciousness of a younger generation is peculiarly set for life (cf. Ephesians 6:4).

Psalm 78 speaks to us in our day of great societal complexity and myriad secular specialisations that God's people need professional history-tellers and guides, that means, disciplined professing (= professional) story-tellers and searchers of God's ordinances, especially those laid down in God's glorious creation, to help orient the coming generation in understanding how to walk obediently before the Lord's face in faith, love and hope. The founders and earliest supporters of the Association saw that setting the consciousness of their children and children's children in this new land was a life and death problem. Next to home and church they wanted an institution – to which they could at least point, as to a light not hid under a bushel basket – where one could study history and all aspects of the world. This study would be done so thoroughly, systematically, so passionately in the grip of allegiance to the Lord that any young ones coming under its sway would come to know experientially the faithful, merciful, promising, saving Creator God of heaven and earth, of family, liturgical worship, socio-political relations, of doing business, the God of timbrel and harp, poetry, sackbut and flute. These young students as next generation would have a sense of biblical direction and the Lord's presence as they struggled to work out shalom, despite the sin constantly messing up their lives.

If there's one message Dr Runner (then, as now, Philosophy Professor at Calvin College) proclaimed as he roamed the continent in those years it was this: the word of God packs a Holy Spirited power able to rip us out of the secular traditions of people and to set us firmly in the scriptural Way of the Lord; and there is a vision of God's Kingdom and human vocation in history broached by the Reformation that has found cultural, philosophical articulation in the Netherlands we should not neglect; in fact, we have a calling to transmit that spiritual legacy of historical reformation to this continent, particularly focused on Scripturally directed learning because that's where you catch leaders. With God's strength in our weakness we may work and pray for an inner reformation of scientific studies, and whether it be Patristic or Oriental studies, economics or aesthetics, we have a beginning, Christian philosophical perspective that can truly bring encyclopaedic wholeness to such disciplines and their import for a life-consciousness. And we must not be parochial, do it just for our own kids; the secular multi-versities have run stuck: we must rally the brightest students of North American Christendom to the Reformational genius of the biblical vision nourished by our cultural roots.

From youthful enthusiasm to greater sobriety

In time the Institute took shape, in 1967 at 141 Lyndhurst Avenue, in the shadow of Casa Loma. During those first years the Institute served as a cross between the Free University of Kuyper's day and a L'Abri counselling service for displaced believers of the 1960s, and as a hangout for a brace of Christian gurus who on demand could speak on every ordinance of God under the sun. These bearded young fellows dropped out of the European sky like phosphorous bombs following up a decade of Runner reconnaissance. There were some fireworks, not to say explosions. Rocks got thrown and lots of windows were broken; toes were stepped on with the greatest concern. There was a heady excitement that some believed prefigured the rapture. Others experienced it more as if there were young foxes running wild in the Christian Reformed Church wheat fields with firebrands tied to their tails.

Finally it was discovered how hard it is to do scholarship on the run, and maybe, to avoid the risk of seeming to be a surrogate church with itinerant lay preachers, it was felt that one should spend solid research time tightening up the quality of one's advanced theory and make earnest with the difficult redirection of one's field of study in a genuinely interdisciplinary way – to show people you are a centre of Christian scholarship worth a couple of years of a young person's life-time.

This last move struck some as a retreat toward an anti-revolutionary, élitist establishment. Others were glad for the maturing wisdom it showed, as messianic reform movements go. I, for one, am fervently thankful to God for God's patience and forgiveness in leading us this far, and to the members of the AACS all over the world who for the sake of the vision of the glory of Jesus Christ also over scholarship have continued to trust and hope and bear with our fallible work in its twenty-odd year history. We have this festive afternoon attended by people from five continents of the globe only because of the faithfulness of relatively few people of God on earth and the everlasting, inscrutable mercies of the Lord.

But I have pointed to our Psalm 78 origination and recounted sketchily and somewhat playfully what developed since, only to make the point that the millennium has not happened. Hart did not turn the Canadian Philosophical

Association upside-down in ten years and as its president reshape the direction of philosophising at Canadian universities. Olthuis' ethics have not yet become a major new, media force redeeming family, friendships and marriage in the secular high school, middle-class, and cocktail society circuits of our modern day. Zylstra is not the prime minister of Canada – that millennium did not come. But this is why Malachi 3 is so appropriate for our hearing today, half a dozen years after God miraculously put a building at the edge of the University of Toronto, 229 College Street, into our mortgaged hands: we should *not* pride ourselves on such Christian Canadian Philosophical Association dreams, models of friendships made-in-heaven, or Christian prime ministership millennial prospects.

When the Day of the Lord comes, when Yahweh Sabbaoth revealed in Jesus Christ acts in that final, historic way – not just as an epilogue! – to extirpate violated troth, vain logic, cruel inequities, illness and death, and shoots the sunshine of shalom all over the place, hauling in the illicitly tended glories of earthbound rulers (as Revelation 21:22–7 puts it), *then* it's time for God's people to stampede like young bulls breaking loose from the Calgary stockades, since Victory Day will have arrived, hope has been realised, the Kingdom of God shall be fully come! Meanwhile, as we keep busy at healing sickness, trying to correct injustices, refocusing life-style, humbling theories in the name of Jesus Christ, our dances and camp-fires do well to remain pregnant and our songs of encouragement to keep a future pull in the melody so that the earnests of shalom we do receive come more like surprises from the hand of the Lord than as our own hard-won deserts. The joy of our Christian life in this age lies in its being one of faith, being rooted, fed and surrounded by the *reality* of things not yet fully seen – birds in the bush, if you will – that we *know* are real, so that our struggling daily life is couched in a thankful, anticipatory suspense of God's *chesed*, the Lord's great, happy-making, covenant-keeping deeds from ever and anon and for ever coming.

Tasks for inbetween time

What must I do to be saved? Whether you be a government official, a rich young business person, or an ambitious student, says Scripture (Proverbs 2; Matthew 19:16–20:16; Acts 16:25–34), sell everything you hold more dear than discipleship of Jesus Christ, throw away whatever of your life is not rigorously, singularly offered as God-service. Get rid of it! And that may include a sense of personal worthlessness, or a holier-than-thou humility, or an inability to lose, to lose face, or coveting success that abrogates a life of faith. What must I do to save the world? Says Christ (Matthew 10:16–19; John 21:15–23), forsake your messiah complex and feed my sheep with all the circumspect wisdom and no-harm-giving love you can muster.

What must we do to be found faithful when the Lord returns? Says Malachi 3:22–4 and Christ explicitly in Luke 16:10–31: keep the law of Moses, fulfil in deeds of faith all the careful ordinances and ordering judgements I have made known to you; and obey the prophetic Word of the Rule of the Lord, of hope that breaks your hard hearts into repentant pieces of flesh that my Holy Spirit shall sew together and make alive in a communion that will unite grandparents and parents and grandchildren in holy laughter. Your task, my people, is to institute ways that will make it possible for your children, the generation around you, and the younger generation even of neighbouring strangers to live more obediently before my Word than you did, as I the Lord prepare to come.

The normative calling of the Institute for Christian Studies, Toronto

As I understand it, the Institute for Christian Studies specialises in the task of having an older generation of God's people tell stories to a younger generation in order to discipline and set their consciousness in the royal way of the Lord (the *paideia* and *nouthesia* of Ephesians 6: 4). Or, to be more specific, the Institute for Christian Studies specialises in having a somewhat older generation who embody insights of the Reformation Christian tradition at a certain stage of historical development pass it on *live* to a new generation as they together, senior and junior men and women, struggle to posit anew in depth what God's will is for human life. And this story-telling and searching exploration which the two believing generations do together at the Institute happens in the arena of scholarship.

We all know that this instilling of a certain Reformation vision by word of mouth from one God-fearing generation to another has gone on through the centuries in many ways. Children learned the family business from the ground up, and if the Reformation sense of vocation and service shaped the enterprise, you learned not only how to size up fresh fish and to sweep the sidewalk in front of the store with Reformed diligence, but also the ins and outs of setting a just price and how to improve people's eating habits, in human dialogue with customers. All this slowly got transfused into your blood by watching, asking and being told this and that by the older ones. Old-style Reformed families or those with a family tree and a European sense of extended family traditions on everything from naming children to celebrating Old Year's evening, shaped the consciousness of the young ones in that family circle on manners, conversational style, devotional habits, respect for work and authority. They implanted an enviable presence of personal composure, security of kin, and purposefulness of life that all helped one weather storms of broken troth. And this world-and-life view habit became part of you not by

Plate 16 Gideon Strauss, Seerveld, James Leach, Gerrit du Preez, Egbert
Schuurman; Centennial Dooyeweerd Conference in Bovendonk, Netherlands, 1994

lectures so much as by the few right words spoken at certain critical moments
in your development at home.

Such a *live* transfer of scripturally visioned wisdom (which has been of particular concern, I think, for those who come out of a biblically Reformed
milieu) is the very gut of the Institute, undertaken on behalf of all God's
people who want to make earnest with the continuing imperative of Psalm
78 as it speaks to schooling, scholarship – which is only *one* (institutional) way
God's people can claim the Lord's faithfulness for the generations who care
about God's covenanting promises.

Scholarship at the Institute is mainly philosophical

The Institute in Toronto exists to thank God with scholarship. The Institute
exists to wed an older and younger generation in scholarly praise of the Lord,
and so to build up God's people, give away richer insights to neighbours, and
turn the other cheek of Reformationally advanced scientific studies to enemies
of the gospel. The Institute research focuses upon forging the key ideas of
special sciences like political science, economics and aesthetics – that's why it's
called 'higher education', I suppose, although a better name might be 'deeper-
down education' (or 'buckled-over education').We want to get the most pivotal
leadings of a discipline intrinsically conformed not to the traditions of people

but to the Will of God. This means, at least for my generation, that Christian scholarship at the Institute will be principally philosophical; senior and junior men and women will need to do sustained, Christian philosophical systemic analysis in order to discover the basic limiting categories and methodological contours that will allow us to raise the scandal, in concert, for example, of a Christian political philosophy and Christian philosophical aesthetics.

I've got to explain this a minute, in popular language if I can, because too many people think (Christian) philosophical analysis is full of vague generalities because it doesn't deal in concrete practicalities, and what's advanced scholarship for if it doesn't change things, if I can't see what I get out of it?! Let me make the point this way: you hurt a family, I believe, if you treat it like a business, where ma and pa are partners in the establishment and the kids are hired to do the chores for so much allowance per week. There's incentive pay (like bribes to be good) when you're younger, and quasi contractual arrangements when you get older and have an outside job to pay for your room and board. You're still a family, but the home starts to become a rooming house with favoured trading partners. Thrift, economy and money matters are not subordinated and incapsulated in the gentle rule of parental protection and filial devotion. Although a family does have an economic side and family bills, it can become denatured into a work unit where service for pay credits and debts dominate the betrothed blood bond. And when this happens, the love relationship between parents and children quite easily shifts into a cash-register gear of supply and demand, or buyer–consumer–producer and broker–analyst. You can also ruin families as families by acting as if you are a miniature state, either of the totalitarian sort where a father's first word is also the last word, or a democratistic one where every member is continually being polled and votes are taken for decisions – the majority rules and you live by committees.

I mention this to make the point that the Institute is by its nature a school, a school for grown-ups, sometimes called an 'academy'; and it would hurt the Institute to force it to act like a business or a factory. The Institute could also be ruined if it were treated like a church, or one big happy family, or like a miniature nation run by a constitutional monarch or a Central Committee, for that matter. The Institute is an institute for studying, for doing scholarship. And it is wrong to ask it to function like some other kind of institution – although the Institute for Christian *Studies* naturally has government functions, troth, confession and industry of its own kind, a scholarly kind. Many people, including Christians with the best intentions, get bamboozled here in our commerce-ridden day.

The question of practicality

Look, if you want support as an Institute, give us a product people can use. If you're in the business of ideas, OK, give us an idea people need or a highly visible one we can advertise – that's the only way for ICS to become a best-seller in America!

But schools – gradeschools, high schools, university-level schools – don't (or shouldn't) mass produce any thing. And the best ideas are highly invisible. Ideas *grow* legs, I'd say; but deeds of theory are not born with post-theoretical bodies full grown in society any more than marriages are supposed to come ready-made with children. Besides, any Christian ideas the Institute develops are not for sale. We give them away.

> *Dear Sir* [and I read this with a smile even though it's not a joke, it's too seriously sincere for joking]: *Please send us half a dozen Christian political insights. Our Action Group is hard-pressed to come up with a distinctively Christian platform. In fact, we face extinction unless you help. Please send by return mail special delivery.*
> *Sincerely, in Christ ...*

You see, I know that various Christian philosophico–political insights sifted out of the sieve of the Marxism seminar at the Institute during the last academic year, but Christian insight is not something you can pile up in the corner or send off in a list of disembodied propositions through the mail. Communal Christian scholarship is more like an open-heart, open-mind surgery, that produces a new horizon, a different slant, certain sunshine dimensions and riches to a human sensitivity and consciousness that has undergone it.

> Oh! You mean, when students get mixed up intellectually and messed up spiritually at a secular place of learning, then we should send them to the Institute, and your Christian scholarship activity straightens them out; and later on, when they become Christian leaders, the benefits kind of dribble out into society, and that's the way we get our money's worth.

That's closer. Although the Institute is no more a reformatory than a Christian gradeschool, high school or college, we've served that purpose, I suppose you might say. The Institute thanks God that men and women who have entered into and contributed toward the 'deeper-down' Christian scholarly surgery going on in its environs are now business agents with the Christian Labour Association of Canada, researchers for the Committee for Justice and Liberty, counsellors, pastors, missionaries and teachers in the church and Christian schools. The Institute does not train labour union organisers or political lobbyists; it does not show people how to be pastors, counsellors, how to teach reading or do journalism: the Institute invites students serious about such life-long callings to undergo its story-telling and philosophical exploratory searches so as to strengthen their particular future work with a consciousness more firmly set and disciplined by a living, biblically true, Reformation-Christian perspective. And to have a teacher with the right perspective, a business agent, researcher, pastor or journalist living deeply out of a Reformation-Christian consciousness is not a dribble in society. Such people are worth their weight in gold, and that holds also for those who continue

Plate 17 Presentation of *Pledges of Jubilee* to Calvin and Inès Seerveld by Lambert Zuidervaart and Henry Luttikhuizen, at Calvin College, Grand Rapids, Michigan, 1995

specialised studies at secular universities (and we'll not worry about who gets the 'credits' after the movie is over).

Studying is work too

There are two little reasons, I think, why scholarship often seems remote from people who are not active in study. Firstly, children go to school before they're old enough to work; kids have the time, the leisure, to study; it's not loss of manpower; but for grown-ups to go to school and do study that's never going to stop does seem odd. Secondly, the proofs of the pudding with schooling seem so intangible for, let's say, truck-drivers; it's especially difficult to pin down the results of *advanced* study because 'the scholarly world' has for centuries lived in a humanist ivory tower far away from the world of truck-drivers.

> When I learned judo in Chicago, our club consisted mostly of truck-drivers, bartenders, and assorted huskies. They really enjoyed my membership, I think, because I was the first 'learned person' they had ever had at arm's length. 'C'mere professor!' Whammo! They wanted to see whether scholars bounced. Scholars don't bounce any more than truck-drivers do, and truck-drivers are as closed or as open to what time it is historically as scholars are.

I just want to testify that scholarly analysis which goes beyond dilettante dabbling is hard work. Professional studying has its own sort of nervous tension, tedium, and promise; it is often very lonely work, and the pressure not to fail is very great. Results of scholarship in a person's life are as real as a coma or a *spiritual* headache that no aspirins can relieve, or as real as tingling *gereformeerde voelhorens* – those radar antennae *Christian* truck-drivers have for detecting what is on or off the biblical track. My testimony so far is simply that because of the special human talents involved and the stakes for priming cultural leadership, it is a terrible waste of creaturely effort, a horrible shame, for scholarship to take place if it is not *Christian* scholarship, studies consciously carried out and philosophically couched in the shadow of Christ's coming, shaped by the directives of the Lord's written Word.

The scholarly task limited but necessary

But I should still like to celebrate (rather than debate) with you the normative calling of the Institute for Christian Studies – story-telling the *magnalia Dei* and philosophical special-science analysis of creational ordinances. I'm so thankful to be able to celebrate that scholarly task as a limited but necessary, crucial ministry of Christ's body on earth especially for the crunch of our day. If there's anything that confronts and can confound the spirit of our age, characterised by rootless opportunism and hateful cruelties that bash through all limits, it is the quiet voice of professional story-telling that raises the sober expectation of Christ's Coming, welding together the hearts of human generations. If there's anything that confronts and disconcerts both the godless fools of our generation in power and the many respectable antichrists satisfied with the evil status quo, it is analysis which points in the direction of sure ways we must walk to overcome our various crises of responsibility, sophisticated ignorance, and busy-busy hopelessness. Such redemptive story-telling and Christian philosophical analysis is doubly important precisely in our day because God's people in many places, especially in the USA and Canada, are experiencing a revival of faith and a sense of wanting new biblical hands. And to have God bless biblical revival in people's hearts with christian reformation in the land, embodied in the very way our culture operates, will take revivified and re-formed minds. The very rooted consciousness of our generation needs to be reset, re-educated, stamped and outfitted with a perspective that can indeed discern what the will of God is for life-style, business policy, political infighting, use of news media, and much else (cf. Romans 12:1,2).

I'm not saying that Institute Christian studies are the single best answer to the oppression and loneliness flooding world society. Christian philosophical studies do not determine measures for stopping violence on the streets, for monitoring corruption in the market-place, for feeding the starving with distended bellies in India, because Christian political scientists are not policemen and Christian philosophical aestheticians are not investigative journalists by trade, and Christian theologians have not been certified as Red Cross rescue workers. Christian scholars face evil all right, at learned society meetings (even if it is only a struggle with shame and pride), and, more importantly, contend with principalities and powers scrounging the universe to cripple student lives. Christian philosophical study works day and night at stopping *academic* violations, *academic* corruption, *academic* starvation, all the lies filling millions of study books in the name of 'straight thinking' or 'Humanity' or who knows what dumb idol (I know that our academic God-service is full of holes, fails, needs to be stepped up, concentrated, etc., but that's not my point now). I'm saying that there is great confusion with devastating impotence. There is a staggering amount of learning going on piecemeal at the secular multiversities, brilliant sailors without a compass often headed convincingly in a wrong direction.

So the Institute speciality by design is not to figure out a specialist's answers but to give trustworthy direction, for example in reconceiving a field of study ('what happens to your idea of art — songs, furniture, style — if "nuancefulness" rather than Beauty is found to be the proper law for aesthetic reality?') The Institute speciality is not to solve problems of public or private neurosis, but to diagnose foundational hypotheses of given sciences ('is bio-energetics therapy a faddish method or implementation of a more integrated anthropological model?') The Institute does not attempt to direct trends coming and going but to rethink established problematics (if one had a biblically reformed philosophical hermeneutic on how Scripture speaks and a Christian philosophical theory of knowledge, you would never get boxed into the fix of 'creationism' versus 'evolutionism', and be trying to wrestle the Bible, geological and biological data into a tight embrace). That is, the speciality of the Institute is peculiarly attuned to the impasse of most secular scholarship today and is right on target for the need of the current generation of reflective Christian thinkers who are looking for ways to move from general Christian philosophical systematics into special fields of analysis, bearing redemptive fruit.

If the Institute, in community with other Reformational Christian scholars, would receive the patient understanding and strong prayer support from God's people at large for its open-mind surgery, it could really be free to restrict itself to exorcising *academic* demons — and not every devil walking up and down on the face of the earth — and the academic healing would spill over, I believe, into many other ministries even more than it does and there could well be multiple celebrations among the angels in heaven.

A real problem ever with us: historical priorities

Very nice, Seerveld, celebration of advanced Christian scholarship as a normative calling, a necessary mission-outreach or ministry to the intellectual and a bulwark for reforming Christian leadership. But you haven't seen anybody starve lately, have you? What does philosophical aesthetics have to do with world poverty, not to mention the American truck-drivers riveted to their beer and TV sets?

Once upon a time God created a man and a woman, and it was so good. And the man and woman had children who fought and killed one another. This hurt God. One day the Lord wrote down a text called the Ten Words. Later God raised up wise men and wise women to help people understand what God wanted done. But such grievous things went on – each one doing what seemed right in their own eyes – that God raised up judges too, who ruled in the Holy Spirit and spoke justice among the easy-going and the woebegone. The judges and prophets were heralds of God's Son who was coming.

Don't evade the problem by telling stories! Starving people don't need story-telling and analysis; they need food! Give the near-dead in Asia at least a glass of water and bread! Give the non-persons of the third world economic identity and self-respect first! Stories and analysis that only students can understand is the last thing they need – not talk and thought but deeds of love!

It's true, some unfortunate in the world need *Christianly* tendered food and drink, not advanced Christian scholarship. But telling someone stories is a deed of love and, as a matter of fact, goes far in giving the hearer self-respect. Elie Wiesel describes how to the Jewish children slaughtered at Auschwitz stories meant as much as crusts of bread.[1] Like the poor jester in the medieval story who only had jokes to give to God, philosophical aestheticians maybe have only analytic insights to offer; but there are also unfortunates in the world who need a cool drink of analytic life.

Doing aesthetics in the face of hunger

I have not witnessed the horror of world famine. Only for a couple of weeks did the blind beggars surrounded by flies in the streets of Cairo, Egypt, grovel and jostle me for alms. And I only remember one time when I was very hungry as a child in the early 1930s that my mother said, 'There is no more food for today.' But I have read Gabriela Mistrale's poem *La Casa*. She is the South American Christian woman who won the Nobel prize for literature in 1945. Let me read it to you in translation:

---

[1] 'Art and Culture after the Holocaust', *Cross Currents* 26:3 (1976), 258–69.

The table, son, is laid
with the quiet whiteness of cream,
and on four walls ceramics
gleam blue, glint light.
Here is the salt, here the oil,
in the centre, bread that almost speaks.
Gold more lovely than gold of bread
is not in broom plant or fruit,
and its scent of wheat and oven
gives unfailing joy.
We break bread, little son, together
with our hard fingers, our soft palms,
while you stare in astonishment
that black earth brings forth a white flower.

Lower your hand that reaches for food
as your mother also lowers hers.
Wheat, my son, is of air,
of sunlight and hoe;
but this bread, called 'the face of God',
is not set on every table.
And if other children do not have it,
better, my son, that you not touch it,
better that you do not take it
with ashamed hands.
My son, Hunger with his grimaced face
in eddies circles the unthrashed wheat.
They search and never find each other,
Bread and hunchbacked Hunger.
So that he find it if he should enter now,
We'll leave the bread until tomorrow.
Let the blazing fire mark the door
that the Quechuan Indian never closed,
and we will watch Hunger eat
to sleep with body and soul.[2]

If I may be personal about it: I do aesthetics with that image on my mind.
Maybe I lose weight because of the poem, but I do not forsake the calling I
accepted before the Lord at my inaugural, to be busy with the next generation reforming aesthetic theory until it be conformed to the Will of God. *Both*
theory *and* food must become servants of the Lord in our hands. Nobody can

---

[2]From *Selected Poems of Gabriela Mistrale,* trans. Doris Dana (Baltimore: John Hopkins Press, 1971).

detheorise theoretical work because there are pressing non-theoretical evils; and it would be misguided, I believe, to withhold reflective analytic attention from aesthetic reality until death caused by greed and world food-distribution problems have been resolved, because then Christian aesthetic theory and most tasks other than the basic ones of supplying food, drink, shelter and clothing to the massive world population will have no grounds to be started and can be pushed aside with good conscience.

All of life needs redirecting

I am just highlighting one major problem God's people face in our day: how do we decide on the relative priority of the many different tasks within our single ministry of world-wide reconciliation to which the Lord calls us (cf. 2 Corinthians 5: 17–21)? Can we find a way to proceed with obedience before the Lord in all areas of creaturely life so that we and our children and neighbours not be compromised by forces at work in certain cultural fields still largely unreformed (as happened in earlier reformations in history) while we labour principally in other fields of service?

Since the problem of priorities will never stop bothering God's people so long as we remain responsible in history, it becomes important for us to keep vivid in our sensitivity the basic vision that our calling is cosmic: none of life is off-limits from needing to be reformed and conformed to the will of God, and *all* zones of creaturely life require office-bearers outfitted with a passionate heart, gentle mind, and strong feet that bring tidings of great joy to the world. That means, quite practically, that we must go out of our way to shun the temptation to pit one ministry *against* another.

For example, at a recent conference where I spoke, a Christian student who had just come from a workshop on world hunger asked in my sectional on aesthetics: 'Last year I had to spend $2000 to complete a film for my BA with a major in cinema. Few people will ever see this beginning film with all its faults. I've been told $2000 could save 12 whole villages of people in Africa or Asia from starvation for years. Did I do wrong? Should I continue learning to make films when poverty is so devastating far away?' My answer could only be: the body of Christ must certainly be busy relieving world hunger *and* also encourage sons and daughters of the church to redeem cinematography. Both need doing, because hundreds of thousands of people are dying in North America every Friday and Saturday night at the movies!

Each cultural activity has its own splendour

We must also recognise the truth that one sort of cultural activity is not the model for another sort of cultural activity, although each sort is called upon to be a foot or an arm or an eye and an ear for the other in our common, single-minded ministry of reconciliation.

For example, the tightly knit-together team of teachers you need for true *schooling* (to effectuate an integrated curriculum and to have genuine, communal reinforcement in the teaching) is structurally different from that proper *political* caucus (where you knock heads together in an all-night marathon session, reach a compromise with the hardest heads dominant, and issue a press release). The *communion* normative for a Christian (or humanist) body of practising academic scholars teaching a new generation is not the model for a Christian (or humanist) political party, and the functional *equation* normative for a Christian (or humanist) party of active political leaders coping with the civic exigencies of the day is not the paradigm to be recommended for schools (also not for church confession groupings of believers). Further, the time-consuming reflective fabric of *academic action* and the necessity for professors and students to conduct analyses in one's academic field constantly referring to centuries of world history in the discipline would block, if similarly imposed on it, a responsible exercise of political activity; and the necessity for *political reflection* to be so focused on the complexity of current options as to be able to initiate corrective, administrative measures would warp, if similarly prescribed for it, the responsible sifting and pathfinding activity of academic work. However, *scholarship* is called upon to distil counsel for statesmen (and all societal neighbours), and *political office-bearers* and staffs are called upon to legislate justice for academic educators (and the populace at large).

Cultural activities must reach out to each other

I could dramatise the point this way: Gerald Vandezande as public spokesman of the Committee for Justice and Liberty is out on a limb every day – that's where he belongs – just as scholarly I belong hidden like a mole in my basement study (just as some of you belong walking the streets daily buying and selling fresh food). Of course Vandezande retreats again and again to the books, to lawyer John Olthuis and the political case-researchers delving in the CJL offices, while I continually emerge to give specific seminars at ICS and occasionally to appear in the public editorial eye. But radio interviews of newsworthy characters and journal articles on Kant or Gadamer are legitimately different kinds of projects and take different kinds of research preparation and savvy.

All of us in our proper jobs need to pray hard that the limb Gerald walks out on holds, and if it starts to crack, help him back to the trunk of the political journalism tree so he can try another one higher up or lower down, so that *our* slack political-journalistic witness not be an offence in the nostrils of the Lord. And I am required by God as philosophical aesthetician, in so much as I am able, to furnish our Christian political journalists (as well as elders and pastors, fathers and mothers, labourers and shopkeepers, social workers and deaconesses, magazine editors, professionals like doctors, lawyers and therapists, artists and repairmen – all appropriately) with Christian ideas from my field on the nature, norm, and relative worth of style, recreation, art and advertisement, for example, as it might impinge upon possible political policy regarding diplomacy, meaningful vacations, murals for schools, streets and day-care centres, bill-board taste, etc.

No apologies for theoretics

If I may also speak, quite personally, for the scholarly moles buckled over in their Christian studies throughout the world: I will not accept the guilt-trip of being out of touch or irrelevant just because my theoretical scholarship is not making headlines. The whole world comes into my study, ages of it; there are frightening images, tempting ideas, devilish promises made by books old and new that I constantly confront in the flesh with my senior and junior colleagues. Even though the Christian theories developing are shrivelled and immature, I am convinced that a mastery of eighteenth-century European cultural history and the problematics of aesthetic theory in that period rather than an in-depth knowledge of the contemporary Canadian political or socio-economic scene is the correct point of incision for orientation and beginning a Christian reconception of the field of aesthetics.

I also know without a doubt who the Redeemer of my scholarly work is and am lifted up again and again on eagle wings far above and beyond the chill of my basement, knowing as a matter of fact that our Christian theory has been used by the Lord on occasion to save student lives for service among God's people and society at large. Christian academic theory is inescapably 'relevant', that is, 'formative' upon somebody sometime. The overwhelming question is simply whether the theory is pregnant with shalom or a miscarriage of wisdom, a signpost bearing new life and hope or a misformative idol of foolishness and death – both hermetic and politicised theory is vain and evil.

Although I am not certain just what the contribution of a Christian political centre should be to institutions for academic activity, I do know that it would be wrong for me to think that the CJL is failing so long as the ICS lacks a government charter and our students have to suffer the injustice of not being able to get provincial loans for their advanced Christian study. That is no more so than that the ICS fails Patmos, CLAC, CJL and the church so long as it does not graduate each year a brace of art-curators, labour economists, political researchers or teachers of dogmatics. This problem of cultural priorities and joined specific tasks is not a temporary difficulty peculiar to the

Canadian locality but is built into the historical reality that God's people will face everywhere when they respond to the call for world-wide reform and have only limited workers and resources, it seems, for harvesting fruits simultaneously in all the kinds of legitimate ministries. I'm saying we must move forward historically together, acutely wary of falling into the age-old, categorial trap of wrestling the matter into factional terms of (contemplative) 'theory' versus 'practice' (i.e. with results), and then presume to solve it technocratically by pleading for a breed of communication specialists to bridge the gap.

Instead, I believe it is biblical wisdom to carry out faithfully the activity proper to one's specific gifts and creaturely task and to serve one another in that capacity directly in the deeper bond of non-specialised, confessional fellowship and wisdom, even to the extent of laying down one's time and salary for one's brother and sister in Christ. That is, each priority should cry out its needs with urgency for all who have ears to hear, but not with bullying impatience. Office-bearers in each priority should serve the others with critique but not with suspicion or self-righteous reproaches. Each priority must appeal for support ingenuously and unhypocritically offer its insights to one's neighbour, not covertly belittling the other's contribution to cultural obedience. Only when this humble spirit will underlie the several specific ministries in development shall the Holy Spirit attend the reformation in the land with the festive communion for which we all yearn.

A second real problem: working spirit

What should be the contours of our working method of reformation toward Christian cultural shalom in scholarship and in other life activities? The answer depends partly on the grit of one's confessional perspective, the spirit driving one's life-time, and also on one's assessment of our day.

Attitudes toward past, present and future

I myself believe the richest biblical contours are fairly clear. Firstly, with respect to the past, God's people should be neither pharisaical conservatist nor revolutionary pragmatist (cf. Matthew 5–7). If past tradition is made the law by which one lives rather than the matrix out of which one posits new obedience, you come to settle for a scholastic philosophy and a synthetic Christian, Victorian morality which is truly out of date. And if you are so unfortunate as to have no sense that tradition is a once-only kind of thing – a certain past in a particular present – and that once the tradition of a community is broken off, discarded or exchanged for something else, you can scarcely ever again breathe, think or love in rooted fashion, then you are easily tempted to make a principle of trying something new to succeed for the day, since tomorrow is only another today; then one's would-be Christian cultural enterprise will hang blowing in the wind.

Secondly, with respect to the present, God's people should neither rest in accommodation to the cultural status quo nor jump into the throes of counter-cultural movements (cf. Romans 12: 1,2, Ephesians 4:7, 12–17). If present-day societal patterns are accepted as the best of most possible worlds rather than as a deeply distorted and dehumanising violation of creaturely shalom, one will never see the need to make a living sacrifice of one's professional life for building an alternate, minority culture that can openly praise the Lord, but one will soon sink into comfortable, middle-class status. And if the cultural present is stigmatised as unredeemably reprobate so that Christians have nothing to lose but their chains, one easily rules out faith (as dealing mostly with birds in the bush!) and has little compunction about entering the lists of the tradition(!) of anarchy. Then edifying cultural projects are precluded and the damage of unrighteous anger prevails.

Thirdly, with respect to the future, God's people should be neither Utopian nor defeatist in outlook. If one acts like Christ's disciples after the resurrection and expects the millennium to come now (Acts 1:6), either by dropping out of heaven or accomplished by our own dedicated achievements, one acts like an over-anxious housekeeper in God's world, counting the longed-for chickens before the eggs hatch, and needs to hear Christ's reproof that it is not for you to know the Father's timing in the coming of God's Rule (Acts 1:7,8). And if one forbids a whole range of cultural activities, like marriage and art, philosophy and laughter, because of one's own guilty conscience, let's say, from eating while others starve (cf. 1 Timothy 4:1–5), then one in fact sets part of life in the world off-limits, withdrawn from Christ's healing power in history and inhibits Christ's body as a whole from stepping out thankfully in faith, love and hope in the creaturely affairs of laughter, marriage, art and philosophy.

Pioneering may mean temporarily doubling up

I believe that the contours of our communal working method should be one of hopeful, principled flexibility disciplined and vivified by a prophetic holy spirit. That means concretely, for just one example in line with my remarks about historical cultural priorities, that various kinds of reforming Christian cultural activity may need to double up also as other forms of Christian cultural obedience, for the time being. I've not thought this matter through completely, and it must not be interpreted casuistically (to give opportunists loopholes for aggrandisement) or primitivistically (to retrench over-all control in the hands of a few). But just as the institutional church pioneering its mission on outposts in lands where biblical Christianity is unknown needs to double as Christian school (catechism classes), Christian press (bulletin news), and Christian labour union (diaconate finding jobs), in order to show new believers in Christ the full-orbed healing the gospel in action proffers, so too in our land of cultural chaos where societal breakdowns and abnormalities are normal and a biblical Christianity consecrated to embodying God's Will on earth (rather than just in heaven) is practically unknown, our beginning Christian organisations may need to double up their services for a time in order to show the full-orbed healing power of the gospel worthy of Jesus Christ's Name until distinct ministries can flourish.

But to erase the different offices and sorts of cultural responsibilities would invite utter turmoil, ruinous jurisdictional disputes, and compound the cultural confusion. For example, the Christian Labour Association of Canada rightly doubles for a while as a haven for immigrant workers terrorised by secular unions, but it would be wrong for the CLAC to aim to serve those workers as church. The Committee for Justice and Liberty rightly doubles up its political-legal action with journalistic salvos on CBC radio in language the general public understands; but it will need to choose sometime later on between becoming a bona fide Christian political force (with a public education sub-task), an independent newspaper or journalist voice, or a charitable citizens' watch-dog with Christian bite. The Institute for Christian Studies rightly offers emotional steadiness to students who matriculate in its programme and correctly doubles up on its normal graduate seminars by organising or participating in conferences geared to provide prognostic and back-up advice for CLAC and CJL; but it would be wrong for the ICS to be forced to structure its academic programme as a think-tank for CJL, CLAC, or some 'interest-group', or to become a counselling service for displaced students – then the Institute would no longer have the integrity proper to an academic centre for Christian studies.

Running together with joy

The guideline of principled flexibility – where different sorts of Christian cultural activity, constrained by the love of Christ, double up on their task temporarily as each moves historically toward a full-fledged, differentiated cultural witness in concert with all the other sorts of communal Christian endeavours – is conceived to keep faith with the host of witnesses behind us and to promote the well-being of the new generation we wish to lead in praise of the Lord, uncompromised, if it please God, by our historical deficiencies. Crucial, however, for the sanctified implementation of such principled flexibility is the presence of mutual trust among all those involved. Mutual trust can grow only when the same spirit is at work in the many hearts and a similar assessment of our cultural circumstances drives us together. To put it bluntly, we need an unequivocal, communal answer to the following complex of questions. Are we living in a permanent emergency (as the old-fashioned existentialists preached)? Is the societal fabric of our (Western) secular civilisation so thoroughly godless we should say, as a people of God, 'We must obey God rather than men, and the way modern humankind forces us to live is intolerable; so we opt out. "The night is dark, and we are far from home"' How can Christ have concord with Belial?

The answer we must give together, I believe, runs this way. We stand continually under the *crisis* (judgement) of our mercifully just God's face, but we do not totter on the brink of cosmic catastrophe. The faithful Lord is calling us in this generation to build up alternative Christian cultural institutions to bear witness of Christ's Rule, confronting godless scholarship, secularist labour unions and political parties with born-again insights – see how the Lord God gives us room to struggle at it historically this very day! And it is a lie that 'The night is dark, and we are far from home': that sentiment is counter to every psalm in the Bible, including Psalm 130! Rather, I believe that my *sin* is very cruel, and it gripes me with tears that together we are not holier servants of the Lord with eyes and ears that see and hear continually Gabriela Mistrale's little boy, but the Lord God is present with God's overwhelming comfort leading us to continue God's work in our specific tasks, despite *my* sin, with great joy.

No, Seerveld, you're giving comfort to the people who ought to be shaken right out of their socks and self-satisfied doldrums! Don't pacify the conservatives who give guilt money to Christian causes out of their tithes but won't change one millimetre of their bourgeois way of life! How can you be truly prophetic if you don't rock the boat!?

Then you read me wrongly, my friend. There can be no peace for those who insulate themselves from the woes of the world (cf. James 1:19–27; 1 John 3:11–18); their inflated security blankets will be moth-eaten before they die or by the next generation (cf. Luke 12:13–21). But a New Testamented prophetic call to the Truth must be at core intercessory rather than denunciatory (cf. Matthew 7:1–5; 1 Timothy 2:1–7). We must not lay Pharisee yokes upon the faithful, trying to push their habits into biblical line. People need to be coaxed, maybe shamed, exhorted, argued, and wept with to hear the Lord's winsome demands to wash their hands clean on pain of going to hell (cf. Isaiah 1:10–20; 1 Corinthians 9:19–23). But people need to be led on a path, not shoved through hoops.

How then shall we as God's people live if we would be found faithful to the end, when the Lord returns? 1 Corinthians 7 says we should live creaturely life to the hilt if we are also able to let it go. 1 John says that love of God without diaconal love for neighbour is a sham. Psalm 91 brings sure comfort for the worst of times: though a thousand drop dead at your side, the plague of the evil one will not get you, my children!

The day described in Ecclesiastes 12 may someday confront us when, it says, girls and boys shall no longer be able to sing. The weeping and wailing in Bangladesh, Rhodesia, Lebanon, and on the hillsides of South America, and the lack of even lethargic sounds from the ghettos in North America, and the pulverised silence and stupor that follows in the wake of a punk rock orgy may be portents of that Day of the Lord. But James Ward, Blanchard, Romanowski and Judy Jordet must never stop writing and singing new Christian songs, not until their throats are literally slit rather than just muffled by the monolithic, secular record-distributing system and lack of concern among Christians in the land. And Institute senior and junior members must never stop pursuing advanced Christian scholarship, never turn their hand back from that academic plough, not until they are literally carried away by police in the night, not stop just because the bank may threaten to padlock the door. Why? Because the tale and analysis we tell is not that told by an idiot full of sound and fury, signifying nothing, but is the story, the thoughtful praise and praising thought told by children of the King who is faithful to the thousandth generation of those who love God and keep God's commandments.

And all of us, all of you, in whatever Christian calling, who want to run for the Lord without getting weary must not run scared. For God's sake, run with joy! tears streaming down your face, thorns in the flesh hurting, stumbling over your sins, but with a doxology and creedal song in our hearts and on our lips, because the future and the pregnant present belong to us who believe in Jesus Christ and God's Kingdom coming!

Part 4

Work and Daily Life

1 Christian Workers, Unite!*

There is a ring to the closing lines of that famous Manifesto from the hurly-burly year 1848:

> The Communists disdain to conceal their views and aims. They openly declare that their ends can be attained only by the forcible overthrow of all existing social conditions. Let the ruling classes tremble at a communist revolution. The proletarians have nothing to lose but their chains. They have a world to win. Working men of all countries, unite!

Those words do not have a hollow ring. The appeal of Engels and Marx rings hard and clear to the discontented labourer of any age, catching at his or her legitimate grievances, cutting through the sham of society's words and indifference to economic misery, a call appealing directly to the greed and violence that lodges in one's human heart too since the fall. It has a devilishly daring, strident, God-damning ring, setting person against person in class struggle, flaunting its economic demands. Few other sounds have rung through the labouring world since.

Where has the Christian manifesto been hiding? Do those who believe in Jesus Christ come to set humankind free, truly free from their chains, have nothing clear to say to the workers of the world that rings, rings true to the Word of God?

Because you have been bought with the price of blood, because you are bound together by Jehovah's jealous love, because your common calling is to act in the name of Christ unashamed, to turn the world upside down in the power of the Holy Spirit, Christian workers – let us shout it from the housetops – Christian workers, unite! for Christ's sake! unite!

That is an imperative, you recognise, a biblical imperative under which I speak, to be heard and obeyed. It is not something carefully thought up by me, somebody who has studied a little logic, theology and philosophy, whose opinion you can argue with, weigh, and discard. I mean to confront you with the imperative of our Lord, who does not pussyfoot around but speaks boldly and asks of those who bear the Lord's name, Christian, everything! If it is not me but the thrust of God's Word before us this afternoon, then there is hope!

---

*Edited version of an address delivered to the 1964 National Convention of the Christian Labour Association of Canada.

and direction for a Christian manifesto. Then the Christian Labour Association of Canada has a terrible sword to wield, for biblical imperatives, unlike human opinions, provoke a response of faith or disbelief, united Christian action or sharp splinters of opposition. I pray that the Holy Spirit who has broken bread with us break the hardest hearts and send us home not incredulous, bitter and unmoved, but thanking God for God's Grace, with a prayer to be kept faithful together in our work, which is the Lord's.

Biblical view of work

Listen first to Psalm 146:

Hallelu Yahweh!

I must hallelu Yahweh!
I will hallelu Yahweh in my (daily) living.
I shall sing it out to my God as long as I live!

Do not join yourself trustfully with tyrannical lords:
in humans there is no salvation at all;
on the day that a human stops breathing and turns back into dust,
that person's well-conceived plans are gone, just like that!

That man or woman is blessed, however, who trusts the God of Jacob for help,
who expects things from Yahweh, their God!
the God who made heavens, earth, sea, and everything in them,
who maintains God's faithfulness on into eternity,
the God who shall execute justice for those pressed down deceitfully,
who does provide food for those going hungry.

The LORD God sets captives free.
The LORD God opens blind eyes.
The LORD God straightens up again those who were bent over.
The LORD God loves deeply those who deal justly.
The LORD God cares for strangers, children without fathers and mothers,
widows and widowers, these God helps hold up:
but the brutal practices of those denying God –
their life God ties into a knot.

Yahweh is king now and forevermore!
Zion! your God rules from generation to generation!
Hallelujah!

Plate 18 Seerveld giving the address *Christian Workers, Unite!* at the Christian Labour Association of Canada, Toronto, 1964

That is what human work is to be according to the Bible: a hallelujahing Jehovah!

Work is not something optional to humankind; it is built in to human nature, an ordinance of God laid upon every person – no one can escape it. God made humankind originally as a worker, a creature to work the earth (Genesis. 2:5), to cultivate and preserve it (Genesis. 2:15), i.e. to act upon the world, to do things in the earth, sea and heavens not just in general but to show up his and her lordly creaturehood, to reveal how glorious God's handiwork is, how rich and good a creation God made for historical development. Without any work a person deteriorates. Whether it be forced old-age retirement, prolonged unemployment or spiteful idleness, no work seems to break a person into doddering pieces, no self left to respect. This is because work is peculiarly inherent to being a human creature.

Sin did not obliterate this God-given structuration of humankind; he and she remained workers. But under sin work became labour, troublesome, tiring, frustrated under the punishing curse of weeds and sweat, sorrow and later wild animals. Outside Eden human beings remained workers but our work was radically deformed, prone to vanity, a betrayal of our lordship under Creator God.

That fact has remained a puzzle for centuries to people untouched by biblical revelation: why do people work so hard and suffer in its tension? Would it not be wiser to work less, and therefore suffer less? The best thinkers of ancient Western civilisation despised any work that would bring sweat to a man's brow. Pythagoras, Plato and Aristotle preached contemplation, to be a candleholder and look on; manual labour – except for heroic! war – they found unbecoming to the master race of Greeks, fit only for the slavish masses and barbarians. So they spun their grandiose theories while Athenian society disintegrated. The opposite and more dangerous unbelieving analysis of human toil crops up strong in the modern period after the Enlightenment. Enlightened men like bitty little Benjamin Franklin worshipped work and promised an Horatio Alger millennium to those who counted their pennies, minded their maxims and ambitiously plugged away at success in the brave new world of America. Money makes the world go round, honest work is the way to money; therefore, in work lies our eventual human salvation. This subtle perversion of humankind's glory, our working condition, is closer to our lives than we think. And it is not far from Marx's idolatry of work which is more ugly only because it is more shamelessly consequent, comprehensive and impatient of law.

The biblical view of work, however, pulls humankind's activity into a sharply different focus. Labour is neither disparaged nor idolised. That a person works is good, say the Scriptures. But that a person's work outside Eden is conceived in sin as a curse or deludedly twisted into a false god is evil, say the Scriptures. In fact, unless a person's work in time since the fall is redeemed by the Lord, is conceived in Grace, is actually and intrinsically a hallelujahing Jehovah! that person's work is indeed a curse, a marvellous distraction, a busy-bodiedness that ends only in the grave, and all rewards of clothes, cars and fame (what moths can eat, rust corrupt, and men forget) are sops! That working person has been bought for a human price, cheap! his or her life-time prostituted for a word, rust and an empty hole. And those sophists who say, 'yet unredeemed work is not useless to civilisation', have turned the truth into a lie and are ascribing what God salvages from God's sinning creatures to the proud justification of humans. The Bible is clear on this matter: our work is a built-in opportunity to praise God, and if our work is not genuine praise of the Lord God born out of faith, then it is dead work, damned and dead.

This is the good news! of the Scriptures to those who have been bought with the price of Christ's blood, that Jesus Christ himself purifies our heart from dead works and turns our acts into worship of the living God, *Godsdienst* (God's service, i.e. worship; Hebrews 9:14). Only then, when human work is worship of Jehovah,

I (simply) *must* hallelujah Yahweh!
I *will* hallelujah Yahweh in my (daily) living!

I shall sing it out to my God as long as I live!

only then does work lose its human chains; only then does that narrow-minded demoniac drive to get and get, erotically satisfy oneself, become stilled, converted into an open-ended rush of joy. Only when Grace covers the toil, the rising up early, the sitting up late, eating the bread you worried about providing, only under and out of Grace does work find meaning, and can a person go on content.

Christians need to take concretely and seriously what the Bible says about work. It is literally so – or isn't it?! – that unless Jehovah be building the house they labour for nothing who build it (Psalm 127:1)! The wise man of Ecclesiastes wondered, 'What's the use? What is left over of the labour to which a person exerts him or herself ?' And the Spirit-prompted answer to his troubling question goes deep:

I have come to understand that a person can do nothing good oneself, that for a person to be glad, to be well-off, even to be able to eat and drink and enjoy oneself in the press and change of daily life – all this is purely a gift of God (Ecclesiastes 3:12,13).

So simple an answer. So simple-minded it seems to those who complicatedly trust in tyrannical lords and the contemporary schemes of people. So simple and deep and comforting an answer to those who belong to God: that person is blessed who trusts the God of Jacob for his or her help, who expects to receive things from Jehovah, his or her God! Work!, Paul told the early Christians, to show the unbelievers you mean business on earth, so that you do not become a public charge, but quietly with your own hands may procure for your family and for giving to those in need the daily bread God provides (1 Thessalonians 4:11, 12; 2 Thessalonians 3:10–12; Ephesians 4: 28). Always in Revelation, Old Testament or New Testament, God – who works too! said Christ (John 5:17) – God, it is revealed, intimately attends, inspires, cradles gently the frail work of God's adopted children who trust God alone. The living God Almighty stands ready to gather up our daily offerings of sweat and tears and change them into a hallelujah song; God's Grace (*charis*) makes believing human work (*eucharistia*) thanksgiving!

That is what I am after by saying that according to the Bible human work is to be a hallelujahing Jehovah, thanksgiving to God, spontaneous faithful response to God's call to worship God each new morning. And God's call to worship ranges the breadth of God's creation; nothing is too mean for God to stoop to and save. Every Christian worker may hold on to that biblical truth that the Lord God works in us both the will and the deed to act out our salvation with fear and trembling and joy to God's good pleasure (Philippians 2:12,13) in whatever calling, with however so many talents God's Grace finds us.

My father is a seller of fish. We sons know the business too, having worked from childhood in the Great South Bay Fish Market, Patchogue, Long Island, New York, helping our father like a quiver full of arrows. It is a small store, and it smells like fish. I remember a Thursday noon long ago when my Dad was selling a large carp to a prosperous Jewish woman, and it was a battle to convince her that the carp – 'Is it fresh?'; it fairly bristled with freshness – had just come in, but the game was part of the sale. They had gone over it anatomically together: the eyes were bright, the gills were a good colour, the flesh was firm, the belly was even spare and solid, the tail showed not much waste, the price was right. Finally, my Dad held up the fish behind the counter, 'Beautiful, beautiful! Shall I clean it up?' And as the Jewish lady grudgingly assented, ruefully admiring the way the bargain had been struck, she said, 'My, you certainly didn't miss your calling.'

Unwittingly she spoke the truth. My father is in full-time service for the Lord, prophet, priest and king in the fish business. And customers who come in the store sense it. Not that we always have the cheapest fish in town! not that there are no mistakes on a busy Friday morning! not that there is no sin! But this: that little Great South Bay Fish Market, my father and two employees, is not only a clean, honest place where you can buy quality fish at a reasonable price with a smile, but there is a spirit in the store, a spirit of laughter, of fun, joy *inside* the buying and selling that strikes an observer pleasantly; and the strenuous week-long preparations in the back rooms for Friday fish-day are not a routine drudgery interrupted by 'rest periods', but again, a spirit seems to hallow the lowly work into a rich service, *Gods-dienst*, in which it is good to officiate. When I watch my Dad's hands, big beefy hands with broad stubby fingers each twice the thickness of mine, they could never play a piano: when I watch those hands delicately split the back of a mackerel or with a swift, true stroke fillet a flounder close to the bone, leaving all the meat together; when I know those hands dressed and peddled fish from the handlebars of a bicycle in the grim 1930s, cut and sold fish year after year with never a vacation through fire and sickness, thieves and disaster, weariness, winter cold and hot muggy summers, twinkling at work without complaint, past temptations, struggling day in day out to fix a just price, in weakness often but always in faith consecratedly cutting up fish before the face of the Lord: when I see that, I know God's Grace can come down to a man's hand and the flash of a scabby fish-knife.

Let me go one step further: the dirtiest job in the fish store is Friday late, load up the truck with a dozen large, metal barrel cans full of fish scraps, bones, guts and left-overs, any rotting boxes, other refuse and seaweed, and drive the six miles outside town to dispose of it all in the city dump. It looks like a movie set for Dante's Inferno as you approach the dump past uninhabited scrublands, wildcat fires scattered about its perimeter, grotesque mountains of sliding cans and rubbish, animated bulldozers poking and pushing and cursing through the smoke. You back the truck up in rather soft sand to the edge of the cavernous hole, not too close lest it give way but right to the brink, throw open the doors, and then one by one try to trip the heavy cans of slops over your leg down into the abyss without slopping all over your shoes and pants, without losing the can in the pit or falling in yourself. I've sometimes thought as I stood there stinking in the summer heat, catching my breath in a maze of flies, eyes smarting from the stench and smoke, what a perfect place for Chaucer's line on the yeoman, 'But it was joye for to seen hym swete!' That's biblical! I am not romanticising, but putting work in a biblical perspective so strange to modern thought: the meanest work can be done to the Lord and is a holy service. My brothers and I at work in the dumps, laughing and struggling, happy to be bodily alive there too: it is like a little hallelujah chorus sung by the South Bay Fish Market, the kind of earthy hallelujah, priestly service, angels fain would sing, but God has reserved for the believer, the Christian worker.

That person has missed his or her calling whose daily work is not a thanksgiving to the living God. The person whose work is thanksgiving, praise of the God of heaven and earth, he or she has a daily joy, a solace, unmeasurable in human coin. I am not saying that the Bible automatically sanctions any old job. Rather, the Bible calls workers to hallelujah Jehovah in whatever job they have and promises that the Spirit of God shall sanctify the work itself of those who respond in faith to the divine calling. I know, the increasingly mechanised and specialised factory work is making it more and more difficult for a worker to understand his or her job as a sacred calling. That is why the fellowship of the working saints is all the more imperative! The hairs of our head are numbered to God Almighty; the intents of our heart privy to God alone. God probes intently, jealously; the work of our hands, all of it!, is no less dear to God, because we were bought with God's own Son's blood, we are completely God's! If we lose this biblical vision we perish from God's sight.

I remember it this way, from my name: Seerveld is a medieval nondescript place-name like van den Berg (from the mountain). Some serfs scattered about on lands outside the feudal lord's castle were probably called *des heren veld* (of the lord's field). In time the d dropped off, the h was elided, and the rest smoothed out to *seerveld*, a field of the lord. God has thoughtfully provided me, it seems, with a kind of gentle reminder of my creaturely working status.

All I am is a nondescript field of the Lord for God to plough and cultivate and bring forth fruit in; God asks me only to be responsive, hallelujahing ground, a place for the Holy Spirit to have free play in. Everyman – van den Berg, van der Vennen, van der Ploeg – should also be *des Heren veld*. That is our *logical* service, say the Scriptures.

Reformational Christian living

You all know that passage from Romans which describes Christ's total lordship of creation:

> all things are from God and through God and to God: let there be glory given God for ever and ever, amen! Therefore, brothers and sisters, remembering God's mercies, present your bodies as a holy, living sacrifice pleasing to God, I beg you – that is your logical service! Do not be conformed to this world. By the reformation of your mind be so changed that you all discern what God's good, pleased, full will is (11:36–12:2).

Scripture never leaves us cliff-hanging. It speaks with refreshing, pointed authority: that's the way things are; therefore, do this. Paul constantly follows up the indicative with an imperative that would seem quite a jump generally to Aristotelian logic. Because Christ is absolute Lord of everything, and God has mercifully changed you from a death-house (Romans 7:24) into a living creature (Romans 8:11), it's logical – I beg you! – it's logical, brothers and sisters in Christ, for you not to be conformed to the deadening spirit of the age you live in, but to be so transformed that you bring your whole bodily existence into line with the saving will of God, that you become a veritable living sacrifice, a praise offering going up in smoke before the Lord, wholeheartedly, wholebodily hallelujahing Christ's name, holding nothing back: that is your logical service in the face of God's mercy.

It is this biblical directive to subject a person's *total* life to Jesus Christ, and the injunction to do it by getting a new consciousness different from the old one you had, a new perspective, a new heart led now by the Holy Spirit: it is this biblical directive which governs Reformational Christian living. By Reformational Christian living I mean human life dominated by the biblical motive of re-forming traditions of people, re-forming existing social conditions, re-forming projected human structurations of life that will set the pattern for generations to come, re-forming activity in all areas of reality until it be all conformed to the lordship of Jesus Christ. That is easier said than done, but that is what a person's life-time is for doing! Reformational Christian living has the gritty temper, the vigorous, outspoken bite that was the genius of the Reformation in sixteenth-century Europe when ecclesiastical constriction of life was broken and every butcher, baker and candlestick-maker was enjoined to go back to the Word of God for a renewing of your mind, for direction to your daily work in the world for Jesus Christ's sake. Reformation is not something that happened once upon a time and must be celebrated once a year. Because people are fallible and history is God's patient, fatherly dealings with God's often childish covenant people, Reformation is necessarily to be an ongoing way of life. Reformed people must not be past tense! The mandate of our Lord is to be a living sacrifice, to be reforming our outlook, *re*forming our action to God's specifications, *re*forming the age in which God has placed us. To do less is not to be logical.

As a teacher of philosophy I know the difficulties of subjecting philosophical investigation completely, unconditionally, to Jesus Christ. A person always has some pet ideas which eventually show up proud, self-satisfying, rather than humble, God-glorifying. To take back a proud idea you have stood for is to lose face; and what person likes to lose face? I know, many thinkers would challenge the statement that 'ideas' can be 'proud' as a badly mixed metaphor. However, the great Dane Kierkegaard, defending his analysis of the world sicklied o'er with the pale cast of thought, got a hold on the truth when he wrote (in the Preface to *The Sickness unto Death*): 'From the Christian point of view everything, absolutely everything should serve for edification. The sort of learning which is not in the last resort edifying is precisely for that reason unchristian.' If you rub out the despair and withdrawal Kierkegaard brought to that thought, you have a biblically Christian goad: so much philosophical thought does not edify because in the last resort it is proud, not constrained by the love of Jesus Christ, and precisely for that reason unchristian.

'Show me how this logical analysis is related to Christian commitment!' The shoe is on the other foot, brother or sister in Christ: how is your scientific analysis edifying? I am commanded by the Lord of heaven, earth, sea, and everything in them, as a teacher of philosophy, both in developing a biblically Christian philosophical systematics as well as in thoroughly, critically, studying pagan, scholastic and secular philosophies: I am commanded by my Lord to be 'breaking down arguments and every obstacle raised up (sophisticatedly) against the simple knowledge of God, bringing *every thought* away captive, in the subjection of Christ' (2 Corinthians 10: 5). The jealous Lord God revealed in the Lord Jesus Christ, by the operation of the Holy Spirit demands not a whit less of you in your work, whatever it be, if you dare use the name Christian for your life, because Christ asks total capitulation, bodily sacrifice, and God is not a God reserved for academic work but is the Lord of tent-makers, tax-collectors, fishermen's work. In fact, say the Scriptures, God prefers to use the foolish things of the world to disgrace the philosophers; God prefers the weak things of the world to confuse the strong things (1 Corinthians 1: 27). The full Gospel is this: all of human life is precious to its Saviour; therefore, be busy in Reformational Christian living – whether you eat, drink, or whatever you do – hallelujah Jehovah! – even if it be out of joint with the times and cost you trouble. That too is graciously given you!, say the Scriptures, not only to believe in Christ but also to suffer for Him (Philippians 1:29).

Comes then the subtle darts of the Evil One, whether in the mouth of angel, man or snake: 'Has God said that all? Life is to be conformed to Jesus Christ? Is there not *anything* indifferent to Christian conviction? Surely what God wishes is your heart, your personal commitment to Jesus Christ as your individual Saviour; this confession is what God wants. But really, sweeping the streets with a broom is sweeping the streets with a broom, whether the handle is held by a believer or an unbeliever. *Qua* broom-sweeping there is no difference. Of course, a person's behaviour and attitude and motive can be Christian or not, but not broom-sweeping *per se.*'

This line of thought may be unpremeditated, but it is murder. It kills the Christian worker and leaves behind a Christian that also works. Work is then no longer my work, a person is not in his or her working or in her or his work product any more, but work is turned into a kind of abstracted *qua per se* mechanical function to which I seem to be locally attached, as it were. Such a rootless, purely theoretical conception of the nature of work conflicts radically with the biblical view of work and undoes the whole drive for Reformational Christian living because it separates a person's faith from her or his livelihood; that is, makes faith something mental, 'spirital', extrinsic to one's actual bodily activity. Such subtle reasoning about work *per se*, work-in-general, secularises the Christian's daily walk as devastatingly as talk about a God-in-general ruins a Christian theology. Sweeping the streets is no longer *Gods-dienst* but simply something you do to earn a living; cutting up fish is no longer *Gods-dienst*, but a common, naturally human busyness. It cuts the heart, the life-blood out of Christian work! '*Christian labour*', strictly speaking, becomes nonsense. Bodily labour becomes a neutral necessity, that's all.

There is no lack of Christian proponents for this evil idea. Strange bed-fellows accept this barren conception of work divested of its hallelujah character. Roman Catholic theory, Barth's theology, do-gooding liberals, and a wide run of Fundamentalists all agree, in varying ways for different reasons, that there is a zone of reality not intrinsically touched, dominated, to be changed by God's saving Grace, that there is an area of the world which simply is *there*. These groupings sharply debate among themselves the exact dogmatic content of Christian belief and also argue sharply among themselves just how important and what constitutes this 'other realm' and how is it to be related to matters of salvation, but they all hold basically that certain created states of affairs, like work, for example, are essentially mundane.

It is not my purpose to judge the hearts of such Christians. My intent is, in passing, in the context of my whole thesis, to point out that their common, deep-going thought-pattern, this life-directive of Nature and Grace, the natural and the spiritual, neutral matters and specifically sacred matters: this age-old, persuasive religious perspective – which cannot be argued once one takes one's stand there – this engaging religious perspective does not discern the full will of God as revealed in the Scriptures. The mistake of such thinkers is to ascribe to the structural ordinances of creation a being independent of creator God's absolute lordship in Jesus Christ and then further confuse things by misunderstanding some concrete human actions (why only some?) as though they be these previously abstracted non-religious Forms in reality. The short-sighted sin to such thinking – who is ever free from it altogether? – is that it admits Jehovah's rule over only part of reality, over humankind's 'heart' motives, valuations, but not over all a person's actions nor over the whole world at large. God's sovereignty, Christ's lordship, is restricted in a person-alised, humanistic manner, and whatever is conceived by these thinkers as not peculiarly human deeds is declared off-limits for God: that is neutral terrain.

This point is not negotiable, I think, for a biblically Reformational Christian faith: nothing in creation is neutral before Jesus Christ! Even the stones, trees and stars hallelujah Jehovah with their mute speech, and wild animals prowling from their lair at daybreak in search of prey are hallelujahing Jehovah, say the Scriptures, telling us a mystery, not just tickling our fancy. And if all creation is struggling, groaning, waiting for the day of redemption of us who sinned, if all things are from Christ and through Christ and to Christ, on what grounds, on what biblical grounds, can one doubt or deny that whatever our human hands bring forth also falls directly under the sway of Christ's sceptre, that *whatever* we sinful humans *do* it is – thank God – a sacrifice of obedience, a hallelujah, or it is an empty vanity? All human production – a philosophical critique, an art object, a clean swept street or a fish dinner – all of it can be and is to be done as unto Christ, who Himself cleaned feet and ate fish. This biblical point of Christ's cosmic totalitarian compass is not nego-tiable to a Reformational Christian perspective.

Because Reformational Christian living is difficult to do consistently, and because Reformational Christian action may be sometimes indiscernible from unreformed action to the naked eye, is no reason to say that human action such as skills and human social life such as organisations are therefore exempt from Christ's claim to be conformed to Christ simply because they are skills or an organisation. Because sin and Grace cut across believing and unbeliev-ing lines is also no excuse to proclaim a neutral-no-man's-land untouched by either sin or Grace, or let us who bear Christ's name forget the extent of our logical debt of gratitude to Him who bought us at an extraordinarily costly, totally merciful price. The concept of neutral spheres of human endeavour is foreign to the biblical imperative, and no amount of keen theoretical argu-mentation, ipse dixits, or sophistry shall be able to hide that fact.

Gradually I have come to see the plight of us American Christians with Reformational roots: for many years we have had strong Reformed theory, but we have been largely satisfied in praxis with the easier accommodation of Nature and Grace. The discrepancy has been noticed, partly because a younger generation is drifting more in the winds of secular prosperity, willing to go along with the lip-service to Reformed theory but becoming increasingly sceptical at pretending it is practical in America. Alarmed conservatives have rallied round the theological doctrines and pushed the *theory* harder. Sincere pietists bred among us have warmed up missions and pushed evangelism in the hope of biblicising our praxis. But neither scholastic conservatism nor devotional evangelism gets at the roots of our dilemma, penetrates through to the full counsel of God.

Two radical, positive alternatives have been broached for our problem, however. The one is to get our theory in line with our daily praxis. The other is to get our daily praxis in line with – not our theory, that was the first bad step! – to get our daily praxis in line with the living biblical imperative to Reformational Christian living, thought, word, deed! This last positive alternative has everything against it – human nature, the weight of tradition, the spirit of the times – except: you may laugh and count the Lord of the Scriptures, the God of heaven and earth and sea on this side, for this is what pleases God.

You foolish working people, banded together here for Christ's sake?! a drop in the bucket of American labour! Are you mad? drunk with new wine? Let it be said to all who can hear: the Christian Labour Association of Canada is not a scheme of human devising, but a humble, fallible, sinful, human attempt to stand up for the Lord's side, to respond hallelujahing to the good, pleased, full will of God, even to the biblical imperative of Christian workers, unite!

Why Christian workers are to unite

Listening to the Scriptures with your heart open, letting the Word sink in to form and re-form your deepest desires and whole consciousness till it lead you out into the world wise in the power of the Spirit: this is the daily joy of the searching believer and the mainspring for any truly Christian leadership. There is this striking passage in Ephesians we should try to hear:

> Grace has been given us, through Christ's largesse, to each one of us in order to strengthen us saints for the work of serving, *building up the body of Christ*, until all of us reach the unity of faith and discernment of God's Son. (*Grace has been given us to be building up the body of Christ*) towards our becoming full-grown, mature in Christ's fullness, not childish anymore, blown about by every teaching, changed this

way and then that way at the dice-throw of people. (Instead of living) in the cleverness of people aimed at the strategy of manoeuvring around, let us simply grow up, presenting the truth in selfless love, *let us lead all things to grow up in Christ who is the head of us all.* The whole body of Christ – every single part in its specific working closely joined together – the whole body of Christ – integrally knit together by every connection there is – *the whole body of Christ will grow up, be grown up out of Christ then, building itself in a love that gives whole-heartedly* (4:7, 12–16).

Christian workers are to unite because Scripture commands us each in his or her own specific workings, closely joined together, to be building up the body of Christ.

What is the body of Christ? It is that union of people who profess that they, with body and soul, in life and death, are not their own, but belong to their faithful Saviour Jesus Christ out of whom, through whom, and to whom they live as their head. The body of Christ is this communion of people called together by the living Word, all those who respond, willing to submit their whole lives openly to Christ's lordship. It is the world-wide community of God's faithful, not just theological professors, ministers and missionaries, but you carpenters, construction workers and office clerks, hands and feet, arms and legs, ears, eyes and mouth, all different walks of life, each with its special function, bound together by the love of Christ into one body. It is this body which the Scriptures command us to be building up, with Jehovah God blessing our hands.

Is that not a rather ingrown, provincial, self-concerned attitude, building up yourselves? Don't you believe the insinuation. Secular historians are wrong that the Christian community be a hard-bitten sect which has obstructed world progress whenever it had a chance to dominate. The Christian community as the body of Christ is what history is all about! Not 'world' religions nor earthly conquerors but the slim body of believers, to which we belong, because it is a special work of God and a question of the glory of God's Son!, is the truly outgoing dynamic at large in the world. It is the little stone broken off from the mountain which is growing, developing, building up from the centre out till it fills the whole earth! It is not for our interests we build, but for the Lord who is coming back to claim his body publicly.

People everywhere are invited, if you confess Christ's name you are commanded – that is why Grace is given you! – to work hard in strengthening this body. No monolithic, universal ecclesiastical institution is intended. The biblical mandate to build up Christ's body aims its imperative directly at every single part of that body in its specific workings. Believing teachers, for example, are enjoined to grow together, to study in concert, to mature in university so that the educational eye of Christ's body may get keen vision, with depth. The Lord asks you Christian workers, for another example, to edify one another, that is, to build one another up, to encourage and help the other believers in their working capacity, to consolidate your resources, to unite! so that the labouring arm in the kingdom of God be supple and strong – that's logical! That's biblical. I know, 'edify' has a prim sound, because it has mostly degenerated to smugly self-righteous pats on the back behind the protection of Sunday School walls but 'edify' in the biblical sense of 'building up the household of faith' on and *in* the job before the stare of unbelief takes more guts than a moralistic platitude. The Word of God requires of you, Christian worker, and every member of Christ's body in the sphere of his peculiar activity, to stop manoeuvring around for the esteem of humans and straightforwardly, freely, come out banded together for action openly in Christ's name, in active communion of the saints, in telling, strengthening union of allegiance to the Lord in your vocation. How can it be otherwise in the face of the biblical imperative? Or is your daily work not a living sacrifice to *God*? Building up Christ's body is not a matter of human preference or not: it is a matter of God's directive.

Do you mean then that building up Christ's body entails separate labour organisation, you 'separatists'? If that is a dirty name for some people, like 'Christian' once was a dirty name for some people near Antioch, accept it. Christians are separated, by the Lord: some people belong to his body, and some people do not. That's a separation. Or does the fact that only some of humankind belong to the covenanted people of Jehovah not mean anything? To be covenanted with God does not mean you have a theological life insurance policy with a clause of irretractability once you have made profession of faith in church. To be covenanted to Jehovah means you live constantly under God's Son's specially loving imperative: build up my body in the world! lead all things to grow up in my name, including labour relations! And because those called to be saints, those sensitive to this covenanted responsibility to the Lord of all creation show that fact, think, work and act corporately as they are indeed constituted: in what name under heaven is such organised labour association called 'separatist', divisive? It is a false prophecy that recommends bifurcation here – split the Christian community to save solidarity with the secular community. True, obedient fulfilment of the covenantal vow to Jehovah does not put Canada or America first, nor the human community first. It puts the kingdom of God, the body of Christ first!

United Christian workers are not 'separated' from fellow human beings and unbelievers – that's a laugh! We confront them daily. They have had your back to the wall here in Canada. The question is how are God's workers to confront them? As individuals, secure in your personal faith, doing a silent, honest day's work in the factory, keeping out of trouble, witnessing briefly at lunchhour conversations? Does that answer Revelation's call for you to shape, to lead the factory's labour-management relations to grow up in Christ's name?

I do not mean to play down personal witness, but I do challenge the *reduction* of 'witness' to individualistic testimony. And I call into question the mean spirit of a current atomistic Protestantism which has no sense of Christ's lordship over earth, sea, sky and society, which is content to 'save souls' for heaven, and which has made inroads in American Reformed circles mostly because the rich biblical Reformational directive of 'communal witness' has not been an operating principle in our lives. The Christian is not in this world simply alone, but is a member of Christ's body. And the Christian's task in the world is not to be conceived in terms of missionary evangelism, but evangelism is to be vigorously carried out in the context of building up Christ's body! To be fuzzy on this point is to surrender the deep biblical insight and focus of a covenantal faith that is relevant for time as well as eternity. Once this biblical injunction to build up Christ's body is lost, with its intensive orienting power for every saint's creational existence, the converted fruits of an individual's witness and the church's preaching have no framework, directive, programme to follow to express the effected salvation of their life – it is the *life of a person* in its full-orbed reality which is saved, is it not? Once this biblical imperative to lead all things to grow up in Christ's name is removed, made optional or 'secondary', you Christian believers have no basic biblical right to be carpenters, construction workers or office clerks, and the very hallelujah character of your non-evangelistic work is being undermined.

However, you Christian workers, who are not only individuals but together an arm of Christ's body in the world, in your office of Christian worker you have the high calling of proclaiming and implementing Christ's lordship in the field of twentieth-century labour. God knows it is not easy. It is not easy to develop a biblically Christian perspective, biblically Christian judgement on concrete labour problems in the secular 1960's.

I was told of one of your locals discussing terms for a new contract. To the item of Sunday labour one said, 'We should ask double pay if we have to work.' But another said, 'If the conditions are in the contract that we do not work on Sunday unless there is an emergency, maybe if it is an emergency on Sunday we should work for nothing.' The *richness* of faithfully struggling together to bring earning your bread and butter into conformity with God's commands! Such enriching communal striving to find out God's will for your factory, construction, transportation, officework, to make your forty-hour week truly Reformational Christian living: such communal seeking builds one up to a maturity in Christ's fullness.

This whole difficult, invigorating endeavour to norm labour actions by the Scriptures, by the very cultural nature of the enterprise, calls out for Christian workers everywhere to come together in the single-minded spirit of Christ to help, to take active part in meeting all the labour problems in His name, from basic ones like establishing the voluntary nature of a labour union to the applied ones of developing a Christian understanding of a 'just' wage and working condition. Cultural forming of any of society's many activities – Christian or non-Christian cultural forming – always needs a grouping of persons, a community. Isolated individuals, no matter how great, do not produce cultural movements. It takes a united body of people, perhaps relatively few, but a body of people united on common ground, fused by a single driving motive, showing one common vision as they spell leading principles out to the fine print: it takes a live consorting of committed people, perpetuated for a generation or more, to effect a cultural force, to influence modes of social action. The whole business is bigger than individuals.

That fact reinforces the biblical mandate – for all those who have not renounced their task of Christian cultural action – that you Christian workers are to unite as Christian workers, as a peculiarly Christian, Bible-grounded association. Your calling to submit North American labour relations to the lordship of Jesus Christ, as a revealed cultural task, cannot proceed otherwise than as a new consorting with common point of departure and a common unifying power at work in you body of people involved. The only foundation on which to build such Christian cultural activity and the only cohesive for directive Christian labour action is the dynamic Word of God, written and revealed in the person of Jesus Christ, moving people to wholehearted, all-out allegiance. This Jesus Christ and the Scripture as final authority for all life and practice is simply not common ground to people in general. Christ's Grace spills over on all people through the creation He is reconciling to Himself and touches many through the deeds of his contemned body of believers, and Christ speaks graciously through His Word to all who listen; but Christ as Lord and the Scripture's radical directive is not commonly accepted and held naturally by humankind since the fall. Therefore, a distinct Christian labour organisation is not separatism but obedient Christian sanity for attempting Christian cultural formation, holding fast in hope to the rock of our common salvation. The sand of human agreement cannot bear the construction of a hallelujahing temple to the living jealous God of heaven and earth and society.

Why are Christian workers to unite? Always this answer: the Scriptures charge those who have received God's saving Grace to be building up the body of Christ in every area of reality. Communion of the saints is the fundamental, joyful reality underlying the whole life of each one who confesses Jesus Christ. And this communion is not inert on earth, just a pinch of salt preserving society from decay, like preserving social and labour relations in a napkin, but is God Almighty's chosen viceregent of creation, the living instrument of the Holy Spirit to let God's will be done on earth as it is in heaven!

This is the glory and the hallelujah shining through the frail efforts of you Christian workers united: Christian organisation is simply a direct, formal expression of the organic oneness believers have in Christ, and the presence of the Holy Spirit in the midst of their organised activity makes it a different kind of organisation from those led by human and unholy spirits. A truly Christian labour association is not a labour union like any other, a power group waiting for the opportunity to get increased benefits for its members, dominated now by a majority of Christians. A Christian labour union is not a lobby for a special minority, for the Church, or even for the Lord; it is not a force organised to get something pragmatically done at a certain strategic moment. That wrong-headed, secular idea of labour organisation (as a purely technical method for obtaining wages, benefits and working conditions) is precisely what it repudiates! Because it knows that people must not live by bread alone, a Christian labour union cannot treat God's creatures abstractly as socio-economic instruments when it studies and manages their socio-economic problems. And because it realises that the actual power for changing economic conditions and relations comes from and belongs to God's Spirit, a Christian labour union is structured, reflects and acts with Power that seems impotent to the unbeliever. A labour association is not Christian merely because it exercises power morally and responsibly; and a labour association is certainly not Christian if it tries to coerce disbelievers into minding ecclesiastical rules. A labour union is Christian when it holds up to all workers the biblical view of work, when it promotes conditions that further Reformational Christian living, when it instructs and directs both labour and management to correct labour patterns in conformity with God's Law and moves to enforce these considered claims with the charity and reticence and convicting power of the Holy Spirit.

God will bless the nation that honours and hears a Christian labour association, for God's ordinances enacted are easy and light upon people's shoulders and promote peace. You workers know better than I that a Christian labour association is the only labour organisation which shall free labourers from the false and bitter struggles Marx capitalised upon – employee versus employer and collectivism versus individualism. Only Christian labour organisation can subdue class struggle and totalitarian evils in society because only its union directs people beyond themselves to an Other who can hold society and individual, worker and work-giver, together in love: Jesus Christ.

The opposition of people

When Christian workers unite under the Lord, whenever a radically biblical, positive Christian thesis is presented in thought, word or deed, the opposition of people inevitably comes to the fore, as has happened to you. The opposition of unbelievers who hate our Lord against the action of united Christians is so fierce because they do not want wickedness re-formed, turned upside down and brought to light. The secular unions cannot brook the witness of a Christian labour union as Christ's body abuilding, dedicated to bringing labour relations under the lordship of Christ, because such dedication ruins their would-be secularisation, totalitarian grasp on a person's life-time. The secular union's disdain, first, and later harassment of your Christian labour association is evidence of the hard core of religious intolerance behind their humanistic facade of common solidarity with all people. They cannot stand your Christian witness because it destroys the unchristian motivation underneath their goals, the hidden power in people's hearts to which they appeal. But such strong opposition to your flesh-and-blood Christian thesis, such a strong, clean-cut anti-thesis is good!, as Kuyper said, because it faces onlookers with the issues of life and death: choose today with whom you will serve! And in your consolidated weakness before such massive opposition lies your Christian strength; you will make no mistake on where to look for help. Lift your eyes to the Lord.

There is also the lethargic opposition of believers who are rocked in the rhythm of Sunday worship but dormant, so to speak, through the week, who do not care to trouble themselves about problems seemingly foreign to their comfortable round of activities, those who in ignorance lead a narrowly defined Christian life and simply do not see the rainbow-like spread of a biblical faith: their opposition is more a drag than anything else. When faced with the challenge of organised Christian action they are wont to reply, 'I don't see how – I don't see why – can't we do it another way?' The claims of Scripture should be pressed upon them patiently, not surface argument which obscures the religious question, but the root of the matter, 'What does our Lord require of you as a member of the body of Christ?!' It takes a long time sometimes for a person to stop excusing him- or herself and to see that his or her individual commitment to Christ necessarily and happily has the great biblical dimension of one's being committed to action with Christ's body! You must have the Grace to be patient with such believers till they grow up to discern fully what God's Son asks of them. You must be patient as some were patient with me. Jehovah opens blind eyes.

Strangely, the worst opposition to Christian communal action can come from believers, learned people who dislike the imperative character to the call 'Christian workers, unite!' and whose attitude seems to be, 'Who are you to tell me what I have to do, and then, if I don't comply, call into question my personal belief in Christ?' The testiness of such a reaction is telltale; it betrays a touchy uncomfortableness on the matter about which no person may speak for another. People can not and may not judge another's heart; and when your heart of faith and obedience is judged by another, for example, as the source of 'grandiose plans for separate organisation', examine yourselves and turn the other cheek, but do not return the offence. However, what can be questioned and should be judged is the spirit and direction in which God's people are led – put the spirits to the test, examine whether they be of God!, said St John. Maybe that's the rub, what provokes such virulent, however softly sheathed, opposition to the new call for corporate Christian labour, political and social action, which till recently has been largely mute in our brave, new world history. Could it be that Reformed leaders on the American continent feel as if the spirit and direction of their leadership has been questioned and resent it? Naturally so, no one of us wishes to be found delinquent. Otherwise I cannot explain the lamentable pettiness of such learned believers' antitheses.

★ ★ ★

As Professor Dooyeweerd put it nearly thirty years ago: it is dangerous, and I would add, shoddy, reasoning to say that because one might be forced to leave Christian organisation undone in certain circumstances, therefore *whether* one should develop a Christian labour or Christian employer organisation *depends* upon circumstances.[1] Those given to fine logical distinctions could take note of this. Believers who respond to God's Word with Christian organisation are aware of the complex socio-historical conditions, the important differences between kinds of societal structures (e.g. clubs, school, businesses, family, political parties, church, power organisations); they are aware that God's people do and must co-operate in our sin-disrupted world with unbelievers when we are involuntarily thrown together with them (e.g. in a state) or need their services without being bound to prostitute our very commitment (e.g. a student at a secular university); and they are painfully aware of the difficult, discussionable human judgements needing to be made among themselves about exactly how, in precisely what form, with what timing Christian organisation is to be enacted in a given field: *they are aware of all that, but take its measure solely under the biblical imperative to be building up Christ's body in the world.* That is why the Spirit infusing and directing the thought and lives of believers active for Christian organisation is not one of common sense involvement in existing social structures plus an individual voting testimony, with the possibility of sometime later, when we deem it strategic, of going an extra, separate 'Christian' mile. No,

---

[1] "When it happens in certain kinds of business – I'm thinking especially of large industry and the wholesale trade – when it happens in such cases that a Christian organisation simply doesn't let itself materialise because there are so very few Christian employers involved, then one must give in for the time being. However, to say: because the socialistic world-and-life view and its class struggle ideas have not penetrated the sphere of employers much, as they have the workers' circles, and because Christian principles seem to be fairly active among non-Christian employers too, therefore Christian employers can get along very well for now without an employers' organisation set up on a Christian foundation – that kind of reasoning strikes me as extremely dangerous' (translated from *De Strijd om het vraagstuk der christelijke Vakorganisatie van Werkgevers*, p. 24). Dooyeweerd's whole analysis points out how the Nature–Grace perspective of reality vitiates the call to establish vocational organisations with Christian basis and orientation.

rather, the Spirit, the priming, driving, dominating, leading religious motive of our lives is that of responding directly, fresh, to our Lord's imperative for communal re-formation of all life and of social organisms extant. This Reformational Spirit and communal direction is zealously followed because it is seen by these covenanted believers to be a biblical imperative that Christian cultural formation is to be done by the mobilised community of the saints concertedly, openly unashamed in Christ's name. God is gentle and sorrowful when human corruption overwhelms God's faithful and they cannot immediately respond but must fast and pray and wait and work for the day that follows the night of unfulfilled longing. But there is no ambiguity on what God's Grace has been given us for! Building up the body of Christ! Unfolding all things in praise of Christ the Lord!

Take away that imperative as the guideline for our covenanted lives together, and Jehovah becomes jealously angry for God's Son's honour. Whenever 'Circumstances' replace this biblical imperative, the Scriptural norm, as rationale for communal Christian action, then you have sold out the Lord and ironically raised Expediency! Efficiency! Strategy! to the status of unalterable abstract principle! And 'Strategy' is not a biblical directive! 'Strategy' as a rule for Christian action preens human cunning rather than trusting faith. The 'principle' of 'Strategy' condemns Christians who would follow it to be always counterpunching, ten to twenty years behind times, jumping in to change things when it is (almost?) too late, never out front leading, shaping human events to come in the power of the Holy Spirit. God does not want us on the level of such well-conceived, strategically effective sacrifices. God wants us initially with the bodily obedience of a broken heart and a spirit malleable, responsive to God's call for communal saintly action.

We anti-revolutionaries, we who would be busy about our Lord's business in re-forming the world, simply because the Lord asks us to! must not be sidetracked from the positive development of what Christ requires of His people. Let us push on in faith, combating the strong opposition of unbelievers with the boldness of the Spirit, winning support of uncommitted believers by witnessing deed and patient discussion, challenging learned believers who are in antagonistic opposition to meet us on the level of Scriptural imperatives.

Our Lord's imperative

The Lord requires of us everything; we may hold nothing back. That is what 'Lord', kurios, means.

Send us Grace, Lord, so that we can unite openly and perform works worthy of You, works of repentance! This is what the Lord requires of us! Not what fits nicely into the pattern of Christian living! Not what is 'effective' on the American continent! Our Lord, *kurios, Caesar,* asks us to repent! turn around, turn to God and work out deeds worthy of repentance, of a changed mind, of a turned-about heart (Acts 26: 20) – repentance of self-willed stratagems, of half-and-half measures, of busyness without the connecting vision of faith under God, God of generation after generation, the covenanting Lord God! Profession of irenic love and peaceability with people is quite trite next to what the Lord demands: public, spontaneous, zealous deed, full bodily action for Christ (1 John 3: 18)! trusting his mercy, protection and guidance, not works which are hid, a cunning infiltration, but work which is open to the light of day, because, as the Scriptures say, 'If we say we have fellowship with Christ but walk in darkness, we lie But if we walk in the light, as He is in the light, then we have fellowship one with another, and the blood of Jesus Christ, God's Son, will cleanse us from all sin' (1 John 1: 6,7).

The imperative under which I have spoken to you was for me too. Only recently have I really come to grips with its biblicalness. By comparison, the rationalistic framing of the question whether Christian workers should unite always, never, or sometimes, seems out of touch with life and faith, like playing academic fiddlesticks. I see how one can become impatient at such talk, while secularism strangles the life-breath from the Christian community, from you Christian workers, and church becomes a pep-talk centre for moralisms and theological discussions instead of dispensing bread and meat for the believers' daily life. What can be preached to you Sundays for your workaday life, intrinsic to your business, except pious generalities and prohibitions if the biblical dimension of the communal task of the saints to lead all things to grow up in Christ's name, if recognition of that imperative is missing? The logical service God asks of us is bodily sacrifice, a daily building up the very body of Christ. If this proclamation does not come from the pulpits and educational institutions, then let it indeed come from the housetops: Christian workers, unite!

The dynamic imperative – Christian workers, unite! – can never be the result of a chain of argumentation: it comes from a deep Spirit-moved conviction dominated by the Scriptures. Never lose the biblical imperative to your association! Do not replace it with a human argument. From the biblical imperative comes your present élan; it is what captures the hearts of people including mine, and brings out the opposition of those who would rather remain comfortable yet in their Sunday best. So long as the Christian Labour Association of Canada is not what your hands have done and keeps faithful to the vision of being a hallelujah response, a union worthy of repentance, a bodily sacrifice to the Lord, it shall prosper. And when you become discouraged in the daily details, remember, you live under the Lord's imperative! you are building at the Lord's body in faith! God is willing to own as God's own what is given God with humbled, openly dedicated hearts.

When God comes looking in the cool of the evening of history for God's people – 'Where are you? Where are you?' – not many faithful shall be found, says the Scriptures. Why? Because everyone has gone his or her own individual way and got snuffed out in the dark?

I pray that you here united in Christ be joined by many more whose eyes Jehovah opens, and that they learn to love the new sound in the world of labour on the American continent, and that a Christian Manifesto be published in time so large that those who only read as they run through life to the grave shall see it. Because each one of you has been bought with the price of blood, because you are bound together by Jehovah's jealous love, because your common calling is to act in the name of Christ unashamed, to turn the world upside down in the power of the Holy Spirit, Christian workers, unite! so that as one body, the body of Christ! you shout from factory, office and home with one voice, Hallelujah! Jehovah!

Reading list

* Of special clarity and pertinence on the topic treated

*Antonides, Harry. 'The Basis of Secular Trade Unions', *His Dominion. A Quaterly Review* 12:2 (1 May 1963), 6–10.

—. 'Some Thoughts on Christian Social Action', *His Dominion. A Quarterly Review* 12:3 (1 August 1963), 10–15.

Brillenburg Wurth, G. 'De Mens en zijn Arbeid', in his *Het Christelijk Leven in de Maatschappij*. Kampen: Kok, 1951, pp. 232–89.

Dooyeweerd, H. *De Strijd om het Vraagstuk der Christelijke Vakorganisatie van Werkgevers in Het Licht van een Oude Strijdvraag in deChristelijke Levens-en Wereldbeschouwing*. 's-Gravenhage: Christelijke Werkgeversvereeniging, 1936.

Habermehl, D. H. *Ons Dagelijks Werk: de Christen in de Industrie*. Kampen: Kok, 1959.

Kooistra, R. *The Free Canadian*. Rexdale, Ont. Christian Labour Association of Canada, 1962.

Kuyper, A. *Architectonische Critiek. Fragmenten uit de Sociaal–Politieke Geschriften van Dr A. Kuyper*. Ed. W. F. de Gaay Fortman. Amsterdam: H. J. Paris, 1956.

'De Christelijke Organisatie', in *Pro Rege of het Koningshap van Christus*. Kampen: Kok 1912, III, pp. 184–94.

Runner, H. Evan. 'Scriptural Religion and Political Task', *Christian Perspectives 1962*. Hamilton, Ont.: Guardian Publishing Co., 1962, pp. 135–257.

Taylor, E. L. H. *Why Work? The Christian Answer*. Rexdale, Ont.: Christian Labour Association of Canada, 1962.

Van Andel, H. and R. Kooistra. 'Expediency', series of articles in *Church and Nation for Reformed Faith and Action*, VIII (1964), nos. 1–8.

Vandezande, Gerald. *Must Christians Form Power Organisations?* Rexdale, Ont.: Christian Labour Association of Canada, 1964.

*Van Riessen, H. *Mens en Werk*, in J. Stellingwerf (ed.), Christelijk Perspectief, (Amsterdam: Buijten & Schipperheijn), 1962, II, pp. 7–77.

Zuidema, S.U. *Kan een Christen Lid zijn van de Partij van de Arbeid? Uit het Delftse Debat.* Delft: Van Keulen, 1952.

*Zylstra, Bernard. *Challenge and Response*. Rexdale, Ont.: Christian Labour Association of Canada, 1960.

2 Labour: A Burning Bush!*

I should like to begin with a story.

Once upon a time Moses, shepherd for Jethro, his father-in-law, a priest of Midian, took his sheep herd way back into the desert till he came to the mountain of God (called) Horeb.

An angel of the LORD appeared to him then in a flaming fire inside a bramble bush; and Moses saw – look at that! – the bush burning with fire was not burned up!

So Moses said, 'I've got to stop and take a look at this striking phenomenon! why this bramble bush is not consumed.'

When the LORD God saw that Moses stopped to take a look, God called out to him from inside the bush, 'Moses! Moses!'

And Moses said, 'Here I am.'

God said, 'Don't come any closer. Take your shoes off your feet, for the place where you are standing is holy ground. I am the God of your fathers, the God of Abraham, Isaac and Jacob.'

Moses turned his face down, afraid to look at God.

'I have truly seen the oppressed misery of my people down in Egypt land,' said the LORD. 'I have heard them crying under those who drive them on; I know intimately how they are suffering. So I am come to save them from the hand of the Egyptians, to lead them out of that land to a good land where one can breathe freely. … Now come, I shall send you to Pharaoh to bring my people, the children of Israel, up out of Egypt land.'

Moses said to God, 'Who am I to go to Pharaoh to lead the children of Israel out of Egypt?'

God said, 'Will not I be with you?'

Moses said to God, 'But if I go to the children of Israel and tell them "The God of your fathers sent me to you" and they ask "What's God's name?" what shall I tell them?'

God said to Moses, 'I am who I am. So tell the children of Israel "I AM sent me to you… the God of your fathers, Abraham, Isaac and Jacob sent me to you" – that is my name for all time! that's worth remembering for generation after generation.

'… The King of Egypt will not let you go, I know that, by his hand of power,

*Address delivered to the 1965 National Convention of the Christian Labour Association of Canada.

but I will stretch out my hand and smite Egypt with all the unheard-of wonders that I shall do there; after that he will let you go.'

But Moses said to God, 'Please, Lord, I'm just not a man of words neither before nor after you have spoken to me as "your servant". I'm somewhat slow of speech, tongue-tied –'

The LORD God said to him, 'Who made humankind's mouth! Who makes a person dumb or deaf, seeing or blind? Don't I do that, the LORD God Yahweh?! Get going now. I shall be with your mouth and teach you what to say.' (Exodus 3:1–8,10–15,19–20; 4:10–12)

How many of you go to work in the morning barefoot? As you walk through the factory gate over the dirty cement or shift cold secretarial feet under the desk or stamp a big flat foot down on the truck's brake, are you there without shoes? Or is the place where you sit and stand to work not holy ground? Do you labour not before a burning bush but just out in a desert somewhere? Does steel and glass, routine and mass duplication stop you from seeing 'that every creation of God . . . received with thanksgiving is made *holy* by the Word of God and prayer' (1 Timothy 4:4,5)?

North America is not Egypt and Moses is long gone, but God's people and more than God's people are held captive still there where labour is forced, constrictively prescribed so that one cannot breathe freely, and the suffering of each little person is worse than meets the eye because it is treated so callously on such a large scale in the name of all that is falsely holy. But if Moses is long gone, who shall lead God's people crying under the injustice out of such captivity?

The New Testament only complicates, intensifies these matters, for Jesus Christ says to those who would follow him:

… I am come to strike fire on the earth!

Do you suppose I appeared on the scene to offer peace in the earth?

Not at all.

I tell you, I came to bring disunion in the earth! From now on of the five in one house there will be three divided against two, and two opposed to the three; father will be estranged from son and son from father.

When you see a cloud rise in the West at once you say, 'A thunder shower's coming,' and so it does. And when you see a South wind blowing immediately you say, 'It's going to be scorching hot,' and so it happens.

You hypocrites! you know how to tell the features of the earth and the heavens; how come you don't know how to tell what time it is now! Why don't you decide just out of your own selves what the right thing (to do) is?

When you head for court with your opponent, make work of it to be quit of him or her on the way there before he or she hale you before the judge and the judge turn you over to the officer and the officer throw you into prison. I am telling (each one of) you that (once judged and) in prison you shall never get out till you have paid the last red cent.

… Guard yourselves against the yeast which is hypocrisy, the yeast of the Pharisee. I tell you that whoever confesses me publicly before people the Son of Man shall openly speak up for in front of God's angels, but the person who disowns me in the face of people will be disowned (by me) before the eyes of God's angels… (Luke 12:49,51–59,1b,8,9).

The bite to Christ's speech that picks up that Old Testament story and gives it an apocalyptic edge is this, that God's appearance burning in a bush is not accidental, but God incarnate came specifically to set the earth, humankind and society on fire, a living witness to God's glorious, powerful presence in creation; and those unwilling to *be* a burning bush on fire for the Lord must beware lest they burn, as Jesus puts it, judged in prison forever.

Are these sayings hard? I speak to you as Christians, that is, people who put their jeans on one leg at a time like anybody else but who are willing to listen to the Holy Scriptures as the Word of God who made and maintains, rules heaven and the earth on which we live and move. Therefore, not with faint heart but with open ears we must catch from the Bible the cue for labour today, that is, come to know truly where our labouring bondage lies, what direction workers are to take, whether the fire under us be of God or the kind that consumes. If we bushes that look like people are still, dormant dead scrub, we should know the reason why; so I start there, uncomfortably close to home.

Pharisee yeast vs. repentant deed

Do not let the yeast of the Pharisee settle inside your skin, within your chummy group of associates, says Christ, because a little yeast leavens the whole lump and pharisaical hypocrites go to hell just like unbelievers (Matthew 23:33,51; cf. Luke 12: 47).

The uncomfortableness and difficulty of talking about hypocrites is that it is always one talking, especially if one has Dr, Rev., or Prof. in front of one's name, though the unlettered need not look past their own noses either. But if we recognise that, that all of us are Pharisee-prone, because the hypocritical Pharisee yeast is so serious to God and confounding in the world, maybe if we listen together we can be pricked to life by the Word, chastened and renewed.

The Pharisee is a believer whose Sunday right hand does not know what his or her six-days-a-week left hand is doing. On Sunday he or she is impeccable (that means, you can't pick any fleas off him or her), impeccable! In matters of Sabbath observance, Canons of Dordt doctrine, moral law and life, it is observed to the letter. He or she is a principled person who takes the church, God's Law, being righteous, with a seriousness Christ never laughed at. The Pharisee lives with an open Bible, studies it hard, memorises, quotes, applies it to case after case arising. But the crux of the matter is missing: a repentant heart flowing over in love to God to *obey God in deed.*

The Pharisee lays 'Thou shalt!'s and 'Thou shalt not!'s upon the backs of his or her fellow brethren, says Christ, and doesn't move a finger to make the burdens lighter (Matthew 23: 4); he or she is dogmatically cold as ice to the offensive unbeliever, offers not at all to bind up his or her wounds but passes by on the other side. He or she talks right but never *does* anything with his or her lily white right hand (Matthew 23: 3). The most grievous sin of the Pharisee is omission: salt without flavour, the kind of vipers that constrict and bite but cannot kill – they just squeeze all the joy out of life, its passion and fun (1 Timothy 4:2,3), unaware or blinded to this, that a person's strong left hand, feet and lips, legs and voice, also should be *directly* tied in with one's salvation. But no, the hypocrite stops zealous reform of left-handed matters with talk! – 'The tyranny of the Roman government is a just chastisement of God upon the sins of God's people; let your forbearance be known to all, for the Lord is at hand' – pious talk that simply, basically betrays a failure to take the *world,* God's world! seriously. And whenever the yeast of pious other-worldliness rises in the life of a believer he or she is not much earthly good to the Lord of heaven *and earth.*

As Jesus puts it, the pharisaical, with all their theological acumen, have lost, thrown away the key of knowledge (Luke 11: 52), the one illuminating focus that opens up the Scriptures and shows its relevance for all here and now: the cosmic lordship of Jesus Christ to be shared and exercised, suffered for by his body of believers in the communion of the Holy Spirit (cf. Colossians 1:16–20). That God loved the world so much God, the Almighty one, came into it to wear diapers, ply the carpenter's trade, teach fishermen's sons, be judged in court, sleep, eat, nothing too mean to hallow in God's Son's name as Christ died to set believers free, is overlooked by the Pharisee who makes the Bible say more and more about less and less, pulls it away from ordinary people and deposits it with the learned exegetical experts who then shall interpret it for the rest as to doctrine and morals.

The Pharisee in us reads the Scriptures with a restrictive veil over the eyes (2 Corinthians 3:15–17), proof texts it to death, staying unmoved by its living spirit that once loosed in a person's life, drives one to praise God gladly where one is every day, fervently to build up the faithful, love one's neighbour (you know who your neighbour is?). The hypocrite in me and in you is tempted to think that knowing about the Truth and speaking the Truth is enough; then one can always say at the judgement day, 'But I didn't do anything wrong.' Yet it is precisely that nothing doing, lack of action, which is the believing servant's terrible guilt when the Master returns to see what has been traded for the talents given, because He redeemed us, says Revelation, to be priests and kings, to rule over the earth (Revelation 1:6; 5:10). That holds for every stiff-necked, murmuring adopted child of God today, especially for every modern-day Moses trained at the nation's universities who runs away from Egyptian labour and politics to tend academic sheep for a generation – no wonder Moses hid his face when God said, 'The cries of my people hurt in Egypt land without leaders trouble me greatly. ...'

Christian believers must act, work out their faith, else it is dead. Not just any old kind of action pleases the Lord, especially not the formalised offerings, pompous sacrifices in which Pharisees delight. I've had enough of that stink, said God to God's Old Testament people, the straight-laced, tight-faced sacrifices you make flattering your own egos (Isaiah 11–14). Serve me informally once, outside the door of the temple, not in the holy place but in some 'unholy' places; show me you love me there too, all the time. Your specified acts and vain gifts remind me of burned up leftovers from yesterday's meal! Give me something fresh for once, truly first fruits, not the lives of your kids on the mission fields, but your life-time (Micah 6:6–8). It is what Samuel (1 Samuel 15: 22), Hosea (6: 6), Jesus (cf. Matthew 9:13) constantly tried to get across to the earnest but self-satisfied believers: God wants deeds all right, those that manifest sincere repentance, keeping of the covenanted promises, intimate, openly heartfelt obedience to the Holy One as Father. Correct, piecemeal worship, when, like a rich young ruler, you still hold back what is dearest to you or would keep it separate, uncommitted, spoils it all in God's eyes. God asks for the heart of God's child and thus all, in *repentant* action.

I don't know how many of you men ever washed your own underwear in a sink. I used to do it as a student in Amsterdam. It is a very human experience, washing underwear; you can't imagine an angel doing it. There is something humiliating and tender about it, like loving someone. Your knuckles get all red and sore; the fingers shrivel, finger-nails become snow-white. The kind of deed that God requires of us, action born out of repentance, out of a humbled, radically turned-around-to-God approach, will always bear a person's hand-washing-underwear character, somewhat clumsy, good-hearted, a little painful, ludicrous to the professional wise in the ways of the technical world, because repentance always shows up passionately, suffering but simultaneously exultant! – foolish to unbelief. Repentance in the Bible is not some kind of morbid, scrupulously breast-beating, self-accusing introspection: it is rather the change-about, breakthrough, Amen! turning of a person newly set in Christ which then spurs him or her on to act trustingly, surprised, wondering – all things are as new! (2 Corinthians 5:17) – keyed-up expectantly, not nervous but urgently busy in preparation for the feast coming, the victory celebration! yet knowingly child-likely weak, shyly happy at doing menial service for the Great Day coming. It is repentant deed before God – whether you are talking economic sanctions, political deals or plain gradeschool teaching – repentant deed in all its tender tough-mindedness, tucking the shadow of pain and sorrow for sin inside the laughing security of forgiveness, of being kept close to God: it is repentant deed that marks peculiarly Christian action.

Most of us, I suppose, were sprinkled before we knew it and therefore tend to miss the awful significance of baptism where it is signed and sealed upon your forehead that you are buried in the sufferings and death of Jesus Christ; and because God's shining glory raised him up out of the dead you are signed, sealed and delivered also in Christ's resurrection. Are you stupidly unaware of that? says Paul; that is why you should live, work, walk around in a wholly new, resurrected way (Romans 6:3,4)! Every baptised person has been officially anointed into the body of Christ, has a signed contract of sonship with God Almighty, has been instated in the office of believer, Christ-follower. If that office of believer held by a person, marked on his or her forehead, is not exercised, if there be no repentant, resurrected type action – it is much worse than defaulting on a thirty year mortgage, running out on your army papers; this is signed and sealed with Jehovah God! If there be no repentant deed daily, then you are playing dead, like a Pharisee.

A believer's office and God's ordinances

Where should a baptised person exercise his or her office of Christ-follower? Right in the corner where you are, as father and mother, carpenter, lawyer, teacher, preacher, evangelist, business person, citizen: genuinely repentant, wholly new, resurrected type action worthy of God who has washed, called you to work along in God's kingdom (1 Thessalonians 2:12; cf. Colossians 4:11), the kingdom of God! the sovereign reign of God's Son, which stretches over the whole earth – all earthly kingdoms, principalities, powers, nations, labours of human hands fall under the sway of God's rule. God's kingdom Rule is one of righteousness, peace and joy in the Holy Spirit (Romans 14: 17): while it cannot be humanly forced and won, it must be sought hard, say the Scriptures; while it shall not be completed till Christ come again, it is already begun among humankind (Luke 17:21) where believers obediently, patiently, sufferingly proclaim, enact the Word and rule of Jesus Christ. Every baptised believer has the ministry – you are *all* ministers – the ministry of reconciliation, of implementing Christ's reconciling the world to God (2 Corinthians 5:18,19).

Do you know what the Bible means by that? Maybe you once heard about that strange line of poetry 'A rose is a rose is a rose.' It may not be poetry anymore but it is true that 'A home is a home is a home' and 'A school is a school is a school' and 'A labour union is a labour union is a labour union' and

'A church is a church is a church'. And when a baptised father breaks bread in a home, cuts meat for his wife and children and asks the blessing of God upon their meal together, he is officiating in the ministry of reconciling bread and meat, man–wife, parent–child relations to God in the name of Jesus Christ. And when a teacher teaches the children to look at a rose, to understand the refraction of light with a ruler in a glass of water, gets them to sing in two-part harmony, all within the soft-spoken vision that this is our Father's world, she is officiating in the ministry of reconciling plants and laws of light, the gift of music to men, reconciling it all to God through Jesus Christ our Lord. When a labour union begins its meeting with a psalm, Scripture and a prayer not to be greedy, pleading for the presence of the Holy Spirit to help them add up the cost of living and a fair wage, then you have people, 'the people' as Jesus lovingly called them, who are officiating in the ministry of reconciling work, sweat and money to our Creator God for Christ's sake. And when a group of elders, after seventy times seven visits' agonising soul-searching, constant forgiving and probing, decide regretfully to begin censure on some wayward one, they are officiating in the ministry of reconciling the confession and life of men and women pure before the Lord.

A Christian home is a home, not a church, and a Christian school is a school, not a home, and a Christian labour union is a labour union, not a school; and the church is a church, not a law court of the state. Yet Christian home, school, labour union, church, each with its own peculiar formation of the ministry of reconciling creation to God through the redeeming work of Jesus Christ, in so far as each is the meeting place of the Holy Spirit, the uniting of two or three persons in Christ's name, a manifestation of God's covenanted people whom God has gathered to praise God – in so far, Christian home, school, labour union, church are manifestations of what the Bible calls the mysterious body of Christ, faint revelation of God's glorious Rule upon earth, weak, faulty, broken by us humans though it be.

Any one who denies this, denies that the Christian home is a member of the New Testament body of Christ, who denies that Christian labour union and Christian school are sincere, if sinful, responses to seek the kingdom of God concretely, historically, before we believers be haled before the judge, and as blessed by God are the beginning embodiments of God's Rule: whoever denies this and thinks *ecclesia* in the Scriptures refers exclusively to the institution serving us the wonderful sacraments, disciplining us by proclamation of the Word, comes perilously close to what Christ cut off the Pharisees for: you shut the door to the kingdom of heaven right in the face of people; you don't go in yourself and you stop others from going in (Matthew 23:13), pulling the Bible out of their unordained hands! Whoever says that the sacramental–confessional nature of the holy house of God must *characterise* the Christian home, school and labour union or it is illegitimate, is in error it seems to me, and has lost the biblical genius of the Reformation which has taught us that not an ecclesiastical creed and structure but only Jesus Christ as confessed by the Scriptures binds us, frees! us to the daily expression of our common priesthood, prophetic task and kingly office as believing family, school, labour association. If a Christian labour union, Christian school, Christian home are not organs of Christ's body in their own right, co-labourers in the one kingdom of God, different articulations, yes, of the Spirit-filled *ecclesia*, knowing the holy, Catholic communion of the saints, then either most human social groupings are swept out of the province of God's renewing Grace or you invite in an impossible and unbiblical clericalism. It is not at all Reformational to ask a labour union to subscribe to the Belgic or Westminster Confession when it constitutionally and organisationally confesses in its doings that 'Your Word is candlelight for my walk, a shining light on my well-beaten path' (Psalm 119:105). And it is not at all Reformational to ask an educational institution, bound together by profession of the truth that 'In Jesus Christ are hid all the treasures of wisdom and knowledge' (Colossians 2:3), to incorporate also the Canons of Dordt into its articles. Such requests are closer to Rome.

I realise much more needs to be said (and do not misunderstand my pointing out differences to be negations). It is most true that the institutional church in which we believers are fed the body and blood of our resurrected Lord, are refreshed by the comfort and Truth in the preached Word, are buoyed up by being specially assembled to adore God our Father and know God's holiness, it is most true that the institutional church is a singular manifestation of God's Grace, of Christ's body, of the kingdom of heaven too. The church institution – you were baptised there! – holds the weighty keys to the kingdom of heaven – which the pharisaical leaders have lost! they can't open the doors to the kingdom of heaven, they just keep them closed! said Christ. So the church institution has an exceptional, unique, terribly critical position in the midst of society to break the Word of *Life*, to minister sacramentally, churchily, in its peculiar office, to home and school, labour association, state, business, you name it. Would to God that Reformed, Baptist, United or whatever pulpits spoke out boldly on what TV-ised homes, pragmatised elementary schooling, brutalised labour unions, cynical businesses, irresponsible politics is doing to the confession of the faithful in the pew! Maybe then, if Jesus Christ's lordship were truly preached, there would be more children in Christian schools, more workmen willing – God knows it is a fearful fire! – to put their jobs on the line for Christ's sake; then there would be more love in the home that is long-suffering, behaves decorously, still to gossip (1 Corinthians 13:4–6), more laws on the books that protect righteousness, more movement for Christian action in politics.

You see the point? The church institution, pivotal in opening up or closing the eyes of its congregated faithful, must speak through elder, deacon and bishop to all of life in its missionary outreach, fearlessly but churchily. It is called not only to preach Christ to individuals but also to admonish other kinds of social bodies – municipality, school, family, political party – with pastoral concern for their action touching its believers' confession; but it is not to invade society and try to churchify such varied institutions. It does not have authority from the Lord to impeach judges, fire school-teachers, punish deserting parents, and when it assumes such authority and pontificates, tries to act as a social civil rights commission, pacifist political lobby, or even as a collection agency for Christian schools, it has missed the fine line of its God-appointed task and moves toward a would-be totalitarian order. The jurisdictional authority of the institutional church is limited by the Lord to business within its confessionally qualified communion; God, says Paul pointedly to the Corinthians, shall judge those outside its confines (1 Corinthians 5: 13).

For this reason, because the church like any bona fide institution has a *limited office* to exercise before the Lord *in all of society*, similarly, the Christian Labour Association of Canada does not discriminate against a person's creed any more than against his or her colour, race or national origin. A Christian labour association is not a church institution but a labour union, and it is not a labour union's business to police its members' creed and doctrine (which does not mean it considers doctrine unimportant or indifferent). A labour union's business is to administer labour problems; and a Christian labour union seeks to articulate, implement, redeem the working person's responsible labouring prerogatives in a way that obeys Jesus Christ, the Lord's guidelines of love and justice as revealed in the Holy Scriptures. A Christian labour union is still a labour union and not a confessionally watered down ecclesiastical ecumenical movement. There should be no confusion here: right indeed is the institutional church's concern into what kind of social groupings its church members carry their particular church's confession, but wrong is the institutional church's demand that other kinds of institutions adopt its churchlike restrictions. A Christian labour union accepts members from any church or the unchurched if they willingly and actually support the constitutionally committed basis to honour and ground its labour programme on the 'principles of social justice and love as taught in the Bible'; and the labour union will be Christian if those building, forming, leading its policy and day-to-day operation are filled and directed by this basic biblical perspective – despite the dues-paying presence of backsliders, formalists, hypocrites that analogously the institutional church has too. If the church institution has lost its fire and hold upon its members in daily life, the solution is not for church people to blame Christian organisations for stealing their thunder and try to turn labour unions into churches, but for them to get back to their churchy business and with single-minded,

Spirit-packed intensity and authority – for which every Christian worker is even now pleading before the throne of God – preach the powerful Word and full counsel of God rather than sermonic homilies, sensitively make the sacraments really dispensations of Grace, enter meaningfully into the centre of a person's life rather than standoffishly cold shoulder non-church institutional life. All life is of a piece and until the institutional church too reforms its apostate desire to be first among equals and instead gets down and washes the feet of its believers clean, that is, makes clear to them that *all* life is of a piece, until then the coming of God's kingdom in America will certainly seem dim rather than burn brightly.

Is it possible to convince the sceptical Christian of the ordinary believer's ministerial office and this crucial matter of God's ordinances, the diversified creational, structured order to the world and society, that a rose is a rose is a rose? Does it say so in the Bible?

The Bible says that God created every thing after its kind (whatever that specifically means). Even Paul, talking about the mysterious resurrection, seems to allude to it loosely and matter-of-factly in passing – different sorts of flesh (1 Corinthians 15:39–41). And throughout the Scriptures point is made of the God-orderedness to things in which the psalmist delights, at the same time their temporality and relative work which humankind absolutises in vain (cf. Ecclesiastes). It is this pervasive tenor of peculiar boundaries to creatures and their doings, without splitting God's world into disassociated pieces, the general revelation, for example, of the strong authority of government (Romans 13) nevertheless limited by God's law for humankind (cf. Acts 5:29): it is this cover-to-cover perspective that led Kuyper to his genial social canon of mutually 'sovereign spheres', a biblically sensitive insight that Vollenhoven and Dooyeweerd have deepened with philosophical richness. But let no Christian, sceptical of such historical applications of the Word, be fooled into thinking that the different ordinances of God, and corresponding diverse gifts which people receive from God's hand to respond with, are some kind of theoretical construct formed to special plead pet ideas. Rather, this is the truth that affords a blessed order to society when obeyed and brings comfort and meaning to every barber, cleric, student and garbage collector that can hear the Word, as it says in 1 Peter:

> With the gift each one got let them minister with it to the others as a steward of the many coloured, multi-sorted Grace of God. If he or she be a speaker, let them speak godly words. If he or she be a servant of some sort, let them serve with all the might God has given one so that in all (kinds of) things God be glorified through Jesus Christ in whom is glory and power for ever and ever. Amen!

That brings us to the matter of rheumatism.

Our secular captivity

You have an *ism* when you have too much of something, an exaggeration of what is not proper to a matter, or when what is tangential, peripheral, is given central importance. In Social*ism* one gives an exaggerated importance to society; in Calvin*ism*, technically speaking, too much value is put on Calvin's teachings; rheumat*ism* describes the condition of having too much rheuma in the joints of one's bones. I wish to speak about Secular*ism*: too much world. Or, how did Jimmy Hoffa's violent teamsters get here – by parachute from Mars? The sexy advertisements for hair tonic, soap and deodorants, did they just crawl up out of the printing presses into your newspaper? I do not propose to give a history of Western civilisation in four minutes, but I should like to give an idea of what has happened to us.

Once upon a time people believed their Bibles, especially because the infallible, interpreting church of the Bible had all the answers – to everything. Around 1500 AD Copernicus said: the earth and planets move around the sun; what does the Bible mean in Joshua (10: 12), 'And the sun stood still'? The sun does *not* move around the earth!

In 1600 Galileo checked it out: the earth is not the centre of the universe; scientific calculation shows it with certainty. But the church said: Are you an atheist? Do you deny the Scriptures say that the sun stood still. So Galileo said: Look in my telescope, O priests! Instead, the church banned his books, put him under house arrest.

And the institutional church was wrong. Since 1600 most intelligent men have *trusted* Galilean scientists, *reason*, rather than the institutional church and the Bible. After all, the church of the Bible was very wrong on a very simple matter, whether the sun is moving around the earth or the earth around the sun. So leaders looked to science, art and philosophy, to solve the problems of humankind; and it got assumed that keen human reasoning might even bring heaven upon earth eventually, the millennium. Some became impatient waiting for the glorious City of Man to be achieved by this educating, evolutionary process: evolution became revolution! But the Establishment of European businessmen, politicians and thinkers like Hegel in the nineteenth century kept the rational lid on. The actual world is as it ought to be, said they; God is in control, that is, Universal Reason is on the throne and It is on our respectable aristocratic–bourgeois side, don't bother us with empirical detail.

Marx arose with the Communist Manifesto: I am interested in some of that empirical detail, facts like exploitation of the poor, me and my fellow neighbour, by the rich. You good capitalistic sons of Christianity take my money at 3 per cent and lend it back at 6 per cent. You tell me, 'Go to church'! If I don't work, I don't get paid, and so don't eat. I see them in church singing 'O for a closer walk with God', resting, and earning 6 per cent on my money on the Sabbath day too. So I'm a materialist? At least I'm an honest one! Money makes the world go round. Tell me what you do with your money, and I'll tell you whether you are a Christian. What does it mean to be your brother's keeper? And Marx set about changing the world: raising individualistic greed to mass greed.

About that time Kierkegaard said, 'The church is dead.' A little later, the son of a minister, Nietzsche said, 'God is dead.' And those looking at the world in August 1914 said, 'Now, Society is dead' – World War I, World War II, and now – in my country at least, we are planning things for – The Great Society! in which there will be no poverty, no ugliness, no ignorance, no inequality. Let us not be timid: 'We have the power to shape the civilisation that we want.'

Secularism! The heart of the matter is gone: the glory of *God*, the reign of *Christ*, the power of *Holy Spirit* is missing! God is irrelevant to most of the world. Jesus Christ is a myth or a man or an ideal to most of our countrymen. All that is left is the World, the expanding universe, with men in control? of pieces of it? There is too much World, only the World counts: this is the Big Lie of Secular*ism*. And with it is coming the whirlwind.

Because humankind is made to give whole-hearted allegiance to God; if God is gone and Jesus Christ does not count, since a person cannot jump out of his or her created allegiance-giving skin, they are bound to serve some thing; and today's civilised persons alone in this great big World generally pick their worldly self. The result has been Evil Lawlessness, or worse, gradual movement toward Totalitarian Controls.

Rootless, directionless anarchy, lawless revolution is somewhat muted today in our countries. It is the fashion with existentialists, hot-rod youth who do not know about war, and it has found a respectable and dangerous form in civil disobedience, that is taking more and more to the streets. But the pendulum of human idolatry has swung more towards 1984 regimentation. The Devil no longer divides and conquers; he is learning to unite and destroy. It is most subtle: the liberal, socialist, communist, fascist in Europe, or the Republican and Democrat in the United States, or the Progressive Conservatives and Liberal Party in Canada are all growing toward one another, into One grouping. It is not respectable today to be extreme left or extreme right. The sophisticated shadowbox both sides and support: the extreme centre, dead centre, in the mainstream, on the bandwagon, a central*ism*! which leads to the tyranny of the majority and the despotic power of a pharaoh. The majority rules utterly even if it is wrong ('Two million people can't be wrong, buddy,' an AFL–CIO official told me) and violates God's norms. Significantly, John Dewey once insinuated that Christianity is an un-American activity because it does not have potential for being the common faith. Is that the handwriting on the wall most people cannot read?

Under such centralised secular*ism* things begin to shift and spin: ordinances of God are confused. A school becomes an agency of the state; church becomes a voluntary organisation like a Great Books club, labour unions become identified or identical? with political parties, and a rose is not a rose is not a rose, it is a tomato. And a rose is called a tomato for the best reasons, the noblest motives. The church takes over the school to save its financial existence, the federal government enlarges its control over localities in the name of justice; the farmer does what the state says because he gets a higher subsidy; the worker kicks in an extra dime because the union enlarges hospital coverage – no questions asked. In this process important social changes take place.

> *Closed* shop? It's a free country! If you do not want to join our union, you do not have to work in this city. You are *free* to move lock, stock, wife and barrel somewhere else (although the fine print says: we intend eventually to set up a closed shop everywhere).

> An East German roommate I had in Switzerland used to tell me how free women were in Russia. They are free to work just like men. Had a baby? The state provides permanent baby-sitters within ten days so you are *free* to go back to work.

I know, there are AFL–CIO locals composed of Dutch dairy farmers in upper Michigan that are so moral they wouldn't hurt a milkmaid; nobody bothers you so long as you pay the dues to the national organisation. I also know an independent trucker cannot operate around Chicago; and if he does, he ends up with the steering wheel around his broken neck. But the point is *not* morality and corruption here or there. The point is that so-called 'non-ideological' neutral unions are *secular: all* we are interested in is better wages, hours, and working conditions – The World is *all* that there is. And that is a lie the Lord God will not buy. How may those who belong to God buy it?

It is so easy to be seduced by the secular way of life; it gets inside your very bones, like rheumatism. People accept it as a given and then try to make the moral best of it. When Ford Motor Company gives the highest possible pay and the most possible free time so the worker does not miss too much the lack of joy in his or her work, one has been bought with a sop. When a college or radio station or commission needs money to meet the payroll, is one moved to pray to the Lord and make a straightforward appeal to God's people for money because our work is for Jesus Christ, or is a publicity expert hired who looks for a gimmick that sells the cause? It's Pepsi for those that think young, and the middle-aged reach for a glass. It's the Great Society and the New Canadian Life for the immigrant and the people who are not timid, so the meek who would inherit the earth say me-too.

With Secularism there is much more at stake than a person's livelihood, protection on the city streets for one's partner, conservation of natural resources and matters of injustice. At stake is the honour of God, the Rule of Jesus

Christ's name! That is, the battle being fought is not one against flesh and blood but against evil powers in high places (Ephesians 6:12). God's honour is not at stake – the victory is assured – except that those who profess to be of God, have they forgotten that this battle – the body of Christ, kingdom of God *vs.* secular kingdoms, the foul-smelling dragon of Revelation – have they forgotten that *this battle* is what is really going on in the world and its history? 'How can my people have forgotten my name?' God asked the prophet Jeremiah, 'I who wanted to wear them as intimately as a girdle into battle. Where are they? stuck in the mud?'

The lawlessness and totalitarian tendencies in Western civilisation are fused at present, especially in our countries, by the Pragmatic Spirit in which truth and action is judged by 'probable future success'. Pragmatism finds that expert technical knowledge – whether on your liver or logistics for air-traffic control – expert technical knowledge yields the best results. Hence comes the rise of expert advisors to people in power, an almost idolatrous concern for efficiency and this worship of success (which covers a multitude of sins). The Pragmatic Spirit believes scientific reason shall bring on the Great Society. If only we can bring our scientific know-how to bear upon all life's problems we will not only get a man on the moon but solve our economic problems, correct our military and political policies, agricultural surplus, racial tensions – if we will only try hard enough and all get together – all get together behind the infallible scientific method – it works! – we will plan us all into one great big happy, successful community where indeed no one will be more equal than another and where freedom means total security

Secular*ism*: a shift from communion of saints subjected to the Absolute Lord into a community of citizens subjected to their Absolute selves! together, as a whole. Once one accepts this Pragmatic Spirit and the subjective norm of group decision as final, there may seem to be colourful variety – when no principles direct a nation, but rather scatter-bugged interests of pressure groups, there will be continual change, instability – but once the Pragmatic Spirit and the subjective norm of group decision is accepted as final, I see no rationale to stop an increasing monopoly of life by some one governing force; and the pragmatic efficiency of such a common total control will be the secular argument more and more advanced for it! This is not a jeremiad against automation: machines are a threat to human life when the skills to run them are viewed independent of the religiously committed person performing them. This is also not overlooking the difference between altruistic Peace Corps, and the undisguised bullying of a Sukarno dictator, the difference between a gangster-ridden union and a so-called 'clean' humanistic one. But I put a question-mark behind our current society's security and well-meant humanism as being parasitically post-Christian rather than the fruit of a living faith. Things are so well-off secularly not because of the Babylon we have built, but only because God is giving God's people opportunity to confess God's name. We shall not live happily ever after if Jesus Christ is denied or ignored as lord of society.

People were wont to rebuke the German Christians of Hitler's day, 'Why didn't you do something?!' But it was no sense to rebuke them: they couldn't do anything. It was too late. It was their German parents and grandparents who stayed out of politics and labour and social problems who should be rebuked! They were the ones who, banded together, under God could have turned the German nation away from the Nazi curse. Maybe in Canada you are at the stage of the grandparents? In my country already could it be fathers' day? Who knows and who cares!

You hypocrites on the sidelines! says Christ, burned-out faggots! You can count the change in your pocket. You can figure out which way the wind is blowing. You read the newspaper headlines last night. How come you don't know what time it is now!?

It is the time for Christian action rather than talk in our secular captivity – for the Day of the Lord is at hand! – not to win the world for Christ, but to be obedient to Christ's command to confess him openly in deed, and expect God's fiery blessing.

Christian cultural power

We Christians have several alternatives for action. We can mind our own business, hang onto the proverbial horse by the tail while it loses hair by hair so slowly you don't notice it till suddenly you have no tail to hold the totalitarian horse still by. Or we Christians can spend all our efforts on saving individual 'souls' for eternity while society and its daily institutions goes to hell. Or, as *body* of Christ called to be saints in the world, to show our love for God above all and to care for our neighbour as if for ourselves, we can move together – for Christ's sake! – to bring the light of God's Word and Christ's easy yoke to bear upon our many-faceted society to free people from their captivities.

That last Christian alternative means certain far-reaching things for the cultural face of the earth. It means first that the whole world is there waiting to be discovered in a way that pleases the Lord. The *whole* world is a burning bush! not just academic, intellectual, mental, 'spiritual' areas, but local politics, bread and butter issues, teaching children how to read. Life and labour without this insight has one profaning God's world, clomping all around with one's big shoes on. That person profanes the earth, profanes labour, profanes the creation of God who finds and uses the world about one as just a common ordinary natural thing. Whoever thinks that the growth of a tree is natural and not miraculous, whoever does not see that the ordinary eyes of an animal are extraordinarily made, whoever would deny that the regular normal breathing of a baby intimately involves the Creator of heaven and earth: he or she has profaned the earth under them. Everything is holy, says Scripture, in the very precise sense that all of creation signifies and seals itself as being the handiwork of the Lord God and only so is to be enjoyed and cultivated, however subconsciously. To write off sex as natural laws, to explain atomic marvels as natural laws, to discuss socio-political phenomena as a natural course of events is to end up with a Mother Nature and reduce the Lord God Almighty's glorious burning bush of a world in all its immediate witnessing power, reduce it profanely to a deserted, ingeniously inert stump of a reality.

To restore the vision of burning bush to people in the factory, in the school, in government, in culture being built by human hands, takes the eye of faith, and to recognise the *direct* connection of our world with its Lord will take the eye of faith developed in a communion of saints, fellow believers consorting together to build one another up, not only because a cultural formation in history is always the product of a *body* of people but also because the body of Christ busy culturally naturally acts in concert, thrown back tightly together by the oppression of evil powers, as it labours to bring its two mites of cultural obedience to the sovereign Lord. Sparks fly in society – and in a person oneself, where secular independence, pride and covetousness never wholly gives in to the discipline of the Holy Spirit – sparks fly whenever Christ's followers try obediently to see and seek the kingdom of God *first*: those who place Christ last, tenth, or second make it difficult for such believers. In the teeth of such difficulties plagued by their own weaknesses, God's people need communal embodiment of their faith to be responsible stewards.

On pain of the worst hypocritical idolatry it must be thoroughly understood that communal Christian action is *not* focused to benefit *us Christians*. Communal Christian cultural action, rather, is engaged to save the lost with the ministry of reconciliation, bring comfort and balm in the name of Jesus Christ, institute Christ's order to life for those caught in the old bondage, as Paul puts it (Galatians 5: 1). That is, Christian political action is not out to get a state which forbids Jews to do business on Sunday but to get laws that protect the right of various groupings to perform their task in the common weal. Christian labour action is not out to secure special privileges for Christians but rather to bring the play of voluntary freedom the Christian faith knows into ordering the structure of labour relations, freedom for whoever it may be – Christian or otherwise. The saints are indeed separate from the world, that is, operate out of a different spirit, but we love and move among those in the world passionately for Christ's sake. This alternative of communal Christian action in society also means the use of sanctified power: not might, constraint, compulsion, force as the unbeliever conceives it, but the power of the Spirit, of the Truth, of opening up creation culturally in the way God normed its development, with a convicted awareness that prayer is neither magic nor hot air but, when believers ask in faith, not doubting, it avails *much*, also for labour negotiations, because God, the Almighty covenanting Jehovah God, Christ, to whom *all power* is given in heaven *and on earth* (Matthew 28: 18), God is directly involved in the formation of history and cares that those who confess Christ's name culturally be not shamed before people.

A Christian labour union, Christian political action, Christian education knows the norm for truly dynamic historical formation. It is not revolution which throws out tradition, breaks continuity, tries the impossible of starting over; and it is certainly not the reaction of conservat*ism* which tries to close down cultural differentiation that has taken place. But this: open up society minding the sovereignly structured rose-is-a-rose ordinances of creation so that individuals and the various social institutions are enabled, with increasing integrity, to freely (unconstrainedly) interact each according to its rose-is-a-rose created nature – this is the directive Christian cultural action pursues. That a Christian labour union does not want to be a political party, and Christian political action does not want to man the universities or run the nation like a business is the strength! of such corporate Christian action. The cultural *power*, vitality of a given Christian cultural formation lies in its knowing (fallibly) its designated, limited place in God's creation and its not trying to suppress the flowering of other created social orders in unrighteousness. The Hitler type of primitivism which would erase complex society back into a simple Aryan *Volk*, or the Total Planned Community in the blueprint stage by the Organisation Men, both violate God's norm for historical fruition and are bound to end in catastrophe.

It is the secular blindness to the ordinances of God and a person's burning-bush nature, blindness to the fact that genuinely historical cultural power flows from forming life within certain God-ordained guidelines: it is this blindness that makes secularists truly impotent, despite their destructive bravado, to effect what they say they wish. If the secular labour union does not know the difference between a rose and a tomato, it is no wonder they give stones for bread and scorpions for fish to the worker.

And why do you think a labour Goliath from Washington DC flew out this week just to see CLAC leader Gerald Vandezande, and the two-hour conversation ends in the spirit of: 'You can't stand up to us! So you have the God of the Bible on your side! Are we dogs you come to fight us with sticks! We'll finish you off completely with all the power at our command ....' Do the secular unions, confronted by your Christian programme and Christian cultural action stupidly sense that the mysterious hand of God is stretched out over the Christian Labour Association of Canada like a fiery pillar in the night and that maybe wonders, wonderful things for the name of Jesus Christ, which they cannot control, are in the offing, yet like a hardened pharaoh will not let you go your way?

The power to communal Christian cultural action is sanctified in that it is born out of obedience to Jesus Christ and is conceived in joy! – the unbeliever cannot fathom that, it is aggravating! That a Christian labour union, Christian political action has this sense of ministry, reconciling labour and governing to the Lord, willing to administer Christ's rule in *hope*, waiting for God to finish it when Christ comes back; that your business agents organise forgotten people in little pockets and hamlets far from the concentrated city wealth and industrial strike control, that your goal is *not* secular success but saintly communion and obedience, responding to the biblical imperative of 'bring every thing subject to Christ's footstool': against this simply joyful obedience, which eludes their comprehension, comes the fire, the hate and opposition of frustrated unbelief.

As Christians act together obedient to Christ in the world – in our malformed culture where Christ's name is found increasingly irrelevant – there will be more of the fire on the earth Christ spoke of. Your life as a thanksgiving burnt offering will take on the burning of fiery trials: don't think it strange, say the Scriptures, but rejoice! as you live into the sufferings of Christ, so shall you be happy when Christ's glory is revealed (1 Peter 4:12–14). They persecuted me, said Christ, and they shall persecute you – the servant is not better treated than the master (John 15: 20); but such is the fire I came to strike upon the earth! Don't you know, said Paul to the Philippians (1:29), it has been graciously given you not only to believe in Christ but also to *suffer* for him – *graciously* given? 'If we suffer, we shall also reign with him. If not, not' (cf. 2 Timothy 2: 12).

You who are oppressed and weary, who have troubles outside and inside your hearts for the sake of Jesus Christ, who burn with the suffering and jubilance that love of Jesus Christ brings, know that such a fired burning bush is not consumed but perseveres to the end.

The glory of the Lord God

So! has the Christian Labour Association of Canada with two whole business agents, one full-time secretary and a raggedy band of scattered amateurs appointed itself the Moses to lead God's people and Canada in general out of the bondage of secular taskmasters?

The sneer or pseudo-modesty in such a question poisons the well of faithful response to God's Word. The CLAC in all its passion does not claim to be immaculate, saviour of the country, nor does it promise workers whole or half of a secularised millennium. It does, however, hear today God's command given to Moses long ago and would in the boldness of *faith* – God forgive us our sin! – respond obediently to go tell it on the mountain, in the desert and everywhere that Jesus Christ came to make labour a burning bush of thanks-giving. And if the Christian Labour Association of Canada exercises this prophetic, priestly and kingly office together in the communion of the saints, hand to the plough not looking back (Luke 9: 62), salted! with fire! (Mark 9: 49), actually enacting ordinances and grievances that fallibly but surely testify Jesus Christ is Lord of economic life too!, and helps the weak, the intimidated, those exploited by secular powers to breathe freely in the Truth of love and biblical justice, let those of little faith not jibe or hang back but come to know what is at stake in the Van Manen and Mostert cases and that the time is late.[1]

It is high time that the Christians in Canada, and in my own country, wake up to our centuries-old secular captivity before the end come, and realise that today Christianity is identified with an acceptable civilised way of life, as *one* of the pillars of Western civilisation, but that's all. Let Christians today face up to the fact that when a believer claims meekly but passionately that only in the *lordship* of Jesus Christ will peace be found on earth in labour, politics, education – then comes the fire . . . of suffering, struck by our Lord himself in the world. It is time that those Christians unconvinced by arguments, waylaid by the pettiness and sins of others and themselves, dilly-dallying around, it is urgent time for them to band together compassionately behind the CLAC and act: act like bread without yeast, as Paul tells the Corinthians (1 Corinthians 5:7.8), purged of the pharisaical talk-leaven, and become a living sacrifice, a burning bush thanking and suffering together, because the Night is coming when no one shall be able to work at Christian organisation, when the fire of thankfully suffering patiently that is struck on the earth now shall become the fire of judgement burning in prison.

It is time for those with wives to act as if they had none, and those that buy as if they had no possessions, and those that use the world as if they could let

---

[1] The Christian diesel mechanic Clarence Mostert was discharged by the British Columbian firm Hoffars Ltd in June 1964 after it signed a collective agreement with the secular International Association of Machinists (IAM) union which compelled workers to be members and pay them dues. Mostert said that, as a Christian he could not subscribe to the IAM constitution which committed its members to class struggle. So he was fired

Tony van Manen had been an accomplished janitor for ten years in Weston, Ontario. He was let go because as a Christian he could not in good conscience join the secular Canadian Union of Public Employees (CUPE) which believed in compulsory union check-off dues for all workers when it signed an agreement with an employer. Van Manen belonged to the Christian Labour Association of Canada (CLAC), and pleaded to give his dues to a charity rather than to CUPE, which supported a brand of socialist humanism that went against the faith by which he lived. The Committee for Justice and Liberty (CJL) fought for both these Christian labourers in the respective provincial Supreme Courts of Canada.

A little later, in the similar matter of Dirk Hoogendoorn, who was faced with the same tactics by the United Steelworkers of America – closed-shop policy, compulsory check-off dues – the CLAC and CJL fought the case through the courts to the Supreme Court of Canada which in 1967 finally ruled in favour of CLAC and Hoogendoorn, and made 'freedom of association' a right extended to labourers with regard to unions in Canadian law. Wherever CLAC organises a shop or business, workers are not required to join it as a condition of employment. CLAC continues to be opposed by secular unions which favour compulsory control tactics.

it go (1 Corinthians 7:29–31). Why? Because the overwhelming Glory of our holy God Jehovah and the sacrifice and claim of God's Son upon our lives in 1965 does not let us do otherwise!

I close with that passage from Isaiah (6:1–9):

> I saw the Lord sitting on a huge throne way up high, and the Lord's (kingly) robe covered the whole room. And there were seraphs with six wings hovering all around up there by the Lord – they used two wings to cover their face, two to cover their feet, and they flew with the other two. And these (fiery) seraphs kept chanting out loud to one another:

> > Holy! holy! holy! is the LORD God of Sabaoth!
> > God's Glory fills the whole earth!

> And the very foundations of the room were trembling at the thunder of their chantings. Then the room began to fill up with smoke…

> And I said: Woe is me! I am finished! For I am a man with a dirty mouth, that is what I am. And I live among people with dirty mouths. (I am finished) because my eyes have seen the King, the LORD of the Angels !

> At that moment one of the seraphs flew toward me holding a red-hot coal taken with a tongs from the altar and he struck my mouth with it. Look, he said, this has touched your lips: your foolishness shall stop; your offensiveness is forgiven.

> Then I heard the voice of the Lord saying: Whom shall I send? Who will go for us?

> And I said: I am here. Send me.

> And the Lord God said: Go!

Go down, Moses, and all the New Testament saints of Hebrews 11 and believers today who have not forgotten my name, the God of Abraham, Isaac and Jacob …

Go down, Moses, way down in Egypt land, whether as gifted lawyer able to plead the cause of Christ's body before the Supreme Court of Canada and maybe someday before the Queen, who knows? – should God so wish to press God's claims upon the Canadian conscience – or simply as a labourer with gradeschool education patiently putting *The Guide* in some recalcitrant elder's mailbox …

Go down, Moses, way down in Egypt land and tell old Pharaoh, let my people go !

Let us go now, each one, as a burning bush – mouth smarting from the angel's coal of fire, body hurting from the secular enemies' attempt to crush believing labour – building, painting, cleaning fish or parsing Greek, collecting garbage or developing philosophy, each believer may have the vision that his or her labour is a burning bush, fired pentecostally by the flame of the Lord: that's our birthright as believers, our gift by adoption, our promise of life even more abundant to come. And if the burning of the bush wear on you workers, endure it yet a little while, my people, says the Word, for Christ is coming soon, not tarrying (Hebrews 10:36,37), and shall set you to building, farming, constructing and manufacturing in the city whose streets are of gold, where justice, peace and joy in the Holy Spirit rule without end. Do not be found wanting when Christ comes. I tell you, says Christ, that whoever confesses me *publicly* before people, (a burning bush) the Son of Man shall openly speak up for in front of God's angels; but the person who disowns me in the face of people will be disowned by me before the eyes of God's angels.

Bibliography

*Of special clarity and pertinence on the topic treated

*de Gaay Fortman, W. F. *Aims and Purposes of Christian Trade-Unionism*. Utrecht: International Federation of Protestant Workers' Association, n.d.

de Graaf, S. G. *Vuur op de Aarde! Predikatiën*. Goes: Oosterbaan & Le Cointre, (1930), I, 5–13 (Lucas 12:49–69).

*Duvenage, S. C. W. *Kerk, Volk en Jeug*. Vol. I of *Die Verhouding van kerk tot Volk*. Zaandijk: J. Heijnis Tsz., 1962. See especially 'Begripsbepaling: Kerk' (pp. 40–62); 'Hervormde Visie: Solidariteit' (pp. 151–65); 'Gereformeerde Visie: Antitese' (pp. 218–60); 'Verdere Prinsipiële Besinning en Slotbeskouing oor die Verhouding van Kerk tot Volk' (pp. 261–87).

Goudzwaard, B. 'Hoe geven wij "Antwoord aan deze Tijd"?' in *Anti Revolutionaire Staatkunde*, xxxiii (Oct. 1963), 304–20.

'Bijbel en politiek' in *Anti-Revolutionaire Staatkunde*, xxxiv (April 1964), 93–108.

*Kuyper, Abraham. *Christianity and the Class Struggle*, trans. Dirk Jellema. Grand Rapids: Piet Hein Publishers, 1950.

Mekkes, J. P. A. 'Antithese', in *Ter Discussie om een Evangelische Politiek*. Zutphen: J. B. van den Brink, 1958, pp. 5–9.

Prins, J. H. *Politiek als Geloofsbeleving*. ARJOS studie-konferentie. 's-Gravenhage: Nationale Organisatie van Anti-Revolutionaire Jongeren Studieklubs, 1964.

Spier, J. M. *De Waardering van het Kerkelijke Instituut*. Dordrecht: N. H. Dekkers, 1938.

van Riessen, H. 'Maatschappij, Techniek en Vakbeweging', in *Verslag Tweede Algemene Vergadering, Nederlandse Christelijke Beambtenbond*, Amsterdam, 1953, pp. 13–23.

— and J. Firet. *Moderne Algemeenheid*. Kampen: Kok, 1963.

Vollenhoven, D. H. Th. *Sphere Sovereignty as seen by Kuyper and us*, Trans. N. De Bree. Available at Grand Rapids: Groen van Prinsterer Society, n.d. (mimeograph).

Zuidema, S. U. 'Einde van het Christendom', *Anti-Revolutionaire Staatkunde*, xix (1949), 65–88.

— 'Gemene Gratie en Pro Rege bij Dr Abraham Kuyper', *Anti-Revolutionaire Staatkunde*, xxiv (1954), 1–19; 49–73.

— 'Kerk en Politiek', in W.P. Berghuis, J.A.H.J.S. Bruins Slot et al. (eds.), *Bene Meritus. Bundel Opstellen uit Dankbaarheid opgedragen aan Dr J. Schouten*. Kampen: Kok, 1958, pp. 70–84.

3 The Rub to Christian Organisation – or, Christian Camel Drivers Unite?*

In those days John the Baptiser appeared on the scene in the Judean desert proclaiming:

Turn yourselves around!
The ruling order of heaven is just about here!
(This John is the one the prophet Isaiah talked about when he said:
A voice crying out in the wilderness:
'Prepare the way of the Lord!
'Make the paths for the Lord level and straight!'
This John wore a camel's hair cloak tucked up by a leather belt; his food was locusts and wild honey.)

Jerusalem, even all Judea, and all the country surrounding the Jordan travelled out to (hear) John and were baptised by him in the Jordan river after they openly, publicly confessed their sins. When John saw a lot of Pharisees and Sadducees coming for a baptism he said to them:

You sons of a snake!
Who told you that you are saved from the coming anger (of the Lord)?
Do (something!) bear fruit worthy of a radical change-about!
Don't keep on talking to yourselves: 'We have Abraham as father.'
I tell you God can raise up sons for Abraham out of these stones here.

Already the axe is put to the trees' root. Every tree not bearing good fruit is to be cut down and thrown into the fire. I baptise you with water into a radical change-about. The one following me up, so much more powerful than me – whose shoes I am not fit to carry – he will baptise you with Holy Spirit ... and fire! Pitchfork in hand he will clean up what's left after the harvest on the threshing-floor, collect the grain into his storehouse and burn the chaff up in a fire you cannot put out. (Matthew 3:1–12)

---

*Polemical address sponsored by the Groen Van Prinsterer Club of Calvin College, given at Calvin Seminary in Grand Rapids, Mich., on 3 March 1965. It was later published as a pamphlet by the Christian Labour Association of Canada.

The rub to Christian organisation is that it demands public confession of sin and deeds worthy of a radical turnabout to God. Public confession of sin, open testimony of needing God's Grace here and now, is not very popular with us humans; we would rather justify how well we have done and are doing. And deeds, not just talk, actual concrete performance meeting the measure of repentance, of a radically new outlook, disposition, perspective, *deeds* that are worthy of such a deep-going turnabout in a person come hard; we believers are more comfortable *discussing* the faith or confining our acts to unmolested churchy activities.

But it could be, unless baptism is an insurance rite automatically conferring Abrahamic status, it could be that without openly repentant deed moved by a holy (= set apart) spirit, it could be that the sprinkled covenanting mark of God on our foreheads only sets us up for the next baptism by fire, the Lord's winnowing judgement, on this generation of vipers and at the end.

This is the tack I should like to take and the level, so to speak, at which I think Christian organisation needs to be confronted. How, before the jealous Lord of heaven and earth, is a believer to acquit himself or herself historically in creation? With what spirit is the Christ-follower to meet his or her given culture? With the spirit of re-forming its patterns of life till they be conformed intrinsically to the way of the Lord? or, with the spirit of accepting what is good in existing institutions, Christianising points where necessary, influencing established ways as much as possible by personal example and wisdom?

Only when examination and decision fall on such directional matters will it become clear what can and what cannot be argued with respect to Christian camel-drivers, Grand Rapids factory workers and Chicagoan scavengers. Let me begin by the back door.

Christian organisation

There is nothing worse than a Christian organisation that lacks the Holy Spirit's presence. A Christian labour union without Christian dynamic, a supposedly Christian college that does not breathe the spirit of Christ in its classrooms, a church dominated by rancour, mistrust and manoeuvrings, are all terrible farces, prostitutions of Christ's name. So-called Christian institutions, organisations, can be sepulchrally white hiding dead people within. Just because an organisation is put together by Christians or has Christian in its name (Christian Reformed Church, Trinity Christian College, Christian labour association) is no guarantee of actual holy-spirited, Christian witness and activity.

Dooyeweerd's comment on religious antithesis should squelch further any misconceived idealisation of Christian organisation:

The antithesis is not a dividing line between Christian and non-Christian segments of the population. It is rather the eternal struggle between two spiritual principles which cut right through ... all of mankind, irrespective of the safe castles of a Christian framework to social groupings... We must never forget that the antithesis cuts right through the Christian life itself ... apostasy, schism, discord within Christian groupings witness to the fact that especially there the turbulent Spirit of darkness wages war against the Spirit of Christ, producing the most obnoxious phenomena.[1]

Christian organisation is necessarily not perfect, even if you make ARSS[*] membership humanly airtight. And the miserable wisdom of the philosopher–king in Ecclesiastes should touch us too at the start:

> I didn't enjoy all my toiling work struggled for under the sun because (I knew) I had to leave it to some man who would come after me, and who knows whether he will be a wise man or a fool? but no matter which, he shall manage all I have done, sweated for, trying to be wise under the sun ... God gives wisdom, insight and joy to the person who pleases God; but to the sinner God gives the trouble of collecting and stacking things up – so that God may give it to one who is lovely to the eye of God. (2: 18,19,26)

That is, Christian organisation is vexatious and vain unless it be conceived, maintained and practised within the immediate blessing of God.

So what is a truly Christian organisation and why go through all the trouble? A Christian organisation is first of all an organisation, an association of men and women, a body of people whose communal existence involves more than the sum of its individuals. A family is not simply the addition of an individual father, mother, two sons and a daughter; a given family has a structural family bond to it which, while never separable from the constituting members and not created to override or extinguish their varying individualities, does hold them correlatively embraced in a typical, temporal family identity. So too with political parties and chess clubs and more organisations quite different from a blood-based family: they are groupings of people who have many other interests, activities and roles. But in this specific matter, viz. use of reflective leisure demanding chess competence or moral concern for what political principles best shape the nation, individual people cohere together more or less. They are united in this particularly qualified grouping which has neither the cohesion of a living organism nor the supposed personality of an *Ueberperson* yet is more than a collection of atomic parts. A political party or a chess club, like a family, has an identity, generally a proper name; it is a certain

---

[1]Dooyeweerd, *Vernieuwing en Bezinning* (Zutphen: J.B.Van Den Brink, 1959) p.3.

[*]Association for Reformed Scientific Studies, an association of Christians attempting to begin a Christian university-level institution.

THE RUB
TO CHRISTIAN
ORGANIZATION
OR . . .

Plate 19 Pamphlet cover designed by Willem Hart, Toronto

community that can act as a unit in its sphere (differentiation of officers is called for by this oneness), even if it is only to set the time for the next meeting. Important to me here is simply this, that *organisations are human social structurations*.

You all recognise that there are importantly different kinds of human social structurations. Marriage is a sexual love union so intimate and lasting only death of one of the two breaks it, while you belong to a high-school basket-ball team at the most four years and are in-again-out-again depending on your marks, athletic prowess and whether you can find time to practise. Some human social structurations you cannot help but be a member of, like a family – the tragedy of bastards and orphans notwithstanding. You are necessarily born into a family, but an American is not born into the Democratic political party (unless you come from Indiana and the name is Zandstra).* The church is a singular organisation to which hypocrites and genuine believers are bound within a definite confessional response to the specially central working of God's Grace, if it be a true church, upon the congregation through sacrament and preached Word and corresponding doctrinal discipline. And the state today is a human social structuration ordained by God of which one is invol-untarily a citizen, against whose binding power revolution is a serious evil; whereas a labourers' association or corporate chain of grocers is by nature a voluntary type organisation, here with a peculiarly economic orientation.

One could go on, but the point is: there are importantly different, specific kinds of human social structurations, unions, institutions, organisations extant – some with an historically transient relative character, others with the cosmic duration of a creational ordinance, some voluntary, others inescapable for people (how one analyses and encyclopaedically orders the myriad number of organisations in our complex, civilised society will say much about one's philosophical and even religious perspective) – yet they *all are alike in being open to the sin of humankind and the Grace of our Redeemer*.

I must try to be clear. It is not so that a marriage of unbelievers is not a mar-riage but continuous fornication; before God their betrothed cohabitation is a marriage. And it is not so that a family who has its confessional papers with an orthodox church is thereby a Christian family. If an evil spirit sit on its back, infest the family talking, eating, living room, it is an unholy horror even if there be a double tithe on Sunday. I mean to say that Christian believers have no corner on creational order, no monopoly on human social structura-tions, except the church. And no concrete organisation, including the church, is Christian just because its paperwork, constitution, statement of purpose, is formally in order.

---

*Zandstra was a well-known family in Indiana, one member of which was elected as a Democrat in a strongly Republican area.

Testing the organisation

That seems to leave precision of Christian organisation rather up in the air. Can you ever – when would you dare – call a college faculty and administration a Christian organisation? a Christian college?

When the leading spirit driving an organisation is one of selfless passion to show God's presence, Christ's blessed ruling order at work in its given social area, then that concrete, temporal human social structuration is a *truly Christian organisation.* Its sins may cry out to heaven and incompetence plague its operation; but if its living conception, dynamic, direction is one of openly impassioned, joyful struggle to incarnate the Lord's wisdom, then you have a human grouping moved by the biblical faith, whether a marriage, family, state, basketball team or chess club. But still, if Christian organisation is determined by this spirit of utter dependence upon God, a constant searching, claiming the promised guidance of the Holy Spirit, isn't discerning the spirit of an organisation a pretty subjective thing? Be specific once. Is the *Anti-Revolutionaire Partij** in the Netherlands today a Christian organisation or not? What have they been doing since Schouten – in their journal, is that an autopsy or open-heart surgery? Or, do you say the Christian Labour Association of Canada is a Christian organisation and the Christian Trade Union of Canada an unChristian one?¶

If that kind of detail question is couched in the usual disinterested spirit of divide and kill, begging Christian to judge Christian, it does not deserve an answer. But if it is an honest question I would answer that there comes a time when one has to decide where the line is to be drawn, what is the language of faith and what of ratiocination. Maybe it falls on article 2, that despite the Ontario Labour Relation Board's charge of discrimination§ you decide you

---

*The Anti-Revolutionary Party was founded in the Netherlands in 1879 as an organised political movement of those who believed that it was a parental responsibility to have schools-with-the-Bible, and that this should not be usurped by the state which wanted education to be formed in schools without the Bible. Abraham Kuyper chaired the ARP continuously until his death in 1920, except for the years 1905–07 when he was abroad. Under his leadership, and against the opposition of both liberal and conservative politicians, the ARP was able in 1880 to pass a bill that led to the establishment, on Reformation principles, of the Free University of Amsterdam ('free' from policy control by state or church). During the 1880s the ARP was able to form a coalition government with Roman Catholic legislators, which passed reforms for allocating tax revenues to support schools shaped by fundamental faith convictions, whether these were Reformed, Roman Catholic, Jewish or Humanist. Jan Schouten was chair of the party from 1933 to 1956, except for the war years 1941–6.

¶The Christian Trade Union of Canada and the Christian Labor Union in the USA held to the 'closed shop' policy (a labourer had to pay dues to the controlling union if he or she wanted to work in that firm) whereas the Christian Labour Association of Canada supported the 'open shop' (a labourer did not have to belong to a union). Opponents to the formation of Christian labour unions exploited this difference to call any such communal Christian activity into question.

§In the late 1950s the Ontario Labour Relations Board refused to certify the CLAC as a legally recognised trade union because its constitution, referring to biblical principles, was judged to discriminate against non-Christians. The Board's decision was overturned in 1963 by the Ontario Supreme Court.

must continue to publicly express that we base our 'programme and activities on the Christian principles of social justice and love as taught in the Bible', and some with the best strategic Christian intentions leave. Or one has to decide whether the solid *anti-revolutionaire* principles are being existentialistically adapted to a welfare-state temper, or are they just being freed from rationalistic accretions? Prayerful discerning of the spirits is an agonising business, takes time; and it is not wise to chit about it from the outside. However, because a given testing is difficult and fallible does not permit one to abdicate one's responsibility under the slogan of 'subjective', unless you mean to call into question the very reality of the Holy Spirit's guidance in a group of people.

Truly Christian organisation may be elusive to pin down observationally and to build up actually – the Holy Spirit does not let God be boxed in so easily – but it is not therefore neo-orthodoxily indecipherable or a matter of momentary visitations by eternal Grace breaking within the time barrier. God's Word according to Matthew 3, I read, speaks quite definitely about the action God wants from his saints: *open confession of Jesus Christ's lordship* and *deeds touched by single-minded repentance, a facing-God praise response*. Such a temper and fruit only comes when the Holy Spirit is at work in the hearts of people, and only such fruit is worth a man's baptism.

Again, I know the temptation to decipher 'good fruit' positivistically, to add up the number of college graduates in the last five years, for example, who become Christian school-teachers, subtract the graduated number who left the church, multiply by the number of missionaries, divide by the number of sex deviates, and if you get a certain score you are a successful Christian college.

Whether a college or magazine, labour union or family is a Christian human social structuration – much depends upon the leading personalities in the organisation (editors, committee chairperson, president, power behind the throne) – its *Christian* character cannot be quantified (to use North Central Association jargon), tabulated circumstantially. Wormy fruit may be born of consecrated labour, and good apples may be a pure gift of God in spite of the rotten tree. Nevertheless, the spirit of an organisation in its approach, expression, within the very cultural force it sets in motion is telltale, fine but discernible. When that spirit is one of reforming historical patterns of life till they be conformed to the way of the Lord, under the skimpy shade of that sour apple tree of an organisation I as a believer feel at home and am ready to give the Lord there whatever I've got.

Christian organisation has somehow gotten a bum steer: 'separatism', 'factional', 'grandiose schemes', 'how can it succeed?' And to damn Christian organisation because of its weak and sinful proponents seems to show a lack of biblical wisdom and Christian charity. Or could there be an other reason?

A Christian labour union is no more a 'separate' organisation than a Socialist labour union in society. Christian organisation is not a forced construction superimposed upon the unwilling faithful: it is rather the embodiment you would expect of believers sharing a deep communion in Jesus Christ who are busy socially. Christian organisation is not a frenetic imperialism to win the world for Christ our way against all odds. Its fight and passion is one of joyful obedience to God to bring the light of God's Word and Christ's easy yoke to bear upon our many-faceted society to free people from their captivities. A Christian political grouping will not be the machinery of an élite band of political scientists, who now are Christians, telling the faithful mass where to apply pressure; but Christian political action like any communal Christian cultural endeavour on earth will be a slow, generations-long build-up of the believing community's sense of Christian political office till they are wise enough to use the power of the sword in a biblical way.

Christians in secular organisations

Some Christians disagree with the call to Christian organisation for quite weighty reasons, the best of which is this: Christians can break through to the world, be a more effective witness to the gospel in existing non-Christian organisations, and can do so in good conscience until such organisations become anti-Christian. I think this position is common, respectable, and wrong – better said, informed by a different spirit than the one that meets and grips me in the Scriptures. And since this position of 'Christians in secular organisations' is sometimes supported not as the happenstance situation a Christian may be historically stymied in and need to work himself out of, but as the leading policy believing Christians should follow today in Western, at least Anglo-Saxon, civilisation, till it is no longer feasible, I should like to analyse briefly a few disconcerting things it presupposes.

The existence of neutral organisations is assumed, like chess clubs and a civic group organised to clean up the shady lady sections of Grand Rapids and make it a better place to live in; neutral organisations, i.e. where by constitution and practice every religious opinion is welcome (atheist, Christian, Jew, Muslim, Dodoweirdian…) and the sole objectives are limited goals common to all members.

One could say, I suppose, there are chess clubs and there are chess clubs. Platonic chess clubs were organised for homosexual dalliance. Soviet Russian chess clubs are organised for political advancement or to bring honour to the state.

But I mean just a plain old human pickup chess club. I don't want to earn a merit badge in the Calvinist Cadets – I just want to learn how to play chess. Can't I, mayn't I join a good secular chess club in my home block?

You certainly can. You may too without even committing the stature of a venial sin.

This sophistry may dazzle, confuse, and trick those unschooled in rhetoric into giving bad answers, but it is most tawdry, like the sort of question. 'Is there a Christian way to brush your teeth?' That is not an honest question, sincerely asking for information; it is a pseudo-question, pure bunk, to which a nonsense answer is 'brushing up and down is humanistic, sidewise pagan, and Christians do it deftly in the form of a cross'. That sort of question about brushing teeth *assumes* some areas of life are not directly subject to God's redeeming Grace; therefore, if you accept the question, you cannot give an answer that *assumes* all life is religion in operation without appearing ridiculous.

Likewise for this business about chess clubs and more importantly Grand Rapids civic groups: to move from the description of fact that Christians and unbelievers can, do, may co-operate in organisational structures not breathing adoration of Christ's name, to raise that current empirical practice to the status of norm, or if not quite normative certainly more than permissible, as the best policy ('best' – with all the built-in relativism of that concept), make this compositional practice the best policy for Christians to pursue in cultural matters, assumes, if I see it rightly, a secular definition of organisation that denatures or idolises humankind, removing a truly significant area of historical concern from the rooting power of the Gospel.

To encourage Christians to take active part in non-Christian organisations as the way to fulfil their cultural responsibility to our Lord God gives me problems, because non-Christian organisations by their nature would suspend, be non-committal about the basic reasons, motive, purpose for doing what they are doing. And those basic matters are not simply theoretical addenda, *super-additum* addenda, but constitute the very dynamic, spirit, of the organisation's doings. When the Christian rationale is levelled on a par with unbelieving rationales, the resulting spirit is a horizontally noble human spirit listing where it reasonably will but that inevitably will constrain the pentecostal way the Holy Spirit flows into and through and out a believer's life. One could deny that organisations have a spirit deeply embedded, moving in its workings, but that presents an insoluble puzzle for those Christians who admit that everything an individual does is before the face of the Lord Jesus, in God's name or not, no third possibility: when two or three individuals are gathered together, suddenly what they do is in nobody's name, neither for or against Jesus Christ, it is a neutral affair.

Something is wrong then, it seems to me. Either you must deny that organisations are God-given *human* social *groupings* and conceive them secularly as space–time constructs, an arena in which Fichtian, monadic egos temporarily act in concert – which denatures human association to a technical relation and conceives social phenomena abstractly as religiously detached – or you must deny that *everything* an individual person does is to be directly subjected to his or her faith-commitment in Christ, that only interpretive, typically human confessional–ethical, mental–reflective acts are peculiarly Christian or not, but not stuff like playing chess and organisationally cleaning up Grand Rapids. Either alternative has serious consequences for the Christian world-and-life view and one's daily practice.

I would not dispute that sometimes somewheres Christians must wait with Christian organisation and work within secular institutions. Afghanistan may be closed to Christian missionaries, but the government invites two highly competent Christian MDs to staff posts in its medical university. It would probably not be biblically wise for them to found the Christian Medical Association of Afghanistan that year. Or in a remote province of Japan where there are a dozen converted young Japanese couples who despite the vision of what a Christian school education would mean for their children simply cannot bring it off: you need a Christian community to act christianly communally. That is why 'Christian Camel-Drivers, Unite!' would not make much sense where I live; there are not many camel-drivers in Cook County. But if in Jordan and Palestine there is a growing body of Christians driving camels, the exhortation would be most biblically appropriate, so that they might surprise their fellow Arabs, Jews, and secular Western business people with the cash value of all that high-falutin talk about the relevance of the Christian faith for daily social life.

And it is so that, because an individual is not ontically swallowed into the makeup of an organisation, a Christian is able to convince himself or herself that one's membership in the National Education Association of the United States is not incompatible with subscribing to the church's creeds because one doesn't really commit oneself to the beliefs of the NEA as it says one does on page 54 (1964–5 Handbook) nor orient one's spiritual injunctions to 'the American way of life' (p. 70). Also, I would not take it ill of a believer who, conscious of one's brief life-time and the critical state of the Christian community, judges that organised development of certain culturally insignificant areas need to be neglected by him or her.

But all this historical turmoil, shifting, qualification *in* which Christians live and move must not be that *from* which they take their cue. And because non-Christian organisations are tolerated and used by believers in our broken-down historical situation does not imply they are neutral before Jesus Christ! much less that they are the straight and level ways *of the Lord* we should be building. Such suggestions are false, misguided directions without biblical support. There is a fine line between the lukewarm compromise of mental reservation and the *biblical* sanity of living out of faith in enemy territory. What spirit fires a person and drives one on determines the issue.

That points to the other disconcerting feature I shall mention detected in the position proposing Christians infiltrate secular organisations: a peculiar ahistorical temper. It seems to be assumed that the Christian faith is not to produce culture but rather critically influence it, not employ worldly power but speak to it, not change the world but interpret it. Paired with this, how shall I say it, otherworldly mission attitude of testify-pull-back-we-have-no-abiding-city-here, paired with this ahistorical temper seems to go a strangely high valuation of humanistic culture plus the conviction that the only really necessary Christian organisation is the church, conceived in high church fashion as the controlling refuge which makes all things well.

I do not think one can gainsay this position once a Christian firmly adopts it. You can find proof-texts for this evangelical withdrawal, compartmentalised adoption, rigorously ecclesiastic standpoint; pacifists, fundamentalists, Roman Catholics, latter-day Anabaptists know their Bible too. All I can say now is: the ahistorical bent of this position, pulled from an absolutisation of the, to be sure, crucial mission task of God's people is foreign to the biblical Reformational Christian faith as I have always understood its genius.

I learned from Dr W.H. Jellema a long time ago that you deform the biblical richness of the Reformed faith if you reduce Christian witness, which is an activity of *civitas, civitas Dei*, reduce it to a matter of personal, individualistic testimony. And I have gradually learned from Dr Runner that doing good competent work in a field, *also* thanking God for it in church, is a meagre, split response of a believer who wants to live singly, wholeheartedly, wholebodily, directly and fully, totally out of the hand of God focused by God's directing Word.

I am aware that the ahistorical bent of this mission-emphasis position does not limit one to candle-holding, bench quarterbacking on Vietnam, pastoral admonitions, that it can foster Roman Catholic confessional sub-groupings of workers within the secular AFL–CIO union. But its grasp of cultural problems always maintains the weightedness of an unreformed ecclesiastic scholastic mentality (which no amount of neo-orthodoxy can erase) concerned more with ends, practical goals than means, that tends to dismiss the important difference between the indisputable *co-operation* of believers with unbelievers and the *association*, the intimate sharing-in-with, mingling partnering communion only believers have together (cf. 1 Corinthians 5:9,10; Ephesians 5:7,11), dismiss the difference as semantics, that would be willing to blur, for a practical mess of potage – God knows Esau was hungry! – the difference between Christian and parochial school.

Again, I know these last remarks may seem derogatory of the church to many scribes and theologians, but these special leaders of God's people never show up well in the New Testament for the very matter on the docket: scholastic presumption of the institutional church to stand authoritarianly between believer and God Almighty.

★ ★ ★

It would be helpful to get straight what is at stake in the debate on Christian organisation. It is not the question whether so-and-so believes in Jesus Christ (secularists who are nominal Christians can hide piously in secular organisations and zealots with false pride can nest easily in Christian social structurations – each one look to oneself). And it is not the question whether so-and-so's understanding of what is happening on the American cultural scene is accurate (fellow Christians may analyse current trends somewhat disparately). Those are not the matters to discuss and impugn.

The question that must be faced is this: with what spirit is the Christ-follower to meet his or her given culture? With the spirit of reforming its patterns of life till they be conformed intrinsically to the way of the Lord? or with the spirit of accepting what is good in existing institutions, christianising points where necessary, influencing established ways as much as possible by personal example and wisdom?

In the balance is the Reformed faith. The Reformational Christian faith as quite distinct from the Roman Catholic, Anglo-Catholic, Fundamentalistic, Neo-orthodox Christian faith. Within which spirit – no matter how you label it – a person decides to frame his or her life is unarguable; that is, if you do not hear the Scriptures tell you all life is religion in operation before God and the body of Christ is to act like one, I who hear this to be utterly, simply, biblically true cannot convince you of it. The pity is you may have a personally rich grip on our common Lord. What differentiates other Christian faith from the Reformational Christian faith is the makeshift reservations, human blind constructions and divisions, unhappy mixtures it seems to a Reformational believer the other's grounding, driving religious motives tries, for whatever good reasons, to insert confusingly into the biblical dynamic. Nothing less than *everything brought subject to Christ's footstool* satisfies the Reformed faith.

The closest one might come to an argument on Christian organisation (not argumentation! – if you know C.S. Peirce's careful distinction) is this:

If *all human life* is religion in operation before God, including a person's organisational and social life; and

if the Holy Spirit drives a person to live single-mindedly *for Christ into the world of history* (not with a gospel chip on one's shoulder but openly, unrestrainedly, publicly); and

if the *saintly communion* which members of Christ's body share truly means its *prayer* that *God's Will be done on earth, establishing the work of our hands* – in that scandalous, humble assurance that *the Christian faith has the singular Truth* and is not just one of the spiritual pillars of Western civilisation, and in the fearful knowledge that prayer without works is dead and works without obedience are vain –

292

then the Christian community, in all its many human social structurations, will be impelled by the constraint of Christ's love to work out the baptism of water on its forehead with the baptism of the Holy Spirit to show the Lord God's gloriousness to the world at large socially, economically, politically...

This 'argument' will not touch the heart of a person insensitive to the playful vision of the reforming, edifying (= building up) Holy Spirit, but I think what Dooyeweerd said once is so:

> It is imperative that without looking to see who-is-what we frankly decide for ourselves on the question *reformation* or *accommodation* because that question determines the Christian way-of-life today too. And only the moving force of God's Word-revelation is able to give us the answer.[2]

Maybe it has struck you that those in Christian organisation act as the opponents of Christian organisation say we should – in confrontation with the world – while those propagating a Christian presence in secular organisations seem to be generally acting as they say Christian organisations would – reflectively on the sidelines as far as outspoken Christian confession and repentant deed goes. That should bother Christians who would be busy trading their talents in the marketplace as they anticipate God's kingdom fully come.

Those baptisers Antonides and Vandezande have been troubling Jerusalem.* I pray they trouble all of Israel, especially all children of the snake who say 'We have John Calvin as father.' The Word of God says that the Lord can raise up children of Calvin out of the stones, the blockheads of Canada. It is not who your father is or how successful your deeds are that counts with God, but whether the work of your hands be fruit of obedience to the Word, the profession of turned-around people sanctified by the Spirit, performed in undissembled love for our jealous God.

---

[2]H. Dooyeweerd *Vernieuwing en Bezinning* (Zutphen: J.B.Van Den Brink, 1959), p.110.

*Harry Antonides (b. 1931) and Gerald Vandezande (b. 1933) were the original leaders of the Christian Labour Association of Canada in the 1960s. Acclaimed by their supporters for their visionary zeal and courageous practical witness to the need for Christ's love to be present in organising the marketplace, they were persecuted by many secular unions in Canada. They were also heavily criticised by a number of leading professors in the Christian Reformed circles of Grand Rapids, Michigan, an area which was known at that time among members of Christian Reformed churches as 'Jerusalem'.

4 The Meaning of Silence for Daily Life and Sunday Worship*

John, the theologian, reports in Revelation that when the seventh seal was broken open 'there was silence in heaven for about a half hour' (Revelation 8: 1). What I somewhat foolishly propose to do now is speak about the meaning of silence and its relation to Christian worship, for about a half hour. Theology is not my field of study, so I am not able to bring coals to Newcastle; but because this is a student banquet and you are presumably on holiday from your critically scientific theological pursuits, professorial robes and seminarian vestments have been left at the shop – and you are gathered rather jovially as believers to fellowship, eating and drinking as the Son of Man came into the world – I thought it might be an opportune moment for me to bring a few clinkers to Westminster.

Should silence, perhaps, not be more structurally incorporated into our meetings of Christian worship? How student banquet-like should our Sunday services of God be? These are not academic questions for the faithful whose weekly celebration of our Lord's resurrection is an impoverished routine of formality and streams of words. And to get at the propriety or nonsense of silence in Sunday worship we need to know what silence means for the six labouring days of our daily life.

No one analyses things without an assumed perspective, even if it be the perspective that he or she happens upon reality with a blank mind. I realise that the nicety of secular speech-making is to pretend that we go to the facts of the matter with little or no bias, with the result that it is sometimes not till the person turns and leaves the podium that you can notice their philosophical slip showing. For the sake of Christian honesty, decorum, and perhaps clarity, I should like to sketch briefly, right away, within what kind of perspective I mean to zero in on silence and church worship.

Human life in God's theatre, AD

In his *Institutes* Calvin sets Vergil and the filthy dog Lucretius' deification of Nature biblically straight by stating that nature is an order prescribed by God

---

*Address given at a 'student banquet', a festive meal organised by students of Westminster Theological Seminary, Pennsylvania. First published in the *International Reformed Bulletin* 10:30 (July 1967), 6–19.

(I,v,5). The whole creation, says Calvin, echoing the psalms, is a most splendid theatre in which God's spectacular work is visible to those whose eyes are focused by the Scriptures (I,vi,1–2). You get the idea that a Christian housewife who watches the icy wind billow her pillow cases dry (if she does not have an automatic dryer) or a Christian student who becomes fascinated by the earthiness of Old Testament Hebrew language, that Christians watching dogs bark at strangers or cut flowers droop in a vase of stale water, Christians can rightly marvel at how God daily provides, providentially orders all things, down to the fall of sparrows and the hairs of one's head, and that these ordinances of the Lord are blessings. Temporal, creational structure is not merely some 'natural law' participating in eternal reason or the impersonal imitation Heidegger curses: the structured setup to every created thing is the lovely, merciful law of God that proceeds out of the same faithful mouth which sent Christ into the world to reconcile it back to God (cf. Colossians 1:17–20).

Peopling Jehovah's vast theatre are myriad creations, and all of them, groaning along with us humans, says Paul, are somehow expectantly waiting for the redemption of our *bodies* (Romans 8:19–23). That humankind exists bodily is important. From the very beginning humankind was made male and female (Matthew 19: 4). Jesus Christ became flesh and bloody (John 1: 14); the fullness of godhood inhabited him bodily (Colossians 2: 9). And the Holy Spirit who wars against Evil in our 'members' makes the believer's *body* God's temple (1 Corinthians 6:19). Any spiritualising of human nature, just because humankind, unlike all other creatures, walks around on earth with a peculiar sense of deity built into one, spiritualising of men and women mistakes the concrete, body richness which God has gone out of the way, as it were, to fashion, hallow and sanctify. And when the glory of humankind's corporeality is ignored, strange, unbiblical ideas and practices replace the wide open, consecrated significance of human action in God's creation.

A person normally acts all kinds of ways: he or she thinks, feels, speaks, breathes, takes up space and the like. And a person acts all these many ways quite differently simultaneously! as a father, mother, citizen, student, maybe as pastor, business person or amateur golfer to boot. That is, whether a person is aware of it or not, he or she functions very richly as an individual and necessarily operates as a member of various human groupings. It was the biblical insight of the Dutch statesman Abraham Kuyper to assert that these human groupings are not just conveniences adopted by people in learned reaction to environments, but that the family, state, school, church, business, and such like human associations, are institutional bonds set by God for society to manifest itself in historically. And Kuyper's famous point, if I may use Gertrude Stein for a minute, that 'a rose is a rose is a rose' and not a tomato, is that a school is a school is a school, and not a church or the state or a business or football team or what have you.

While some fathers philander and some citizens are civilly disobedient, some business people criminally cheat and some pastors, like parishioners, affirm creeds with tongue in cheek: the fact that they individually betray their particular social responsibility does not release them from its God-instituted demands. Further, when the state over-extends itself to be a school or a church swallows up businesses, such disobedience to God's laws inevitably brings tyranny and corruption. So, people are called by God to act all ways faith-fully and to incarnate the rule of Christ in all these spheres of life in a way that maintains the interrelated differences of family, state, church and the rest. In fact, being busy in effecting this 'Rule of Christ' world-wide is what seeking the kingdom-regime of God first! (Matthew 6:33) is all about – getting the Redeemer's Rule at work in the hearts and *lives* of people cultivating creation.

All people live today AD, after the death of our Lord Jesus Christ (and after Christ's resurrection!). That means we are in 'the last days', as the Bible calls it, before Christ comes again, back to earth to complete subjecting all things to his footstool. Therefore, we must not be fooled by the noise made nowadays in God's cosmic theatre by the bodily action of most people, which seems to be driven by a restless spirit of revolution dialectically tangled with a demonic faith in cybernetics: we must not be fooled into thinking the world is heading for a dead end. Especially we faithful live AD, post mortem! with the beginnings of eternal life in Jesus Christ now; we are alive truly in an advent of apocalyptic proportions! In this perspective I should like to begin a peek at the phenomenon of silence.

The meaning of silence

Is silence an ordinance of creation? Is it a special kind of gift God has blessed us with? Or is silence by nature a lack of something – absence, cessation of sound, response, movement? Is there something incomplete, possibly evil in silence? Before creation there was silence, says Max Picard, only dark silence; he makes it into a kind of demonic antipode to God who finally spoke the Word, shattering it with light.[1] Is there more to silence than meets the ear, so to speak?

The Dutch mime, Frans Reynders, performed at Trinity College a couple of years ago. Pack the audience in tight, front centre and then back, not a break in the seating, he said; this density is needed to get the best silences. And he told me of the different kinds and levels of silence he was sensitive to getting as his programme of mute imitation developed, from a flying eagle coming to rest on a crag to an old blind man crossing the street to sit forlornly on a park

---

[1] *The World of Silence*, p. 38.

bench. If it was right, some silence was just under the threshold of laughter and other silence was deeply intense, suspended, incredulous, or sorrowfully still.

Freshly fallen snow meets one silently outside one's door in the country on a winter morning. Wisps of clouds slip quietly by in a hot summer sky if you can lie on your back and look up with no one but the grass and dirt near. Plants, however, whether fruit trees breaking into blossom in the spring or oak trees shedding their leaves in the fall, seem less still than inanimate creation. Is that because plants are less passive objects to our subjective human manipulation?

Animals, of course, glory in sounds. Not noise. Noise is a peculiarly human product, I dare say. There is a qualitative difference between the screech of auto brakes, the roar and throb of electric motors, the din of heavy roadway construction, a difference there from the insistent hum of locusts in the night, lowing of cattle, the barking of hunting dogs that Shakespeare called 'sweet thunder', and the furtive, friendly chirps of birds. Animal sounds have a restful appropriateness; even the rage of a trapped lion or the stupid bleep of a hunted cricket are cries but not 'noise'. Noise is manufactured and always has a forced, inappropriate character to it. (One could say, maybe, that as music becomes more noisy it does not become more bestial but rather more typically pervertedly(?) human.) Animals often are mute, it is true, work and suffer without being able to speak as Balaam's ass did; yet animals stay busy, change, are capable of sound, even in sleep. Some are purposely still as they lie in wait for prey, and all animals are completely silent when they are dead.

I am saying then, so far, that silence as an inarticulate presence, perceived or not by people, is a feature that attends all creation more or less, whether wind or flower, fish or beast. The key to the meaning of silence, however, lies further on, revealed in its human analogue.

Men and women are silent at different times toward different objects for different reasons. There are the painful silences. When a girl is embarrassed by a remark to which she has no comeback, there is a hurt blush of silence. When a person is thrust into a circle of cognoscenti or intelligentsia above his or her head, one's ignorance soon reduces one, if one is wise, to an uncomfortable, pitied silence. People newly met will sometimes chat on superficially as good friends never need do until presently there comes a halt and stillness, an impersonal stillness that coldly betrays this will be the first and last meeting.

Then there is silence which is compelled. Catastrophe can force one to a closeted silence: why has the father of my children been struck down with incurable cancer? Poignant resignation, terrible repression, stubborn protest, all tend to be voiced dumbly. And when one is caught red-handed doing wrong, before the excuses come, there is a moment of silence dominated by the 'impossible possibility' of being caught. Or ushered in before some authority, the suppliant is compelled by the objective weight of the other's office to be silent and wait for proceedings to begin. An audience before a speaker is a parody of the situation; and everybody knows that when a teacher or parent has to explicitly order silence – Keep still! – it is a command showing weakened or disobeyed authority.

Other silences are more happy ones. When a couple is stilled to admiration before a majestic panorama of mountains or deep in a forest, alone before the gigantic, anything but silence to let the beauty sink in would be a disturbance. The contact of love too is realised in stillness, where an exhilarating, mutual trust softly fills in the chinks, powerfully and completingly increases the attachment one for another; love happens best silently, with the eyes and the hand. (This is why love-letters are a burden.) And the homely quiet of sitting down to do nothing, as it were, after a hard day's work, with the one whom you love, and not need to talk, just enjoy the other's nearness, is a rich quietness full of relief. Silence of this reflective sort always has an intimacy that breathes rest and completion.

And there are critical silences among people. The simple hesitation on how to answer an important question put by one's superior or antagonist, the stymied fear at secrecy, uncertain as to what will happen next, keeps one concentratedly hovering in anticipation while afraid to move. The silence that attends crises, whether trivial or mortal, seem to mock the indecision rather than beckon onward. Such silence does not give direction.

So what does this incomplete encyclopaedia of painful, compelled, happily restful and critical silences show? That when a person is inadequate to cope with a given situation he is pushed to silence; or, when a person is satisfied, content, silence discloses that peace and command most fully. Silence surrounds one's self like one's skin distinguishes one concretely from other individuals. You can have excruciating intestinal pain and a person standing right next to you, deeply sympathetic, cannot share the agony. Silence surrounds a person with similar privacy. It is the mark of a person's being a single, self-conscious, individual creation. This is why when a person is threatened with shame, with public exposure of his or her innermost secrets and failings which while hidden help him or her maintain self-respect, when what is closest to one's very self is to be violated, then as a last resort a person withdraws, pulls back into one's cloak of silence, trying to keep intact and out of reach at least something that is one's own. It is precisely what torture is after, to break a person determined to be silent into crying out, to have broken through his or her final reserve not to willingly give in – the exposé Sartre hates but sadistically feeds upon in his earlier philosophy. Herein lies the tormenting evil of being asked a question to which silence *is* a telltale answer.

Thus silence is a given with created individuality; only in human creatures, however, blessed with selfhood, does silence assume the full reflexive, protective character that establishes privacy. Animals may be possessive but only people have privacy. And it is into that silent privacy that a person affronted or faced with overwhelming evil retreats and consciously or unconsciously tête-à-tête with oneself before the Lord, or if one be an unbeliever, before one's idol, he or she seeks reflectingly to know him or herself and what to do. Silence gives a person room to move around in oneself, presents a reserve for regrouping one's forces; instead of needing to keep on responding outwardly, a person can in silence, consciously or subconsciously, concentrate on ordering one's past thoughts, intentions, desires, one's present makeup. The healing of psychotherapeutic silence is instructive here. The so-called 'recognition' which is instrumental in restoring health is not a magical release from repressed drives against social norms, Freud notwithstanding, but is the fact that the troubled one can respectfully become themself in silent tête-à-tête trust with another person whom they know has come to accept them as they are given. Then a person has the wherewithal, is willing, to speak again, you might say.

That human silence can be hopeful, deeply expectant at decisive moments, is an important matter still coming.

Some of you are certainly aware that silence has been overvalued and undervalued in the history of humankind. Not that people did not hit upon the Aristotelian mean in their judgement, but this: silence has been idolised for centuries by what one could call loosely the mystic tradition, while today it is largely lost sight of in the West, with disturbing consequences.

If one were to try to put one's finger on the key to mysticism, Zen, Yoga, or Trappist monasticism, one might well centre on what its climactic silence is thought to mean. After the long, usually ascetic, purifying preparation, in the extremity of spiritual concentration, comes finally the great Silence with a blinding flash or a dully dark merging of one's entering in with the transfinite, meta-individual transcendent One-All-Whole God or whatever you call it. Perfect silence to the mystic affords *gnosis* (inspired, intuitional knowledge). This Silence is the enveloping, ineffable noetic revelation in which I attain Buddhahood or enter Brahma or 'blend into God' as Meister Eckhart would say. That is, in the silence, presumed suspended from time, the individual mystic experiences *unmediated union* with the Infinite (or at least transfinite) Spiritual Presence. It is that presumptuous affirmation, however it be hushed and humbly circumscribed with words, that exposes the radically unbiblical character of mysticism (cf. John 11: 6) and its wilful denial or antagonism toward the bodily creational nature of humankind in God's temporal theatre headed for the *eschaton*.

Relatively few people have pursued the mystical way and its rigours of professional silence. It has always been easier for the run of humankind to act out stupidly, in Heidegger's terms, their fallen *in-der-Welt-sein* (being-in-the-world), as worldling. The truth is, people do try naturally to escape facing the ultimate questions and prefer to live, day in night out, as if who they are and why is sufficiently taken care of not to need reflect on the matter. Long ago the mystical saint Augustine chided others, somewhere in his *Confessions*, for travelling abroad while leaving themselves undiscovered. Pascal picked up the same theme and mocked his courtly contemporaries of seventeenth-century salon society who chased rabbits on horses, amused themselves endlessly chatting and cutting decks of cards, who busily faked their figures with corsets, bustles and cosmetics, and tried tirelessly in all diversions to hide from their miserable selves. And it would not be hard to make a case that the maximum of machine-made noise people have in their hands today is used – teenagers hugging blaring transistor radios to their breasts, adults fastened fascinatedly to the smokey blue screen – is used wittingly or not to avoid the silence which is an ordinance of creation inviting one to self-knowledge. Because the modern person seems bent on ruining the opportunities of silence to know one's self and thus runs from God-knowledge too, it is no wonder a Western civilised trend seems to be toward a youth of frenetic movement, middle age of luxurious boredom and an old age of operations and medical complaint, rather than Christian joy, leadership and elderly wisdom.

I must be very clear right here. I am not advocating silence of introspective philosophising as a nostrum for our wild times: our day is indeed an age of psychoanalysis and it has not stopped wholesale preoccupation with trivia and distracting noise. I am also not supporting the romantic pipe dream of a Thoreau who, in the wake of eighteenth-century primitivism, sought to escape the madding crowd in a typical cynic, anti-social way by retreating to Walden to rejoice contentedly in the melancholy threnodies and morose notes of hoot owls. The old Christianised mystic at least attempted withdrawal for response to God; its secular parallel is a sloughed off movement to be unresponsive to society. The contemporary cults of beatnickish Zen and yogi in America only carry transcendental Walden with its gentle civil disobedience to a logically absurd, apostate conclusion of irresponsibility to God, state and society: vociferous silence is made a fetish. Rather than suggest some watered down form of mysticism, perhaps in the line of Böhme and the German pietists, as an antidote to our globetrotting, mass-media hysteria, I should like to point up the necessary, peculiar, sane place of church worship in human life. It is terribly true that all those who go noisily chasing after strange gods, Jehovah quietly destroys (cf. Psalm 73: 27).

Peculiarity of church worship

All human life is religion in operation, I would argue; that is, all human action is adoration, sacrifice and thanksgiving to the true God revealed in Jesus

Christ witnessed to by the Holy Scriptures or is obedience to an idol. I mean daily life – kissing your wife or husband good-bye, shifting gears to pass a motorist, watching birds fly South, solving theoretical problems – all of it is expression, witness! of what could loosely be called service, 'worship' of God or tokens of human vanity. Because the very corporeality of a believer, because our bodies are temples of the Holy Spirit (1 Corinthians 6:19,20), Paul commands us 'whatever you do – eating or drinking – do it to show God's presence' (1 Corinthians 10:31); and he prays that our love of God increasingly overflow into our perception, every sensation (*pase aisthesei*)! (Philippians 1:9), till we become veritably living sacrifices going up in smoke for the Lord (cf. Romans 12:1).

So every consecrated deed is *latreian* (worship), a ministry. However, certain acts of a person not only embody and show his or her underlying God-attachment but seem to reflexively stand still and reiterate while reflecting that basic faith-commitment. Prayer not only manifests one's faith but in a doubling back, specially concentrated way that does not characterise Christian working, thinking, feeling, eating and drinking, prayer is a type of recapitulating faith act. Such human action that has a built-in reflexive, turned-toward-God posture can well be called peculiarly 'confessional' action; and while every thing a person does has a confessional moment to it, sport, business, legislating, for example, are not structured, qualified by the still, reformulating type confessional way that constitutes the nature of prayer.

Confessional-type human action does characterise exactly, however, what goes on in the institutional church of Jesus Christ. Certainly, the church is a grouping of people called out and rooted in the Lord Godself. And there are many unchristian confessional groupings of people: sects, lodges, klans, brotherhoods with their bastard temples, office-bearers and creeds. But in the kingdom of God, among the many institutional human associations dominated by the Holy Spirit – Christian families, Christian schools, Christian labour unions, Christian burial societies, Christian roses, tomatoes, gladioli and the like – that one historically founded creational structure which binds people to a confessional union for its temporal social existence is the institutional church, whether the bond be a confession of the 1500s or the 1960s. The church institution is a confessional body of believers. All its legal disciplines, finances, language, art, atmosphere, doctrines are to be confessionally dominated and limited: to forget this is to denature the church into an ecclesiastical state or business or social agency (but that is not my concern now). The peculiar task of the institutional church, its ministry, 'worship' is *leitourgia* (liturgy), that is, public, official, corporate, confessional worship of God.

That means for me that church worship, where God's people together draw near to meet God for God's promised blessing, all that happens there is to be ordered, driven, permeated by the concentrated, adoring-God, reflexive intensity that is a special mark of confessional matters. The whole Christian life of worship (*latreian*) needs to be focused, confessionally recapitulated, symbolically performed (*leitourgia*) before God's face out of and back into its living source, the reconciling Grace Jehovah presents to the congregated faithful in Jesus Christ. The institutional church baptises a person, initiates them into the covenantal relation with Jehovah, calls them to repentance, kerygmatically showers them with the Good News, refreshes them when tired with the blessed banquet of the Lord, lovingly, pastorally admonishes them to more pure, thankful good works. The fact that the institutional church handles authoritatively these weighty keys to the kingdom of heaven demonstrates how critically central its doings are in the life of a person. And if the church goes bad as representative distributing the means of Grace, if it offers stones for bread and weak acid instead of living water, and if it has no clearly biblical idea of how the thankful confessional response of God's people is to be determined and practised, what should mark its Sunday service – this is my primary concern right now – then it will hobble, cripple a believer's life-time or may even keep some people not far but still outside the door of God's holiness.

Silence before The LORD? Festivity?

That leads me, finally, to drop the couple of clinkers I brought along as a simple believer to your seminary. Are we before Jehovah in God's holy temple to keep silence (cf. Habakkuk 2: 20)? Are we to make a joyful, loud noise unto the Lord in God's presence (cf. Psalm 98: 4)? Both? How? What role must silence play in Sunday church worship to relate it biblically fruitfully to the rush of human life in God's theatre? And does the peculiarly confessional character of *leitourgia* exclude the spirit present here tonight of student banqueting, a symposium festivity, in God's house on the Lord's day?

To orient our answers we must remember that God is never silent. God is *Logos*. Since the creation of the world God's eternal power and godhood have been manifestly visible (Romans 1:20; Acts 14:17), and especially since the fullness of God became incarnate in Jesus Christ (Colossians 1:19), that mystery too is openly revealed and made known to all peoples for their obedient response (Romans 16:25, 26) – all of which is unmistakably witnessed to by the Holy Scriptures in our hand (James 5:39; 2 Timothy 3:15,16). Therefore, were Jehovah God to be silent, inarticulate, dumbly hide, God would have to undo God's historical revelation and betray God's very nature. If God seems silent (= the sceptic's most subtle dart), it is because people cannot read and hear God's voice in their pride, curiosity or impatience, and do not know that in God's lofty, mysterious way the Lord is busy preparing an answer for believing prayer and unbelieving jibe. Jesus Christ was silent on earth, messianically silent before the bureaucrat Pilate and the quizzical Herod while the theological leaders of the day spoke calumny. Christians too are encouraged in the face of enemies' ridicule and injustice to let their forbearance be known – the Lord God is at hand, and God shall answer them (Philippians 1:5). But God Almighty is the Speaking One, and when the faithful go officially to meet God they can expect to encounter the Word whether read and proclaimed or sacramentally administered (cf. 1 Corinthians 11: 26).

We should go to God silently. The silence spells leisure, the rest of having come apart for a while (cf. Mark 6:31) behind protective stained-glass windows, to listen to the Word. We want to be *all ears*! before Jehovah stirring Godself up out of the seat of God's holiness (cf. Zechariah 2:17). And confronted by the Holy One a person is immediately further struck dumb with guilt, shamedly, painfully penitent for the sin of the past six days and nights that cleaves to one's skin under all the fine clothes. A New Testament believer knows, one may come boldly into God's presence covered by the blood of Christ, one's evil conscience and filthy body washed clean, says Hebrews (10:19–22), but still, because even New Testament believers do not know exactly how and what to pray for and need the Holy Spirit to plead along with inarticulate, unutterable groanings (Romans 8:25), and because we approach God often in weak belief, like uncertain lovers wishing 'tell me once more that you love me', silence! cautious, searching, grateful, intensely waiting silence is the appropriate order for preparing to meet God.

That holds for the liturgete too in somewhat different fashion, the one specially ordained to the apostolic office of breaking the bread for the people (cf. Acts 2:42), who officiates in this unusual, public confessionally declarative glorification of God. The liturgete's words must not obtrude ministry of the Word, and if his or her rhetoric pulls attention and admiration – part of the heresy proceedings against Paul of Samosata in the third century, reports Eusebius (*Hist. Eccl.*, VII, xxx, 9), attacked his pulpit-pounding, popularly successful histrionics getting the congregations to applaud and wave their handkerchiefs at his bursts of 'good old preaching' – if the person speaks too hard to make the point, he or she becomes a false prophet in the mercy-seat. Also, as intercessor for the congregated faithful, the overseer must be chary of words, burdened, seared by the awareness that the all-knowing God is sitting on God's cosmic throne in heaven while they are a speck of dust upon a piece of earth; therefore, let your words – everyone of which is an awful vow! – let your words be few in the house of God, says Ecclesiastes (5:1,2). Long prayers are heathenish, a sign of hypocrisy (Matthew 6:7; Mark 12:40). If you want to pray all night, good, go into your private room, and wrestle with the Lord for God's sheep; make your petitions known to God again and again, troubling the Lord to respond, and God shall grant you what you need (Matthew 6:6; cf. Luke 18:4–8); but public prayer may not be wordy, a show – it is as loveless as sounding brass.

The ordinance of silence should dominate our waiting upon God. Not just that so many more actions could be surprisingly significant if people were set to observe and listen in silence – entrance of the body of four-and-twenty elders, stylised movement of the pastor from lectern to pulpit to table, a halt and pause by the organ before shifting to the next liturgical step, the simple gesture without words of raised presentation of the offerings to the Lord, proper utensils and quiet enough to hear the splash of water on the baptismal font – not just a sense of silence for the possible added meanings is needed. Silence gives the believer time, room, the attention and play required to come to oneself and thus fold out, un-lax, become receptive at heart for the Grace (*charis*) about to be offered. Men and women met for *leitourgia* (specially confessional worship) need more than pleasantries and conversation plus a rather brief, concert hush before the conductor steps up to the podium, because we are not waiting for the pastor to come, quietly polite before he or she enters. A Sunday worship meeting is unusually aimed away from other people: we are all come to commune with the Christ who is in heaven at the throne of God, that is, seek and find Christ in heaven by way of the Holy Spirit who indeed, listing where God wills upon earth, gives there through Word and sacrament what is sought in faith. And for this standing still and attent communion with the Lord a person must be as whole as possible and the congregation must be as all together as possible to receive in its intensity the blessing. Resting – it is Sunday! – focusing silence of wholehearted, communal expectancy is what needs to be kindled. Once Grace has been spoken, partaken of by the faithful, then the whole proceeding takes on a different cast, that of Thanksgiving (*eucharistia*)! This is why my support of silence as the right *preparation* for receiving Grace differs radically from the position of quasi-mystics, Rudolph Otto, Quaker experience, Moral Re-Armament (to bring many variants under one rubric), those who judge silence to be the culmination, consummation of worship.

The error in thinking silence bespeaks the final moment of Truth in worship I do not need to repeat. Our necessity of a mediator *incarnate*, the fact of *written* revelation, the Bible's expressed preference for consciously interpreted preaching rather than glossolalia (1 Corinthians 14:13–19) point in a different direction. But this should be added: those who seek the subjective experience of *mysterium tremendum* as the end to all formalism, dead-wood scholasticism and miscellaneous orthodox evils get caught antinomically in the same or worse traps. Eckhart inveighed against holy asses with their penances and external practices of piety only to shift work-righteousness dialectically inside to the attainment of *Abgescheidenheit* (disinterestedness). Quaker history shows that its early informal spontaneity grew in time its own kind of quietistic, deadening formality.

And all 'revelation' loose from the *Word* has the problem of the Buchmann follower I heard explaining how in 'the quiet time' God appeared and spoke to him. A critic parried, 'Yes, but Christ had a quiet time of forty days and forty nights and then not God but the devil appeared and spoke to him – you have to be careful who speaks to you (by the inner light).' That is, introspective, unfathomable, hierophantic silence taken as the crux of worship ruins biblical *leitourgia*: public worship is malformed semi-privately; official acts are levelled individualistically; and corporate praise by Christ's body is spiritualised.

Christian worship in the Reformed and Presbyterian tradition has not made much meaningful use of silence, to my knowledge, in Sunday services, and in so far as we have practised silence at worship or in a 'week of preparation' before one of the sacraments, we have often suffered, we do suffer from a bodiless, somewhat intellectualistic, not to say spiritualistic type silence because it is not exercised as a momentary prelude toward full bodily hallelujah expression of joy. Reverence for us means *only* quiet; our thankful response to Grace, except for a measured song or two and the teaching elder's sole Amen, is quite introverted. Does not 'preparation' for communion, if taken seriously, frazzle into a few hours of moralistic cross-examination that diverts us from the truth that the only condition to eat with Christ is faith, publican and sinner, not a spotless moral life? And the Lord's Supper itself is a far cry from the laughing festivity of the communal meal we shared tonight – it is generally held in the tones and looks of a wake. But God's people deserve better. And a right understanding of silence could help reform and enrich our Sunday worship by instituting the proper dramatic rhythm of concentrated waiting for Grace to which we then shout Amen!

A few months ago I visited a midnight service of the famous Chicago Negro church, First Church of Deliverance, home base for the Metropolitan Spiritual Churches of Christ, Inc. It was a rollicking songfest of an affair. At the close of his sermon, thanking God for having brought the weak and the sick, the poor and oppressed through another week by God's Grace, 'let's all give God a big hand!' said pastor Cobb. And he clapped across the stage and the audience clapped after him, and then they sang. 'A big hand for God!' he repeated, and father and son, mother and children, they all clapped, clapped hard and long.

In St Peter's, Rome, for an Easter service once, I huddled in the dark long service of chanting and hocus pocus till suddenly! at transformation of the host thousands of lights sprung into candle-power and the choir crescendoed magnificently – something must have happened, a tourist would say. Thank God we do not have the pseudo-miraculous popish mass, and I do not recommend we imitate the beat of African rhythms and exuberance of Chicago's First Church of Deliverance; but I do think it biblically imperative for you seminary graduates to foster the right kind of silence in Sunday worship so that upon proclamation of the Good News or having presented Christ visibly sacramentally to the faithful, you can then turn the meeting into a joyful celebration of *bodily* praise! the whole congregation, children too, participating.

Once believers have restfully confessed their sin, been ritually reconciled to God and given the reality and promises of Grace again, there comes joy! Amen and Amen! There must be bodily ways – are we afraid to use our sanctified inclination? – bodily ways to channel the Hallelujahs and festivity; otherwise people will suppose church worship is an unreal adjunct, a take-it-or-leave-it addition to daily life rather than the burning focal point which concentrates confessionally in capsule form, as it were, the hopes and fears, laughter and tears of all our days before the face of the Lord.

Narrowly Reformed, orthodox Christians have not bothered too much till late with structuring the people's response (*eucharistia*) in Sunday public worship. Zwingli and certain Puritan divines' influence seemed safe, I suppose – they are as good scapegoats as any; or possibly the concern to ensure pure preaching of the Word above all else in the church explains reticence for liturgical reform – attention must not be diverted to lesser matters. But neglect of how the faithful are there to respond simultaneously impoverishes understanding how Grace is to be brought. If the presence of covenanted children were really given more than lip-service, might it not lead us to discover the Lord's Supper biblically once more as an intimate family-style love feast *with* the Lord in anticipation of God's coming, a banquet together with our children in holy holiday spirits! rather than as a memorial service with children as spectators? And would not the nonsense of sermons being didactic lectures or homilies trying to meet certain individuals' introspective needs or testimonies capitalising on religious experiences of the week, would not the nonsense of this be doubly clear if it were seen that the faithful are quietly, silently waiting expectantly for exhortational exposition of *the Word* so that they may grow in *Grace*!

Our daily life is a busy one and the needful silences are pressing fewer. As the end time nears, the crowding out noise and secret malevolent silences of the enemy's hate will grow more intense for those who openly confess Jesus Christ. So we should get set, fortify our consolidating silences. And that is where the church peculiarly comes in. A person without the church is utterly worse off than a person without a country: all he or she has then is bedlam and stolen reprieves. Because the church is truly the pause that refreshes in the work of the Kingdom, the church must not fall down, may not fail in giving us hard-pressed children of faith, so often tired beyond our years, give us a holy silence at Sunday worship that edifies, builds up because it concentratedly sets us up for the laughing burst of praise that sends us back into the battle of the world, refreshed and fighting.

Without proper silence built in to Sunday worship, its celebrating character will faint because the fact that *something happens in church!* is muddled. It seems to be only an academic lecture surrounded by special numbers or a pep talk or exercises for trained seals, to an outsider, rather than that *the living Word of God is spoken*! disclosed in a listening silence to flesh and blood labourers and teachers and young people who are aching to be outright captured, convicted, comforted by the Word of Life *for* life on the morrow and are then literally moved by the Spirit to commit their bodily lives and show it in liturgical practice. Unless it be a false church where minister and consistory have nothing to say in God's name to the worker, housewife, student, and soldier, unless it be a voiceless sham, both the silence and celebration of church worship AD will be pregnant with hope. It is always advent for the saints, and this hope – faith, hope and love, and the most human of these is hope – this certain hope of our Lord's coming to complete God's worldwide kingdom deserves to be intensely enjoyed, silently and then bodily, every Sunday. You who are shepherds of the faithful may not rest until believers come to wait and worship God, celebrate the resurrection Sundays with the anticipation lovers have of greeting one another in the holiday season after a long absence – first the silent approach and then finally the rush of joyful, bodily embrace. That Christian worship is not always so lies in large measure on our not understanding and not having learned the humility of silence and the bodied character of praise.

Bibliography

Baden, Hans Jürgen. *Das Schweigen*. Gutersloh: C. Bertelsmann Verlag,1952.

Cadier, Jean. *La Doctrine Calviniste de la Sainte Cène*. In Etudes Théologiques et Religieuses, xxvi:1–2, 1951.

Gaurer, Hildegard. *Die Psychologie des Schweigens in England*. Heidelberg: Carl Winter's Universitätsbuchhandlung, 1937.

Greene, Alice B. *The Religious Uses of Silence*. New York: Columbia University, 1938. Dissertation.

Greene, Alice B. *The Philosophy of Silence*. New York: Richard R. Smith, 1910.

Harvey, T. Edmund. *Silence and Worship: Study in Quaker Experience*. London: Swarthmore Press, 1923.

Le Bost, Barbara. 'Silent Transfigurations', *Cross Currents*, xv:3 (Summer 1965), 295–301.

Otto, Rudolph. 'Schweigender Dienst', *Die Christliche Welt*, xxxiv:36 (September 2 1920), 561–5.

Picard, Max. *The World of Silence*, trans. S. Godman. Chicago: Henry Regnery, 1961.

Thielicke, Helmut. *Das Schweigen Gottes. Fragen von heute an das Evangelium*. Hamburg: Furche Verlag, 1962.

Tournier, Paul. *To Resist or to Surrender*, trans. J. S. Gilmour. Richmond, Va.: John Knox Press, 1961.

van den Berg, J. H. *Over Zwijgen en Verzwijgen*. Utrecht: Kemink en Zoon, 1949.

Part 5

Arts and the Aesthetic

1 Art: Temptation to Sin or Testimony of Grace?

Is Art Something Holy, Something Seductive, or Something Else?*

In the warm-blooded land of southern Greece long years before Christ, young people gathered in the spring to sing, dance, practise art, and make love somewhat indiscriminately in honour of Dionysus, the god of wine, art, and fertility.

It is a shame that the natural flow of youth and art in the springtime is not captured today in the name of Jesus Christ. Young Christians busy with art should come to know it as a holy business; they should know that they can practise art to show their love to God, to revel in the fact that God is king of the whole earth. Because the Creator has adopted them as God's children, they should understand their ability to enjoy God's world and should be happy to express this enjoyment in music, colours, shapes, rhythmic writings, and speech. It is time in this affluent society for the body of Christ to get at the downright fun of glorying in artistic gifts God gives God's people, to realise that the Christian faith deserves artistic expression, and then to probe trustingly, critically, into the Christian use of art.

Believers have long treated art as a devilish temptation. The church unfortunately began to think it so early in its history. Art, it said in effect, is sensuous, and the sensuous is a seductive road to hell; therefore, stay away from art. Children should not be allowed to play with matches; why should God's children be permitted to dally with art? What is art good for? Our purpose in life is to believe and become fishers of people, win souls for Christ, sojourning here till we leave for heavenly mansions not built with human hands.

The early church rightly exposed Caesar's song-and-dance spectaculars, the Bacchic art festivals, as unworthy of Christian patronage. But it wrongly disparaged art itself through guilt by association. The church at times suppressed art unless it was turned into a pedagogical instrument (paintings in the church to teach Bible stories to the illiterate) or used to dress up the institutional means of special worship (decorations in the margins of prayer books or

---

*First published in *Christianity Today* 10:5 (3 December 1965), 239–41.

trumpet notes on Palm Sunday). In other words, art was sometimes used gingerly, perhaps for a 'spiritual' end – but even then, watch out!

It is easy, of course, to criticise what was wrong. In the beginning the Christians did not have time to write poems or go beyond pictures in the catacombs. Their minds were taken up with formulating confessions against heresy and codifying doctrines to stop civil misunderstandings. However, it is a different matter when Christians piously argue whether art is worth less than other human activities, generally implying with classic pedantry the old error that art is a romantic spasm unfit for Christians, unless it somehow be bent to church worship.

But if the Christian community maintains a prohibitionist or, at best, a permissive conception of art, it has missed a critical area of Christian action and affronted God. If the Church does not like the jazz, painting, and literature of today, what does it expect if it does not encourage its baptised children to produce something Christianly different?

Whenever God-created drives or talents in people are denied meaningful exercise, there is trouble. Humankind's glories then become a temptation to sin. Temptation is much more complicated and casual an affair than a scantily clad woman accosting a hungry St Anthony in a wilderness of stumps, logs, water, and grass. Temptation is always the opportunity for one to satisfy one's God-given needs and desires in ways that ignore God's loving ordinances for the exercise of human abilities.

When God's adopted children who are especially talented in being sensitive to the wonder of the world and culturally and artistically responsive to it are frustrated by Christian kill-joys (cf. 1 Timothy 4:1–4), then the devil, who covets culture and its human makers, knows how to twist art into temptation to sin. He subtly gets believers with artistic talent so wrapped up in the truly God-created enjoyment of art, especially in reaction to unbiblical prohibitions, that they forget that art itself must be practised before the face of the holy God and Lord. Disregarding that, the artist becomes tempted to think and act as if his or her artistic deed had its own right to be and was naturally revelational of God's Truth rather than being a humanly conditioned response to God's glory. Unless art is conceived and practised (albeit subconsciously) as a channel for the Holy Spirit's witness to others of one's being a perceptive child of God, it should be forgotten. Otherwise one has made art its own lord and has swallowed the devil's bait. Unless art is itself a praise response, a hallelujah to God in the world – not churchy moralism, not a forced, derived, lugged-in Christianised witness, but a joyous, ministering hallelujah praise, it will be still-born – no matter how elegant the music, painting, prose, and poetry may be.

A peculiar thing about art that offends so many serious-minded Christians is its playful, leisurely, imaginative character. If we want art to walk in through the front door of the Christian community rather than to be quietly smuggled in the back door, it must be made plain to the uninitiated that writing, painting, singing, and playing are hard work of a highly talented sort – that their make-believe is not faking, pleasant nonsense, but an excruciatingly careful, symbolical formulation of what the artist knows or supposes the world to be about. In a famous exchange, Matisse was told by a woman in an art gallery who was looking at one of his curving, twisted black swirls, 'I never saw a woman like that.' 'Madame,' said Matisse, 'that is not a woman, it is a painting!' And his painting was not unreal because it was not a woman, nor was it false and unimportant because it was 'exaggerated'; for Matisse discloses and affirms in colour the voluptuous viciousness of a wanton that could perhaps be shown no other way.

If adult painters were merely working out some of their subconscious shrieks in colours and if musicians were performing simply because their mothers made them practise the piano early in life, then art would indeed not deserve to be taken seriously by the public. But since art is a man's or woman's modest but intense contribution to his or her neighbour's grasp of corners of reality, states of affairs, levels of meaning not often explored but present in creation all the time – caught by him or her as artist in symbols for the other's appropriation – what the Christian artist does is significant for building up the body of Christ and speaking to those who will listen.

If we could convey to the sceptical in the church that the artist stands like a child toward the world – not, to be sure, innocent, not void of moral obligation, but childlike, fresh, open, giving himself or herself to discover, penetrate, and grasp what is out there in creation as well as inside his or her self-consciousness, wondering for Christ's sake; if we could make church people see that the artist needs leisure, the kind of leisure college students have near the end of a semester when they work day and night, not meeting carefully apportioned deadlines but concentratedly busy at a pitch of excitement; if we could convey something of this, then perhaps we could break through to the Christian mentality that understands missions, preaching and teaching – hard work as service to God – but has trouble relaxing in laughter before God's throne. There is a lot of laughter, of love, of *Sunday*, to art rightly understood, features for which Christians are uniquely constituted. Christians can give themselves to the task because their involvement is not artificially manufactured for selfish or pragmatic reasons but is simply a matter of spontaneous thanksgiving because God in God's world is so great and merciful.

By *Sunday* I do not mean a legal holy day bored through with interminable talk, stuffy formalism, and lap lunches, but rather the day of rest God gives us, the God-created leisure, the vacationing celebration people may have and need, no less than a six-day week. Sunday is to be a joyful anticipation of the coming resurrection in which believers will blossom, each according to his or her own talented nature (1 Corinthians 15), bringing the glory and honour of the world's kingdoms fully to Jesus Christ (Revelation 21:24,26). Art has this innate festive character – not that it is specially holy (that is the companion error to judging it inherently suspect) but that it is a specially tempting occasion for a person in the sense of Psalm 1 to bring forth fruit leisurely ripened to please God. Because artistic talent is God's gift to God's creatures, we should take seriously the scriptural imperative to develop that talent if we have been blessed with it, to discipline and hone its craft-element, so that when the Lord comes back to see how we have passed the time of day with what God has given us, when God comes to judge our artistic efforts, we can be quietly glad that the five, two, or one talent is doubled. That is the biblical, apocalyptic background to studying, performing, and criticising one another's art in a communion of saints.

What is the church and the believing artist to do with all the modern art that mistakes the world, perverts creation in despair, or, giggling nervously, is empty of praise? Responsible Christians must make a point of examining such art critically in order to be exactly aware of the culture they are caught in, so that they can be stirred to develop the art of praise. Believers frequently cut a sorry figure in the contemporary world, because they practise an unbiblical otherworldliness. Recently our college organised a tour for a large group of young Christian artists at the Art Institute of Chicago. We told the director we wanted a tour concerned with the intrinsic relation of art and faith, that we wanted the guides to show us the biblical truth that a person's final commitment to whatever he or she holds dear and inviolate necessarily, though subtly, appears in his or her work.

The director said, 'You mean medieval art, crucifixes, and church symbols?' 'No.'

'Perhaps our Buddhist, Hindu, Oriental religious art treasures?'

'No. Rather what does, for example, contemporary art say about the world? What does the artist mean with his or her canvas? Could you explain to us, who come from Trinity Christian College, what spiritual expression modern art conveys?'

'Oh, yes, but you wouldn't like it,' he said. 'It is not very pleasant, sometimes.' 'But that is what we want!'

In the tour coming out of this conversation we saw some highly articulate vomiting, symbolically expressive anarchy, whimsicality, cursing in art, as well as random playful comments on human foibles and the unutterably pathetic blue canvas of Picasso's man with a guitar. It became clear to those with eyes to see that contemporary artists have largely turned the world topsy-turvy, that they ask God questions and berate God for not answering, while all the time God is asking, 'Do you love me?' and people are not answering. Such perversion does not stop us Christians from learning bits and snatches from these terribly perceptive, acutely gifted, unbelieving artists, because they are bound (if they would communicate) by the laws of God for art in this world – laws they would like to violate! But their godless art, the blank, distorted, dead-end picture of the world they present, is a lie! That is not the way the world is; that is the way the world looks when seen without the Gospel today, without the Good News of Jesus Christ.

The evangelical, Reformational Christian upshot to such a confrontation is not to demand that all become eunuchs for the kingdom of God (Matthew 19:12) but rather to plead that believers, having seen such art, should go home and exercise their artistic birthright, pained that God does not hear hallelujahs from this planet above the cries of secular disbelief. While society becomes increasingly secularised, war-torn, and giddy, the artists in Christ's body should be encouraged by us all to embody – whether in poetry, painting, music, or speech – hope in their sorrows, to show love through their disappointments, to communicate to whoever listens, in an idiom intelligible in their day (and that may mean no major chords, no prim representations, no heroic couplets), that the struggle in the world by those who believe is done joyously for a sure prize, the glory of God we now already share in Jesus Christ.

The direction Christ's body must take is clearly shown in the Scriptures. As the manifesto of Psalm 150 says:

> Hallelu! Yahweh!
> Hallelu God in God's holy place!
> Hallelu God through the heavens which God rules!
> Hallelu God for God's sovereignty!
> Hallelu God in the overwhelmingness of God's grandeur!
> Hallelu God with the blast of trumpets!
> Hallelu God with harps and bass violins!
> Hallelu God with (bouncing) tambourines and dance!
> Hallelu God with stringed instruments, with flutes,
> Hallelu God with ringing castanets!
> Hallelu God with cymbals crashing joyfully!
> Let every thing that has a breath hallelu Yahweh!
> Hallelu Yahweh!

If a Christ-follower holds Jehovah God as his or her Lord, then for the sake of their Lord let them sing, play, paint, and write God a hallelujah in the presence of the faithful and of God's enemies. Such is the joyful ministry of the Christian artistry we need to be engaged in.

2 Human Responses to Art: Good, Bad and Indifferent*

I should like to begin with a paragraph from Revelation 18: 21–4:

> And one strong angel picked up a rock, big as a millstone, and heaved it into the lake, saying: That's the way – boom! – the great city Babylon shall get the heave and never be found again. The sound of guitarists and folk-singers and flautists and trumpeters shall nevermore be heard in your city; no artist, in any of the arts, shall be found any more in your great city. The sound of the millstone grinding shall be heard among you no more forever, and the lamp-light shall shine no more among you forever, and the voice of bridegroom and bride shall nevermore be heard among you, nevermore – your businessmen were the bigshots of the earth! – nevermore, because all the people were misled by your clever artistry.
>
> They found blood too in that city Babylon, blood of prophets and saints and all those believers who were butchered to death on the earth.

Art by its presence demands a response from you as a human person

In our culture today, whether you live in Sioux Centre, Toronto, or New York City, you are confronted by art. Even if you don't read, you still go to the movies. If you close your eyes, you still hear somebody's radio with its mix of music and commercials. If you should use ear-plugs and a guide dog, you would still feel the pattern of city streets as you ride in the back of a taxi, or sense the architectural shape of the building you are entering as you walk through a revolving door. Art by its ubiquitous presence demands your response, even if it is rejection.

The Bible is concerned that our response be filled with a holy spirit that knows what is good and what is evil so that what we sense, see performed, read, hear, and understand does not poison or butcher us. The Bible wants us

---

*First published in *Human Responses to Art*, ed Mike Vanden Bosch (Sioux Center, Iowa: Dordt College Press, 1983), pp. 1–18. Originally given as a lecture at a conference in 1981 at Dordt College, Sioux Center, Iowa, where Seerveld and Paul C. Vitz (professor of psychology at New York University) discussed the problem of left-brain and right-brain activity as it related to human responses in culture. Dordt College is a Christian liberal arts college whose programme is shaped by the Christian philosophical perspective of the Reformation.

to learn how to be edified and compassionately deepened by what we perceive, so that we know and exercise what is important for a child of God (cf. Titus 1:15; Philippians 1:9–11).

That is our topic: examining the human response to art. By way of introduction let me say that this is a very complicated problem. When a Dordt theatre-arts major and a farmer go to the same play, they *see* the same performance very differently. It's up to the theatre-arts department, the *Diamond* as college newspaper, and the Public Relations department of the college to mediate those different perceptions. Even though they are looking at the same canvases, a Christian Reformed Church ladies-aid society looks at an arts professor Norman Matheis' art show very differently from how Clement Greenberg, the New York art critic, would. And the direction of the art department at Dordt depends upon which perceptions the leaders take seriously. When a talent scout for the Chicago Symphony and an almost tone-deaf, prospective donor for musical instruments listens to the Dordt orchestra, they *hear* very differently the same sounds.

I'm not talking 'good guys' versus 'bad guys', as if there were an elect élite and a reprobate mass of people responding to art. In fact, I tend to trust the naive person more than the sophisticated one, particularly if the simple person is a Bible-believing Christian, unaffected by TV, who wants to serve God on earth. I'm simply trying to show you that there are many subjective factors at work in the experience of artistic events and artworks. A dramatist should be aware that there may be farmers in his or her audience; a mid-western artist needs to know about the New York art scene, and the Dordt choir must realise that few people can actually hear the intricate structure of a madrigal. But our focus now is on the farmer, the city critic, and church audience: how should one respond to art? And can we examine it in a way that acknowledges that one and the same art object will occupy, briefly, the attention of a wide variety of people?

This problem can be made concrete in connection with this lecture. If you are an educational philosophy student required to attend and take notes, it affects what you hear. If you just dropped in, know nothing about art, but are interested in being educated, you will *hear* things differently. Now the philosophical question is: how do people receive artworks, performance, and books of short stories? Are there right ways for people to experience art which will unlock its flavour and meaning? What are the key problems theorists (have to) take a stand on with regard to seeing, hearing, and reading of art?

Marxist, Freudian, or Idealist theories of response-to-art will mislead us in regard to our perception of art

As a Christian thinker I would say, first of all, that one should beware of oversimplified answers, and test the spirit in the theory of response-to-art you examine. A Marxist approach normally curses the middle-class WASP enjoyment of a piece of art as a smug evil, and blesses all those who demand that art be a useful weapon for stamping out injustice in society. A Freudian approach tends to advocate 'letting yourself go' at a concert. Since art for the Freudian is essentially a substitute for sex, the simulated orgasms at a punkrock festival are much better for emotional stability than the polite, inhibited applause after a cantata at First Church. An Idealist theory focuses on the idea-content of an artwork – if you get that, you've got it all; anything more is either gravy or distraction. What I am saying is that a carefully thought-out response to art assumes a theory of art as well as a theory of knowledge, a philosophy of perception. If you take art to be a therapeutic stimulus or a sugar-coated idea, propaganda or a luxury item like chocolate cake, you will experience art within that defining framework. I know that artworks normally have a point and always mean something, and that the emotion-stretching component of art is very important, and that art objects show the artist's commitment to be or not to be societally responsible. But an Idealist, Freudian, or Marxist theory of response-to-art each overexposes its cherished elements and therefore misleads by blocking out other crucial factors, thereby warping perceptions of art into an ideological rut.

The task of a Christian theory of aesthetics, and also of a Christian theory of perception, would be to set out the key features of a normative, aesthetic response-to-art. It should also spell out pivotal factors one should look for, listen to, and wait for in the various art forms, so that we will be saved from one-sided, short-sighted, and other wrong responses. A Christian response-to-art is not automatically guaranteed by one's knowing the contours of a Christian theory of response-to-art; nevertheless, a theory of aesthetics, if it embodies Christian insight, can help grind the lenses of the eye-glasses and temper the diaphragms of the earphones of your art-experience.

Thesis: For us not to respond to art as a piece of *art*, imaginatively, is to miss the meaning of its artistry

A human creature should respond to art in kind if he or she intends to make the acquaintance of dated/located artworks in God's world. A piece of art is a piece of art. Art is not a stimulus to nerve-endings; it is not an instrument to complete a plan; it is not a signpost, nor a mathematical problem to be figured out and solved. A piece of music or theatre or a painting normally is stimulating and formed to get something across; an artwork usually says something and needs to be understood. But its stimulating, constructed, signifying, and thought-provoking come-ons are features of its character as an *art object*. An artwork or an artistic performance must be responded to first of all *imaginatively* or you miss its meaning. Artworks are *imaginatively* stimulating, *imaginatively* formed, *imaginatively* discussible, *imaginatively* thoughtful. That's what an artwork is, if it is art – an object made to be known and responded to imaginatively by human subjects in God's world.

Inadequate reactions

In my judgement this means it is inadequate to respond to a choreographed dance by only saying, 'I like it,' or 'I don't like it.' Don't get me wrong: it's OK to have likes and dislikes. Likes and dislikes are rooted in our God-given sensitivity to pleasure and pain. But if our chief response to a ballet movement is, 'It turns me on,' or 'It turns me off,' then we have a very undeveloped, not to say stunted, response to an artwork. To be chiefly turned on or turned off by art as a person is not very intelligent activity. Such a stance mistakenly treats an art object as if it were akin to a body rub or a cold shower.

A more involved and common but still inadequate reception of art is conveyed by the exclamation 'Neat-o!' or 'Cool, man!' Such judgements often prize the skill displayed – for example, the sheer virtuosity of the guitar-playing by Jimi Hendrix recorded in the film *Woodstock*. This kind of response, inadequate though it be, requires inside knowledge of technique. One responds to a musical performance as one responds to a good double-play in baseball or an expert, delayed-pass routine in football. One can't put it into a lot of words, maybe, but you are enough of a rock or Bach buff to know the finesse or slightest error in fingering or intonation. You admire or disapprove the act with cold-blooded, arm-chair professionalism. This kind of specialist-trained ear or eye – and it often is not academically trained – is personified in the knowing look and hip language sign of approval or the kind of cutting remark heard sometimes at intermission: 'The horns were flat in the second movement.' If this is the limit or the focus of listening to music, then pieces of music are treated not as artworks, but primarily as technical operations.

Over-reaching responses

Next to these two kinds of inadequate, mistaken art receptions, which I'll call the *grunt reaction* and the *umpire perception*, I'd like to mention briefly a couple of others which overshoot the mark, you might say, instead of reducing art to stimulus for a grunt or to a trick worth watching to see whether it's a ball or a strike.

Some people are inclined to meet theatre or cinema, for example, only at the verbal level. They read movie reviews and, after they've gone, can talk a blue streak about what the actors did, describe in detail episode after episode in a film, tell you the story line, the message, and specify its contents clearly. Very literate. But such a literate recounting of *Equus* or *Clockwork Orange* seems untouched by a poignance of make-believe human horses with heads and hooves of empty, shiny metal, or by the distorted, looming, ant's-eye camera shot of the rape and the lurking presence of Beethoven's Ninth in the soundtrack. This is a talkative way of seeing and hearing, of experiencing a play or film, that tends to overlook and miss the exact nuances most difficult to translate into words. The person seems satisfied with what can be paraphrased. So one could identify this kind of misfocus as the *paraphrastic* response.

Another kind of approach to artworks or artistic performance is with a lattice-work, as it were, thrown up in front of your face that allows you to see only what can be precisely, analytically put away. You treat a painting as if it is in a laboratory and you are dissecting it, probing each element microscopically for germs of thought, examining and explaining all the causal connections you can rustle up, staying alert for any ideas there may be, but discounting what is not conceptually interesting as the packaging one needs to unwrap. Aestheticians, psychologists, philosophers, and university graduate students who are not careful may err this way when they leave the classroom and go to a concert or an art gallery or read a novel. Applying a theoretical grid straightaway to a Bach fugue, a Moore sculpture, or a Watteau painting pre-empts their experiencing it in all its lovely polyphonic or polysemous ambiguity. This overreaching approach to artwork I'd call *scientistic attention*.

So far I've been reporting on what I think are inadequate and overreaching ways to perceive artworks – four mistaken kinds of ways of responding to artistic presentations. There are more wrong ways to confront artworks, which do not respond to art in kind, but I'll let them go for now (cf. my *A Christian Critique of Art and Literature*, p. 107, n. 3). But let me make two notes to head off misunderstandings until I can get more of the whole picture spelled out.

Firstly, you will seldom find pure, air-tight specimens of these mistaken types of art reception. We respond inadequately as human creatures, but the Lord graciously compensates for us, keeps us from totally ruining our lives when we have a severe case of Gruntitis or Umpire pox or suffer from Paraphrastic diarrhoea. It's not even the end of the world if we're struck down by Scientistic fever, although all these wrong ways to respond to art will be a curse of sorts on us and the artists, closing us down and putting a whammy on certain real, creaturely joys. Also, please realise I am not saying there should be a tabu on feeling, know-howing, talking, and thinking when we respond to artworks. In fact, without feeling or know-how, the correct response to art will be weak, and I'll argue that talking and thinking are crucial for a deepened perception of art. The point I'm coming to is that the sensing, know-howing, describing, and thinking activities must be submerged within an *imaginative* openness to the art object. All these normal, operating activities must become functions fused within the act of response which is focused on the piece of art or artistic performance in its *nuances*. All important functions of the response-to-art activity must be focused by the art object's defining quality of allusivity.

Secondly, it is entirely legitimate to analyse a Hopkins poem like 'God's Grandeur' or to decide whether you want to pay 30 dollars to see Peter Shaffer's play *Amadeus* off-Broadway. It's fair enough to decide whether you like or dislike Steve Reich's music or whether the colours of a Picasso print will match or clash with the wallpaper in your living-room – fair enough, if you are willing to respect the art-object character of the artwork in question. In the respects I've just mentioned, artworks are no different from a ton of coal, which you may or may not like to have in your living-room either, with its dust or smell. That is, artworks exist in the world along with tons of mined coal, which is also a cultural object needing to be responded to by men and women *as mined coal* in a number of ways – analysis, price, fitting in with your living-room or not. And it is utterly legitimate to make human decisions on these sorts of external relations of artworks and of coal. So it is fair enough to say, 'I don't want my kids to see Tantric temple sculpture,' and 'The price tag on a Rembrandt is as immoral as what Steinbrenner will pay to sew up a slugger in a Yankee uniform.' There are all kinds of contexts in which artworks find themselves which need Christian concern and where non-artistic judgements are valid – about the art, or coal. But right now we are trying to recognise how to appreciate, pick up, notice, understand an artwork or artistic event in its *artistic* meaning, its particularly artistic character, which is intrinsic to the nature of artistry like painting, music, theatre, and cinema.

Imaginative reading of an art object or of artistic meaning

The prime feature of a human act of response to an artwork is an intent awareness of the pregnant allusiveness of the piece. I should like to contend that the way to get at the aesthetic quality which, for me, defines an art object is that one activate its congealed nuances. And the only way to activate the nuanced meaning which the artist, and performers as co-artists, have brought to an artistic head is to read it nuancefully. That is what I take an imaginative response to be: a nuanceful reading that plays perceptively and intelligently with the nuances of anything. Since an artwork, in my understanding, is always a humanly crafted object that is at its core virtually a metaphor, visual, aural, worded, gestural, or whatever; since a Rouault painting, a Brahms concerto, Ionesco's *Rhinoceros* or *Macbeth* is a qualitatively nuanced artefact of symbolific compression; then an imaginative reading is what it takes to make the art object come alive as an artwork.

Let me explain that. By 'imaginative reading' I mean an intuitional retracing of the art object. You play back in your consciousness whatever the pasty, stained-glass colours and heavy, leaden, black smudges of lines in Rouault's painting of Christ's head suggest, and you mull over the hidden meanings hovering all around and within the images; but you leave it wonderfully shadowy. Or you replay in your consciousness as it takes place the opening scenes of Bergman's staging of Gombrowicz' drama *Yvonne, Princess of Burgundy*, where you'd swear the 1920s-dressed courtiers of the king look like two-dimensional, cardboard props in a ritzy, furniture show window, and you store the caricatured gestures of those puppet people, as an index to their cramped violence. You pick up and keep those telling nuances percolating subliminally while they build imaginatively with a compounding complicity. Or you play along in your consciousness with the sight–sound metaphor of Yehudi Menuhin directing his select string orchestra in a concert performance of Boyce, Mozart, Bartók, and Haydn, and you thrill, with eighteenth-century decorum, at the nicety of the symmetrical musical phrases, the relatively simple melodic patterns, the reassuringly constant tempo that allows such clean virtuosity in subtle changes of timbre and tones; you listen and hear indirectly a world of elegance, arabesques, make-believe and frolic.

That is, a nuanceful reading of an art object like a painting, theatre-piece, or symphony, imagines how the sensible, constructed, nuance-laden nest of allusions means what it does; and your thoughtfully sensitive awareness remains at an intuited kind of retrieval. No matter whether your imaginative knowing is experienced and deep or tentative and beginning, an imagining-active playback (and I didn't say 'feedback') of the art object in all its fused symbolic penumbras of meaning remains curious, prone to re-reading the piece, full of wonder.

An imaginative reading of an art object does not exhaust itself in sense-perception, and it does not aim at a comprehensive understanding that wraps up the piece. There is a genuinely more-than-visible yet unfinished-off ambiguity that is integral and structurally permanent, I think, to an imaginative reception of art because, firstly, that's the defining way an art object is, and secondly, that's the right way to perceive, conceive, receive art – what Kant was trying to pin down with 'taste' and 'aesthetic judgement', what Susanne K. Langer means by 'intuitive discernment of non-discursive import', and what Rudolf Arnheim explores in 'visual thinking'.

Symbolify: the professional norm for making art

Now we are coming to the heart of my remarks. First, the art object. It takes hypersensitive, skill-trained people to lay the foundation for making a piece of sculpture or for composing a sonata. (I know there are all kinds of borderline cases of people who are not overly sensitive nor very skilful who come up with a good song or poem in their life-time, but things are so complicated we've got to take clear-cut examples.) If you are insensitive to the properties of clay and cannot 'think with your hands', as the expression goes, you will make a poor sculptor or potter. If you have no ear for music and are sloppy at organisation, you will have trouble composing a piece for six musical instruments to play that will hold attention for more than five minutes. You don't have to be married or be a Christian or be twenty years old to be a bona fide artist, but you do need, in my book, to show a certain measure of crafting ability in a medium, be it of clay or tones or words or whatever. Being able to design in a medium is the base line, I think, for producing an artwork which deserves the name of art.

An artist also needs a special kind of insight, an aesthetic discernment and imaginative ability to capture meanings at large and transform them, metamorphose them, into a suggestion-rich entity which not only keeps all the delicate shades of suggestion-rich meaning intact, but also somehow has enough integrality and durance to be an object made precisely for aesthetic imaginative attention. That is what I use the terms 'symbolical' and 'symbolical objectification' to describe. An art object is the objectified presentation of certain (other) meanings which a subjective artist has crafted so that its very being-there is of 'symbolical' quality – allusiveness permeates its whole existence. An art object is like an alluring, ambiguous wink hinting at matters worth experiencing, full of knowledge bottled for those who can open up its allusiveness and taste it aesthetically. So 'symbolical' means for me in the context of aesthetic theory 'a professionally fashioned and honed allusiveness'. 'Symbolical objectification' and 'symbolify' are short phrases for describing the most salient feature of artistic activity.

Lots of things could be added. (a) Art objects can be a professional service to help people become more aware of nuances in ordinary, non-artistic circumstances of life. I want to make people aware that art is relevant for all of life – it can open our eyes and ears to creatural glories, if it is right – and I'd like to reform Christianly the idea of professional. To be a professional artist should mean you unblushingly profess the committed mould to your whole life in your artistry, and you believe that what you are being is worthy of mastery – 'professional'. Such an idea would curb the evil of uncommitted professionalism and would also encourage amateur artists. Every artist who earns a living by their artistry began as an apprentice once upon a time. Even 'professional' responders-to-art began as amateurs. And amateur artists don't need to make it full-time work; but they are called, I believe, to do justice to whatever they take up as an artistic hobby, that is, take its 'symbolical' nature seriously, rather than just mess around therapeutically – which would have a different rationale.

(b) Those of you who have read in *Rainbows for the Fallen World* know that I understand practical jokes and surprises as *aesthetic* objects or events, also typified by allusiveness (pp. 49–59) which can be as real, important, and memorable as many a painting or poem. But unlike artistic objects, which are professionally 'symbolified' artefacts, aesthetic objects are more effervescent and meshed with shifting societal contexts, it seems to me. So if nobody gets the joke or surprise, maybe it wasn't there, but if nobody gets the play or the musical composition, it is still more there somehow than the intended joke was.

(c) The history of reflection on 'symbol' can be investigated at length until finally you take your own stand somewhere and try to use the term wisely. 'Symbolical' for me is the norm for art. Symbolical, as I said, is the allusive feature heightened professionally, the allusive squared, you might say, or taken to a higher power of refinement. So a 'symbol' is different from a sign, which signifies something clearly. An '=' is not a symbol in my vocabulary: it is a mark designating mathematical identity or logical similarity. Words too are essentially signs, pointers, with a syntactic framework and a range of meaning even though words have a built-in symbolic layer – their connotations. When English sentences are turned into poetry, the connotations take the lead, incorporate and overshadow the denotations; so poetry is less clear language than ordinary sentences because it has become symbolically heightened language.

'Symbolical', then, is the criterion for whether something is art or not. Whether an artefact or handicraft is art or propaganda, art or the exercise of an expert, and so on, depends on whether its defining characteristic is symbolical. I know people will differ in judging a particular event. People even differ on whether 'symbolical' is the norm for artistic structure. The same is true for deciding whether or not a given act belongs to a biblically Christian life-style. But we may not abdicate a stand because of Christian disunity. We need to posit, in community, imperatives for which the Lord holds us responsible, also in artistry and aesthetic theory, if that is our office, otherwise we forfeit 'feeding the sheep' of the Lord. As a theorist at this stage of my development I am willing to stand by 'symbolical' as the decisive factor for art.

Nuanceful lineaments of certain arts

I still want to offer, as pertinent for exploring our responses to artworks such as paintings, pieces of music, theatre and cinema, an incomplete, a playfully philosophical checklist of artistic features that will reward and can deepen our imaginative perception, conceptual notice, and judgement surrounding our aesthetic reading of specific art objects.

When you face a painting, you do well to look for its nuances of colour and try to imagine how the nuances of the painting's constitutive properties such as size, foreground–background, surface-texture (i.e. brush strokes, palette-knife gobs, airbrush sheen) and the nuances of its hues and design contribute to what it as a whole symbolifies. Also, try to discover intuitively how simple or complex it is with respect to other painterly dimensions: does it depict? are there emblems? are there recurrent motifs in the artist's paintings which allude to a peculiar novelty of interest? You do well to become imaginatively aware of how tasteful and engaging its symbolical quality is and how nuanced the thrust of the piece is, if you want to plumb its artistic meaning.

When you listen properly to music, you need to hear and recognise its musicality. You need to hear the nuances especially of its rhythms. Constitutive properties of music include its tempo and loudness, its vertical pitch patterns and silences. You need to become aware of the pregnant emphases and intended oddities of phrasing, intensity (i.e. the attack, sustenance, and decay of sound), the nuances of timbre and delicacies of orchestration, for all contribute to the allusive-squared meaning of the music. Aesthetic listening to instrumental music will be enriched if you can intuitively be aware of the expressive, innovative, entertaining and cherished tonal nuances – all the lineaments that make up the symbolic thrust of the piece.

I'm fairly certain that professionals in theatre and cinema arts could delineate features that might help harness our habits of perception and intelligence to a more imaginative reading of such artworks and artistic performances too. But let me make my most careful comments about the imaginative response to art, which I believe is basically the right kind of response to art. I want to make these comments after giving those sketchy lists of artistic features in paintings and music. We may need to study and learn how to respond to art beyond the grunt and slogan level, but art response must not become scholastic. Art response deserves to be imaginatively deep and aesthetically rich.

A partial diagnosis of imaginative reception of artworks

To receive film, novel, cantata, choreographed dance, or a drawing imaginatively, we must perceive the work without losing its impact and richness through a pre-emptive analysis. Nevertheless, to experience the richness of that perception, we must be aesthetically sensitive and artistically aware of the different lineaments of the artwork. Gush kills taste, and expertise can paralyse imaginative perception; but we will not enter the music or the painting or the play aesthetically without empathy, without perception that can simulate and remember intuitively the technical founding elements of the artwork.

325

Also, to read an art object imaginatively and maturely we shall come to interpret and compare forms. It is a natural tendency for our aesthetic play-back of the artwork to put into words and into concepts what we are aesthetically undergoing, to show we are indeed whole people who are discriminating viewers and listeners able to express what we experience intuitively. But that normal tendency of our imaginative reading to become expressive and discriminating must not slip into the realm of disinterested description and explanation, because then one rides roughshod over the symbolic qualification of the art and its proper reading, and substitutes talk and thought for imagining. Art criticism, analysis which delves and exposits and distinguishes facts predominantly by similating* and comparing, can develop the calibre of one's primary aesthetic responses to artworks. Art interpretation which highlights and points to symbolical distortions and imaginative over- and underexposures can facilitate sound art reception. But art criticism and art commentary cannot take the place of original art reception and imaginative reading of the symbolically qualified piece of gifted human artistry.

I would like to develop an aesthetic theory and philosophy of perception that would save you from imaginative paralysis when you face artworks and artistic performances. I want to respond as a child of God who is called to rule this culture in God's Name. It is a romanticist lie that thinking and speaking about art necessarily kills art reception: to be dumb and blank-minded and filled with a turmoil of inexpressible emotions is not the state of imaginative reading. But it is also a lie that we need to bring this irrational art business under some rational control, or at least clip its wings with some decent reasoning. I've tried to say 'No' to both of these responses. I've posited that aesthetic activity has its own prime ontological structure and task interwoven in human life, especially in responding to art.

In closing, a double note that's important to me. (1) Because every artwork has a date and a tradition and inescapably carries around in itself like a ghost the spirited perspective of its human makers, to read the work accurately we must see the spirited perspective embedded in that very sensible, crafted, allusion-rich artefact. Many humanistic theories of response to art block out the question of whether art has this horizon of final commitment in its flesh and blood. And too few would-be Christian theories of response to art are willing to confess the sobering fact that at bottom one's response to art is going to meet the question of whether one is faced with what serves the Truth or the Enemy. Powerful art – and that could mean the power of established tradition rather than banks of amplifiers – will butcher believers in the last days. In fact, in our technocratic day, art is a more simple and attractive idol than science to

---

*Similating: term coined by Karl Aschenbrenner, in *Concepts of Criticism* (Dordrecht: D. Reidel, 1974, p. 313), to mean offering appraisal by relevant comparison of similar and dissimilar characteristics.

many (cf. Matthew 24:22–4). Therefore, we need to taste, sense, perceptively enjoy, remember, interpret, compare, and especially read artworks imaginatively with passages like Matthew 7:1,2; 1 John 4:1; Philippians 1:9–11 giving us the cue. No snap, self-righteous aesthetic judgements will do, but imaginative testing of the spirits of those pieces of art. We must be in the sure grip of the Holy Spirit so that our very sensation knows the overflowing single-minded love of Jesus Christ.

(2) When we visit the theatre tonight or attend the musical performance tomorrow, we will likely be a motley crew, from anti-music auditors, indifferent receivers, partisan fans, and emoting grunters, to professional art-expert listeners, inexpert theorists, psychology professors, and maybe even one or two good imaginative readers of theatre and music. What could pull us together would be a unifying, normative sense of what we are responding to (a symbolified object) and a communal working conception of how we can thoughtfully perceive and sensitively think within our (imaginative) response to what goes on as it reaches out to us. That is an edifying, methodical programme, I think, of how to proceed.

But I'll make a provocative comment in the hope it will be picked up: to look or hear, perceive and respond to an artwork or artistic performance as if it is itself not *historically embedded*, just as we art-receivers are, is like trying to guess the meaning of a quote out of context, often a foreign-language quote at that. We American Christian academicians – speaking for myself – have often sinned, I think, by treating artworks as if they never grew in historical dirt, as if they grew in an antiseptic laboratory of art formation. But an artwork is truly historically dated and contexted, and we must allow it the time to let the historical context of an artwork worm itself slowly into our experience, informing us of the world it breathed and breathes. Otherwise we interpret the art object according to what ails us. We may delight in Mozart's music so much because its genial loveliness entices us to escape from our secular rush of deadlines, strikes, and machines going on the blink, and thus we may over-hear, miss and dismiss its rococo spirit. Or we may falsify artworks and sterilise imaginative responses in our performance practices when we bring artworks to the stage with little regard to historical setting. The striking difference between concert and theatre programmes in Munich, London, and New York makes my point. The German programme holds a short, reflective essay in layman's language, giving the historical setting of the piece and something of its afterlife. The British programme gives a few art critical remarks about significant features of the work. The American *Playbill* lists the cast with their credits and many advertisements of other shows in town and nothing else – you're on your own.

My closing remark is to ask each of us to realise that when we examine human response to art and try to delineate its proper structure, we are only treating the ABCs of an art response. But I am glad we are doing it, because it is important to grasp even the ABC's of factors in art response with the innocent circumspection of Christ's proverbial dove and snake (Matthew 10:16).

Bibliography

Arnheim, Rudolf. *Visual Thinking*. Los Angeles: University of California Press, 1969, 1972.

Barzun, Jacques. *The Use and Abuse of Art*. Princeton University Press, 1973.

Blanshard, Frances Bradshaw. *Retreat from Likeness in the Theory of Painting*. New York: Columbia University Press, 1949.

Brooks, Cleanth. *The Well-Wrought Urn*. New York: Harcourt, Brace & World Harvest, 1947.

Broudy, Harry S. *Enlightened Cherishing. An essay on Aesthetic Education*. Urbana: University of Illinois Press, 1972.

Bullough, Edward. "'Psychical Distance" as a Factor in Art and an Aesthetic Principle' (1912) in W.E. Kennick (ed.), *Art and Philosophy: Readings in aesthetics*. New York: St. Martin's Press, 1966, pp. 534–51.

Buytendijk, F.J.J. *Prolegomena van een Antropologische Fysiologie*. Utrecht: Aula-boeken, 1965.

Casey, Edward S. *Imagining. A Phenomological Study*. Bloomington: Indiana University Press, 1976.

de Graaff, Arnold H. *Psychology: Sensitive Openness and Appropriate Reactions*. Potchefstroom University for Christian Higher Education, 1980.

Ehrenzweig, Anton. *The Hidden Order of Art*. Berkeley: University of California Press, 1967, 1971.

Gibson, James J. 'A theory of pictorial perception', in Gyorgy Kepes (ed.), *Sign, Image, Symbol*. New York: George Braziller, 1966, pp. 92–107.

Gombrich, E.H. 'On physiognomic perception' (1960) in *Meditations on a Hobby Horse*. London: Phaidon, 1963; 3rd edn, 1978, pp. 45–55.

Greene, Theodore Meyer. *The Arts and the Art of Criticism*. Princeton University Press, 1940.

Guggenheimer, Richard. *Sight and Insight: a Prediction of New Perceptions in art* (1945). Port Washington, NY: Kennikat Press, 1968.

Hine, F.D., Ronald Silverman et al. (eds.) *The Aesthetic Eye: Generative Ideas*. Los Angeles: National Endowment for the Humanities & Office of the Los Angeles County Superintendent of Schools, 1976.

Lanz, Henry. 'Aesthetic relativity', in *Stanford University Publications, University Series Language and Literature* 7:1 (1947), 3–20.

Lipps, Theodor. 'Einfühlung, inner Nachahmung, und Organempfindungen', *Archiv für die gesamte Psychologie* 1:1 (1903), 185–204.

—. 'Zur ästhetischen Mechanik', *Zeitschrift für Ästhetik und Allgemeine Kunstwissenschaft* 1(1906), 1–29.

Schapiro, Meyer. 'Mr Berenson's values', *Encounter* 16 (January 1961), 57–65.

Schwartzmann, Helen B. 'Research on Children's Play: An Overview, and some Predictions', in *Proceedings of the Association for the Anthropological Study of Play* (1977), ed. Michael A. Salter. West Point: Leisure Press, 1978, pp. 105–15.

Seerveld, Calvin. *A Christian Critique of Art and Literature.* Toronto: Association for the Advancement of Christian Scholarship, 1964, 2nd edn 1977.

—. 'A Christian Tin-can Theory of Man', *Journal of the American Scientific Affiliation* 33 (July 1981), 74–81.

—. *Rainbows for the Fallen World: Aesthetic Life and Artistic Task.* Toronto: Tuppence Press, 1980.

Sibley, Frank N. 'Aesthetic concepts', *Philosophical Review* 68 (Oct. 1959), 421–50.

Springer, Sally P. and Georg Deutsch. *Left Brain, Right Brain.* San Francisco: W.H. Freeman, 1981.

Steensma, G.J. and Harro W. van Brummelen (eds.) *Shaping School Curriculum, a biblical View.* Terre Haute, Indiana: Signal Publishing Co., 1977.

Tashiro, Tom. 'Ambiguity as aesthetic principle', in Philip P. Wiener (ed.), *Dictionary of the History of Ideas.* New York: Charles Scribner's Sons, 1973, 1, pp. 48–60.

Wolterstorff, Nicholas. *Art in Action.* Grand Rapids: Eerdmans, 1980.

Zuidervaart, Lambert. 'Introduction', in *Kant's Critique of Beauty and Taste: Explorations into a Philosophical Aesthetics.* Toronto: Institute for Christian Studies, M.Phil. thesis, 1977, pp. 1–16.

3 A Christian View of Aesthetics*

A Christian view of aesthetic theory differs from a secular perspective on the discipline in showing how the field and its development relate to the lordship of Jesus Christ.

Development of a theology of beauty

For centuries before the historical incarnation of God in Jesus Christ reflection on beauty, epitomised by the dialogues of Plato, set up what became perhaps the major stumbling-block to a fruitful theory of art, a down-to-earth sense of the aesthetic, and a hermeneutics that can trust imaginative knowledge.

Plato posited an absolute beauty outside the visible, temporal world as a pearl of great price men should desire to know. A good Greek mind would persist in pursuit of such transcending perfection until it came to contemplate the unspeakably well-proportioned, noetic form of Beauty itself. Then one's soul would be saved from the curse of bodily, earthly transience (*Symposium* 209e–212a). The only prayer in Plato's works has Socrates intone the words, 'O Pan, grant me to become beautiful inside' (*Phaedrus* 279b8–9).

The Hellenist Plotinus and even Augustine carried on the Platonic tradition with a chain-of-being ontology that allowed them to declare everything is beautiful insofar as it is. Worms are beautiful (*On true religion* 41:77), and evil too with its punishment fits harmoniously into the balancing mosaic of God's goodness (*Confessions* 7:18–19). Although Thomas Aquinas thought in Aristotelian categories and maintained an analogical distance between creature and Creator, his doctrine of beauty retained the highly mathematical, Platonised dogma that proportion, perfection, and now brilliance constituted the attribute of God the Son (*Summa Theologica* I, 39.8) which pleases us in its more mundane form as 'the beautiful'.

The Reformer John Calvin understood the visible beauty of creation to be a mirroring of God's glory; art then became God's gift to humankind to help men and women recognise beauty, a kind of general revelation of God. The 1898 Princeton lectures of Abraham Kuyper followed through on Calvin and

---

*Entry in Walter A. Elwell (ed.), *Evangelical Dictionary of Theology* (Grand Rapids: Baker, 1984), pp. 16–18.

formulated somewhat idealistically what has become almost the mainline tradition among evangelical Protestant thinkers: art has the mystical task of reminding those who are homesick for heaven of the beauty that once was lost and of the perfect lustre that is coming.

In the context of comparative religion Gerardus van der Leeuw developed an apologetic for the 'beautiful' as an ancillary or penultimate step toward what is 'holy'. Thomist Jacques Maritain in his 1952 Mellon lectures presented a complex theology of artistic and transcendental beauty in which he confessed 'that all great poetry awakens in us one way or another, the sense of our mysterious identity, and draws us toward the source of being'.

Christian thinkers who adopt a theology of beauty are beset by the problems which attend natural theology and all theodicies: how radical and disfiguring is the reality of sin and the necessity of Christ's redemption? Can beautiful nature and art be evil? And, if human art is beautiful, is it not naturally good? Also, whether beauty is taken to be an elemental harmony in the world or a fitting and satisfying quality of human artefacts, the concepts of balanced order, form, and delight are at best analogues of aesthetic reality. Such properties of 'beauty' do not define the peculiar character of artistry, nor do they explain art's special province of oblique meaning.

Struggle for a foolproof hermeneutics

Modern debate in aesthetic theory has largely converted beauty into a problem of taste and then argued about the kind and reliability of 'aesthetic' judgements. There is concern with how to read and interpret art and literature with a critical mind that can be sure its exegesis is correct.

In the eighteenth century Alexander Gottlieb Baumgarten conceived the aesthetic realm to be one of fused image-knowledge, which lacks the precise distinctness of ideas that is requisite for higher, logical knowledge. Immanuel Kant identified taste as an autonomous, disinterested form of sensitivity which involved the satisfying use of one's cognitive faculties but which was not a source of knowledge; human sensitivity to beautiful and especially to sublime affairs was important to Kant, because such aesthetic activity is analogous and propaedeutic to morality.

Hegel, however, was influential in cutting concerns about taste and aesthetic judgement at large more narrowly down to examination of art, and art as a kind of secular theophany. Such romantic idealist philosophers of fine art as Herder and Schelling strongly supported the idea of artistic genius and intellectually intuitive creativity, which give art, music, and especially poetry a revelational character that transcends logical examination. Critique of literature soon became largely a matter of empathic discernment of the 'spirit' of the

Plate 20 Seerveld visiting Dirk van den Berg of the Department of Art History, Bloemfontein, University of the Orange Free State, South Africa, September 1994

text and its prophetic meaning for the present; past historical settings became largely immaterial for interpretation, next to the imaginative inspiration for humanity afforded by the piece.

Wilhelm Dilthey aimed to overcome the problem of historical relativity of artworks by making a rigorously descriptive, psychological analysis of the structure shaping poetic imagination. He believed he might be able to fashion a scientific method for interpretation that would distill the lasting, typical knowledge of literary art relevant for any time thereafter. Positivist I.A. Richards undid this hope in English-speaking lands by divorcing poetry as important emotive language from scientific prose that had semiotic referents. It remained for a new critique of poetic language (the 'new critics'), harking back to Kant, to find a format that would keep distinct yet in synthesis the formal, textural devices of poetry which demand close, professional reading, and the paraphraseable message.

Marxist thinkers like Georg Lukács and Leon Trotsky made more clear than many confessing Christians how deeply permeated all art and literature is with the committed perspective of the artist forming the work. Marxist aesthetics is normally so partisan, however, and its literary hermeneutic so dictated by class-conscious, orthodox political dogmas, that the theory and the reading of texts became more a predictable diatribe than genuine analysis and exegesis. Quite differently, Hans-Georg Gadamer has reintroduced a Hegelian dialectic, humanised and authorised by Platonic dialogue on the beautiful, as the model for critical interpretation or art. Gadamer's hermeneutics mutes Heidegger's belief in the oracular nature of poetry to a conviction of the mediating power of language to bridge time and transmit the cultural heritage or literary art, if a reader's consciousness is free to be playfully charmed out of the darkness of prejudices into the light of 'adequate knowledge' of the speaking text.

Christians working in literary theory and the aesthetics of art and literary criticism, as well as ordinary expositors of the Bible, have usually, unfortunately, followed secular trends at a distance. The neo-idealist concern for the 'spiritual content', never mind the technical details, converted to Bultmann's demythologising attempt to get at the *kerygma* core of Scripture, let the trappings go. The subsequent positivist creed, that only rational, logical knowledge (preferably scientifically verified) is trustworthy, has encouraged a teaching of literature that separates cleanly (1) neutral, technical description from (2) orthodox evaluation of the world-view. The idea that holy Scripture is not a true story so much as 'propositional revelation' also owes a debt to the positivist commitment. Current schools of French structuralist aesthetics and the 'deconstructivist' critics who treat texts with the arbitrary originality of dada artists, and whose focus is above all on the reader and the spectator, seem to have a curious echo in the praxis of those who do not mind exegesis of the biblical Scriptures so long as the result is an orthodox point. There seems to be great ferment and much confusion at present, because imaginative (literary) knowledge still lacks a Christian philosophical home as bona fide knowledge.

Problematics of systematic aesthetic theory

A theoretical aesthetics informed by knowledge that we inhabit a world created by the Lord God revealed in Jesus Christ will posit an ordinance for aesthetic reality, for the style of ordinary life, and for the professional construction of artworks. An aesthetic theory that has its analysis cast from a biblically Christian orientation will also recognise that performers and critics as well as leaders in style and composers of artworks have breathed a holy or evil spirit into their respective artistic results, and each needs to be examined as to how the legitimate exercise of his or her tasks has served the public with insight or with curses.

One major attempt to think these matters through with Christian sensitivity takes the incarnation of Jesus Christ as the paradigm for artistic acts. Artists give the 'flesh' of sensible matter to the content of spiritual ideas. Such a 'theological aesthetics' tends to accept a theology of transcendental beauty, to think within a God–artist analogy, and to proffer an apologetics that treats all art as essentially sacramental.

A different current attempt to formulate a radically Christian philosophical aesthetic theory asks for a thoroughgoing reformation of received tradition and thinks out of a different categorical framework. The defining law of God for the aesthetic side of life and style to be obeyed is the ordinance of allusivity, where activity is to be ruled by playfulness and surprise – what would make God smile. Artists are called to catch things and events in creation with an imaginatively crafted miming characterised by the quality of nuancefulness. Artists are understood not as imitators of Christ taking on flesh but as diaconal workers skilled in forming symbols pregnant with meaning for whoever has eyes to see and ears to hear. Artworks are at core metaphors and parables that need to be treated as expressions of seriously committed, living human subjects under Christ's coming Rule. If the artwork is vain, it needs to be charitably humbled; if weak, it should be aided by informed wisdom; if fruitful, it should be praised with thanks. Christian aesthetic theory will fashion an encyclopaedia of the special arts and literature that avoids any ranking hierarchy. It will welcome art bound to special tasks such as commemorative portraiture, monuments, advertising, and liturgy, but will also promote theatre, concerts, paintings in museums, and novels, which have their own special contribution to make as art in society. Christian aesthetics makes clear that our style, artworks, critique, and theory of the aesthetic and artistic in history will be judged for its redemptive fruit on the final Lord's day.

Bibliography

Frei, Hans W. *The Eclipse of Biblical Narrative: A Study in Eighteenth- and Nineteenth-Century Hermeneutics*. New Haven: Yale University Press, 1974.

Kuyper, Abraham. 'Calvinism and art' [1905] in (Stone) *Lectures on Calvinism*. Grand Rapids: Eerdmans, 1961, pp. 142–70.

Langer, Suzanne K. *Feeling and Form: A Theory of Art*. New York: Charles Scribner's Sons, 1953.

Lentricchia, Frank. *After the New Criticism*. University of Chicago Press, 1980.

Maritain, Jacques. *Creative Intuition in Art and Poetry*. Cleveland: Meridian Books, 1954.

Murray, Michael. *Modern Critical Theory: A Phenomenological Introduction*. The Hague: Martinus Nijhoff, 1975.

Scott, Jr, Nathan A. (ed.) *The New Orpheus: Essay Toward a Christian Poetic*. New York: Sheed & Ward, 1964.

Seerveld, Calvin. *A Christian Critique of Art and Literature* [1968]. Sioux Center: Dordt Press, rev. ed., 1995 [with more bibliography].

—. *Rainbows for the Fallen World*. Toronto: Tuppence Press, 1980.

Tatarkiewicz, Wladyslaw. *A History of Six Ideas: An Essay in Aesthetics*. The Hague: Martinus Nijhoff, 1980.

Van der Leeuw, Gerardus. *Sacred and Profane Beauty: The Holy in Art* [1932], trans. by David E. Green. Chicago: Holt, Rinehart & Winston, 1963.

Wolterstorff, Nicholas. *Art in Action: Toward a Christian Aesthetic*. Grand Rapids, Mich.: Eerdmans, 1980.

4 A Way to Go in the Problem of Defining 'Aesthetic'*

How can one determine whether aesthetics be a special science with its own domain, and if so, the prime nature of 'aesthetic'? Is there a way to avoid either the dogmatism of an apriori decision and designation, perhaps derived from one's basic philosophical stance, or covert scepticism toward any conclusive definition of 'aesthetic', because one is really only chasing a bevy of ghosts through a viciously circular bog of language?

The fact that aesthetics is increasingly recognised today as a special science and seems charmed with a phoenix persistence after every logical murder is adventitious and still does not advance our professional reflection on the problem. It has even become fashionable in North America to commit methodological suicide, as nominalist George Dickie recently did,[1] recommending we institutionalise all definition-mongers and then rest content with whatever such beautiful people in the art-world christen as 'art' or 'aesthetic', since it is so by fiat.

But if one realises that oracles are out of date, and wants to establish securely rather than take for granted that there is a definite, aesthetic field of investigation, one has to deal seriously and philosophically with certain inescapable states of affairs.

Methodological problem of definition

On the matter of strict definition, a neo–idealistic thinker is tempted to posit that there be certain prime realities which are ultimate and which therefore have to be accepted or denied as primary data; primes have to be immediately apprehended or they remain unknown, they are not susceptible to further logical parsing.[2] A pragmaticistic mind demurs, however, especially with

---

*First published in Rudolf Lüthe and Stephan Nachtsheim (eds.), *Die Ästhetik, das tägliche Leben und die Künste* (Bonn: Bouvier Verlag Herbert Grundmann, 1984), pp. 44–9.

[1]George Dickie: *Aesthetics: An Introduction* (New York: Bobbs–Merrill Pegasus Book, 1971) pp. 101–8; *Art and the Aesthetic: An Institutional Analysis* (Ithaca: Cornell University Press, 1974), pp. 28–52; and 'What is Anti–art?' *Journal of Aesthetics and Art Criticism* 33:4 (Summer 1975), 419–21.

[2]Theodore Meyer Greene: *The Arts and the Art of Criticism* (Princeton University Press, 1940), pp. 6,14.

respect to art. Definitions on the nature of art may be slogans for reforming critical appreciation of what is commonly called art, but that there be a set of sufficient and necessary conditions which things must possess to be art is seen in traditional aesthetics as the egregious, original sin.[3] The test of whether 'blanket' terms are ever justified depends upon the consistency of language and the coherence of subsequent practice when such terms are employed,[4] but the existence of an (aesthetics) 'essence' is simply an old philosophical pothole.[5]

This stalemate between intuitional, *ipse dixit* idealism and pragmatic operationalism, in my judgement, points to a way beyond both as well as beyond the non-committal indecision of Urmson,[6] Weitz,[7] and Rader[8] on whether 'aesthetic' can cover birds of the same feather.

Idealists usually sense that the quest for philosophical definition is unlike the positive search for identifying whether so-and-so be cancer or a vitamin deficiency and is unlike the logical exercise of specifying commonality and differentia so as to distinguish umbrellas from shotguns. Philosophical idealists normally recognise the legitimacy of delimiting, in an open-ended way, certain irreducible features of things that cannot be conceptually determined. Although reflection on basic, irreducible aspects of things is simply not dreamt of in a philosophy which restricts language, truth and logic to matching up atomic sensa with conventionally hyphenated phonemes like 'yel-low' and 'sweet', idealists are on the right track, I dare say, in claiming that the task of 'transcendental' definition (positing discernible, categorial conditions) affords meaningful knowledge. Idealism goes wrong, however, in ascribing entitary reality to what is abstracted modal structuration, as if *modes* be *things* which they are not.

Pragmaticistic analysis, on the other hand, tends to undo any hypostatisation of structure, whether it be Platonic noéta, Scholastic *essentiae,* or Kantian noumena. Pragmaticists, by and large, are also happy to functionalise entities, and by a kind of perverse, kenotic logic convert any internal, nature-defining criteria of something into various external use-relations, so that things only be what they function as. It is a markedly pragmaticistic penchant to dissolve

[3]William E. Kennick: 'Does Traditional Aesthetics Rest on a Mistake?', *Mind* 67:267 (June 1958), 319, 325, 330–31.

[4]W. B. Gallie: 'The Function of Philosophical Aesthetics', *Mind* 57:227 (July 1948), 304, 310.

[5]Marshall Cohen: 'Aesthetic Essence', in *Philosophy in America*, ed. Max Black (Ithaca: Cornell University Press, 1965), pp. 115–17.

[6]J. O. Urmson: 'What Makes a Situation Aesthetic?', *Proceedings of the Aristotelian Society*, Supplement 31(1957), 87–91.

[7]Morris Weitz: 'The Role of Theory in Aesthetics', *Journal of Aesthetics and Art Criticism* 35:1 (September 1956), 31–3.

[8]Melvin Rader: 'Introduction: the Meaning of Art', in *A Modern Book of Aesthetics. An Anthology.* (Toronto: Holt, Rinehart & Winston, 4th edition, 1973), p. 5.

defining typicality into circumstantial functionality. That means for philo-sophical definition that one can never pin-point a centrally cohering, irre-ducible feature of something; it must remain permanently indeterminate, the protean object of an ongoing process of approximation.[9]

So prescriptive definitions never seem to escape a measure of arbitrariness, and ostensive definitions remain basically mute, while bumping empirically into objects whose relevance is never sure. Alternative options to date have been the fall-back suicide position of eclectic gamesmanship, or to hang fire in a statesmanlike polemic as Osborne does, declaring that the repudiation of definition for 'aesthetic' has been premature, and that if there be no validity to an artistic kind, there can be no genuinely art-critical appraisal – which is manifestly false.[10]

Limited task of definition

A different, new philosophical way to go, rooted in the insight of a minor Christian tradition close to the *theatrum Dei* perspective of Augustine, Calvin, Pascal and Kuyper, is the following.

1. Take for granted that there be creational ordinances which hold for all kinds (and sub-sorts) of things extant. That there are various, mutually irre-ducible, interrelated but prime, relative structurations which order all things, events, acts and whatever, as members of some kind (and sub-sort) or other, and that this structuration is a mark of creaturely reality, is held to be a credible given. If one happens to believe it is the biblical Lord God's covenanting 'Let-there-be', ordaining Word which effects the real, rainbow-rich groupings of things and activities, the kindred ways creation is extant, then the philosophical 'cash value' of the orientation is this: the structuring is honoured as real, holding for creatures, but the structuration is denied *any* self-validating being. The basic categorial modes of existence conditioning the many lawful patterns of order and disorder we may be busy discovering are simply the cosmic, limiting Word of God at work.

2. Within this conceptual framework, the rightful task of philosophical defi-nition is understood to be identifying *how* something is *qualified* (and

[9]In 1956 Gallie rejects his earlier 'informed scepticism' of 1948 (see note 4) about whether 'Art' 'stands for any one thing', and tends to agree with Passmore that '... we must be able in some degree to circumscribe the field within which these probably bogus concepts have been applied' ('Art as an Essentially Contested Concept', *Philosophical Quarterly* 6:23 (April 1956), 100 n. 2,110).

[10]Harold Osborne: 'Definition and Evaluation in Aesthetics', *Philosophical Quarterly* 23 (January 1973), 16, 23.

perhaps founded, if you are dealing with concrete things and events). This kind of definition, so important for orienting systematic inquiry, tries to disclose the characteristic limiting factor of what is given. Traditional theory of definition has made the mistake of twisting the characteristic-way-of-being-there, the question of typically-how-meaning into a what-question. Looking for the essence, ideal exemplar, or even minimal conditions, overshoots the mark and misleads one into thinking you have to penetrate to the total being or to the causally sufficient facts of the definiendum. But philosophical definition, rightly conceived, gets at only *one,* albeit crucial, factor of what may be several necessary ingredients to what you are investigating,[11] and the ontic status of the defining factor which gets defined is an (abstract) how, not a simple what–totality.

3. Further, defining matters such as 'aesthetic' becomes less tendentious if one does not confuse the complementary heuristic and verificational stages of the process.[12] Discovery is what occurs in definition; so there is bound to be a tentative, exploratory moment. And corroboration occurs in definition; so it is normal to grow gradually in certainty about the defined characteristic. The trouble comes when verification and discovery are coalesced. Then comes the pressure to have your initial hunch certain (else it be dubious) or not to claim any reliability till there be complete enumeration of particulars (an impossibility) – hence so much conundrumic mystification surrounding definition. But tentative knowledge is normative for the theoretical examination that makes up defining things – again, you are grappling not with the revealed be-all and end-all of something, but with its characteristic-how; and verified (scientific) knowledge does not result from bare logical activity, it is born from analysis deepened by risking a stance and that thus takes on affirmation inexplicable as mere thought processes.

It seems evident that one is compelled to take a stand on a crucial meaning aspect of something in defining it. That is one reason why definitions are not won by the bread of analysis alone. It is also a reason why theoreticians driven by an *Aufklärung* spirit of 'tolerance', often display a febrile deviousness to avoid defining things, taking a stand on anything, except as a convenient handle. However, philosophical or transcendental definitions have the calling to help order our understanding of the world. Not that right definitions ensure a life

---

[11]Karl Aschenbrenner has correctly observed that there are several, necessary structural elements to art, all of which legitimately press important claims for theoretical analytic attention – its internally configured constitution, its (representational or not) relation to other reality, and the special bond it bears toward its human maker and beholders 'Aesthetic Theory – Conflict and Conciliation', *Journal of Aesthetics and Art Criticism* 18: (September 1959), 106–8.

[12]Lambert Zuidervaart: 'Principles of Modal Theorization', seminar presentation at the Institute for Christian Studies, Toronto, February 1975.

of shalom and wrong definitions compromise the limiting ordinances God has set. If you define a person as a 'rational animal', he or she still functions as a human creature before the face of God, although people living by Aristotle's definition may try to tune their neighbour's drives and control his or her ratiocinative mechanism instead of loving him or her as a 'worshipping creature'. Meals may be 'defined' by the packaged-food industries as an 'efficient exercise in digestive health' rather than as a 'fellowshipping repast', and meals still get served in the world of TV-monitored North America: it is just our usual experience of them that may be denatured. But definitions which acknowledge their limited, leadership task will lose the nervous compulsion to be as exhaustive as a pinhead game of chess,[13] and develop the more humane dimensions of being a professional service to scholarship and the public at large.

Structural qualifying function of art: a clue to 'aesthetic'

Working out of this redefinition of the nature and task of definition, one has a new way to go in defining 'aesthetic' as a fundamental mode of existence, as a definite and prime dimension of life interwoven with other aspectual 'strata' of creaturely reality, which men and women do well to recognise, understand and obediently enact. One goes looking and listening for the qualifying function of artworks in our civilisation, which comprise a kind of family of human-made things that bear an object-functional characteristic irreducible to the qualifying function of other kinds of cultural artefacts. Unless one perversely denies that such things, for example, as artistic sound compositions (music) and artistically composed gesture-sequences (mime) exist, one has an observable place to start the investigation.[14] Whatever the identifiable, qualifying, object-functional characteristic of art turns out to be (which does indeed guide the bona fide appearance of 'aesthetic objects'[15]), indicates what we may call the nuclear moment of 'aesthetic' reality at large.

---

[13]Cf. Paul Ziff: 'The Task of Defining a Work of Art', *Philosophical Review* 62:1 (1953), 62–4.

[14]It is a philosophical commonplace that the locus where theoretical identification starts is roughly the most acceptable and reliable pieces proper to the neighbourhood of one's scrutiny, not borderline cases. Cf. C. K. Ogden and I.A. Richards, *The Meaning of Meaning* (1923) (New York: Harcourt, Brace and World Harvest Book, 1946), p. 19, as well as Mikel Dufrenne, *The Phenomenology of Aesthetic Experience* (1953), trans. E. S. Casey et al. (Evanston: Northwestern University Press, 1973), pp. ivii–lviii.

[15]Mikel Dufrenne (*The Phenomenology of Aesthetic Experience*, pp. 218–33) and Roman Ingarden ('Phenomenological Aesthetics: An Attempt at Defining its Range', *Journal of Aesthetics and Art Criticism* 33:3 (Spring 1975) 262–5, 268) correctly aver that it takes a human aesthetic–functioning subject ('instaurative action', in Souriau's terms) to activate the 'aesthetic object', the typical vocation of a purported artwork. Also important to me is a recognition that the characteristic quality which ensures the possible realisation of such an 'aesthetic' vocation belonging to an artwork is not some epiphenomenal ascription by occasional human subjects (leading to Margolis' 'intermittent' artworks, cf. 'The Mode of Existence of a Work of Art', *Review of Metaphysics* 12:1 (Sept. 1958), 32–4, but is ontically an existential (aesthetic) object-functional-how of authentic art projects themselves, perduring and binding upon all and sundry subjects.

It is assumed that an *aesthetic-how* is thoroughly meshed with other kinds of original ways concrete things function, and that the distinguishability of the 'aesthetic' moment is simply more sensible when 'aesthetic' predominates as the qualifying object-function of art. The fact that it has taken centuries of civilisation for crafted sacral objects and performances to become differentiated into art-as-such[16] should not bluff our defining 'aesthetic' into uncertainty; historical unfolding of things takes place within structural parameters and can neither create nor negate such ordinantial bounds.

The crucial point of this proposed method is that it posits a prime structural how-reality for 'aesthetic' (which truth idealistic definition mis-takes substantially) and goes about approximating the nuclear kernel of *aesthetic-how* reality by an ongoing scrutiny of artworks (which truth pragmaticistic definition vitiates in bad faith by precluding any structural specificity). Hence, with this approach, defining 'aesthetic' can be both serious and relaxed, for one is not trying to capture and certify the sum total of art with one throw of a loaded theoretical dice. Rather, one is only pointing to the structural, qualifying object–function of art as telltale of *aesthetic-how* reality. Whether 'allusiveness' (which I merely mention here)[17] correctly suggests that characteristic 'aesthetic' structural feature and will help bring order into the many varying, historical attempts to define 'aesthetic' should be tested, not by the out-dated criterion of universal acceptance, but by its catalytic fruitfulness among defining men and women of good will who are busy examining art.

---

[16]Paul Oskar Kristeller: *The Modern System of the Arts* (1951–2), reprinted in *Renaissance Thought II. Papers on Humanism and the Arts* (New York: Harper Torchbook, 1965), pp. 163–227; and Meyer H. Abrams: 'Art-as-such: the Sociology of an Aesthetic Concept', an address given at the fifth plenary session of the Fourth Congress on the Enlightenment, held at Yale University, July 1975.

[17]Cf. C. G. Seerveld: *A Turnabout in Aesthetics to Understanding* (Toronto: Institute for Christian Studies, 1974) and *Aesthetic Life and Artistic Task* (Toronto: Wedge Press, forthcoming) [published as *Rainbows for the Fallen World* (1980)].

5 Christian art*

Art that is Christian will be Christian art because the artwork meets the norm for art in the Lord's world and breathes a spirit of holiness which recognises that our creaturely existence plagued by sin needs to be reconciled back to God in Jesus Christ.

Holy spirited art in history

During early Bible times the Lord raised up choreographers (Exodus 15:20), sculptors (Exodus 25:9–40), silversmiths (Exodus 31:1–11), songwriters (Psalms), composers (2 Chronicles 5:11–14), story-tellers (Judges 9:7–20; also Christ with His parables), poets (cf. Isaiah 40), and artisans of many sorts (1 Kings 7:13–22), who made a joyful noise to the Lord and praised God's name with the artistry of their hands, unafraid of violating the commanding Sinai word against making stupid images that might tempt people to idolatry. Despite the ancient oratory (Genesis 4:23,24) and architecture (Genesis 11:1–9) that was a testimony of godless vanity, artistry was from the beginning a gift with which God endowed human creatures (cf. Adam's poem about Eve in Genesis 2:23); God wanted artistry to be exercised as an obedient and edifying caretaking of the materials, sounds, shapes, sights, words, gestures, and the like which God had provided for men and women to tend.

Catechetical art and iconoclasm

By the time the church became a world power under Constantine, who converted to the Christian faith as emperor (AD 313), arguments on whether images were incipient idolatry (Clement of Alexandria) or a proper, pictorial book of instruction for the illiterate (Gregory of Nyssa) had set the problematics for centuries of controversy on visual art.

Byzantine painting in Constantinople (after AD 330) synthesised earlier attempts at Christian art into a style of rich ornamentation but little figuration. The artisans employed to beautify the churches of Ravenna (sixth

---

*Entry in Walter A. Elwell (ed.), *Evangelical Dictionary of Theology* (Grand Rapids: Baker, 1984), pp. 82–4.

century), however, heirs perhaps of Syrian Christian insight, broke new ground in art. The monumentality of Graeco–Roman temples and the illusionistic depiction of actual things, common in hellenistic mimesis, were replaced by a simple, jewel-like splendour in mosaics that showed a sacramental quality. Whether human figures bearing gifts like magi or scenes of pastoral perfection representing the new earth were formed, the visible images of these Christian craftsmen seemed to make present and to certify a reality that was not yet visible. Even the originally Coptic, zoomorphic emblems of angel, lion, calf, and eagle for the evangelists bore a celebrative note that rather overpowered any didactic focus: the depictions and motifs in Ravenna are more richly liturgical than devotional.

The stand of Pope Gregory the Great (590–604) for catechetical use of images, a position later reaffirmed by the moderating Charlemagne (800–814), became embattled by the 726 edict of Emperor Leo III, which banned image worship; Leo's son, Constantine V (741–75), pursued a vigorous, outright iconoclastic policy that even suppressed images of the Virgin Mary. The Second Council of Nicaea (787), however, explicitly enunciated a doctrinal rehabilitation of images, using the precise distinction formulated by John of Damascus between veneration (*prosynesis*) for images and worship (*latria*) due to God alone. Although antipathy toward picturing God persisted strongly in the church until 867, gradually popular practice not only received the requisite doctrinal justification for using images to teach the Bible stories but also, in line with the neo-Platonic position of Pseudo-Dionysius adopted by John of Damascus, affirmed that holy images were a means of grace. Icons, especially of Christ – who had come to earth in visible flesh – became beloved as mnemonic, mesmerising aids, approved by the ecclesiastic hierarchy, for mediating communion between God and the ordinary worshipper.

Churched art and reformation

Monastic reform movements in the West from the tenth to twelfth century affected art with the ambivalence built in their combined tenets: *luxus pro Deo* (splendour for God, the Cluniac programme of temporal power) opposite mystical renunciation (the Cistercian and later Franciscan Orders). Romanesque architecture insulated a determinate, impenetrable space from the lighted, outside world. But subsequent Gothic building of cathedrals, with flying buttresses and stained-glass painting, embodied the principles of scholastic theology in which reason was meant to clarify faith with an exhaustive, concordant order that embraced everything under the sun and soared into a towering anonymity. The increasing presence of *Andachtsbilder*, cavernous *pietà* sculptures with relic overtones, and gargoyles hinted at an increasing individualistic and apprehensive fascination with the reality of death that stalked life.

A different spirit coursed through the *Canterbury Tales* of Geoffrey Chaucer, breathed in the graphic art of figures like Holbein, Dürer, Cranach, and Lucas van Leyden, and found shape in Huguenot psalmody of the Reformation. Now there was a colloquial bounce and an appreciation for creaturely phenomena and a joy of this earthly life lived before God's face, where faith was not seeking analogical understanding of the mysteries of God so much as itself providing a way to walk through the glories and miseries of historical turmoil. Unlike Dante's masterful, allegorical *Divina Commedia*, an *itinerarium mentis ad Deum* (the mind's road to God), Chaucer presents a kaleidoscope of society breathing pious grit and bawdy laughter that makes pilgrimage but does it with flesh and blood and peevishness. Following Luther's movement of institutional church reform, woodcuts and engravings began to flourish in northern Europe. Unlike sculpture and frescoes, art that was on paper lost the stigma of being an idol: you could hold the image in your hands and respond to its message anywhere, outside the precincts of the church. Luther's songs and the original psalm melodies of Louis Bourgeois and others in Geneva also drastically altered church music. Those who were not trained in Gregorian chant and its vocal decoration could now learn tunes with one note per syllable and with repeatable stanzas, so that song-praise came into the mouths of ordinary people, like folk-songs.

Although the Council of Trent (1545–63) reasserted the priority of churched art in all its mannerist, baroque splendour as a proper catechetical tool, the possibility for art to be Christianly spirited but not under church hegemony – a striking tenet of the Reformation – became a culturally important legacy. In the seventeenth century, painting in the Netherlands by Rembrandt, Vermeer, and many others gave viewers eyes to find blessing in what is homely and to see glory in the creaturely commonplaces of sky and water. The great poet John Milton altered the reforming movement by combining an independentist streak in Protestantism (cf. his treatises on divorce and *Areopagitica*) with an enormously educated classical and Christian humanism, so that the art which embodied such a hybrid world-and-life vision took intellectual pains to 'justify the ways of God to men' (in *Paradise Lost* and *Paradise Regained*). John Bunyan, however, became mouthpiece for an unadulterated biblical faith which was content to pass through life as a pilgrim while making progress not to an earthly Canterbury but toward the Heavenly City.

Confessional art after secular enlightenment

Cultural leadership passed out of Christian hands in Western civilisation as the deep-going secularising trends of mathematical and empiricistic science,

Encyclopaedist philosophy, and warring mercantilism came to dominate European life in the 1700s. Disciples of Christopher Wren still built churches in England with a delicate, refined gravity; Isaac Watts and the Wesley brothers wrote hymns of simplified quatrains that comforted the many poor in society with gospel; but pietism, also flourishing in Germany, inhibited Christians both from losing themselves in a show of art and from giving direction in such matters of sensibility. In the new world of America, however, an amalgam of neo-classical rationality and the transcendentalist idealism of Emerson could not stifle the resident Puritan consciousness of good struggling against the evil heart of darkness which surfaced in the rich, symbol-laden narratives of *The Scarlet Letter* (1850) and *Moby Dick* (1851) by Nathaniel Hawthorne and Herman Melville, respectively.

As industrialisation complicated and upset traditional cultural patterns of privilege, and as a spirit of positivism, along with inventions such as photographic cameras (c. 1830), faced art with the possibility of being levelled to mere fact, Christian artists like the Pre-Raphaelite Brotherhood in the mid-nineteenth century opted conservatively to fashion painting in an earlier illustrative style, with true-to-actual-daily-life detail and devout biblical or literary themes. Canvases like William Holman Hunt's *The Light of the World* came to serve as Victorian icons of sorts, mirrors to stimulate the viewer's subjective piety. The initiative of William Morris was more forward-looking, intent upon curing urban ugliness with good design and attention to craft; but the 'arts and crafts movement' still had a curious, old-fashioned, medieval feel to its programme even while it trimmed architectural form and decorative arts to uncluttered lines. When Christian artisans are not busy setting the cultural pace of their day but look for norms and patterns of relevance in the past, they either tend, it seems, to introduce the faith thematically for confession inside their art or to suffer from touches of obsolescence.

Christian art in a pragmatistic culture

Given the setback to cultural idealism in World War I and the profound jumble of avant-garde euphoria and huckster fashions since European dada and American jazz of the 1920s, the gradual supremacy of technocratic and commercialised interests over art has come to face professional artistry with a crisis: either art goes popular for a mass audience (television and tabloid), or art pulls back into an expensive, esoteric ghetto (the New York art gallery scene, for example). In such a pragmatistic and monopolistic context art that would be both viable and truly honouring of the Lord's Rule in history will be relatively rare and of exceptional quality, or it will find a marginal home in Christian communities outside the hardcore, secular mainstream.

The engravings and paintings of Georges Rouault reinvest the Byzantine tradition with a sombre, stained-glass seriousness that is definitely biblical in its horror of modern dehumanising atrocities, and is truly compassionate in composition, colour, and gritty style that bespeaks Christian art, whether the topic be kings, prostitutes, or Jesus Christ's passion. The Nobel Prize winner for poetry in 1945, Gabriela Mistral of Chile, updates a Franciscan holiness and gives it a poignant, singing voice that casts haloes of comfort around girlish hopes, forgotten prisoners, and even the nests of birds. Canadian painter William Kurelek weds a love for the Bruegel world of low life with a Roman Catholic slant on the poverty of success gained without the presence of the cross; his mark of pristine folk happiness is normally touched by an existential sense of nuclear war apocalypse, so the careful observer can never rest easy. Significant about such varied Christian art born out of Catholic sensitivities today is its unchurchly, world-wide, sorrow-sensitive aura.

A more hidden, 'autonomous', or even tangential expression of biblical faith in art of the twentieth century deserves mention: the sculpture of German Ernst Barlach articulates with rough austerity a forceful cry in wood and metal for reconciliation with God and neighbour that so incurred the anger of the Nazi government it destroyed much of the work. The New York Jew Abraham Rattner not only conceived an enormous stained-glass wall of apocalyptic emblems for a major Chicago synagogue but also grappled time and again in painting with the crucifixion of Christ, trying to exorcise both Golgotha and Auschwitz, as it were, from Jewish experience. Gabriel García Márquez of Colombia, 1982 Nobel prize winner for fiction, exposes small-town political corruption in South America with fantastic horizons that juxtapose real angels, supernatural forces, and the comic foibles of weak people.

The black spiritual song of American Civil War days takes on new evangelical fervour in the melodies and lyrics of Mahalia Jackson, whose simple Baptist roots act prophetically through the cascades of rhythmic beat and glorious sound. The paintings, prints, and constructions of Henk Krijger body forth reminiscences of both Bauhaus and German expressionism muted and melded into strong, restfully honed shapes and expertly chosen colours that reveal artistry integrated by the Reformation perspective that ordinary life is a vocation to be lived directly before God and to be redeemed while sharing sadness, humour, and hope.

New ferment and reforming categories

Anglo-Catholics everywhere continue to renew the age-old vocabulary of liturgical artistic service. Native people like the Indians and Eskimos of North America and many tribal cultures in Africa, who came to confess Jesus Christ as Lord through missionary efforts of the church, are finding in the current generation their own non-Western idiom for art that shares biblical faith. Mennonites and various holiness communions are now looking for ways to practise Christian art, since the mass media no longer make a secluded escape from artistic praxis feasible. Christian liberal arts colleges in North America have come to form important pocket communities across the land for developing alternative, Christian formation of poetry, painting, music, and theatre. Although the Nashville industry continues to break down Christian songwriters into formula sound that will sell well to the middle-class market, there are even large-scale events like the Greenbelt Festival in England which are probing pop and rock band music with an open-ended desire to find a truly new and powerful, integrated Christian art.

The old categories of 'sacred' and 'secular' are misleading, as if art could be first of all 'natural' or 'neutral', and then sometimes 'holy', if it is fitting for church or spells out a biblical message. It is indeed correct to understand that bona fide art may be appropriately harnessed or 'encapsulated' into the specially limited service of church (for liturgy), state (in monuments), or business (as advertising). But art-as-such, like a novel or music concert, ballet or theatre piece, is never uncommitted at the foundational level of human allegiance to Jesus Christ or to no-god. And art is not holy by virtue of its topic, any particular formula, or being blessed by church officials. When one realises that Christian art is artistry infused with a genuinely holy spirit, in contrast to art subtly dictated by a Hindu, Buddhist, Muslim, or secular humanist spirit worshipping human hands, then the matter of Christian art will be rightly recognised as the fragile task and fruit of obedience in history performed by gifted artisans within Christ's body at large in the world.

Bibliography

Barzun, Jacques. *The Use and Abuse of Art*. Princeton University Press, 1974.

Davie, Donald. *A Gathered Church: The Literature of the English Dissenting Interest, 1700–1930*. London: Routledge, Kegan & Paul, 1978.

Doumergue, Emil. *L'art et le sentiment dans l'oeuvre de Calvin* [1902]. Geneva: Slatkine Reprints, 1970.

Dyrness, William A. *Rouault: A Vision of Suffering and Salvation*. Grand Rapids, Mich.: Eerdmans, 1971.

Eliot, T.S. *The Sacred Wood: Essays on Poetry and Criticism*. London: Methuen, 1920.

Hagstrum, Jean H. *Sex and Sensibility: Ideal and Erotic Love from Milton to Mozart*. University of Chicago Press, 1980.

Harries, K. *The Meaning of Modern Art: A Philosophical Interpretation*. Evanston: Northwestern University Press, 1968.

Hughes, R. *The Shock of the New: Art and the Century of Change*. London: BBC, 1980.

Kitzinger, Ernst. 'The Cult of Images in the Age before Iconoclasm', in *Dumbarton Oaks Papers* 8 (1954), 83–150.

Mâle, Emil. *Religious Art from the Twelfth to the Eighteenth Century.* New York: Pantheon, 1949.

Panofsky, Erwin. *Gothic Architecture and Scholasticism* [1951]. New York: Meridian Books, 1957.

—. 'Comments on Art and Reformation', (1960) in *Symbols in Transformation,* Princeton: Princeton University Art Museum, 1969, pp. 97–116.

Rookmaaker, Hans R. *Art and the Public Today.* Huémoz-sur-Ollon: L'Abrié Fellowship Foundation, 1968.

—. *Modern Art and the Death of a Culture.* London: Inter-Varsity Press, 1970.

Visser 't Hooft, W.A. *Rembrandt and the Gospel,* trans. K. Gregor Smith. New York: Meridian Books, 1960.

Wencelius, Léon. *Calvin et Rembrandt.* Paris: Société d'Edition 'Les Belles Lettres', n.d.

6 A Generation of the Arts before and after 1984 AD*

It is a sign of our times that Surrealism in art looks old-fashioned today. Good folk talk about 'Freudian slips' and the id in normal conversation, and nobody seems to get too upset about the juxtaposition in *Time* magazine of an atrocity photographed in El Salvador placed near a slick ad for Dubonnet liquor. We have become so accustomed to the bizarre in ordinary life and to trivialisation of things deeply human that 'modern art' like Surrealism, in the museum, looks and is *passé*.

Arts like painting, sculpture, and even concert music, have also been shunted off to the side, away from the focus of public cultural attention since the end of World War II, by the increasing and overwhelming popularity of cinema, television, and the hi-fi record industry. Wealthy people may still buy original art as an investment, but most of us have to make do in art with what is mechanically mass-produced, or frequently repeated (like a theatre performance). And this fact of life, that art is tied today as never before to what individual people can and want to afford, is directly relevant to what is going to happen to the arts in the generation after 1984.

★   ★   ★

In 1945, one could say, New York became the capital of art ferment in the world, instead of Paris and European cities which were recovering from the war. With the dominance of the United States in painting, for example, came a brash disregard for the history of art form.

Already back before World War I artists like Picasso, Matisse and Kandinsky had led the avant-garde into explorations which began to change the traditional face of painting and sculpture. But Picasso, Mattise and Kadinsky around 1910 were trying to paint and sculpt their contemporary world with a contemporary consciousness. They were not in revolt against art history so much as in earnest to follow up the artistic challenge of the Impressionist painters and van Gogh and Cézanne, to rid art of the stilted romanticism and aura of luxurious indulgence with which nineteenth-century idealist commitments

*First published as 'Can Art Survive the Secular Onslaught?' in *Christianity Today* 25 (17 July 1981), 968–9, 971–2.

had blessed art. Cubist painting was basically an attempt to mint afresh the standard painterly vocabulary of nuanced composition, enriched colour schemes, and the telling impasto of brushstroke texture, all to deepen one's vision of the twentieth-century lived world. Their shock effect came mostly from the uneducated reaction of the public which was ill-prepared to let go of its magazines filled with ideals, its conviction that the norm for painting was picturesque beauty and that novels should have happy endings. Braque, Brancusi and Stravinsky were not revolutionaries; they only did art with an honest secularity that disturbed comfortable people.

But after two world wars, avant-garde artists came to the fore in New York circles who were revolutionaries, and who made their predecessors look tame by comparison. Jackson Pollock (1912–56) dripped paint onto canvas laid flat on the floor and made it impossible to connect what he was doing with the history of European art crafted since the Renaissance. Willem de Kooning (born 1904) swerved humanoid shapes of paint across spaces that looked simultaneously fleshly and environmental, and critic Harold Rosenberg gave such dislocated splashes of loaded paint-brushes and drip-dry techniques the name and thenceforth pedigree of 'action painting'. Pollock and de Kooning artwork spearheaded an effort, it seemed, to do art that had no precedent, that intentionally censored out the pictorial dimension of artistic painting, and compensated for the loss with a deadly serious, violent, gigantic histrionics in the techniques of raw paint. It was as if the dominant American style of the 1950s, 'Abstract Expressionism', meant to echo the unprecedented explosions of atomic bombs dropped on Hiroshima and Nagasaki in the 1940s, blotting out the memory of Puritan America and even the sunny rationalism of its Declaration of Independence and Bill of (human) Rights.

During the next decade, partly in reaction perhaps, the so-called 'New York School' came to blanket the art-world, that is, the art market of musea, prestigious corporate foundations, and art galleries of New York. The artists who were now fêted by and large reduced their concerns to purely formal matters and riveted their attention solely upon a manipulating finesse with the media of painting. Mark Rothko's (1903–70) cloud beds of shimmering, palpitating colour were still to be taken as invitations to contemplative meditation on Nothing in particular. But Kenneth Noland (born 1924), Ellsworth Kelly (born 1923), Frank Stella (born 1936) and others experimented in the 1960s with stark, simplified designs, incredibly bold stripes of colour; they pushed and pulled shapes into strikingly novel patterns that were first and foremost rigorous exercises in painterly elements (cf. a master pianist playing scales on the piano), nothing more. Critic Clement Greenberg had the position of cultural power at *Partisan Review, Art News,* and *Artforum,* however, to inflate such exercises into icons for the times. Greenberg naturally demythologised 'colour-field' painting, 'minimal' or 'hard-edge' art, appropriately for the

Plate 21 Seerveld with Mary-Leigh Morbey, Professor of Art at Redeemer College, lecturing at the Association d'art des universités du Canada in Halifax, Nova Scotia, 1987

secular setting, but the disciples who flocked to the money springing from this fountain of constructing puzzles and games that did fascinating tricks to one's eyes always tried to maintain at least a Wittgensteinian level of fascination to their art. Nobody pays van Cliburn simply for playing scales or a painter for painting squares, unless the act has been somehow souped up into a fetish.

Also complicating the past twenty-five years of modern art has been the presence on the American scene of what can only be called anarchist art. Rauschenberg (born 1925) combined junk with paint and great imagination to startle onlookers into doing a double-take toward what then became an unforgettable image: a besmirched, stuffed goat stuck in a discarded, spare tyre, or a slept-in bed splattered with goo and paint and hung on a wall, gave you a queer sense that sex or a national emblem or something important was being desecrated, anonymously as it were, but you couldn't be sure. Warhol (born 1930) picked up on the banality of mass-produced Campbell Soup cans and

Marilyn Monroe's kissable face and traded on the novelty, for a few years, of blowing up insignificance to billboard proportions of fame, until he himself became a parody of his PR self, and 'pop art' slipped back into the cheap advertising morass from which it came.

Happenings, documented 'earthwork art', photo-realism, and 'conceptual art' on into the 1970s have often depended more upon promotion gimmicks and the people St Paul (cf. Acts 17:21) and P.T. Barnum talked about than upon artistically honed skill and insight. But it is a superficial judgement to think that the artists are the ones who were fooled or to say that this tradition of dada art in America is meaningless. Anarchism is not nonsense, not even in art. It is the nihilistic side of hedonism.

And that might be a way to sum up the main streams of modern art since 1945 and all the trendy isms that have been in effect in painting and sculpture while *Christianity Today* has existed with subscribers. With important exceptions, avant-garde art in America has tried to break down the iron-clad conventions which have boxed art in from being democratically flexible and germane to our motorised, commercialised, fast-paced life where the medium is the message. Art of the generation before 1984 AD has tried to destroy – whether it be in the heroics of 'action painting', the controlled exercises of 'minimal art' or in the genial pranks of Oldenburg (born 1929) and Lichtenstein (born 1923) – destroy the mentality of pompous sculpture and the sacrosanct rules of order and propriety in the genre of painting.

The double trouble with this tack is that the art of our current generation, which aimed to cut the inviolate privilege of High Art down to size and challenged its dated irrelevance and patronage, assumed, in so far as it succeeded, the very same kind of élitist, cultural tyranny, even more isolated from the real issues of life than the traditional art it faulted. New York formalism fought its tempests in the Soho teapot while the civil rights struggle took place in the streets, and how could 'conceptual art' continue to crack its bad jokes after the murder of Martin Luther King? How can Christo Jaracheff (born 1935) still dare 'wrap up' a million square feet of Australian coastline in plastic tied by rope when there is world starvation? It is a real question too whether the American art which came of technocratic age during 1945–80 has not been co-opted by the power of technique and painted its *artistic* self into a corner.

★ ★ ★

What will happen in art between now and 2020 AD, if the Lord waits to return, depends partly upon where the current teenagers and college graduates will find their artistic roots and upon how wise artistic leadership becomes in the world after 1984. History is neither a predetermined blueprint we need to approximate with an educated guess, nor is the future a blank cheque, utterly unknown. The truth is that God blesses cultural obedience with good fruit, and

God punishes the vanity of godless men and women with frustration and ruin and takes God's gifts away from those who bury such talents in the ground. (God uses people like Cyrus to work God's will too.) At least this is the way the Bible tells it (cf. Isaiah 45, Jeremiah 35, Matthew 25, James). And I believe that norm holds true also for art. So what happens in the next twenty-five years in painting, music, theatre, architecture, sculpture, ballet, narrative and other arts, depends upon how obedient to God's law for art the artistic leaders and their followers in the coming generation be. A few things are fairly certain.

1. There will be more of the same for a while, simply because of cultural inertia and because the Lord takes his time in punishing disobedience. Avant-garde art since 1945 may be dead, but it is still not buried. And musea the world over house pieces of the relics, dealers have large inventories to unload, and it will indeed take a convincing band of prophets to prove the emperor has no clothes on before the monopoly has to jettison its investment to cut its losses.

Even though New York art essentially reduced itself to problems of design and has gone out of its way to be useless, commanding the price of jewels, the legitimacy of fine decoration and the aesthetic reality of ornaments gives its experiments some right to exist, even though its cup of artistic meaning will never be able to flow over. But if decorative exercises ask to be treated like bona fide artworks, after a while the boredom they induce will bring them the oblivion their pride deserves.

As for the anarchist streak in the wit which has at least enlivened the art gallery scene: God knows we shall need humour in 1984, and entertainment is indeed a worthy pastime; but art must be more than an entertaining event to last, and the laughter promoted by the legacy of Marcel Duchamp (1887–1968) is one that is arbitrarily cruel. The mild sadism of neo-dada and the enervating masochism of much 'pop art' is as wasteful of time as certain i ching music of John Cage (born 1912). We may be hopeful that the audience of novitiates for this art will continue to shrink.

2. Art that is explicitly harnessed to specific use will come to be dominant in society, because the pragmatist spirit is the most vital, secular cultural force presently at work in the world. And pragmatism is a protean dynamic that does not rest until whatever it touches is useful for this or useful for that, testing the truth of a cultural product by its societal instrumentality.

This would mean that professional art and its expense must pass the test of utility and guaranteed audience. Monumental sculpture for commemorative occasions, murals on the outer walls of buildings to beautify the city streets, and agit-prop theatre would be in. But novels would be hard put to justify their existence unless they be best-sellers with an Uncle Tom's Cabin type of point; concerts just for listening would be up for grabs, unless as benefits; and easel oil paintings, lyric poetry, and old-fashioned Shakespeare – what are they good for?

Totalitarian governments already have a pragmatist policy on art: the state dance troupe (like the national airline) is used to win prestige abroad and to act like a bread-and-circus safety valve for the tribes at home; paintings and prints are tolerated if they become posters for the ruling party. But less politicised and closer to home: who reading these lines finds it responsible to recommend to his or her child, 'For God's sake, become an artist,' to compose music, chisel sculpture, or write novels for a living? The wandering Chinese poets, troubadours with their lyres, the guild of cabinet-makers, or the bohemian painter living on French bread and a glass of wine, are things *of the past.* Already now, if your art is not a specialised community service hooked into a financial or state network, you cannot live, as an artist, a normal, responsible life.

3. Performance art and artistic acts that are mass-reproducible will gradually crowd out everything else in Western civilisation done by professional artists, because the curse of collectivism and the annihilation of objects as unique valuables is part and parcel of the regime effected by the technocratic idol our culture as a whole at heart serves, with or without militarism.

This means that paintings of individual canvases (like single family dwellings) may disappear as a major art genre just as the art of landscape gardening did after the eighteenth century; the painterly art could be absorbed into advertising or revert to illuminating (= illustrating) the text of books. And hand-carved sculpture may try to stay alive by becoming an appendage of architecture, like a frieze; or sculptors may become consultants to those who build the Stonehenges of America, the multiple-level, intertwined cloverleaf of highways near major cities. Dramatists and choreographers who buy the centralising handwriting on the wall will reconceive their art (as Balanchine is already doing) to fit the TV screen, so different from the theatrical stage we still know. At best there will be pieces like Reginald Rose's *Twelve Angry Men* (1954) and the recent CBC ballet-choir rendition of Carl Orff's *Catulli Carmina* (1981). At worst there will be spectacular kitsch, with high audience ratings.

4. Current American hegemony in the arts will (reluctantly, perhaps with angry, violent bitterness) pass away, because the empire of the United States in the world is due to end, and there is a spirit in South America, Asia, and among many different native peoples in the world of aspiring to a deeper quality of life with the arts as *they* conceive art, if only they could breathe culturally for a generation-long period free from the repressive constriction of Communist terror *and* from the Western blight of hamburgers, plastic, transistor radios, ballpoint pens and coke. (This is so even if many cultural leaders in the USA do not know it.)

It is possible that the poignant painting going on right now in Eastern European countries, underground as it were, in spite of Russian occupation, and captivating fictional narrative like that of Gabriel García Márquez (born 1928), *Cien Años de Soledad* (1967), who recently had to flee for his life his Colombian homeland, will never survive the demise of Superpower art: what we cannot treat as esoteric or lionise on a talk-show may simply be pulled down with the Titanic. And Buddhist, Hindu, Islamic and Oriental art may not have the consistency to withstand the hideous strength of our secularism, but their pagan pedigree could offer other prospects for reform than New York glitter.

★ ★ ★

For the sake of a few righteous in the secular city of art the Lord might still do wonders there in the generation after 1984, and prove judgements 2 and 3 above be wrong. But our record as evangelical Christians in this area of God's Kingdom has not been good: we have had other priorities. (That is why the devil works so well in the arts today among the younger generation.) The conversations of a few superstars does not change the pattern of pop song and rock music on the air waves and in the record shops. It takes a generation of artists with a common perspective to shape an alternate artistic style. And our art critics are tempted to make blanket, negative judgements (so too Ellul in *Le futur indéfini* against Klee, Beckett, Chagall and Bergman, *L'Empire du Non-Sens*), missing rich figures like Barlach, Rivera, Hopper, Brecht, Paton, Rattner, Krijger, those who have suffered much in swimming against the stream. We Christians on the sidelines have a lot of repenting to do when it comes to the arts, I believe.

What needs to come first is the vision that the arts are a 'reasonable service' for the Christian community as we tend creation for the Lord in His absence and break the bread of life to our neighbour, no matter how dark the night become. And then *the christian artists among us* – not the theorists – in concert with Christian art historians, Christian art critics and aestheticians, along with wise spectators, will take self-conscious soundings for fruitful, if aborted, art movements in history and solid artistic figures who may serve as an inspiring cloud of witnesses as they lead us all gently into the coming years. Thank God there is still time, also in the next quarter century of *Christianity Today*, God willing, to gird up our artistic loins as Christians and begin to run this race too in earnest.

Bibliography

Ellul, Jacques. *L'Empire du Non-Sens*. Paris: Presses Universitaires de France, 1980.

Elsen, Albert E. *Origins of Modern Sculpture: Pioneers and Premises*. New York: George Braziller, 1974.

Hughes, Robert. *The Shock of the New*. London: BBC, 1980.

Kramer, Hilton. *The Age of the Avant-garde: An Art Chronicle of 1956–1972*. New York: Farrar, Strauss & Giroux, 1973.

Rosenblum, Robert. *Modern Painting and the Northern Romantic Tradition*. London: Thames & Hudson, 1975.

7   Comic Relief to Christian Art*

Scripture gives us an amusing description of a lazy person. The lazy person turns over in bed the way a door creaks open on its hinges. The lazy person lets the hand sink down into a bowl of food but finds it just about exhausts him or her to bring it back to the mouth. Such a person cries, 'There is a lion in the road! There is a lion in the streets!'

The writer goes on to say (Proverbs 26:16) that the sluggard thinks he or she is wiser than any seven discerning persons taken together; yet here the person is, saying, 'I'm not going to go outside, not me! There's a lion out there!' A lazy person can make fantastic excuses for not going to work, can dream up the most elaborate rationalisations for his inactivity. 'There's a lion outside the door!' So Scripture pokes fun at the person.

A quite different situation occasioned the celebrated laughter of Sarah. When Jehovah told Abraham his ninety-year-old wife would still have a baby, he laughed, and later on she laughed, her joy mixed with incredulity, just as Christ's disciples are reported to have been amazed, not believing because of their joy, when Christ suddenly appeared in the room with them after the resurrection. Sarah, like some Christians today, felt guilty about laughing and lied about it, though after Isaac was born (Isaac means 'laughter') she said believingly, 'God made me laugh so that all who hear about it will laugh with me.'

Laughing along with Sarah – that is the direction our thinking and encouraging of Christian art should take. What makes something funny? The element of incongruity is certainly central; the unexpected juxtaposition or intersection of opposites sets up a humorous state of affairs. Once I ate dinner opposite Gerbrandy, the iron-willed wartime Prime Minister of the Netherlands, who flinched not a bit before the Nazis. I watched him with his huge, white, handlebar moustache sip hot tomato soup and try to keep stray whiskers from getting red. Incongruity! Great courage and dinner-table helplessness.

Exaggeration, too – whether it be that of the Coney Island mirrors that distort the viewer's anatomy, making him or her lopsided and pin-headed with monstrous feet, or the lion-in-the-street impossibility – is an element of humour. Whenever exaggeration is patently false or a grand pretence is punctured, there are the makings of comedy. This is why teachers, preachers, and other people of authority are good prospects for the deflation of laughter. The

---

*First published in *Christianity Today* 12:11 (March 1968), 5324–36.

holes in human importance easily show through. The comical has a way of appropriately levelling people.

But there is always a framework of seriousness behind what is funny. Perhaps it is only the plodding determination of a year–old child to walk, step … step … step, till he or she abruptly stumbles and falls on his or her face in the grass, a delightfully comical, pleasant failure to a young mother marvelling at the fruit of her womb. There must always be some kind of background security, responsible purpose, or norm that gets broken, frustrated, undone, to deliver the element of surprise that is built into something funny. This is why art, if it is indeed intrinsically metaphorical in relating dissimilars, has, because of its serious, constantly surprising character, a subliminal laughter in its products.

Now it is a fact that the same comic discrepancies in reality can be conceived and shared either in Christian charity or in non-Christian disdain. Nietzsche epitomises the delighting scorn a keen observer of human frailties can voice. Jonathan Swift's righteous satire, Daumier's softer yet biting political caricatures, some of Picasso's violent derangements of figures – all these testify to a severe judgement on the out-of-joint character of society. There is ice in their laughter, a touch of the ridicule that the old revolutionary sophist Gorgias recommended – destroying the seriousness of your enemies with laughter and their laughter with seriousness. But the cold remoteness of such a comic critique of life betrays a restless spirit foreign to the biblical gentleness of rejoicing with those who rejoice and weeping with those who weep (Romans 12:15). Such critically comic art and literature seems to play the supercilious moraliser it rightly condemns. I do not mean to suggest that the happily-ever-after endings are a mark of a Christian grasp of reality, or that a tragic, humourless vision like Wagner's bespeaks God's world. I just mean that there is a secular, high-handed, polished, black humour that is deep, that bites deep, and that does not heal.

Much modern art, from music to sculpture to poetry, seems to have lost any sense of humour, to have become so professionalistic that it has its head in a bag of double sharps, acetylene torches, and polyglot acrostics. We should not wish to make jokes about abstract, drip-and-drag art, or about difficult atonal music; that would reveal the tasteless pride of a Christian who does not know the deep agony of hopelessness that has gone into some of these contorted creations. But it is worth noticing that, when art has lost the naive sense of humour, fun, and sheer joy, there is little to protect it from becoming bizarre or barren. And then humourless contemporary art seems to go to one of two ends: either 'The Big Mouth' (Revelation 13:5), where it experiments, sexualises, casts about into dark mythologies with its false prophetic word, becoming something that is absurd for hanging in museums or treating respectfully between hard covers; or a nervous tittering, the unravelled conclusion in pop, op, and bop art to what are indeed the valuable, purging innovations of a Kandinsky, Mondrian, or Stravinsky. One can laugh in art galleries, book

Plate 22 Poster for Seerveld's address, designed by Robin Jentzen

stores, and concert halls today; but often this laughter is not so much comic relief as an embarrassed response to the nitrous oxide and frenetic tickling of tricksters making the popularity circuit.

Christian art does not and will not succumb to the secular sickness and the positivistic inheritance of the Renaissance-schooled intelligence with its ideal of harmony, nor to the Romantic revolutionary and his affinity for anarchy and meaninglessness. Christian art is born out of a perspective revealed in the

357

eighth chapter of Proverbs, where Wisdom says: 'And there I was, all playfulness, laughing daily, continually, before God's face, playing with the inhabited portion of the earth? I enjoyed myself with humankind.'

That is, the biblical Christian is not bluffed by the fashion of Big Mouths or the whine of chitter-chatter, because he or she knows that from the beginning God was in Christ reconciling the world to Godself, and that therefore our created situation is not hopeless – it is an arena in which God's trustworthy grace covers people of faith like a cloak till Christ comes back to earth and finishes righting the broken world that we inhabit. The human condition, to the eye of biblical faith, is funny! Not that sin is a humorous matter, nor that God's covenanting, jealous anger is not a terrifying reality, nor that the evils of war and rumours of war are not enough to freeze the smiles on little girls' faces. But this: revelation shows unmistakably the childish folly of us two-legged people trying so hard to walk by ourselves and falling flat on our faces with our lion-tired rationalisations and our exaggerated estimate of our strivings. Revelation makes clear the joke God has played on humankind, how in a little Jewish baby God answered the questions that for centuries have taxed the brains of the greatest philosophers. And to top off the incongruity, for the ultimate rule of God's world God chooses, not the especially intelligent, gifted, or good-looking people, but the apparently foolish, the weak, the meek.

Furthermore, these followers of faith are it seems, misfits, people who are able to rejoice at death, suffering, and daily persecution when they could be carefree, who thrive on marriage but act as if they were not married, who intensely enjoy the world but can let it go (1 Corinthians 7:29 ff.). This sainthood business is a joke. Disciples of Christ cut the figure of a clown in the world; they are buffoons, going the extra mile, turning the other cheek.

Yet it is this comical reality – funny because God's hand cradles the whole inexplicable, laughing, homely matter in certain hope – this delightful surprise of mercies each new morning despite our sin, that deserves creative artistic form. This kind of buoyancy should typify Christian art.

By comic relief to Christian art, I do not mean an anecdotal temper, a reformed take-off on Salvador Dali's mystifying practical jokes in art, or even Ionesco's visionary dramatic enigmas. Rather, I mean that Christian art – one must be careful not to dictate its forms apriori – in the spirit of Schütz, Bach, Melville, Alan Paton, Rouault, will disclose a spirit of holy contentment not gone to comfortable seed, an apocalyptic prophecy that still encourages reconciliation. It has in it the joyful victory laughter of Psalm 126 sung *before* the final battle, though perhaps mute in time of deep trouble; the relief in toil of Romans 8 ('nothing can separate us from the love of God in Christ Jesus our Lord'); the incredulous, quiet, humanly sinful but forgiven joy of Sarah. This sin-sensitive, Father-in-heaven-comforted comic relief *will* come through subtly in Christian art.

Too often artistically talented young Christians hover on the edges of the church. There seems to be little room for them within a given evangelical communion; they are asked to squeeze their lump of art somehow into a liturgical shape – if they cannot, then what is it good for? This unhappy situation, which is generally foreign to Roman and Anglo–Catholic communions, comes from the inability of most evangelical churches to know how to laugh Christianly or to recognise that there is more to our Father's world than piously delimited space.

There *are* lions in the city streets and country roads of America today. But our task as Christians is to go outside – our Lord is at hand! – to judge what we see in the name of Jesus Christ, to trample lions under foot, and thus to be built up in the faith. Otherwise, what we are inescapably exposed to culturally will judge us on the Last Day. This means that those interested in art must find out what the colour signature of Matisse, or an Emil Nolde, is saying, that they must study the verse form of Hopkins, Emily Dickinson, Alan Ginsberg, and T.S. Eliot, to discern what is excellent and what is not. We may neither flirt indiscriminately with our cultural surroundings (cf. Matthew 6:13) nor try to escape earth for an ivory palace (1 Corinthians 5:10). Here and now we must let the compassionate, purifying love of Christ in us spill over into our daily experience and into every sensation we feel (Philippians 1:9), including our appreciation of art. Here too Christ must rule.

Yet for the Christian community, critique is not enough. Especially those believers who are true to the fundamentals of the faith once delivered to the saints must busy themselves with the positive, full-orbed witness of praise. And if art is anything, according to the Old Testament psalms, it is a vehicle of praise. But art will not grow Christianly strong within evangelical circles unless people see that the proper ministry of art is first of all not evangelising but a praising edification (the root meaning is rough-hewn, earthy building up, not cloying, heavenly platitudes), and unless the Church does not expect full-blown Christian masterpieces from its young artists in the first generation but has the wisdom to be happy with little artistic comic reliefs.

Evangelical Christians should not take themselves too seriously just because they take Christ's mission in the world very seriously. The legitimate 'burden for souls' needs the relaxing biblical perspective that all things present as well as future belong to us, and we 'are Christ's, and Christ is God's' (1 Corinthians 3: 21–3). Therefore, let us work out our everlasting salvation with fear and trembling – and with Sarah's holy laughter.

We Bible-believers do not need an up-to-date dialectical theology that is really as old as the hills, nor do we need to learn to speak with a secular voice to a dechristianised world. What we really need to know is how to laugh for God's sake. Then Christian art, because of its intrinsic comic relief, will be both evidence of the evangelical community's robust faith and a pointer toward the way God's people should go.

8 Cal Looks at Nick: A Response to Nicholas Wolterstorff's *Art in Action**

1. Overview

Perhaps a good way to help a prospective reader understand this carefully written book is to say it details an ontology of art. The core of the argument consists, in my judgement, in the exposition of 'fittingness' and in a description of the artist's 'action of world-projection' (pp. 96–150). These points on 'fittingness' and the artist's 'action of world-projection' are complemented by a running commentary which is critical of Western society's having institutionalised art, our virtually confining fine art to the High Art of musea and concert halls for aesthetic contemplation by an élite. Wolterstorff wants to restore a full, widely diverse, functioning-in-society approach to art. The instrumentality of artworks is a key, underlying thesis. He self-consciously pursues both his critique of the artistic status quo and his ontology of art-in-action as a participant in the Calvinist tradition of human cultural responsibility in history (pp. 78,177).

2. Method

Everything is written with exacting terminological care. You can practically trust the prose that there will be no conceptual confusions. The precision which results from various logical excursions in the text (and in the appendix on 'an expression of', 'expressive of' and 'self-expression') might be daunting for those of us not so trained, but the disciplined clarity of presentation is truly admirable.

Paired with this meticulous care is a disarming casualness. 'Let us say that aesthetic contemplation is …' so-and-so. 'Let me now for the sake of convenience introduce a bit of terminology.' That such a manner is usually not innocent, simply for the nonce, shows up in the control these informal definitions have upon the shape of the argument and the conclusions reached. For

---

*Review of Nicholas Wolterstoff, *Art in Action* (Grand Rapids, Mich.: Eerdmans, 1980), published in *Vanguard* 10:6 (Nov.–Dec.) 1980), 18–19. The same issue held a parallel review by Wolterstorff of Seerveld's *Rainbows for the Fallen World*.

example, which factors of an artwork are 'irrelevant to *aesthetic* evaluation' are determined 'by definition' (p. 159); and that definition of 'aesthetic' has been generated by earlier 'Let us say' (pp. 17–18) and 'for the sake of convenience' statements (p. 42).

Another important example of what is at stake in terms: a 'state of affairs' is not taken to mean any given creaturely reality that can serve as a touchstone to test human subjectivity; but 'A state of affairs may be described as *a way things can or cannot be*. So far as I can see, there *are* such ways' (p. 131). Such use of the term 'state of affairs' allows it to function as a linchpin in Wolterstorff's ontology of imagined worlds and to shape his main answer as to why humans produce art (p. 145).

There is nothing illegitimate here. Every philosopher needs terms and definitions. It may just be important for a reader to realise (1) that 'Let us say' statements in this book are frequently what Aristotle identifies as unargued, primary *premises*; and (2) that definitions, also informal definitions, like stone fences, have a way of walling in and walling out neighbours in a discussion.

I think too that this engaging, casual manner of introducing analysis reveals a fixed philosophical methodology it would be fair to call 'instrumentalist'. Wolterstorff mentions in the section on 'Norms in Art' that he has 'adopted a *qualified* instrumentalist theory of *artistic* value' and of 'aesthetic excellence' (p. 158). I must admit I feel uneasy about how such methodological praxis may affect the root meaning of truth in a Christian philosophy of knowledge about art. (I say this realising my own claim, that there needs to be a characteristically biblical, jealous view of truth applicable to aesthetic theory, may strike an 'instrumentalist' as ill-conceived or as the 'essentialist fallacy' (pp. 7–8,18; cf. my *Rainbows for the Fallen World*, pp. 105–09).

3. Systematic crux

Art in Action is intended as an analytic probe into the basic structural nature of art: 'It is my goal in this book to dig beneath the particulars of how art functions in our society, and beneath the particulars of how art functions in other societies, down to what is universal in art' (p. 11).

Two main judgements emerge. (1) The basic framework for our approach to art should be that 'works of art are instruments and objects of action', on the part of the artist and on the part of the public, and *not*, first of all, that artworks are in fact a particular kind of cultural response that bodies forth human (probably faulty) praise of the true God or (possibly brilliant) service to an idol (pp. 84–90). (2) Thanks to the marvellous power of envisagement God gave us humans – 'envisagement' is an excellent word to replace Coleridge's clumsy 'esemplastic imagination' – the 'world' imagined and projected by artists in their works 'is the most pervasive and important of the actions that artists perform' (pp. 122,130–34).

I continue to wonder why, with respect to the first main judgement, it is so important for Wolterstorff to oppose what he names 'the Protestant view' and to go out of his way (with an exegesis of Romans 1:18–32 that strikes me as forced) to reject the position that religion is the inescapable, defining structure of humankind such that all of a human's actions are actually allegiance to the Holy Spirit or driven by the vanity of sin. I wonder why, especially because he affirms that *the world behind* an artwork (that complex of what an artist and his or her community believe) is 'often' confirmed in *the world of* the work (pp. 89–90,144). Is this polemic necessary? Or, more pointedly (and I don't mean it rhetorically), must this attempt to honour the full, mixed, historical embeddedness of art in our day of fragmenting secularity entail a denial that art is always an expression of faith-vision and that such expression is necessarily of primary concern?

On the second main systematic judgement, regarding the artist's 'action of world-projection', let me only observe that 'projection' is a very modern, post-Romantic formulation of the age-old problem of *mimesis* (p. 123), and it seems to keep stage-centre, curiously enough, the benefit of art's being there for 'consideration' (p. 134), the very purpose art-in-action was meant to relativise, namely, the (perceptual or non-perceptual) 'contemplation that satisfies' (pp. 10,44,83). It is also said that 'pure' music and 'abstract' art are artefacts that are not (ever?) used for projecting imagined worlds (p. 122). If this were so (although I am not convinced 'pure' music and 'non-representational' painting lack such a correlate, imaginary world of meaning), and if it includes 'pure' dance and 'abstract' sculpture as well as architecture (although architecture is not considered a bona fide fine art for the purposes of this book (pp. 7,38)), then such exceptions would seriously impede the theory, it seems to me, from getting at 'what is universal in art'.

4. Historiographic judgement

A brief review cannot do justice to the eloquent indictment made in this book of the sins of the modern art world, its institutional establishment of covetous pride in fine art. The piety and deep Christian commitment of the author spill over into numberless insights backed up by an immense amount of first-hand contact with High Art and 'low art', from African masks to John Barth. A reader and a reviewer can only simply be thankful to God for the testimony offered.

But I question the historiographic interpretation made of the development toward art as we know it at the Tarragon theatre, Harbour Front poetry readings, and art gallery. In my judgement it is not idiosyncratic (pp. 67,178) but normative in any developing civilisation for art to come institutionally into its own as art, just as it is normative for education in a developing civilisation to be differentiated into school institutions for education-as-such in society. Our Christian critique should fault the élitist idolatry and wilful hermeticism of musea and concert hall in Western culture but not its institutionality.

Because of the ambivalence and *fallenness* of our *institution* of high art, which Wolterstorff points out with biblical penetration (pp. 192–3), some of us believe we should not be content as Christians with the strategy of enjoying the peculiarity of new music so long as we spend time beautifying the city streets, or rest with participating in the world of high art, gingerly, saved by knowing it is food offered to idols, while making certain we balance it by developing a richer liturgy in the church. Yes, indeed. But do we not need the horizon both in our theory and in our praxis of throwing our Christian energies into *instituting Christian art galleries* with *institutional formations* appropriate in our day to reformation of the particular societal arena? just as we Reformed people have the theory and praxis of free, differentiated, alternate *Christian institutions* for learning-as-such in society – schools, colleges and universities (cf. *Rainbows*, pp. 182–4).

5. Questions for opening discussion

The remarks Wolterstorff makes about the institution of high art also hold, he hints, for our world of professional, academic philosophising (p. 208). With that in mind I alter his moving diagnosis on page 61 to read: 'The institution of high professional philosophy is a profoundly secular institution – with the result that the philosopher who identifies himself deeply with some religious community will constantly have the experience of being a divided self living in two worlds. The institution of high professional academic philosophy is a jealous god!'

No Christian philosopher in aesthetic theory wants to be double-minded and divided against oneself. It would help us much in pursuing an integrated Christian aesthetic theory, I think, if it could be shown how the 'theoretical equipment' (p. 132) of art-as-instrument for-action-use is cause-generated by his basic Reformed world-and-life view. Otherwise, where does this proposed strategy as 'the basic framework' for our Christian approach to art come from?

I ask myself whether Wolterstorff's strong drive to emphasise the rightful, relative, multiple place of (fine) art in society has not let him mistake a necessary external relation of art for its definitive internal structure. I also wonder whether a more developed Christian *philosophical cosmology* (beyond the matter of 'fittingness') – creation order holds during historical change – might not help furnish us with a stance on norms for art that does not remain with an 'instrumentalist' conception of good art (p. 158).

There are more 'good' questions to ask, because *Art in Action* is a serious attempt to move us onward toward a Christian aesthetic theory.

9   Affairs of the Art*

This well-written book based on the 1984 London Lectures in Contemporary Christianity raises the current level of Christian discussion about the arts. The six authors know from the inside what they are talking about: contemporary painting, television, rock music, theatre and literature. They are that unusual breed of Christian artists who are reflective, historically grounded, biblically sensitive, and unassumingly articulate.

Painterly wisdom

The essay by painter and wood-engraver Peter Smith is alone worth the price of the book. He knows his Rookmaaker, C. S. Lewis, and Peter Fuller, but the biblical wisdom he speaks with grace and simplicity is all his own. Making paintings must never be the prime concern of a Christian's life, he says, but making visual artworks can be legitimately a serious, dedicated act of service to Christ and one's neighbour, even if the paintings are not authenticated by the secular art establishment. Painterly art by Christians must not become 'a kind of religious advertising', and should never be equated with or reduced to 'a clear message, *in verbal terms*'. Painters are called to respond imaginatively to God, as Adam did in naming the animals, by helping others to 'share the delight God has in God's own creation'.

So many things are well put: 'Art is a good servant but a bad master.' 'Tradition of itself is not negative. More often than not it provides the continuity and mind-set from which that which is remarkable springs.' 'There is, though, a certain mentality which views the fallenness of the world as justification for growing vegetables in the garden because they can be eaten but not flowers because they have no "use".'

Peter Smith has the charity to say, as a gifted painter who has suffered the indifference of fellow Christians, that painters who believe it is responsible to provide for one's family and for those in need may need themselves to seek alternative employment. Such testimonies of sacrificial love are rare.

---

*A review of Tim Dean and David Porter (eds.), *Art in Question* (London: Marshall Pickering, 1987), published in *Third Way* 11:1 (January 1988), 16–17.

Watching carefully

David Porter, author and poet argues for a way of watching TV that will teach one's children the process of Christian discrimination. Television is like a friend of the family, because many families spend more time watching television together than any other family activity. So that poses a dilemma for Christians, if your best friend has no sense of sin and holiness, blandly promotes materialism, and reflects current sexual mores. Besides, television depends upon a simplified image, and its quick-change images which are direct, intimate, and compelling, pretend to give viewers the truth; but the contextlessness and rush-to-be-done format distort and reduce the full reality of anything happening, writes Porter. He also analyses how video intensifies and changes certain problems the art of television puts in our laps.

'Television is a committee in search of an agenda. In that sense it isn't going anywhere. It has no future, only a perpetual present.' Porter recommends we Christians engage the media and participate in television not to preach (or to do apologetics with single-issue thinking) but to *witness* with Christian wisdom on news events and cultural problems, side-by-side with those with whom we disagree. Then one becomes a redemptive presence *in* the world but not *of* it.

Musical meanings

'The Message of Rock Music' by William Edgar, musician and professor of apologetics, puts rock music, begun by Elvis Presley, Bill Haley, Buddy Holly, and disc jockey Alan Freed, into historical context with the blues in the black song tradition. Simply by giving that societal, historical setting for rock music and by showing how rock music originally called into question the comfortable success of post-war modern life and its sentimental pop music, Edgar reveals, without needing to say it, how superficial so much critique by Christians has been (e.g. a Communist plot, Satanist subliminal manipulation, nonsense). Rock music at its hard core is against the establishment, any establishment, and like many popular movements seems to be vague as to its aim because it is looking for criteria it cannot quite formulate.

To think 'that rock is not worth bothering about is the approach of the Christian ostrich'. To take the Manichean view that the created world and its culture (lumping all rock music together) is no good – we should wait for heaven – is also to fall short of the biblical injunction to 'test everything; hold on to the good' (1 Thessalonians 5:21). To be an historical relativist and believe that music is neutral is to be mistaken too. Music has musical meaning and, like the food Paul talks about to the Corinthians, is contexted as music either to be received with thanksgiving or as food offered to demons. We Christians need to *filter* rock music in the light of biblical norms, and that means something much deeper than 'do it until the red light of your conscience goes on'. We need, says Edgar, a popular musical aesthetic theory that is informed, honest, and able to identify idolatry *wherever* one finds it.

Theatre craft

Murray Watts, playwright and co-founder of the Riding Lights Theatre Company, most helpfully groups modern dramatists in a way that highlights certain major trends in theatre. He argues well that theatre as an art keeps things complex, as real life is, and is much less open to commercialisation and (advertising) interruption than television. Theatre art demands concentration from the audience.

Watts pleads for Christians to learn the craft of theatre by a thorough-going apprenticeship so that we believers do not fall into agitprop performances. And with hurt eloquence that is very moving he laments the kind of censorship exercised by church people who are shocked by reality and want 'human experience ... edited into brief spurts of propaganda'. Such censorship is insidious 'because it is deeply sincere. Like an invisible ink, it suddenly appears when the heat of debate arises. As soon as there is controversy, and as soon as a work of art is seen as potentially damaging to a successful public relations campaign for God, the protestors marshal their complaints, if not threats.' Every armchair critic of Christian artistic efforts in our day needs to hear this cry for prayerful, informed support.

True judgements

Ruth Etchells, theologian and lecturer in English at Durham University, characterises current trends in literature, and nominates various Christian writers for reading. She believes that one's world-view tips off the kind of literary critique one practises. Because she thinks the Christian faith is 'characteristically *paradoxical*', and that each of us always goes to work 'within *our* absolutes', she asks readers to credit that writers (for whom they may not have so much sympathy) are dealing with the reality of the larger world in which they were created. 'Truly Christian judgement of books is never arrogantly judgemental ... [its task] is to identify ... the deep underlying pattern, the principles that underlie any work of art.'

A similar concern seems to be the overriding interest of Graham Birtwistle, art history professor at the Free University of Amsterdam. He is at pains in the introductory chapter entitled 'Art and the Arts', to avoid any pat idea of art, and to reject, along with Rookmaaker and Schaeffer, any idolatrous grant of special status and prerogatives to art. His piece is also an appeal to the evangelical mind not to jump to conclusions before one has looked at what 'we have, in practice, accepted'. Christians should not dictate to artists from any ivory theoretical tower, in so many words, what the artist's identity and task must be. That is surely correct, and a good caution. Maybe that is the point of the title to this collection of essays: Art in question.

Art in its own right

But to dethrone *idolatrous* capital-A Art (or what Nicholas Wolterstorff calls 'high art') should not lead one to the dissolution of the *specific* nature of art, it seems to me. As Peter Smith puts it: 'Our attempts to remove painting from the idolatrous pedestal it has had built for it are not helped by claiming that there is no difference between designing a margarine wrapper and painting a portrait.'

The 'experimental', though serious, conclusion Birtwistle presents, that art means 'no more than a loose alliance of professions which may or may not share working experiences and problems', to my mind is *not* 'one of the more interesting possibilities open to us in the late twentieth century'. Such deconstruction of art is more like a setback in knowing the specific nature and in finding a fruitful praxis of *art* history. And we will go wrong and be confusing, I think, if we form a makeshift definition of art by pointing to its multiple possible functions. Again, in the choice words of Peter Smith: 'To make the aesthetic function central in a painting is not to isolate it or remove it from contact with the environment in which it asserts itself. The aesthetic element in other areas of life plays its part, if you like, as a servant. In a painting the aesthetic element becomes central and is itself served.' We need 'to struggle to reclaim our [artistic] normality in Christ. [Artistic norms and principles] we discover as we walk within God's structured world'.

This book is a tonic for any Christians with a heart for calling the arts, and media, and thought about the arts and media and culture at large, to concerted, redemptive action. The book also gives food for thought to those Christians who feel distant, disappointed with or hostile to the arts. These writers give you bread rather than stones to eat.

10 The Christian Encounters Censorship, Obscenity, and Sex*

This book puts together the main events which have formed the present US legal and social mentality on what to do about pornography and questionable literature. With dispassionate wit it describes many cases of ill-advised censorship by state and church and community, but never for a moment does the book suggest that the problem of obscenity before the public is a minor one. American Christians today have some serious decisions to make: how to protect freedom to read for those who deny Christ is Lord as well as for the faithful, without abetting moral deterioration of society. The charm of Klausler's book is that he treats all the relevant matters with an earnestness that is not nervous. The cartoon illustrations embody a humility healthy for Christian reformers.

The focus Klausler gives to the Christian encounter with censorship, obscenity, and sex is this: 'For the Christian there is also the continuing matter of steering clear of a stringent legalism while at the same time applying the freedom which the Gospel grants' (p. 74). I am not certain this tension of legalism and a laissez-faire attitude on the part of individual Christians has the structural depth to give our secular society biblical leadership in this area. One can counsel care for the weaker brother or sister, but still let each one do what seems right in his or her own (sanctified) eyes. Such a policy does not set a Christian cultural direction in the land.

It seems to me little headway can be made on our troubles until we see that state, church, school, home, associations of competent Christian art critics – each have a *different* responsibility toward public smut. The state has an authority from God to maintain public order, which is properly quite different from the church's authority from God to keep the confessional life of God's folk strong and pure. Parents have a God-given area of home authority over their children which they may *not* ask the state to legislate, or the church to assume, on pain of inviting totalitarianisms.

Well-meaning Christian parents and Christian clerics, it seems to me, should not try to usurp state powers to ban books and films contrary to their

*Review of Alfred P. Klausler, *The Christian Encounters Censorship, Obscenity and Sex* (St Louis: Concordia Publishing House, 1967), published in *Gordon Review* 11:3 (Fall 1968), 1659–71.

biblical confession; but they may support vigorously 'Christian' laws that make it a crime to push prurient photography and writings into the public arena, because such work undermines the social order. Disciples of Christ are called to give Christian contour to the life of society without compelling all citizens to become Christians.

Further, working with the line Philip Dunne draws 'between compulsory censorship and private guidance' (pp. 71–2) and moving in the direction the Missouri Synod Lutheran Church advises toward 'voluntary agreement rather than compulsion' (p. 91), it would seem to me to be a natural development of Klausler's request for a Christian perspective to have Christian colleges call into existence a body of Christian critics, completely separate from the institutional church, who, by dialogue and communion, reviews and regular commentaries, would gradually form a climate of Christianly critical normativity that could guide those who are alone and at a loss.

> A Christian perspective requires recognition of the sex-obsessed society in which the church finds itself. When modern business uses sex to advertise its products, from cars to perfume, then it is time for the Christians to re-examine some of the presuppositions underlying the American way of life (p. 92).

And that re-examination and positive formulation of Christian perspective, beginning with 'freedom' understood as 'bound-to-Christ,' cannot be won by single, responsible Christians. It is a task which Christian leaders and followers must exercise communally, within the jurisdictional limits proper to the kind of body concerned. The Christian academic community may also not be found wanting.

11 Mennonite Art: The Insider as Outsider*

During the Twelfth Assembly of the Mennonite World Council in Winnipeg this past July (meeting every six years somewhere in the world) an exhibition of vital art by 'artists of Mennonite heritage' was held at an alternate gallery, the Main/Access Gallery in Winnipeg, Manitoba. The exhibition was put together by Priscilla Reimer, a graduate in aesthetics from the Institute for Christian Studies, Toronto, and the subtitle wording was very carefully chosen. Many of the artists in the show were too estranged from the faith-community that nurtured them to be considered good, practising Mennonite church people today. Yet their Anabaptist upbringing has marked their art for life with a sensibility for land, a love for the richness of ordinary things, a tenacity to be non-conformist while celebrating community, and an abiding concern for societal justice.

Reimer's eloquent essay in the catalogue explores the problem of why 'insiders' to the Mennonite community have had to become 'outsiders' in order to remain true to the artistic gifts God gave them. If your faith-community and neighbourhood has no place for art in its committed world-and-life vision, what do daughters and sons of the church do as artists? Ceramicist Grace Nikkel (born 1956, Altona, Manitoba) makes vessels of exquisite delicacy that reveal fragility and durability as perhaps only a woman knows. Vessels can be receptacles that confine and restrict, but vessels can also be a protective chamber carrying life. Grace Nikkel's lovely earthenware bowls hold the promise of growing and flowering safely.

Leonard Gerbrandt (born 1941, Carrot River, Saskatchewan) showed a water-colour and gouache piece, *I love the land*, that is neither 'pretty' nor 'picturesque'. In a very 'modern art' way that has overtones of Cubist and Expressionist structure and colour, Gerbrandt presents the countryside as a vibrant and complex scape of adventure, work, and joy. Les Brandt's *Prairie Icon* (1989) is more traditional for the prairies, but is swimming with a feel for farm, the reliability of old, well-worn buildings dramatically standing out against the endless sea of earth and muddy ground.

Lois Klassen (born 1963, Arborg, Manitoba) illuminates the hospital world

*First published in *Calvinist Contact* 46:2227 (14 September 1990), 11.

Plate 23 Grace Nickel: *Untitled (vessel)* (1989; slip cast earthenware clay, underglazes, glaze, 17 × 37 × 7 cm), exhibited at the Mennonite art exhibition

and matters of human health with installations which really make you do a double-take. *Household lamps* turns surgical uniforms into fascinating, somewhat eerie objects hung from the ceiling, giving light like human lamps. In the hospital where 'the intensely personal is rendered impersonal, the unique is treated uniformly, [and] illness is … commonplace' (Reimer, p. 14), how is an individual human supposed to remain human, when being sterile is so important? Lois Klassen makes this enigma vivid.

Susan Schantz (born 1957, Kitchener, Ontario) enters more rough-handedly into the repression of the peace that destroys many. Her *Ancestral Spirits: Bed* juxtaposes a blown-up old photo of a stiff Mennonite wedding couple standing above a real, cold metal headboard of a bed, and the genital areas of the couple have been decorated, like graffiti, with an erect penis and a womb with baby drawn on the photo. Underneath our respectable appearances often lurks a harsher reality.

Reimer uses the assemblages of Erma Martin Yost's (born 1946 near Goshen, Indiana) as a symbol for what Reimer hopes might be a new understanding acoming of (Mennonite) community, which Calvin Redekop and others have described recently to be in crisis. Erma Martin Yost's constructions are quilt-like paint-fabric sculptures which present 'patches' of interrupted sights, history, images, loose threads, and cloth, that catch together the old Mennonite craft of quilting and the current changing world of art, speed, and loss of orientation. Maybe, writes Reimer at the close of her curatorial essay,

Plate 24 Les Brandt, *Prairie icon* (1989; mixed media on paper, 57.1 × 76.2 cm), exhibited at the Mennonite art exhibition

'The quilt implies in its suggesting form that society will not be changed from the top down or from the inside out, but from the bottom up and the edges in' (p. 25).

This catalogue, *Mennonite: The Insider as Outsider* (with 13 full-colour illustrations), is an important document that lets artists from the Mennonite heritage show and tell where art stands in the Mennonite community today. Some are angry, and little good comes out of anger. Some have perhaps become secularised, without much concern to be part of a patchwork quilt of the Mennonite people of God. Some have persisted in the Mennonite heritage against odds. But with this catalogue Priscilla Reimer has mediated in a most graphic, honest way the kind of resources that artists *are*, willy-nilly, in a faith-community. And when the artistic resources of a faith-community go begging and become lost, for whatever reasons, everybody loses. When God's gifts to women and men are thwarted, perverted, or wasted, even God becomes sad.

The point of this tribute to Mennonite art for the Christian community is this: support your local poet, honour your resident potter, visit the studio of a Christian artist, order a song for the next banquet, get professional architectural help when you have to build a new church, read your grandchildren imaginative stories before bedtime along with the Bible story, discuss *Calvinist Contact* movie reviews, buy Hugh Cook's new novel, *The Homecoming Man*, and so on …

12 'Lenten Emblems' by Gerald Folkerts*

Emblem books were the rage in the 1500s and 1600s in Europe. 'Emblems' were visual images accompanied by proverbs, and intended to fasten in people's minds pictures of how to live. *De Stoelmaakers* is in a book of emblems by Jan and Kasper Luiken (Amsterdam, 1790). 'Chairs' break, but God's Rule holds firm.

Gerald Folkerts' series of twelve drawings called 'Crossroads' can be understood to be emblems telling the story of Christ's passion, a kind of up-to-date, Protestant, stations of the cross. The title drawing uses the cross form clutched by a despondent, bowed figure as a road on which appears a famished child staring at a dead man hanging from a tree, while the pained face of a 'Third World' woman and, sideways, another head nestled in thorns, exist in a forsaken wasteland and cityscape under a dark sky rimmed by the crosses of Golgotha. As a border are written various of the Beatitudes found in Matthew 5. The whole picture with words exhibits the point of Matthew 25:31–46.

Good Friday has the famous Iwo Jima icon of soldiers raising ... the cross! (instead of the American flag), and underneath the linen tunic of Christ protrude Canadian dollar bills, with two dice nearby that came up snake eyes. Here the *Good Friday* emblem doubles as a vivid statement against modern militarism, even if performed with the guise of righteousness. Underneath the glorification of war lies the dirty money of gambling for another's possessions.

Self-portrait shows Folkerts himself startled by the viewer's gaze, pounding a nail into the wrist of Christ on the cross lying on the ground. Curled lip, furtive eyes, aggressive hammer, tensed body, all under churning nest of vipers – it is a well-drawn almost melodramatic drawing of the guilt that lodges in the best of us. Read Luci Shaw's exquisite, spare poem 'Judas, Peter' when you look at Folkerts' more unrelenting, flamboyant drawing, and you will get the message of what the Bible means by 'passion' ('suffering') caught up in the Lord's grace.

Redeemed in the series has left behind the gnarled, troubled teaching by pictures of what Christ's sacrifice entails. An empty can of Pepsi is thrown left, lands, shows its battered, smashed-up condition, struggles as it were to

*First published in *Calvinist Contact* 47:2284 (29 November 1991), 12.

Plate 25 Gerald Folkerts, *Self-portrait* (1989; graphite, 27.9 × 30.5 cm)

straighten up, get out of dents, until finally it is 'redeemed', as a whole new tin can fit for use. This final (partially coloured) drawing gives a new look at the redemption of refuse, and mimes the meaning of humans being made into new creatures, thanks to Christ's historic crucifixion and resurrection at the crossroads of earthly history.

Gerald Folkerts' 'Crossroads' drawings are carefully conceived, subtly drawn, fastidious in detail. Folkerts does 'abstract' painting too, and subtle non-representational colour studies; but the drawings in this show are didactic and accessible to anyone not acquainted with art. 'Emblems' are 'logical pictures', you might say, somewhat like puzzles. So you need to *think* as you *look*, and figure out what the *message* is which the *image carries*. These good drawings exemplify what one might call 'encapsulated art', art voluntarily harnessed to other-than-artistic purposes, the way advertising art and monument art normally is bona fide art poured like powder into the capsule of business or a government act. 'Crossroads' makes eminent sense as art for a church hall, especially during Lent.

Plate 26 Gerald Folkerts, *Crossroads* (1989; graphite with coloured pencil, 27.9 × 33.0 cm)

Gerald Folkerts and his wife, Arlis, teach at Calvin Christian School in Winnipeg. He is a graduate of Dordt College, Sioux Centre, Iowa.

13 Kurelek Art: Preaching in the Footnotes*

William Kurelek (1927–77) has two theme songs running through his painterly art: 'Amazing Grace' and 'Amazing Nature'.

Born in Whitford, Alberta, the son of a Ukrainian immigrant farmer who ran a dairy farm in Stonewall, Manitoba, from 1934 to 1949, young Kurelek was put down by his father as a sissy for wanting to draw and paint. But he kept painting.

Years later, after a nervous breakdown in 1957, he was converted to the Roman Catholic Christian faith. Ever since, Kurelek has lived overwhelmed by the amazing grace of God who saved him. That is why 'I am concerned for the state of man's soul individually and collectively …,I can't help but paint the sense of impending doom of our times; the way of salvation too … I am completely convinced that the Christian answer to life is the true one and being true, it cannot help but be organic (in my paintings). So I preach the message in my art that modern man needs to turn to Jesus Christ while there is time before the nuclear holocaust encompasses us as punishment.'

Kurelek, however, is not a Christian artist with a long face. Kurelek is a country boy who knows and loves the prairies of Canada with a passion. Nature is amazing in its expanse to the horizons! And he paints the country of endless winter snow in Manitoba, the spring thaw and flooded land, the Northern Lights and thunder storms, but also the lovely nights of fireflies, a summer rainbow, sunset at Malton airport and the Don Valley in Toronto. The Nature Kurelek paints is an enormous panorama, whether it is scenic or merciless, dwarfing the men, women, and children who usually show up only as grace notes on the canvas.

The new book by Joan Murray, director of the Robert McLaughlin Gallery in Oshawa, Ontario, *Kurelek's Vision of Canada* (Edmonton: Hurtig Publishers Ltd, 1983), $19.95, hard cover with 48! colour reproductions, is a prize of a book. Both her art-critical analysis and background comment and the

*First published in three parts in *Calvinist Contact* 40 (Oct.–Nov. 1984): no. 1946, p. 8; no. 1950, p. 9; no. 1952, p. 13. Page references in the text refer to Joan Murray's *Kurelek's Vision of Canada*, mentioned in the review. To coincide with the exhibition, Seerveld gave a public viewing and discussion, at the Institute for Christian Studies, of *The Maze*, a forty-minute documentary film made by Cornell University about Kurelek's life and art.

excerpted statements by Kurelek himself about his art, faith, and world-view, make it a good catalogue of the travelling exhibition of Kurelek's paintings going across Canada.

This large show of Kurelek painting will be at the Art Gallery of Ontario (Dundas and McCaul Toronto) from 13 October until 2 December. If you have seldom or never gone to the Art Gallery of Ontario, this is a good time to go once. Admission is free on Thursday from 5.30 to 9.00 pm. Thursday is not a consistory night; it is not the night for midweek prayer meeting; Thursday is not catechism night. Go with the whole family. It will be crowded. Give yourself at least an hour and a half at the exhibition. You should take longer than two minutes to look at various of the paintings, to let the painting speak to you as you ask it questions. Then read the Kurelek/Murray book.

Does it disturb you to see a crucifixion in the middle of the farmer's field, *Dinnertime on the Prairies* (1963)? Does the picture of fellows shooting rats, *Ambush in Manitoba* (1971), remind you of Bruegel? Did you get the *Newfie Jokes* (1974) from the painting itself, or did you have to read them on the frame – does it matter? Which painting did you like best? Which painting was the best *painting*? Did you find a sense of human loneliness or powerlessness in the infinite reaches of earth, grass, and sky, in so many paintings? Is *Beauty and Peace: the Happy Family on Vacation* (1968) true to your life?

Kurelek tells stories with his paintings. That's why his illustrations of *Who has seen the Wind* (1976) speak to thousands of people without any trouble. Boys with slingshots or a lone dog howling at the moon are human interest anecdotes that everybody recognises with a smile. The fact that Kurelek also throws in paintings called *The Parable of the Sower* (1963) or *Not Going Back to Pick up a Cloak* (1971) gives a secular person a jolt. But often times the secular person will take the sermons like a grain of salt because of the surrounding humour. 'I try to distract people with my pretty paintings,' says Kurelek, 'in order to get my foot and Christian message inside their door.'

Since the Art Gallery of Ontario has finally opened its door to Kurelek, it would be a witness to the Christian faith for you to go see it there ...

★　★　★

Kurelek's painterly art embarrasses most professional art critics, because he is largely self-taught and because he is explicitly Christian. When the Art Gallery of Ontario announced their large Kurelek show in *The Gallery* of October 1984, they kept their distance, very discretely:

> William Kurelek (1927–77) believed his ability to make art was a gift from God, and so must be used in God's service. This unfashionable conviction set him apart from his contemporaries ... Kurelek's vision of Canada, opening at the AGO

October 13 through December 2, is just that – one man's individualistic and sometimes quite extraordinary look at his environment … Kurelek as an artist has not always found favour among Canadian curators and critics … (p.2).

Patricia Godsell's lavish book *Enjoying Canadian Painting* (1976) classified Kurelek with 'untrained artists' and someone like Ojibway Indian artist Morrisseau. Marxist Barry Lord's *The History of Painting in Canada* (1974) praised Kurelek's painting for its 'social realism' on farm and working-class folk, but rejected Kurelek's treating people as sinners who were dependent upon divine salvation as something 'unscientific' and bad for his art.

So it is a great strength of Joan Murray's edited book, *Kurelek's Vision of Canada*, to take this self-taught, openly Christian painter who is outside the Establishment sympathetically seriously, and to establish critically that panoramic landscape is the key to the artistic idiom of Kurelek's painting.

To be exact, Kurelek paints *scenes*. Things happen in the endless fields Kurelek depicts. The land is never painted to be just a landscape (p. 10). Yet the enormous stretches of sky and land or snow and water, hills or night, blocked out so carefully like a quilt covering the whole universe, are what dominate in their quiet immensity almost every painting since 1960.

It is true, when figures are closer up and larger (cf. *Ambush in Manitoba*, *Who has seen the Wind*), their lumpish bodies and simplified contours show how Kurelek admired Bruegel's earthy rogues and lowly, boisterous folk. But even then, Kurelek's homely folk do not fill the painting: Kurelek's people are there in a huge world.

And normally the ground – background, foreground, middle-ground – is not a frame for the people but is what overwhelms with grandeur the animals and human creatures who work, relax, marry, play, and bury their dead on the earth. 'Man was given the divine commission to subdue the earth and make it his,' wrote Kurelek in 1973 (p. 76), but the immensity of the world Kurelek paints shows how small and weak humans really are too (p. 71), especially in the face of 'natural' spectaculars (like valleys and mountains, the Northern Lights) and catastrophes (floods, prairies fires).

Kurelek painted the tragedies of ordinary life (*Flu Epidemic in Alberta*, and *Lest We Repent*) as well as the sunny moments. The truth of Ecclesiastes 7:1–4 resonated deep in his heart: it is better to face the day of mourning than to carouse in the mirth of successful parties, because death faces everyone with what life is all about.

That is why there is often a brooding footnote to many of the pleasant vistas, even a crucifixion hidden in the underbrush (*Don Valley on a Grey Day*) or the mushrooming cloud of atomic conflagration at the horizon (*In the Autumn of Life*). Sometimes the disaster pictured is a local one, like a burned barn stage-centre that shows that everything the hardworking family has spent decades building up is destroyed (*A Ukrainian Canadian Prairies Tragedy*). Other times the forlornness is simply felt in the wide-open, empty spaces, with no one visible (*Trustees Meeting on the Barber Farm, Regina*).

The minute attention to realistic detail on every inch of the canvas contributes to the hint of a surrealistic strangeness in the paintings (cf. *The Atheist*). No wonder Kurelek appreciated Andrew Wyeth, Edward Hopper, Ben Shahn, and Alex Colville (p. 14), who often conjured up the existentialistic aura of foreboding crisis by a similar technique.

I think the comparison of Kurelek to Hieronymous Bosch (pp. 13,74), however, is mistaken. Both Bosch and Kurelek believed in the grip of sin on people's lives and painted it; but Bosch's painterly world is a vibrant, topsy-turvy fumble of fantastic imaginings: Kurelek keep his natural theology of beautiful creation ('Amazing Nature') and his supernatural apocalyptic judgements ('Amazing Grace') *next* to one another, not one permeating the other, and the overall feel is one of simple, even placid happenings, no matter how severe or evil they actually be.

Kurelek used photographs a lot in doing his painting (pp. 16,45,49). Such a practice reinforced the simplified, picturesque flatness of the pictures, although the paint-scratched-out details keep one's eye interest jumping before each view. Each painting is out to make a single point. As in a parable or a poster, all the minute, authentic detail aims at reinforcing *one* main story or lesson.

As a result Kurelek paintings have a simplicity to them. *Night Hunters* or *No Grass Grows on the Beaten Path* are not ambiguous. The straight and narrow diagonal line restfully makes you feel immersed in the vast tract of land, and you quietly absorb the thought that animals hunt and kill one another, and grass does not grow where man and beast walk. Very simple, but worth meditating about.

And that is precisely how Kurelek preaches in his artistic painting: in the footnotes or margins, in the titles and themes, a soft-sell with self-including humour: 'It is the sins of men, and that includes mine (that's why I use we, our, us, in my titles) ... Pictures are democratic. If there is a sermon contained in them it can be taken along or left behind when the viewer leaves the gallery' (p. 75).

I don't want to force my message on people, and sooner or later I may offend somebody, says Kurelek.

And I could go on and paint only nice, harmless pictures to serve the great god Art, which people will want to hang in their homes. But I would not be true to my inmost conviction and so I have to risk at least some loss of popularity and income, to paint these things that mean most to me (p. 74).

Other paintings (not in the current trans-Canada exhibition) confront the viewer with cosmic devastation in no uncertain terms, but Kurelek's basic policy is to 'sneak Christian symbols into the composition' (p. 70). And paintings like *The Parable of the Sower* are trying to do what Giotto did, illustrate, 'teach the illiterate masses the Christian story' (p. 74), coax people back into seeing-hearing-knowing the ABCs of the biblical message.

> I realise religion is a touchy subject to a lot of people, and I suppose this is only natural since it reaches down to the very heart of every person – where he or she has more or less decided on the very purpose of life and what to do about it (p. 73).

So Kurelek feels compelled to mix in with the Canadiana travelogue and the stories of little human joys and foibles a call to turn from one's evil ways and to remember Christ's sacrifice on the cross. That is a typically Roman Catholic way of bringing the Christian gospel: you show human solidarity with your neighbour, and then on occasion in your artistry you signal that there is more to life than meets the eye in paintings, there is the additional need to have life complete in the work of Jesus Christ. And Kurelek does this double song of 'Amazing Nature' and 'Amazing Grace' with such disarming ingenuousness, one is taken in.

> The meaning of this picture [*Dinnertime on the Prairies*] is that our sins crucify Christ just as much today as 2000 years ago, and just as much in Western Canada as in Palestine. The farmer and his sons doing the fencing may have had an argument just before dinner or one of them may have enjoyed a lustful thought. Or got an idea how to revenge himself on neighbours, etc. (p. 28).

Plate 27 William Kurelek, *Dinnertime on the prairies* (1963; oil and mixed media on masonite, 72.14 × 44.27 cm), McMaster University Collection, Wentworth House Art Committee Purchase, Hamilton, Ontario

This tactic of Kurelek turns a painting into something like an advertisement or an instrument for making a confessional statement. I think such a policy of 'smuggling in' the message with an obvious sign of Christ tends to keep both the artwork and the art viewer immature in artistic sanctification and wisdom. If you put words under the painting to make the image plain or paint specially explicit note or 'symbol' to make certain people get the point, then artistic painting becomes at best a tantalising come-on for preaching, like a tract.

Is that way, the method of Kurelek art, preaching in the footnotes, the best way to witness artistically of the hope with us of Christ's salvation in history? Yet there it is: an art-gallery goer is faced with a crucifixion he can't just put back into the past like an antique. So we should thank God for artist William Kurelek's paintings.

★   ★   ★

Should art evangelise? For a while William Kurelek did not sign his paintings because, like medieval sculptors and painters who were anonymous in praising God with their gargoyles, Kurelek wanted to do his art in humility just for God. Signing his paintings, he thought, was acting as if he were somebody important (p. 21). He believed art is not something super-sacred, and artists are only working people.

Kurelek is right. His attitude makes him stand out like a Christian sore thumb in the art-world full of prima donna fingers. At the same time, Kurelek consciously painted what he himself called 'pot-boilers', the nostalgic scenes of life down on the farm, that people would buy, so he could make a living, *and* then he *also* painted his 'religious commentary' ones, which accuse us successful, Western materialists of ignoring the starving peoples of the world, or he pushes Christ's crucifixion into our well-fed faces. Is that not a wonderful compromise? First, be pleasantly neutral to make a living; and then make your 'Brother, are you saved?' speech?

But who will throw the first stone? The Reformed Christian way of following Christ is to make the call of repentance and the promise of Jesus Christ's gracious blessing as natural to your life as breathing, so its joy and strength touches people without your trying so hard. Nothing is to be neutral. But you don't walk around with an evangelising chip on your shoulder, chin jutting out to drop an appropriate Bible text at the drop of a curse word. Instead, you become a vulnerable, saintly person who looks normal, acts both sensibly and imaginatively, and is ready to help any neighbour in trouble, and to stop evil wherever you find it, also in consort with others, communally.

When a Reformed Christian person is specifically busy evangelising and preaching, the Word of Good News is to be spoken with winsome directness. (1) All of us are sinners (Ephesians 2:1–10). (2) Those of us who submit to

God's call to become adopted children through the atonement of Jesus Christ then live grateful lives together of praise, service, and care, fighting evil and doing good (2 Corinthians 5:17–21; Ephesians 6:10–18; cf. Heidelberg Catechism question and answer 32). (3) So come, read the Scriptures with us, and meet the LORD who knows your need, whatever it is, and be open to the Spirit of God (cf. John 3:1–21).

Should art be such a specific evangelising tool? I don't think so, if 'evangelising' is simply *one* of the ways we may exercise our calling in being disciples of Christ, as Paul puts it (Ephesians 4:7,11–16; especially v. 11). Not all God's children need to be an evangelist like Timothy (2 Timothy 4: 5) to please God. Some may be prophetesses like Anna (Luke 2:36–8), teachers like Barnabas (Acts 13:1), poets like Asaph (cf. Psalms 50, 73–83), or artists like Bezalel and Oholiab (Exodus 31:1–11). Each member of Christ's body is asked to give back to God and give away to one's neighbour in the world whatever special gifts God has outfitted you with (Romans 12:3–6; 1 Corinthians 12:4–31).

If you are a born ruler, then administer power with justice and gentleness; if you know how to make money, distribute it generously (Romans 12:8); if you have the strength to heal, bring healing with joy (1 Corinthians 12:9); if you are able to discern the spirits of people, test them carefully (1 Corinthians 12:10; 1 John 4:1); if you are an evangelist by calling, then be diligent, vigilant, and patient as a preacher, speaking the Word with a timely, appealing force (2 Timothy 4:1–5); and so on. Of *all* such kinds of human activity – when such activities are sanctified – of such is the coming of the Kingdom of God.

Kurelek thinks that the most logical thing for a Christian to do who wants people saved from the judgement coming upon sin is to preach the gospel of 'repent and be saved'. But if God had meant me to do strictly that, then he'd not have given me the talent to paint and draw. So all angles considered, it ends up that I'm doing exactly what I am supposed to be doing. Paintings may not have nearly the power to convert people that the printed or spoken word has, but each person has his or her part to play in the human and divine drama – some persona just a few lines, others whole pages. To refuse to play one's role at all is not the answer either. It is better to light one candle than to curse the darkness. In the divine economy nothing good that is done is ever lost (p. 22).

So Kurelek does his art of painting beauty ('Amazing Nature'), but also tries to harness his painting sometimes into preaching ('Amazing Grace and Judgement'). He sneaks in the Christian symbols (p. 70), baptises the scene with a title that converts the painting into an allegory of Scripture (*Our World Today*, of a large burning barn with children playing in it, p. 22), or illustrates a biblical parable (*Satan Sowing Weeds in the Church*).

In my view, evangelistic preaching is *one* glorious way to show compassion for those who are lost, and it is indeed the crucial one. No Reformed person may think that you can keep your mouth shut forever and just do your daily moral business, and that's enough to count for being a faithful servant of the Lord. If we are not ready while we live to give an account of the saving hope we have in Jesus Christ (cf. 1 Peter 3:13–17), we shall be found wanting in the Last Day.

But there are more ways for proclaiming Christ's Rule on earth and in giving body to God's Word calling for obedience than a preaching ministry. For example, followers of Christ can reach out with the Good News of belonging to the Lord by giving food for the hungry in Christ's name (cf. Matthew 25:31–46; Acts 4:5–12) and by building drainage pipes in praise of the Lord that separate sewage from the drinking water of destitute people (cf. Zechariah 14:20,21). Followers of Christ can also show what the saving LORD is like by teaching songs and sights that will buoy the discouraged with melodies and colours holding the promise of God's rainbow.

Art that is a worthy response to Christ's sacrifice and resurrection will praise the LORD (cf. Psalms 146–150), grieve at sin (cf. Psalms 6, 32, 51, 130), and woo all who have eyes to see and ears to hear, to be joined as bride to the living Jesus Christ who rules all creaturely existence with norms that shall bless our lives (cf. Matthew 11:28–30; Proverbs 3:13–20; Colossians 1:9–23). But the glory of art is not in specifically preaching and evangelising. The glory of art lies in being a thankoffering to the LORD (Romans 12:1,2), a sacrifice that exercises all who encounter the art into seeing, hearing, thinking, feeling, and imagining meanings that will please the LORD. The task of art is to praise God by making the people who receive it wise in the LORD's ways of compassionate judgement.

Both artistic activity and evangelistic preaching can be full-time service for the Lord (and both can be sinful exercises in vanity). And it is true that God may use artistry as a vehicle for changing people's lives from darkness into light, just as God can use sport contests, business deals, wars and human love, to hound people from sin into forgiveness. But art is called by the LORD to witness in between the lines; it is the creaturely nature of art to be nuanceful. Preaching, however, should always be upfront, outright, direct, and clear, along with its imaginative moments.

That's a problem in Kurelek's attempt to be faithful to God with his artistry. Because artistry is by nature *not* preaching, but because Kurelek thinks preaching is the most necessary thing to do, he tries to squeeze the evangelistic preaching somehow into the painting. As a result, the preaching that goes on in the footnotes makes the art limp a little as art.

Rembrandt's *Jewish Bride*, for example, does not preach in the footnotes; but the painting *does* express to any onlooker, with incredible subtlety and unmistakable power, the deep, enduring giving and forgiving tenderness God wants to be holding between a man and a woman who are to become husband and wife (cf. Song of Songs 8:6,7). Rembrandt does not evangelise in his late portraits, but discloses the glory and misery of our humanity in richly modulated colours that bespeak bearing one another's burdens; the portraits are painted with a consciousness suffused by Galatians 6:1–10.

That is, granted the achievement of Kurelek art in today's secular world, like that of an explicitly Christian teacher grudgingly respected in a secular school, and given our heartfelt support for the fact that in his 'Amazing Nature' and 'Amazing Grace' way, Christ too has been proclaimed (cf. Philippians 1:15–18), there is a still more excellent way to do Christian art, I believe, than preaching in the footnotes.

We must not require our Christian artists to evangelise with their artwork. That would be putting an unnatural yoke on them the way the Pharisees did on people (cf. Matthew 23:4). We need to support and encourage believing artists to let a full-orbed, holy life of sensitivity, knowledge and commitment to the LORD come through the very pores of their painterly competence. That's all. And the Holy Spirit will use the smoke of such sweet-smelling, artistic offerings in miraculous ways.

14 Diego Rivera's Art: Worth Respectful Attention*

The best way to understand what an artist means with art is to see a retrospective show. That means you look at what the artist did as a young student, how he or she changed under the influences of various teachers and friends and then how the artist matured as they grew in years and became skilled in presenting artistically what they wanted to say.

The Detroit Institute of Arts is presenting a retrospective show of art by the Mexican Diego Rivera (1886–1957). Detroit has collected for the occasion the drawings behind the impressive frescoes on *The Detroit Industry* series which covers the large atrium of the museum. 130 exquisite drawings and watercolours, 114 easel paintings in oil, a 30-minute film on the frescoes of Diego Rivera, as well as a photographic display of the artist, his associates and local spots dear to him. This is an unusual opportunity to see how a sometime Marxist commitment and vision translated into art for people that gave the underclasses a sense of self-respect and historical identity.

Diego Rivera painted like the Cubists after studying in Paris, and later he indulged in a fantastic kind of Surrealist artistry for while. But in the 1920s, when the 'revolutionary' Mexican government was intent upon not following everything 'Made in USA' and Europe, Diego Rivera began to paint native Mexican scenes with a simplified line that reminds one of pre-Columbia sculptures, ungainly by Renaissance standards, but homely and strong.

It is the huge drawings in charcoal and crayon, studies for frescoes, which show the master craftsman and the particularly tender strength of Diego Rivera's art at its best. In the drawings one can see the delicate hints of grief and pride in the Indian workers and poor behind the obvious surface point. The watercolours too catch the provocative rhythms of a local festivity so much like Bruegel or Jan Steen, and the raw, noble beauty of a peasant.

The frescoes themselves are charged with societal critique like the prints of Hogarth. In some ways Diego Rivera takes on the artsy traditions as Canadian William Kurelek did, and gives an alternative, although Diego Rivera believes

*First published as 'Diego Rivera's art: worth respectful attention' in *Calvinist Contact* 41:2020 (18 April 1986), 8.

technology and professionalism will save us if we can just get rid of the greedy who exploit other people.

There is something naive about Diego Rivera's faith-filled art, disarming and simultaneously short-sighted, as if evil can be overcome by simplicity, food and a woman with flowers, instead of the reality of Easter. But Diego Rivera's sturdy, skilled art is worth a Christian's respectful attention. It might even give us pause as to how we misunderstand, rarefy, or neglect so great a creatural gift from our Lord.

Part 6

Bible Songs and Dance

1 Songs to Sing Standing Up*

Suppose you had invited unbelievers to a church service around Christmas, to give them a sense of what Christ's birth did for humankind in history and what it means for the church today. Which of the following two hymns do you think would best get across to an unbeliever the message we proclaim: 'Joy to the World!' or 'Silent Night! Holy Night!'?

I know that the text and melody of 'Silent Night' are beloved by many Christians. 'Silent Night' is almost synonymous with Christmas carolling. But it is not so worthy a song as we might suppose. And I doubt whether 'Silent Night' has the right biblical bite we need today to cut through the tinsel and Christmas-tree sentimentality that surrounds so much secular 'celebration' of Christmas.

'Silent Night' has a lullaby cadence and easily slips into a slow-waltz atmosphere. The words give a picture of tender sweetness, the kind of tableau you see in lots of paintings and stable scenes of the Virgin Mary and the little baby boy. Both the gentle music and the text ('All is calm, all is bright') are utterly unreal when placed next to the ten o'clock news of wars and rumours of wars. The pleasant, reassuring tones of 'Silent Night,' I think, are no longer credible today except as nostalgia. It sounds as if Christ's birth were a happy little occurrence once upon a time long ago, instead of a humiliation for the Son of God and an earth-shattering event tied up with his death, resurrection, and second coming.

'Joy to the World!' however, is a sturdy song. The first eight notes descend the octave of the D major scale with power, vitality, and brightness. No mistake about it: the LORD has come down to earth, and the whole world – men, women, children, fields and floods, rocks, hills and plains – can't help but dance around with joy at the marvel. There's a sort of Handel's *Messiah* laughter and hallelujah in the music. And the text repeats the confession: our King has come.

One Christmas my wife and I, living in Rome not long after the Hungarian Revolution had been crushed by the Russian army (1956), attended a hymn-sing with Roman Catholics and Protestants from many lands. Each country taught the group one of its carols. Without fail, all the carols seemed sentimental, even sticky, with rockabye feelings and barber-shop harmony

---

*First published in *The Banner* 117:12 (29 March 1982), 23.

possibilities around the scene of the wonderful mother-with-child. When our turn came, we taught them 'Joy to the World!' at a good tempo. 'My,' said a thoughtful nun, 'that one has *life*! We should stand up to sing that one!'

She was right. Next to 'Silent Night', which you can sing sitting down, 'Joy to the World!' comes through like a brilliant bolt of lightning. Maybe the only good Christmas carols – those that will give unbelievers a sense of the importance and urgency of recognising Christ's birth – are the ones you have to sing standing up.

2 A Note on the Liturgical Dance used with the Sunday Exhortations on Ecclesiastes*

Dance, like music, is expressly enjoined by Scripture for worship (Psalms 149, 150). Dance, like music, was performed long ago in celebration of God's blessing (cf. Exodus 15:20,21), in liturgical processions (cf. 2 Samuel 6:12–16), and in worship services (cf. Psalm 81: 1–4), by persons with gifts, trained for that ministry (such as the Levites in 1 Chronicles 25).

When music played by instruments (orchestra or organ) complements the song of God's people at worship, it is performed appropriately and in good order if it supports the Word preached and is carried out in a holy spirit of joyful confession and response germane to what God has said through the Word proclaimed. The same for dance. Music and dance that are included in a worship service are bound to serve the express purpose of churchly praise of God and edification and outreach among those gathered for worship. Such music and dance is called 'liturgical dance' and 'church music'.

Music in general is by nature tones composed to a rhythm that without words focuses the consciousness of those who hear the organised sounds and leads those people to imagine things. Bach's music, for example, often fashions an ornate world of majestic sound that can impress one with awe. Handel's *Largo*, for example, tells one in sprightly measure of a stately order and uncomplicated happiness.

Dance in general is by nature the rhythmic movement of a human body composed to show without words a lively expression which mimes all kinds of meaning for those who learn to read its movements. Clenched fists and crossed arms and bent body, for example, tells the viewer of bondage, exile, and frustrated helplessness. Dancers circling with skipping feet and clapping hands to cheerful rhythms mimic the simple joy of children dancing in a circle holding hands. A pose of stretched body poised on one foot suggests expectation and hope, for example.

Neither music nor dance can be read as if sounds and movements can be looked up in a dictionary. An arpeggio of a major scale played in triplets does

---

*A letter written to Grace Christian Reformed Church, Toronto, 8 August 1982, at the request of the clerk of the council of elders.

not always mean gaiety, and a cartwheel does not always mean exuberant thankfulness. But a harmonious arpeggio in triplet rhythm does not usually connote sadness, and cartwheels do not reflect imprisonment.

It takes time to understand music and to read choreographed movement, just as it takes time to learn a new song. Both music and dance can deepen the official worship of God's people if the music and dance contribute to heightening the point of the Word preached and enrich the response of the faithful.

Neither dance nor music should be 'special' presentations unrelated to the exhortation, put into the 'programme' as a 'talent show' or to relieve the talk: such misuse of art hurts concentrated wholeness of a worship service.

The liturgical dance performed in response to the good news of Ecclesiastes 11:1–6, which used songs composed around portions of Isaiah 52 and Isaiah 35, followed by a more sober, choral gradual, was conceived and executed to lead the congregation into a joyful expectation of the LORD's Second Coming (in connection with the exegesis of Ecclesiastes 11:7–12:7). The dance portrayed how old and young, the persecuted, the disappointed and the handicapped, someday will shout Hallelujah! and sing and dance before our glorious Lord in unconstrained gladness (cf. Psalm 30:11,12). Since we await that coming by serving Christ intently in the difficult world of today, the dancers – after testifying of the victory surely coming – exercised more sober movements to prepare us assembled more quietly and seriously to walk out of church ('So soon Christ is returning ...') into a new week 'living with each other; gladly we share each other's pain'.

So long as the dancers, like the minister, bring the message of Christ's rule with dedication, the LORD will bless the means used. Those who lead in liturgical matters, and those who supervise the liturgy, must pray hard that they be wise. Those who take offence when the mandate of Scripture is followed to make loud music or to dance for the LORD in worship must beware lest they fall into the kill-joy trap and condemnation that caught Michal (cf. 2 Samuel 6) or the Pharisees reprimanding Christ's disciples (cf. Luke 7:31–5).

3 A Bible Song from Micah 6:8

1 God made a good cre - a - tion. Our hu- man sin brought ru - in.
2 God kept on cov - e- nant - ing, of - fers the Ho - ly Spir - it.
3 God's grace can make us ho - ly; Christ's love pro-vides us shel - ter,

Christ gives a - way sal - va - tion: what does God re - quire?
We need to be re - pent - ing: what does God re - quire?
when we in faith do bold - ly what the LORD re - quires:

Prac - tice jus - tice; show com - pas - sion; love and hum-bly walk with God.

Text, tune and harmonization; Calvin Seerveld, 1991–1992©

7775 447
LUKE

4 Miriam's Song of Victory with Dance, Exodus 15:1-18

1 Hal - le - lu - jah! praise the LORD God! He has drowned the
2 Hal - le - lu - jah! Phar- oah's cap - tains boast- ing best arms
3 En - e - mies said, 'We will chase them, rob and rape— they're
4 Oth- er peo - ples heard the sto - ry, how we marched through
5 Hal - le - lu - jah! praise the LORD God! You gave us a

en - e - my! God a - maz - ing pitched the horse - men
ev - er known stuck in mud, thrashed through the flood, were
good as dead.' But you simp - ly blew an East wind,
on dry ground. They got shiv - ers, cramps, hys - ter - ia,
place to stand. You have prom - ised to make ho - ly

with their beasts in - to the sea. Sing the LORD God!
swal- lowed up, sank like a stone. Sing the LORD's arm!
and they plum - met - ed like lead. LORD Al - might - y!
left us free to walk a - round. Faith - ful LORD God,
all o - bey - ing your com-mand. Heal our hurts, Lord.

Shout the LORD God! Cheer the Sav - iour of our gen - er - a - tions'
Shout the LORD's arm! His ma - jes - tic ang - ry pow - er kin - dles
Ho - ly Sav - iour! None com- pare with your pro - tec - tive, start- ling
cove- nant LORD God, you have kept us safe from threate- ning en - e -
Make us wise, Lord. Gird us strong with your com - mun - ion, truth and

Text: Calvin Seerveld, 1986 ©

87 87 47
BRYN CALFARIA

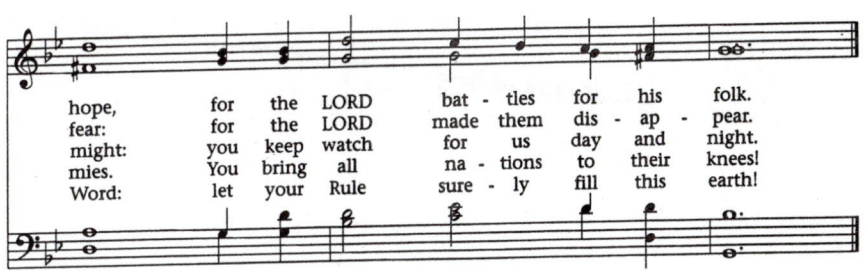

hope,	for	the	LORD	bat - tles	for	his	folk.
fear:	for	the	LORD	made them	dis - ap -		pear.
might:	you	keep	watch	for us	day	and	night.
mies.	You	bring	all	na - tions	to	their	knees!
Word:	let	your	Rule	sure - ly	fill	this	earth!

5 The Song of Deborah, Judges 5

(women) 1 Thank God the men re - solved to fight.
(women) 4 Wake up! wake up! you sons of hope.
(women) 8 Curse those who shirked to help your folk.
(all) 9 Thank God the men re - solved to fight.

(men) We stand pre - pared to give our life.
(men) The tri - umph may be dear - ly bought.
(men) They did it not to Je - sus Christ.
(all) We stand pre - pared to give our life.

(all) Un - armed, a joy - ful sac - ri - fice,
(all) God's An - gel says, 'Press on, fear not!
(all) O God, cha - grin those who lust for loot,
(all) Un - armed, a joy - ful sac - ri - fice,

we trust you, LORD, to lead us right.
Go cap - ture those who think we're caught!'
but make us strong in faith to shout:
we trust you, LORD, to lead us right.

Text: Calvin Seerveld, 1980 ©

L.M.
DEO GRATIAS and DEUS TUORUM MILITUM

398

2 Be still, you heads of blood - y com - mand. The LORD be -
3 But times were grim and no one felt safe; the coun - try
5 True Is - rael came all set to be - gin, while Reu - ben
6 The hor - ses thun - dered o - ver the ground; their i - ron
7 The Ken - ite Ja - el chose for the Lord and killed the

strides___ the earth and leads from Si - nai to the
cow - ered from vi - o - lence. We spurned our God, we
dal - lied and asked, 'But why – ?' Man - nas - seh, E - phra -
char - i - ots stalked us prey. But God shot stars and
fug - i - tive en - e - my, whose head was smashed as

prom - ised land: we'll fro - lic and sing of his might - y deeds!
void - ed our faith; the i - dols we trust - ed were no - de - fence.
im, Ben - ja - min joined Is - sa - char, Zeb - u - lum, Naph - tal - i.
had them all drowned; in Kish - on, God's ser - vant, they washed a - way.
prom - ised re - ward for bruis - ing the heel of the wo - man's seed.

6 The Resourceful Woman Song, Proverbs 31:10–31

1 Find a re-source-ful wo-man and you find
more than the jewels pos-sessed by hu-man-kind.
Her hus-band nev-er need feel in-se-cure;
she gives pro-tec-tion that is strong, ma-ture.

2 Watch a re-source-ful wo-man and you see
one who can buy and sell with in-dus-try.
She has the skill to keep her chil-dren warm;
she makes fine clothes, and saves the poor from harm;

3 Know a re-source-ful wo-man and you know
one who speaks wis-dom and whose car-ing shows.
All who en-joy the good work she dis-plays
re-spect her qual-i-ty and give her praise.

Text and tune: Calvin Seerveld, 1985 ©
Harmonisation: Emily R. Brink, 1995

10 10 10 10 10 10
ANYA RUTH

The Resourceful Woman Song

Run - ning a house - hold, o - ver - see - ing land,
her hus - band mer - its pub - lic con - fi - dence:
While charm and beau - ty mere - ly cap - ti - vate,

she shows both lead - er - ship and sure com - mand.
she fac - es times to come with laugh - ing strength.
a wo - man of the LORD we cel - e - brate.

7 A Christmas Carol, Isaiah 11:1–10

1 From Jes - se's old stump a shoot will spring out:
2 He nev - er shall judge by hear - say or sight.
3 Then wolf with the lamb, the li - on and calf,
4 Since know - ledge of God shall cov - er the earth,

like fruit from the root, a new branch will sprout.
His jus - tice pro - tects the poor in their plight.
the leop - ard with goat, shall gam - bol and laugh:
no crea - ture shall hurt, de - stroy what has worth.

God's Spir - it will bless him with wis - dom and might,
The breath of his mouth stops the ruth - less and cruel:
to - geth - er the heif - ers and bears shall be guests,
The na - tions shall seek him: their war - fare shall cease,

1-3

and awe for the LORD shall pro - vide his de - light.
trust - wor - thy, sure mer - cy shall clothe his new rule.
and ba - bies shall play near old poi - son - ous nests.
and Jes - se's new fruit shall bring glo - ri - ous

4

peace!

Text: Calvin Seerveld, 1986 ©
Tune: Basque Carol, adapted by Edgar Pettmann (1865–1943)
Harmonization: Dale Grotenhuis, 1987

10 10 11 11
NORMANDY

Appendix

Seerveld Gives Mini-Lecture on Toilet Paper*

In response to the *Tempo*'s joking announcement that there would be an exposition of the individuality-structure of coloured toilet paper, Dr Seerveld gave a 20-minute mini-lecture on the topic before one of his December 101 class free-for-alls. If there were no toilet paper, he posed the question, what then? Of course, for thousands of years of human civilisation there was no toilet paper, simply because there was no paper. Pharaohs of the Middle Kingdom used cloths in their ceremonial toilet rites, while the ordinary people probably used their imagination. Chinese paper-making entered the West through Arab conquests in Samarkand in AD 751. One of the first references to rag-content paper is found in the tract of Peter, Abbot of Cluny (1122, *Adversus Indeos*). Perhaps also part of the prehistory to toilet paper is the use of blotting paper which W. Horman in his *Vulgarian* (1519) describes as 'Blottyng papyr serveth to drye weete wrytynge, lest there be made blottis or blurris'.

Dr Seerveld has searched for a pithy definition of toilet paper, comparable to Kierkegaard's description of the way a kiss sounds ('The kiss sounded as when a cow lifts her hindleg out of a swamp') but felt scientific precision would better serve the cause. Toilet paper is the technically formed product linking former organic Subject (vegetable fibres) into a cultured hygienic Object, i.e. a utensil for cleansing. Toilet paper, therefore, belongs to the kingdom of cultured paper artefacts. Its functioning in all modal spheres is obvious, from being 11.5 by 11.5 cm porous sheets susceptible of movement, and having the symbolical object function utilising aesthetically in the rainbow-rich presentation of God's world, to its confessional fetish exploitation in needing to be of an exact texture, colour and smoothness to fit the modulated colour scheme of one's bathroom fixtures.

Dr Seerveld displayed samples of socialist toilet paper from England stamped 'Government property' and promised specimens of capitalistic toilet paper (perfumed, flower-decorated sheets) at a future meeting. He wondered whether the colouring of toilet paper did not embody some of the curse built into secularising technology which gives us less time to ourselves. Now housewives must consume thought-energy deciding which colour toilet paper to choose, and therefore are forced to think more highly of toilet paper

---

*Published in *Trinity Tempo* [student newspaper of Trinity Christian College, Palos Heights, Ill.] (Feb. 1968). Author unknown. A 'class free-for-all' was a session in which students could ask questions on any subject they wished. *The Banner* was a denominational weekly publication.

than they ought to think. Is coloured toilet paper not perhaps Madison Avenue's striding into our bathroom? – where at least a Christian *person* ought to be able to be alone?

As to the nature of Christian toilet paper, Dr Seerveld thought it should move in the direction of being colourless (i.e. black and white) waste paper, substantial enough so not too many sheets are needed but of such a constituency that it least likely clog the sewer drains. 'Toilet paper is simply a convenient means to keep clean in God's world.' Until we get some Christian sanitary engineers analysing the problem in fun, he suggested, the most Christian toilet paper would be two-week-old church *Banners* chopped to four-inch-square sheets.

Perhaps this investigation could be continued, he concluded, next year in a series of Family Action Seminars.

List of Illustrations

13 Junior members Adrienne Dengerink, Judy Jordet, Donald Knudsen, Allison-Ann McSwain, Carol Guen, with Seerveld, during a seminar tour of New York City musea, 1981 [p. 213]

14 Junior members outside the Institute for Christian Studies, Toronto, 1989: (back row) Shari Luttikhuizen, Govert Buijs, Marcille Frederick, Henry Luttikhuizen; (front row) Fran Wong, Barbara and Nigel Douglas, Priscilla Reimer and Seerveld [p. 214]

15 Junior members at a philosophical aesthetics seminar, Institute for Christian Studies, Toronto, 1992–3: (back row) James Leach, Scott Macklin, Greg Nations, Brent Adkins, Hamish Robertson, Craig Bartholomew; (front row) Greg Linnell, Andrea Bush [p. 214]

16 Gideon Strauss, Seerveld, James Leach, Gerrit du Preez, Egbert Schuurman, at the Centennial Dooyeweerd Conference in Bovendonk, Netherlands, 1994 [p. 219]

17 Presentation of *Pledges of Jubilee* to Calvin and Inès Seerveld by Lambert Zuidervaart and Henry Luttikhuizen, at Calvin College, Grand Rapids, Michigan, 1995 [p. 222]

18 Seerveld giving the address *Christian Workers, Unite!* at the Christian Labour Association of Canada, Toronto, 1964 [p. 239]

19 Pamphlet cover designed by Willem Hart, Toronto [p. 284]

20 Seerveld visiting Dirk van den Berg of the Department of Art History, Bloemfontein, University of the Orange Free State, South Africa, September 1994 [p. 332]

21 Seerveld with Mary-Leigh Morbey, Professor of Art at Redeemer College, lecturing at the Association d'art des universités du Canada in Halifax, Nova Scotia, 1987 [p. 350]

22 Poster for Seerveld's address, designed by Robin Jentzen [p. 357]

23 Grace Nickel, *Untitled (vessel)* © 1989. Slip cast earthenware clay, underglazes, glaze, 17 × 37 × 7 cm, exhibited at the Mennonite art exhibition. Photograph by Shiela Spence, Winnipeg. Used with permission [p. 372]

24 Les Brandt, *Prairie icon* © 1989. Mixed media on paper, 57.1 × 76.2 cm, exhibited at the Mennonite art exhibition. Photograph by Shiela Spence, Winnipeg. Used with permission [p. 373]

25 Gerald Folkerts, *Self-portrait* © 1989. Graphite, 27.9 × 30.5 cm. Used with permission [p. 375]

26 Gerald Folkerts, *Crossroads* © 1989.Graphite with coloured pencil, 27.9 × 33.0 cm. Used with permission [p. 376]

27 William Kurelek, *Dinnertime on the prairies* © 1963. Oil and mixed media on masonite, 72.14 × 44.27 cm. Wentworth House Art Committee Purchase, McMaster University Collection, Hamilton, Ontario. Used with permission [p. 381]

★ ★ ★

The author has made every effort to trace the original sources of the images and photographs used in this book. If any omission should come to your attention please contact the publishers to correct it in subsequent imprints.

Other Writings by Calvin Seerveld

*In chronological order of writing

A Christian Critique of Art and Literature, revised edition with 20 black-white illustrations. Sioux Center: Dordt Press/Toronto:Toronto Tuppence Press, 1995. xviii–150. ISBN 0–919071–04–X

The Greatest Song: In critique of Solomon, freshly and literally translated from the Hebrew and arranged for oratorio performance, with music by Ina Lohr and woodcuts by Flip van der Burgt, design by Sypko Bosch, second edition, Toronto Tuppence Press, 1988. 107 pp. ISBN 0-919071–02–3 paper, ISBN 0–919071–03–1 cloth

Rainbows for the Fallen World: Aesthetic life and artistic task. 7 colour plates and 66 black-white illustrations, 1980. 254 pp. [Temporarily out of print]

'Dooyeweerd's legacy for Aesthetics: Modal law theory', in *The Legacy of Herman Dooyeweerd: reflections on critical philosophy in the Christian tradition*, ed. C.T. McIntire. New York: University Press of America, 1985. pp. 41–79. ISBN 0–8191–5034–7

On Being Human: Imaging God in the Modern world. 14 black-white illustrations with 11 psalms, hymns and spiritual songs. Burlington: Welch Publishing, 1988. 104 pp. ISBN 1–55011–068–3

'Concluding Theses', in *Philosophy in the Reformed Undergraduate Curriculum,* eds. John W. Roose and George N. Pierson. Palos Heights: Trinity Christian College, 1990. pp. 79–89. LCC 90–71065

'Christen en Kunst', in *Wit Begint, Zwart Wint*, ed. Pieter van Kampen. Amsterdam: Buijten & Schipperheijn, 1993. pp. 156–167. ISBN 90–6064–804–8

'Both more and less than a matter of taste', *Acta Academica 25:4 (1993): 1–12.*

Philosophical Aesthetics at Home with the Lord:An untimely valedictory. Toronto: Institute for Christian Studies, 1996. 31 pp.

To Photostephano tis Anthropinis Phantasias, translated by Eirene Deontaridou, with 13 colour and 8 black-white illustrations. 61 pp. Thessalonica: Somateiou Ellenon Christianon Kallitechnon, 1997.

La foi et l'art: Les principes bibliques inspirant la démarche artistique, translated Richard Ouellette. Quebec: Éditions la Clairière, 1998. 46 pp. ISBN 2–921840–28–6

'Proverbs 10:1–22: From poetic paragraphs to preaching', in *Reading and Hearing the Word: From text to sermon. Essays in Honor of John H. Stek*, ed. Arie C. Leder. Grand Rapids: Calvin Theological Seminary, 1998. pp. 181–200. ISBN 1–56212–373–4

Through the Waters: Christian Schooling as a City of Refuge. Ancaster: Ontario Christian School and Teachers Association, 1998. 23 pp.

'Minorities and Xenophilia', in *The Role of the Arts in a Europe on the way to Integration.* Rotterdam: International Christian Artists Seminar sponsored by the European Union, 1998. Proceedings 7:38–43.

Take Hold of God and Pull: Fresh words from Scripture for our lives today. 9 black-white illustrations. Carlisle: Paternoster Press, 1999. 237 pp. ISBN 0–85364–910–3

'Reading and Hearing the Psalms: the Gut of the Bible', in *Pro Rege 27:4 (June 1999): 20–32.*

Why Should a University Exist? with Korean translation by Sung Soo Kim. Pusan: Kosin University Press, 2000. 80 pp.

'On Identity and Aesthetic Voice of the Culturally Displaced', *in Towards an Ethics of Community: Negotiations of difference in a pluralist society,* ed. James H. Olthuis. pp. 200–16, with 8 black-white illustrations. Waterloo: Wilfrid Laurier University Press, 2000. ISBN 0–88920–339–3

'Beyond Tolerance to Tough Love', in *Proceedings of the Ninth Symposium on the Role of the Arts in a Europe on the way to Integration.* Rotterdam: International Christian Artists Seminar sponsored by the European Union, 2000. 9:39–43.

'The Necessity of Christian Public Artistry', in *The Arts, Community and Cultural Democracy,* eds. Lambert Zuidervaart and Henry Luttikhuizen. pp. 83–107, with 5 black-white illustrations. London: Macmillan Press/New York: St. Martin's Press, 2000. ISBN 0–333–79469–9

Bearing Fresh Olive Leaves: Alternative steps in understanding art. Carlisle: Piquant/Toronto: Toronto Tuppence Press, 2000. 212 pp. ISBN 0–9535757–3–X/0–919071–05–8

How to Read the Bible to Hear God Speak: A study in Numbers 22–24, revised edition of *Balaams Apocalyptic Prophecies.* Sioux Center: Dordt Press/Toronto: Toronto Tuppence Press, forthcoming 2001. ISBN 0–919071–08–2

★ ★ ★

All these titles are available directly from Toronto Tuppence Press, 332 Senlac Road, Toronto, ONTARIO, M2R 1R3 CANADA.

In the Fields of the Lord and *Bearing Fresh Olive Leaves* may also be ordered from Piquant, PO Box 83, Carlisle, CA3 9GR, UK.